MUXEN TUS.
EMAI ER.
BRAMAS.
Lacus.
SAN CII.
XIAM
HON A O.
QUINCII.
XANTON.
IA
Meaco.
SEPTEMTRIO.
C.Lancamo.
Scala leucarum; quarum nouemdecim, gradum efficiunt.
20 40 60 80 100 120 140 160 180 200 220 240
Vlterius littora incognita sunt.

Generation of Giants

"Now giants were upon the earth in those days."

GEN. 6.4

GENERATION OF GIANTS

The Story of the Jesuits in China in the last Decades of the Ming Dynasty

by GEORGE H. DUNNE, S. J.

University of Notre Dame Press

Notre Dame, Indiana

1962

Imprimi potest
Romae, die 21 jul. 1960
Renatus Arnou
Delegatus Gen.lis pro Domibus Romanis Interprov.libus S.J.

Imprimatur
E Vicariatu Urbis, die 18 aug. 1960
Aloysius Card. Provicarius

Second printing March 1962

Library of Congress Catalog Card Number 61-18401

DESIGNED BY HARVEY SATENSTEIN
MANUFACTURED IN THE UNITED STATES OF AMERICA
BY BOOK CRAFTSMEN ASSOCIATES, INC., NEW YORK

Matri dulcis memoriae

necnon

Yves Henry et Auguste Haouisée gigantibus.

Portrait of Matteo Ricci, S.J., painted immediately after his death by Brother (Manoel) Yu Wên-hui. Brought to Rome in 1614 by Nicholas Trigault, S.J., it was hung in 1617 in the Jesuit residence of the Gesù along with the portrait of St. Ignatius of Loyola and St. Francis Xavier. It is still there.

Foreword

I HOPE THIS BOOK qualifies as a scholarly work. At the same time I trust that it successfully avoids the more deadly features sometimes associated with that phrase. I have aimed at interesting not only the scholar, but the average reader of intelligence who likes a good story. This is a good story. I hope I have told it well.

A special index of Chinese characters for names of persons and book titles has been omitted. The number of scholars to whom it would have been of service is too few to justify the disproportionately greater publishing cost this would have entailed. The occasional scholar who may wish to know the Chinese ideogram for any person or book title which appears in these pages may get in touch with me and I shall be happy to supply his want.

I have very few debts, but they are substantial ones. I am grateful to Thomas Carroll, S.J., of Taichung, Taiwan, for discovering for me a number of ideograms; and to Charles McCollester for typing the manuscript and proof-reading the text. Without the warm personal interest of Miss Emily Schossberger, able director of the University of Notre Dame Press, this book would not have appeared; without her intelligent editing it would better not have appeared. My heaviest debt is to Francis A. Rouleau, S.J., who saved me from many errors of omission and commission and out of the immense reservoir of his own knowledge generously filled the many lacunae in my own.

G. H. D.

Contents

Illustrations

Generation of Giants

PROLOGUE

WHEN IN 1415 the Portuguese captured Ceuta in Africa, they set in motion a series of exploits which made the fifteenth century one of the most remarkable centuries in world history. It was the Age of Discovery, an age of incalculable consequence to the future of humanity.

In the years that followed the capture of Ceuta intrepid Portuguese captains, inspired and directed by the genius of Prince Henry the Navigator, nosed their ships down the west coast of Africa discovering a new continent. In the second half of the century Diego Cao reached the mouth of the Congo, Bartholomeo Dias rounded the Cape of Good Hope. On May 20, 1499, Vasco da Gama cast anchor at Calcutta. The route to the Indies had been found.

Meanwhile the epochal voyages of Columbus opened vistas to the West comparable to those opened by the Portuguese to the East. The famous Bulls of May 3 and May 4, 1493, of Pope Alexander VI and the Convention of Tordesillas concluded the following year drew a line of demarcation between the colonial activities of Spain and Portugal.

Conqueror followed hard on the heels of explorer. Socotra and Ormuz were taken in 1507. With the capture of Goa by Albuquerque in 1511 the foundation of Portuguese empire in the East had been laid.

These achievements were of far-reaching importance to Christianity. The world had enormously expanded. Almost overnight innumerable peoples and widely divergent cultures burst upon the vision of Europe. It was an apocalyptic revelation of the implications of Christianity's world mission.

At the risk of oversimplification the history of the missionary enterprise of the Church might be divided into three stages: the conversion of the Roman empire; the conversion of northern

Europe; the modern age of the foreign missions which began with the discoveries of the fifteenth century. In the long pause between the second and the third stage, ignorance of the existence of that unknown world teeming with people encouraged the assumption that the world mission of Christianity had been substantially completed. In the thirteenth century the Polos did their best to awaken Europe to an awareness of China, but Marco's classic account was dismissed as mendacious fantasy. The notable, and for a time flourishing, Franciscan mission, founded by the great John of Monte Corvino who became the first Archbishop of Peking, scarcely outlived the Yuan dynasty which fell in 1368. So far as Europe was concerned it might as well have occurred in a void. When Franciscan missionaries followed the Jesuits to China in the seventeenth century they were unaware that other sons of St. Francis had preached the Gospel in China three centuries earlier.

The revelations of the Age of Discovery confronted the Church with a task of enormous dimensions, and one for which she was not at the moment very well prepared. The problem was similar to that which the primitive Church had to solve when she emerged from the seclusion of the Jewish community and undertook to transform the Greco-Roman world into a Christian society. On the one hand, there stood a small group of men, mostly of Jewish provenance and therefore of alien culture, armed with only the feeblest of natural resources; on the other hand, there towered the Roman empire, heir to the highest achievements of pagan culture, at the height of its prestige and power.

To have attempted to impose upon Roman society Jewish cultural forms would have doomed the enterprise from the start. Any hope of breathing a new Christian soul into the highly developed body of Roman society rested upon a policy of the broadest possible accommodation of Christianity to the cultural forms of that society. The first debate to arise in the councils of the Church concerned the problem of Judaization versus accommodation. Fortunately, the views of St. Paul, who strongly opposed the imposition of Jewish practices upon gentile converts, prevailed. That debate determined the authentic character of the Christian mission. Christianity was to act as leaven, not as an emetic, in the body of society.

The primitive Church went to great lengths in adapting herself to the cultural milieu of Roman society. In developing a Christian vocabularly she did not hesitate to make free use of Greek and Latin expressions. That those expressions in their pagan context signified something at times quite different from the Christian concept was no deterrent. Since the very notion of the supernatural order was unknown to the pagan world, the Greek and Latin languages possessed no words in themselves evocative of the Christian concepts. Either a whole vocabulary of Hebraic barbarisms had to be grafted onto these languages or non-Christian words had to be given a Christian meaning. The latter policy was adopted. By a process of definition and education the words were emptied of their pagan content and filled with Christian meaning.

The language of the Church, like the dress of her clergy, was that of the people. It was only after the German tribes had overrun the empire and a Roman speech had developed that Latin was installed as the liturgical language of the Church. This was done in order not to expose Christian teaching to the vagaries of new tongues still in a state of flux. It was not until after the time of Constantine that a liturgical vestment developed. When it did, it was modelled after the secular styles of the time.

Candles, incense, oil, and water were freely used in pagan rites. The early Church did not consider this a bar to introducing them in her own liturgical ceremonies. Pagan feast days were replaced with Christian feast days. Because the people were fond of religious processions these found ready acceptance in Christian practice.

The catacombs provide abundant evidence of the broad spirit of accommodation during these early centuries. Christian artists employed established Roman art forms. They adopted and adapted a great part of their symbolism from traditional contexts: the palm of victory, the phoenix of immortality, the olive branch of peace. It is probable that the fish, which appears repeatedly in the art of the catacombs as a symbol of the eucharist, was borrowed from certain ancient pagan sacrifices.

One of the most striking features of the policy of accommodation in the early centuries was the well known discipline of the *arcana*. Some of the most important, but to the uninitiated most startling, dogmas of the Christian faith were withheld not only from the pagans, but also from the catechumens. Not until they had completed their probation and were ready for baptism did they receive initiation into the more recondite mysteries such as the real presence of Christ in the eucharist. This practice was based upon a sound principle of pedagogy. The mind must be acclimatized to the whole Christian view of the divine economy of man's supernatural destiny before the credibility of such doctrines can be seen. Christ Himself had observed this principle. Only gradually did He reveal Himself and His purposes to the disciples. He even carried this pedagogy beyond the limits of His mortal life: "I have yet many things to say to you: but you cannot bear them now. But when He, the Spirit of Truth is come, He will teach you all truth."

In the external forms of life it would hardly have been possible to carry the principle of accommodation further. Old personal names, many of them originating in pagan mythology, continued in use. Christians adapted themselves fully to local social customs as long as these did not involve the worship of pagan gods.

Their own liturgical functions were held quietly and in inconspicuous places. They did not go out of their way to provoke trouble. When trouble came they met it, usually with sublime courage, often with flaming spirit; but there was in their attitude none of that defiance, touched with arrogance, which would seek occasion to flout the prejudices of the pagan society in which they lived. They saved their defiance for the moment, unsought but unevaded, when confronted with the supreme issue. Then they did not hesitate to defy the emperor himself.

Thus the early Church entered thoroughly into the cultural life of the Roman empire. Without sacrificing doctrinal purity she preserved from the old culture whatever was good, transformed whatever was indifferent, and with a view to gradual catharsis from within tolerated much that was considered evil, but not intrinsically or irremediably so. It was cultural accommodation carried to its highest point.

In the process of uniting herself with the highest culture to which pagan society had risen, the Church acquired definite cultural forms. Her governmental, social, and juridical life were cast in a Roman mold. In their essentials these forms would henceforth be maintained. Christianity was no longer simply the Revelation which had come out of Judaea, its cultural forms still in the seminal state. In any future expansion a certain amount of Romanization was inevitable. It was also desirable. The civilizing mission of Christianity required that the fruits of the higher culture be communicated.

At the same time, this healthy form of Romanization was tempered with a large amount of accommodation. Thus while raising the German tribes to a higher cultural level, educating them to Roman juridical concepts and social patterns, the Church encouraged the preservation of whatever was good in the old culture and incorporated it into the new. The draconian Saxon policies of Charlemagne, the first to distort the role of the temporal power in missionary work, was an exception to the enlightened methods characteristic of the time and drew a protest from Pope Adrian.

The great missionaries of the second stage of Christian expansion were Benedictine monks. To them is due chief credit for laying the foundations of European, or Western, civilization. The full development of this civilization was a long process which reached its fullness only in the thirteenth century. The final product was a civilization which, in its external forms, was neither Hebraic, Greek, Roman, Celtic, Germanic, or Gallic, but European. It was characterized by a unity, or rather an interpermeation, of religion and culture. Whatever tares it contained (and since, as the Chinese say, "heaven does not tolerate perfection," they were many), there was universal acceptance of the same ultimate truths, of the same spiritual ideals. There was a common world view. There was general agreement about authentic values.

The Church had been the chief agency in the development of the culture of Europe. She had woven Christianity into its very fabric. That culture in turn had attached itself to Christianity by a thousand invisible threads which could not easily be broken. Nor was this necessary. As there had been room for sound Romanization in leavening the cultures of northern Europe, so there was room for sound Europeanism in any future expansion of Christianity. That the best elements developed in the long history of Occidental civilization should become the possession of the whole world would be the world's gain.

Unfortunately, by the time the Age of Discovery dawned, inaugurating an altogether new stage in the missionary history of the Church, an unhealthy form of Europeanism had developed, the thought patterns of which were hostile to the idea of cultural accommodation. It assured that in the further expansion of Christianity scant respect would be shown non-Christian cultures. The Crusades had left a legacy of militancy and intolerance. Sword and Cross seemed natural allies. All non-Christian cultures seemed the work of the devil. To uproot them and plant Christian, that is to say European, culture in their place was the work of God. Tolerance seemed betrayal. That grace is operative even in a pagan milieu was forgotten.

By the fifteenth century conditions had conspired to produce a particularly dangerous type of Europeanism: close union between the mission and secular political power. As one of the consequences of the interpenetration of Church, Society, and State, princes conceived it their duty to spread the faith. But the weapons proper to princes are not likely to be those proper to saints.

It is impossible to doubt the genuine religious zeal of many Spanish and Portuguese rulers of the Age of Discovery. They were men of strong and ardent faith with a high conception of their obligation to extend the Kingdom of God. It was the realization of this fact which prompted the Holy See to give its support to the enterprise.

In a circular letter of April 4, 1418, to the Portuguese dioceses and cloisters, Pope Martin V urged support of the African expeditions of King John I, since they had as their object not simply the defeat of the Moors, but also the spread of Christianity. In the Bulls *Sane charissimus* of April 4, 1418, and *Cum charissimus* of April 4, 1419, the pope confirmed to the king all lands he should take from the Moors.

Nicholas V, in the Bull *Romanus Pontifex* of January 8, 1455, extended the privileges granted the Portuguese by Martin V and by Eugenius IV. He sanctioned the already generally recognized Portuguese monopoly of discovery and trade in South and East Asia.

Leo X, in the Bull *Dum fidei constantiam* of November 3, 1515, extended these privileges over all lands discovered or conquered, or to be discovered or conquered, "from the Capes of Bojador and Neon to the Indies, wherever situated and even though in our day unknown." The clergy, laity, princes, kings, and even the emperor, were forbidden to trade, or to fish, or to sail the seas in these ill-defined regions without express permission of the king of Portugal.

In return for these privileges the king of Portugal was required to further, as far as in him lay, the spread of Christianity in his sphere of influence. He was to send missionaries into these regions, to provide for their maintenance, to establish churches, chapels, cloisters, and other mission foundations.

Thus were laid the foundations of the Portuguese *Padroado*. Thus was born the worst form of Europeanism, union between the mission and colonial imperialism.

Another factor inimical to the spirit of adaptation was the burgeoning spirit of nationalism. The fierce loyalties peculiar to nationalism do not breed the cosmopolite. By serving as a representative of his own national culture, the missionary compromises the universal character of his mission. As Pope Pius XI was to say in 1929: "Nationalism has always been a plague upon the missions. It is not too much to call it a malediction."

Nationalism was responsible for a peculiarly narrow form of Europeanism. National pride tended to identify national cultural forms with Christianity itself. Nowhere was this truer than in sixteenth-century Spain and Portugal, where the self-assertive spirit of the Christian West was wedded to the most ardent nationalism. To the Portuguese, Christianity in any but a Portuguese wrapping was inconceivable. The same was true of the Spaniard.

There were many notable exceptions, theologians who defended the rights of indigenous peoples, missionaries who respected native cultures. It is not necessary to name them, because what is important here is the prevailing pattern, the rule rather than the exception. The rule in the sixteenth century was Europeanism; and Europeanism as a missionary method can succeed only where certain conditions are fulfilled.

If the superiority of European culture is clearly apparent, it may succeed in supplanting a native culture; but even in such a case, success is unlikely except where European political power has established its domination and brings to the support of cultural penetration all the resources of force at its command. Where these conditions are not fulfilled the system is doomed to failure. The history of Portuguese imperialism makes this clear.

It was India which first fully revealed the deficiencies of Europeanism. Here Christianity was confronted with a rich culture of a high order. In many respects it was a more complicated culture than that of Rome. The problems which it presented would have taxed the ingenuity of missionaries of a more genial age. They were insoluble to the missionaries of the sixteenth century.

The laws and decrees issued in the latter half of that century by the councils of Goa, by the kings, and by the governors reveal a great deal about the spirit of the times.[1] All Mohammedan and pagan priests, penitents, and sorcerers are to be driven from areas under Portuguese domination; non-Christian places of worship are to be destroyed; public practice of any but the Christian religion is forbidden; polygamy is punishable by banishment to the galleys; certain sections of the city are zoned against non-Christians.

In areas subject to them, with all the force of political power mobilized, the Portuguese largely succeeded in Christianizing the Indians. But Portuguese domination was confined to a few strong points on the coast and immediately contiguous regions. Their influence, except as it adversely affected the reputation of Christianity, did not extend to the hinterland nor reach the principal centers of Hindu culture. Furthermore, Christian life was modelled upon that of Portugal. Converts were thoroughly portugalized, obliged to take Portuguese names, wear Portuguese clothes, observe Portuguese customs. They were thus cut off from their own people. Even the native clergy were educated entirely on the Portuguese model. In addition they were treated as a kind of clergy of the second class, little more than catechists. There was no appreciation of their unique qualifications as interpreters of Indian thought.

After a century of these methods the mission in India reached an impasse. The experience shows that Christianity can carry out its world mission in the face of a deeply rooted non-Christian culture only by resorting to a policy of the broadest adaptation compatible with the purity and unity of the faith.

Sixteenth-century China, ruled by the Ming dynasty, posed an even more difficult problem for the Christian mission. Here the missionaries faced not only a high culture, but a unified political entity living an all but completely self-contained existence behind a wall of isolationism. China was more than a state. She was a world unto herself, and a closed world. She saw herself as synonymous with civilization. Outside her borders nothing existed but barbarism. China could be tolerant of that other barbarian world, but only upon condition that she have as little contact with it as possible. The aggressive fever of expansionism which had fired the imagination of the pushing Western world had no counterpart in late Ming China. The spirit of high adventure, lust for empire, for power, prestige, wealth, and zeal for the spread of Christianity, had dotted the seas with Spanish and Portuguese sails. Europeans were landing on every shore, pushing on from conquest to conquest, eager, curious, acquisitive. China was a stranger to this spirit.

China had known her hours of high adventure and of stirring romance. Under the great Wu Ti (140-87 B.C.) of the Han dynasty (B.C. 206-220 A.D.), the soil of Asia had resounded to the tread of conquering Chinese armies and great pioneers ventured deep into Central Asia to establish contact with the outposts of Mediterranean culture. In the golden age of the T'ang, Changan (modern Sian-fu), the capital, was the cultural mecca of the entire Orient. While radiating its cultural splendors throughout the East, it was receptive to influences from without. Nestorian missionaries met with a friendly welcome. Mohammedanism and Manicheism were tolerantly received. Buddhism continued to bring fresh streams of thought from the outer world. Under the Yuan dynasty (1279-1368), when Khubilai Khan's successors occupied the throne of China, foreign faces were a common sight in the dusty streets of Khanbaligh, the later Peking.

These days of glory lay far in the past. It had been long since China stirred to new ideas. In sixteenth-century China, senescence was far advanced. The dynasty was old and unadventurous. Except for its first two reign-periods (1368-1424) it had not been a specially vigorous dynasty.[2] Chinese culture was old and, living in the past as the old are wont to do, contemptuous of anything which did not belong to the past. If this was a sign of stagnation, few thought so. It was complacently assumed that Chinese civilization was a finished product. It had long since found all the final formulas. Nothing new could be added. The great philosophical activity of the Sung period (960-1279) had reached conclusions and produced results which were regarded as definitive.

If the future had nothing to offer, still less was wisdom to be sought among the barbarians. It is difficult to imagine the sixteenth-century European looking to the natives of darkest Africa for enlightenment. It is no less difficult to imagine sixteenth-century China looking for light to the West.

The atavistic and provincial character of Chinese culture in the sixteenth century, contrasting with the eclecticism of certain earlier periods, was due to the domination of political and cultural life by a scholar-official class devoted to a particular school of Confucian thought, the school of Chu Hsi (1130-1200). It was the Han dynasty (B.C. 206-220 A.D.) which first established competitive civil service examinations as the basis of recruitment for government offices and later made Confucian texts the basis of the examinations. This gave Confucian scholars a dominant position in the bureaucracy. Later, in the political divisions that followed the collapse of the Han, the bureaucracy of scholars lost its importance, but under the T'ang the essential feature of the Han political system, rule of an emperor through a bureaucracy recruited by an examination system, was restored.

The position of the scholar-official class was strengthened during the Sung dynasty (960-1279) when all other doors to official careers other than the examinations were closed. After another loss of power during the Yuan period of Mongol rule (1279-1368) the dominance of the class was revived with the restoration of Chinese rule under the Ming in 1368. As the self-appointed agents of Confucian philosophy the scholars made that philosophy a state-sanctioned cultural monopoly, thus assuring their own political and social predominance.[3] Orthodoxy became the touchstone of truth; and the touchstone of orthodoxy became fidelity to the interpretations of the Chu Hsi or Sung school of neo-Confucianism.

The scholar-officials had achieved their position only through a centuries-long struggle. They had no intention of imperiling their position by tolerating new ideas.

This was the China which St. Francis Xavier had vainly tried to enter. This was the challenge faced by the missionaries who followed him. The task of introducing and finding a sympathetic hearing for the unheard of and revolutionary doctrines of Christianity seemed hopeless. If Europeanism proved wanting in India, it would prove totally inept in China.

Towards the end of the sixteenth century a realization of the errors of Europeanism began to appear among a few missionaries. They were chiefly Jesuits, members of the newly founded religious order known as the Society of Jesus. They developed methods of apostolate which represented a sharp break with the dominant spirit of the age. These methods aroused criticism and have been the subject of debate ever since.

Much of the criticism stemmed from the fact that few understood at the time or have understood since what the Jesuits were attempting to do. They were accused of being innovators, of compromising the faith. Actually they were attempting to restore the genuine ideal of Christianity as the leaven of the world; to renew the authentic character of the world mission of Christianity; to revive methods of cultural adaptation which had played a prominent part in the earlier centuries of Christian expansion.

The spirit of the Society of Jesus was admirably suited to the development of these methods of apostolate. The order was young, having been canonically established by Pope Paul III on September 27, 1540. Religious orders, like individuals, generally manifest in the days of their youth a flexibility which is wanting to their more advanced age. With age comes caution: a partiality for the well-worn paths of the tried and true; a reluctance to recognize that in a world which never stands still the tried and true often becomes outmoded and false; an unwillingness to embark upon new adventures.

St. Ignatius of Loyola, founder of the Jesuit order, was not afraid to break new trails. His Constitutions imposed no narrowly defined limitations upon the methods of apostolate proper to his followers. He decided against the adoption of a distinctive habit for members of the Society. One of the first rules of the order required its members to learn the language of the country in which they resided. This seems an obvious thing to do. Yet this first principle of cultural adaptation had been generally ignored. It was the common practice in missionary countries to teach the faith through interpreters. Some members of older orders looked askance upon his innovations and were not easily reconciled. There is evidence that some of the hostility to the methods later employed in China was not unrelated to this attitude.

When in 1542 Paul III sent the Jesuits Bröet and Salmeron to Ireland, Ignatius ordered them to adapt themselves to Irish customs. When another Jesuit, Melchior Nuñez Barreto, was named patriarch to Abyssinia he gave him instructions which breathed a broad spirit of adaptation. He was to multiply schools and hospitals and to develop a native clergy. No violence or force must be used in propagating the faith. He should take with him to Abyssinia engineers, agricultural experts, doctors and surgeons. Echoing the genial instructions given to St. Augustine of Canterbury by Pope St. Gregory the Great, Ignatius warned Barreto not to be precipitate in removing abuses which might have crept into the liturgy, but to remove them gradually so as not unduly to shock deep-rooted prejudices.

It is safe to surmise that the spirit of Ignatius, communicating itself to some of the early Jesuit missionaries, played a part in developing the method of cultural adaptation. It would be a mistake, however, to think that from the outset Jesuit missionaries hit upon this formula or that they were unanimous in its acceptance. It was in China that the first and most notable effort in this direction was made. Even here the lessons were learned gradually out of several decades of disheartening failure.

This is the story of the small group of men who, breaking with the dominant spirit of their times and recalling a distant past, restored the concept of cultural adaptation to a central position in the world mission of Christianity. They wrote a splendid page in the history of the cultural relations of East and West. They were the first in what may be called modern times to establish a successful contact between those two worlds. Their story is worth telling not simply as an important segment of world history, but because it has much to say not only to the Christian missionary of today, of whatever faith, but to a world which has not yet learned to break down the barriers of cultural, racial, and national pride.

NOTES

(1) The text of the decrees is in Levy Maria Jordão, *Bullarium patronatus Portugalliae regum in ecclesiis Africae, Asiae atque Oceaniae bullas, brevia, epistolas, decreta actaque S. Sedis ab Alexandro III ad hoc usque tempus amplectens.* (Olisopone: Ex typographia nationali, 1869), Appendix I.

(2) One should, however, not under-estimate the genuine achievements of the Ming dynasty in the field of public works, law, colonization, fine arts, and literature; cf. L. C. Goodrich, *A Short History of the Chinese People* (New York: Harper and Brothers, 1943), pp. 185 ff.

(3) The excessive power of court eunuchs, especially under the later Ming rulers, challenged that predominance; but that is another story the general lines of which will emerge in the pages which follow.

Chapter I

Reaching for the Moon

When, on the night of December 2, 1552, Francis Xavier, who had opened Japan to the faith and dreamed of doing the same for China, died on the tiny island of Shangchwan, Portuguese prisoners languished in Cantonese jails and China was hermetically sealed. Shortly thereafter certain influential Cantonese merchants, regretting missed commercial opportunities, succeeded through Lin Fu, the governor of Kwangtung, in obtaining from Peking authorization to open a small and carefully guarded door. Canton was opened to strictly limited trade in 1554. The Portuguese, settling on a tiny peninsula on China's southern coast, established a community which, as the city of Macao, was destined to play an important role in the history of the West in the East and to achieve a renown out of all proportion to its size.

Apart from these small chinks in the wall, China remained as firm as ever in her isolation. All efforts by missionaries to break through her ramparts were repulsed. In 1555 Melchior Nunes Barreto tried in vain to preach in Canton. In 1563 there were eight Jesuits in Macao working among the five thousand Macaists of whom nine hundred were Portuguese. In 1565 their superior, Francisco Peres, appeared before an official tribunal in Canton with a formal request to be allowed to establish himself in China.[1] He was treated with courtesy, advised reasonably enough to learn Chinese, and sent back to Macao.

Three years later the Spanish Jesuit, Juan Bautista Ribeira, later to serve as secretary to Francis Borgia, the third general of the Society of Jesus, with characteristic bravura had himself set down on the coast of China whence he proposed to set out unaided, unauthorized, and unversed in the language to evangelize China. He incurred not only the displeasure of the Chinese, but that of his superiors as well. For his pains he was sent back to Europe where he reported the penetration of China to be a hopeless undertaking. "During the three years I was at Macao," he reported to the general of the order, "I did everything possible to penetrate the continent, but nothing I could think of was of any avail."[2] Among the things he had evidently not thought of was an approach to China through respect for her culture. It is not surprising to find him, in the same letter, advocating force: "There is no hope of converting [the Chinese], unless one has recourse to force and unless they give way before the soldiers."

Barreto shared this dangerous opinion. Since he and Ribeira had been together in Macao they probably had discussed it. In a letter of November 2, 1569, he expressed the wish that the Christian princes of Europe would stop quarrelling among themselves and "force the sovereign of China to grant to the missionaries the right to preach and to the natives the right to hear the truth."[3]

Meanwhile attacks upon the Chinese citadel began to develop from another quarter. On May 8, 1565, the Spanish expedition of Legazpi, sailing out of Mexico, had landed on the island of Cebu and within a few years Spanish rule was established over all the Philippines. To the Augustinians who accompanied the expedition and to the *conquistadores* as well, the Philippines were but a stepping stone to the Asiatic continent. On June 24, 1571, Governor Legazpi founded the city of Manila because, as he wrote, he was uncertain whether His Majesty Philip II "wishes us to proceed immediately to China."[4] Four years later the Augustinians de Rada and Marin accompanied envoys of Governor Lavezaris, Legazpi's successor, to China. They were treated with elaborate courtesy by the governor of Fukien, wined and dined and sent back to Manila.

A less happily inspired attempt four years later ended in tragedy. Four Franciscans, scarcely arrived in the Philippines from Spain, landed near Canton. They were jailed and harshly treated. One of them died in prison. The others were released, but deported. One returned to Manila. The other two settled in Macao where they established the first Franciscan house in that city. They added their voices to the pessimistic chorus of those who had tried in vain to scale the Chinese wall. "No monastery of nuns," wrote Tordesillas, "better observes the rule of cloister."[5] And Alfaro, his companion, added: "With or without soldiers to wish to enter China is to attempt to reach the moon."[6] As everyone now knows, even the moon can be reached. It is a question of method.

The methods employed during the twenty-five years that followed the death of Francis Xavier showed no advance upon the narrow Europeanism characteristic of the age. The missionaries who attempted to penetrate China made no effort to overcome their ignorance of Chinese language and customs. An exception can be made for the Augustinian de Rada who in 1575 took back to Manila one hundred volumes of Chinese works on a variety of subjects and, reporting his experiences and observations, gave to Europe the first authentic picture of China and her institutions. For the others, the religion, history, philosophy, literature and even language of China held no interest.

It was an Italian Jesuit, Alessandro Valignano, who gave an entirely new direction to the enterprise. A doctor of civil law and with some years experience in the court of Pope Paul IV, he brought to the Society of Jesus, which he entered in 1566 at the age of twenty-eight, rare intellectual and spiritual gifts. In 1573 the general of the Society appointed him superior, with the title of visitor, of all the Jesuit missions in the East Indies, a geographical expression which included Japan and China.

Valignano sailed from Lisbon on March 23, 1574, with forty-one Jesuits destined for various missions in the East. From October, 1577, to July, 1578, he was for the first time in Macao. The inquiries and observations he made during these nine months gave him both a high esteem for the Chinese ("great and worthy people") and an insight into the cause of previous failures. "The only possible way to penetration," he wrote to the general of the Society, "will be utterly different from that which has been adopted up to now in all the other missions in these countries."[7]

This might well be called an epochal observation. It heralds a definite break with the exaggerated Europeanism of the time. Instead of attempting to graft itself as a foreign substance upon the resistant and unfriendly body of Chinese culture, Christianity was to revert to its original character of leaven. Entering quietly into the body of Chinese culture it must endeavor to transform it from within.

This was Valignano's insight. It cannot be said that he had a detailed program of action in mind. Such a program was not possible. It could take shape only gradually. The revolutionary character of his break with the missiological ideas of his time did not consist in the confrontation of program with program, but in a change of fundamental attitude.

Europeanism is a state of mind. It consists in a narrow and arrogant assumption of the finality of national cultural forms. To these forms it attaches absolute value and is thus incapable of recognizing the values inherent in other cultures. It is a constant irritant to the sensibilities of a people who are perpetually insulted by aliens whom they have received, or been forced to receive, into their homes.

Cultural adaptation is based upon respect for native cultures. It is rooted in humility of mind and is sensitive to human values wherever found. *Nil humanum ab eo alienum.* It was this new, although really quite old, attitude with which Valignano approached the missionary problem that was revolutionary.

He wasted no time in implementing the new policy which he was fully conscious of introducing. The Jesuits at Macao were not equal to the task. They were too deeply imbued with the spirit of Europeanism. (In Macao Chinese converts were required to take Portuguese names, wear Portuguese clothes, adopt Portuguese customs.) Valignano asked the Jesuit provincial at Goa to send him the Italian Bernardino de Ferrariis. He was not available. In his stead the provincial sent Michele Ruggieri, also an Italian.

Ruggieri arrived in Macao in July, 1579, only to learn that Valignano had sailed for Japan two weeks before. He had, however, left orders for Ruggieri to learn "to read, write, and speak" Chinese. It was the first step towards the cultural penetration of China.

In November, 1580, Ruggieri for the first time visited Canton with the Portuguese merchants who were permitted to make two trading visits a year, one in the spring, the other in the fall. En route he persuaded his companions to observe the formalities of Chinese etiquette to which they ordinarily paid little attention. So pleased were the Chinese officials by the improvement in Portuguese manners that they insisted upon Ruggieri's presence at all public audiences.

On his return the following spring he was shown every courtesy. In the official audiences, while all the others were required to kneel as was the custom, he was asked to remain standing. He was given lodging in the building reserved for the triennial visits of the Siamese and Tonkinese tribute-bearing embassies en route to Peking. In the fall, when he was back again, the intendant, the sub-prefect, and the military commander attended his Mass. He was later taken to task for permitting this by the Franciscan Montillas.[8] Thus quite simply, as signs of benevolence multiplied, the doors which for so many years had remained firmly closed in the face of frontal attacks, began to open to the gentle pressure of sympathetic understanding.

If Chinese officialdom appreciated Ruggieri's efforts, his fellow Jesuits in Macao did not. From the beginning he suffered from their lack of comprehension and sympathy. They told him he was wasting his time. Ironically they said that the Chinese was not living who would be converted at the sound of his voice. The Jesuit superior persisted in interfering with his Chinese studies by applying him to ministerial tasks in Macao. Even the energetic intervention of Valignano from Japan failed to end petty obstructionism.

"If Father Alessandro Valignano were not here," Ruggieri wrote to the general of the Society on November 8, 1580, "I do not know what would happen to this business of the conversion of China. I write this because I hear certain ones say: 'What is the sense of this Father occupying himself with this sort of thing when he could be of service in the other ministries of the Society? It is a waste of time for him to learn the Chinese language and to consecrate himself to a hopeless enterprise.' "[9]

Three years later, six months after his own arrival in Macao, Matteo Ricci described Ruggieri's years in Macao as a kind of martyrdom at the hands of the Jesuits there "who, although holy men, fail to understand the problem of the Christian mission."[10]

Upon his return to Macao in 1582 Valignano took decisive action. He removed the Jesuit superior and sent him to Japan. He decreed that Jesuits appointed to the China mission should enjoy a large degree of autonomy from the Macao community and he strongly urged Claudio Aquaviva, the general of the Society, not to disturb these decisions.[11] In addition, he ordered abandonment of the policy of "portugalizing" converts. Chinese Christians were to remain Chinese. Instead of "portugalizing" them, the missionaries were to "sinicize" themselves.

New difficulties arose from another source. On May 2, 1582, a group of Spaniards, led by the Jesuit Alonso Sanchez, appeared at

Canton after having landed in the province of Fukien on April 2. The Chinese, although they had seemingly come to accept the anomalous existence of Macao, were always disturbed by the appearance of foreigners from another quarter. In this instance Ch'ên Jui, viceroy of Kwangtung and Kwangsi provinces, sent a summons to the newly arrived bishop of Macao, Leonardo de Saa, to appear before his tribunal in the city of Chaoching together with the *capitan mayor* of Macao, Airez Gonzalez de Mendoza, to explain the juridical basis of the sovereignty exercised by the Portuguese in that city.[12] Valignano sent Ruggieri to represent the bishop. Ruggieri made so favorable an impression that upon his return to Macao he received an invitation from the viceroy to establish himself at Chaoching. Taking Francesco Pasio with him, Ruggieri hastened to return. A pagoda was given to him for his use. There the viceroy, surrounded by a considerable number of lesser officials, paid him a formal visit and presented him with a eulogy in Chinese verse.

The next storm that blew in from the Philippines had less happy results. Five Franciscan friars landed on the coast of Fukien. They were seized and imprisoned in Canton. One of them died in jail. The others were released through the efforts of the Portuguese at Macao whose charity is the more remarkable in view of the fact that these repeated and intemperate adventures jeopardized their whole position.

In March, 1582, the viceroy was summarily removed from office and ordered to Peking to answer the charge that he had violated the immunity from capital punishment enjoyed by the scholar class. Fearful that, in the state of concern aroused by the appearance of the friars, he might also have to answer for the signal favor he had shown the foreigners he ordered Ruggieri and Pasio to leave Chaoching. Hoping to soften the blow, he wrote to the port commander at Canton directing him to allow them to establish themselves there. Orders of mandarins out of office carry no weight and they were forced to return to Macao.

All the budding hopes seemed ruthlessly destroyed; but within six months the wheel of fortune had come full cycle. It is not clear what led to Ruggieri's recall to Chaoching. Probably the good friends he had made, among them the intendant of the Canton circuit and the prefect of Chaoching, Wang P'an, were responsible. Within a week after Ruggieri had presented to the former a written request for a small piece of land on which to build a house and church, an officer from Wang P'an's office appeared at the residence in Macao with an official document stating that the request had been granted by the new viceroy, Kuo Ying-p'ing.

Pasio had gone to Japan. In his place Ruggieri brought back to Chaoching with him the young Jesuit priest Matteo Ricci, who was less than three weeks away from his thirty-first birthday and who was destined to write, before his death twenty-seven years later, one of the most glowing chapters in the history of cultural relations and missionary enterprise.

Ruggieri and Ricci arrived in Chaoching on September 10, 1583. There they established on the property given them by the viceroy the first Christian establishment in the interior of China. Christianity had been in China before; but all traces of the remarkable Nestorian mission of the seventh and eighth centuries and of the splendid Franciscan achievements in the thirteenth and fourteenth centuries had long since been buried in oblivion. A new phase was now opened. Through whatever valleys of misfortune she may have passed since and however prostrate she may be at this moment, the Catholic Church has never ceased since that day to live in China. Valignano had been justified and the carping critics of Ruggieri put to shame.

NOTES

(1) I have tried throughout to suit orthography to nationality. Thus it is Francisco for Peres, a Portuguese, but Francesco for Pasio, an Italian.
(2) Matteo Ricci, S. J., *Opere storiche*, ed. Pietro Tacchi-Venturi, S. J. (Macerata: Giorgetti, 1911-1913), I, n. 5. Hereafter cited as *Opere storiche*.
(3) Quoted by L. Delplace, S. J., *Le Catholicisme au Japon* (Bruxelles: A. Dewit, 1909-1910), II, 155.
(4) Francisco Javier Montalban, S. J., *El patronato español y la conquista de Filipinas, con documentos del archivo general de Indias* (Burgos: El Siglo de la Misiones, 1930), p. 105.
(5) Quoted by Dr. Otto Maas, O.F.M., *Die Wiedereröffnung der Franziskanermission in China in der Neuzeit* (Münster in Westfalen: Aschendorff, 1926), p. 44, n. 92.
(6) *Sinica Franciscana, Relationes et Epistolas Fratrum Minorum*, ed. A. Van den Wyngaert (Ad Claras Aquas [Quaracchi-Firenze] apud Collegium S. Bonaventurae, 1926-1936), II, 180. Hereafter cited as *SinFran.*
(7) Quoted by Henri Bernard, S. J., *Aux portes de la Chine* (Tientsin: Hautes Etudes, 1933), p. 141.
(8) The Jesuits had faculties from the Holy See to celebrate Mass in the presence of pagans. Cf. *ibid.*, p. 155, n. 51.
(9) *Opere storiche*, II, 397.
(10) *Ibid.*, p. 35.
(11) *Ibid.*, I, 111, n. 2.
(12) For the names of cities I have followed the romanization of the 1932 edition of the official Chinese postal guide.

Chapter II

Ricci Joins the Expedition

IF THE WORK of Michele Ruggieri in opening the door of China has been generally overlooked, it is because of the overshadowing importance of the career of Matteo Ricci. In a deeper sense than Ruggieri he was the pioneer of the mission.

Ricci was admirably suited by temperament and background to carry out the policy inaugurated by Valignano. His letters reveal a man who was exceedingly kind, affectionate and understanding. His entire life in China is a record of monumental patience and exquisite tact. He never forgot Macerata, his birthplace in Italy, as he never forgot his family. The ties which bound him to the one and the other reached across the chasm of time and space. There is an abiding tenderness in his letters to his family: "May God keep you from all evil." There is something deeply human in his affection for the place of his childhood memories: "Continue to write and even in more detail, because it is impossible for me to forget."[1]

In 1568, at the age of sixteen, Ricci left home for Rome to study at the German College. It was a good time to be alive. The Catholic Reform was in full swing. Art and science were both flourishing. The historical associations with which Rome is filled fascinated him.

St. Ignatius of Loyola had been dead only five years when, on August 15, 1571, to his pharmacist father's disappointment, he entered the Society of Jesus. After thirteen months of novitiate he pronounced his religious vows and became a student in the Roman College, from his day to this the alma mater of a long list of distinguished alumni. Among the happiest memories he kept green during his years of isolation in China were those associated with his fellow students in this college: "One of my good oraisons is to think of them," was his charming way of putting it.[2]

The two professors who probably most influenced his development were Clavius and Bellarmine. Clavius, noted Jesuit mathematician and friend of both Kepler and Galileo, was chiefly responsible for the development of the Gregorian calendar. Under his direction Ricci studied the positive sciences. Robert Bellarmine, later cardinal and canonized saint, at the age of thirty-four already enjoyed a European reputation. He inaugurated on September 26, 1576, his famous Course of Controversies. Among those who flocked twice a week to his lectures was Ricci. Bellarmine, brilliant controversialist, great erudite, and genial humanist, put his stamp upon Ricci during these last months of his student days in Rome. The two were kindred spirits and it is not surprising that Bellarmine later manifested great interest in the Church in China and, in 1618, wrote a letter of encouragement to the Chinese Christians.

Ricci, having volunteered for the Far Eastern mission, left Rome on May 18, 1577, for Portugal. Here he continued his studies at the University of Coimbra while awaiting departure for Goa. The faculty of philosophy at the university was at the time engaged in preparing the commentaries on Aristotle which were later to achieve renown under the title of *Conimbricenses*. Ricci, with the aid of Chinese friends, would later translate part of these commentaries into Chinese. He sailed from Lisbon on March 29, 1578, with thirteen other Jesuits, among them Ruggieri and Pasio. Their ship dropped anchor at Goa on September 13, 1578. Here, except for a few months at Cochin, where he was ordained to the priesthood in 1580, Ricci remained for almost four years, teaching the humanities, studying theology, and struggling with poor health.

One of his letters written at this time to Claudio Aquaviva, the general of the Society of Jesus, throws considerable light upon his character and suggests that he was indeed a man predestined to implement the policy of Valignano.[3] Certain Jesuits in India and in Japan, infected with the spirit of Europeanism, which is inclined to undervalue the native character, would have reduced the indigenous clergy to a status of inferiority. In Japan Francisco Cabral urged that Japanese candidates for the priesthood be taught Latin and cases of conscience, but not be admitted to the courses of philosophy and theology followed by European students. Valignano strongly opposed this view. In India there were many who agreed with Cabral and, in 1581, they prevailed. At Goa the Jesuit superiors adopted the system advocated by Cabral. In a letter of November 20, 1581, Ricci registered a strong dissent:

> . . . The reasons advancd in support of this policy seem to me of little weight. It is alleged that philosophical and theological studies will make [native students] proud and that, as a consequence, they will not be content to serve in poor parishes; and that, furthermore, they will look down upon those European [students] who do not do so well in their philosophical and theological studies. But all of this could be said, and perhaps with more reason, of others who study in our schools whether in India or in Europe. Nevertheless, we do not on that account refuse them admittance to our schools. Much less should we do so in the circumstances here, since no matter how learned they be native born Indians rarely receive due credit from whites. . . . Secondly, by this new policy we shall encourage ignorance on the part of ministers of the Church and in a land where learning is of much importance. These students are preparing for the priesthood and the care of souls. It does not seem right that, among so many kinds of unbelievers, our priests should be so ignorant that they will be unable to answer or to propound an argument either to confirm themselves or others in our faith. Unless we are to look for miracles where we have no right to expect them, a mere casuist cannot be adequately equipped for the ministry. Thirdly, and it is this which disturbs me more than anything else, this people have been greatly humiliated in this land. No one has shown them as much understanding as have our Fathers. It is for this reason that they have a special love for us. If now they are to be made to feel that even our Fathers are against them and do not want to enable them to hold their heads high and to make it possible for them to aspire to any office or benefice on a basis of equality with Europeans, as education enables them to do, I am very much afraid that they will come to hate us. Thus will be thwarted the principal object with which the Society is concerned in India, namely, the conversion of the unbelievers and their conservation in our holy faith.[4]

Clearly Valignano could have made no better choice when, in 1582, he ordered the provincial in India, Rui Vicente, to send Ricci to Macao. From the moment of his arrival in that Portuguese city on August 7, 1582, he plunged into the study of Chinese. Valignano also directed him to prepare a summarized description of China: its people, customs, institutions, and government. He was persuaded that a knowledge of Chinese civilization was an indispensable preliminary to an effective apostolate. Of the various descriptions of China which had appeared up to this time, Alonso Sanchez, an acute observer for all his Europeanism, remarked: "Actually all are defective because they include things which do not exist or omit many things which do exist."[5]

Working day and night, Ricci, assisted by a staff of interpreters and instructors and checking his conclusions against the observations of Ruggieri, wrote his description of China. Valignano incorporated it into his biography of Francis Xavier.[6] Based chiefly upon Chinese written sources the description contains many inexactitudes which Ricci would later correct in the light of his own experience and observation. In China as elsewhere, as he later remarked, "the reality of things often falls far short of their reputation."[7] Ricci's account is, nevertheless, important for two reasons: it was the most reliable account of Chinese civilization yet to appear, and it typifies the Valignano approach. Chinese civilization is treated with respect. Twenty-one pages of text are devoted to the admirable features of China and her people. Sincere admiration did not, however, destroy Ricci's critical sense. China's shortcomings receive attention in eight pages of text.

Later rationalistic writers, especially Voltaire, as part of their general attack upon the supernatural, would exalt far beyond measure the triumphs of natural reason, morality, and religion in China and appeal to the authority of the Jesuits in support of their thesis. They were not on solid ground. Neither Ricci nor those who followed him, with the exception of the yet inexperienced Longobardo, were guilty of the extravagances of Voltaire and the *philosophes*. What they chiefly admired was the political organization of the City, in which they thought to see a realization in fact of what Plato had conceived in theory, government by philosophers. Even here what they admired was rather the system than its actual operation. They were not blind to the faults from which it suffered and which they explicitly attributed to the absence of the supernatural. Ricci mentions the "many grave disorders," among them numerous injustices committed by officials through the abuse of their discretionary powers, and attributes them to the limitations of natural reason and morality. The same critical balance can be found in the judgment of later Jesuit commentators upon the Chinese scene, from the sharply observant Le Comte to the less critically admiring Magalhães.[8]

As far as the religions of the Chinese were concerned, the Jesuits had little regard for Buddhism or Taoism, which they imperfectly understood. In Confucianism they admired chiefly two things: its moral doctrines, which for the most part did not conflict with Christian moral teaching; and the theodocian tenets which, in their opinion, characterized original Confucianism as distinguished from the materialistic interpretations of the Sung School. Even here, however, they clearly recognized the essential deficiency of both the one and the other in comparison with Christian moral and theological teaching. Inasmuch as in October, 1700, he was the victim of a resounding condemnation fulminated by a commission of the University of Paris because he allegedly placed Confucian and Christian doctrine on the same level, it is interesting to read what Le Comte's views really were:

"However attractive and comprehensive is the moral [doctrine] of China," he had written, "it represents but the feeble rays of light of extremely limited reason, rays which fade into nothingness the moment they are compared to the divine illumination which religion reveals to us."[9]

Their respect for Confucius fell into the same category as their esteem for Aristotle. If, in a moment of more than ordinary fatuity, the freethinker La Mothe le Vayer "felt himself constrained to exclaim 'Sancte Confuci, ora pro nobis!' "[10] the Jesuits were hardly to blame. The freethinker had to be either singularly obtuse or extraordinarily malevolent to find in the writings of the Jesuits support for his thesis.

Ricci spent six years in Chaoching trying, through patient perseverance against formidable obstacles, to consolidate the newly won position. From the outset it became increasingly clear to him that the primary task was not to multiply baptisms, but to win for Christianity an accepted place in Chinese life. Until this was accomplished the Church was in constant danger of being driven from Chinese soil by hostile officials. It formed no part of Ricci's plans to strive for only ephemeral success, a few years of brilliant conquest followed by the destruction of all high hopes. This was to be the story of Japan. Nor did he have any desire to record a few thousand baptisms each year only to have the whole movement grind to a halt after a few generations. This was already happening in India. His object was not simply to establish a certain number of Christian communities on the fringes of a hostile society; it was rather to build a Sino-Christian civilization. This required that Christianity enter as deeply as possible into the streams of Chinese life; that through a gradual diffusion of Christian ideals and ideas minds be acclimated to the Christian message; that, through the development of an ever widening circle of sympathetic contacts, Chinese hearts be prepared for its acceptance. Through the pacific processes of infusion and diffusion, the Christian leaven quietly at work, was this transformation to be achieved.

Ricci, like Valignano, did not begin with a fully developed program of action. What distinguished his approach was rather an attitude of mind: respect for the people and culture of China, combined with unaffected humility which enabled him to adapt himself to his environment. His methods developed over the years, the product of experience and a rare talent for accurately judging the Chinese scene.

The years in Chaoching were difficult. From the outset there was clear evidence of deep-seated hostility on the part of the common people. In the sixteenth century xenophobia was more prevalent in Kwangtung province than elsewhere. Probably the proximity of the Portuguese was responsible. When Ricci and Ruggieri appeared in the streets they were accustomed to hear "a thousand epithets" hurled at them. The commonest, still common in the twentieth century, was "foreign devil."

Ricci, nevertheless, quickly learned that it was possible to establish friendly relations with many of the scholar-official class. This sympathetic attitude was not characteristic of the scholars as a whole. Most of them, under the influence of entrenched neo-Confucian orthodoxy, shared the hostility of the crowd. Yet there were many who were open-minded and interested in new ideas. To these Ricci directed his principal efforts.

To introduce their numerous visitors to Western culture, he and Ruggieri kept on exhibition their collection of books. Modest though this was, it was the foundation of the first library of European books in China. Throughout his life in China Ricci, in his letters to Europe, asked for more books. He was never satisfied. European art also received its first showing in China in this Jesuit house in Chaoching.

Visitors were specially interested in the European technique of perspective, new to China. As examples of the mechanical genius of Western Civilization they could examine spheres, solar quadrants, prisms, and clocks.

Conversations with his visitors, revealing the deficiencies of Chinese cosmography, inspired Ricci to prepare a map of the world. It was destined to have a profound effect upon Chinese notions of world geography.[11] During the years which followed he re-worked, corrected, and amplified this map which, as he later wrote, "was printed time and time again and circulated throughout all China, winning for us much credit."[12]

In 1581 Ruggieri had written in Latin a work of apologetics, which he called a catechism, and had some of his interpreters translate it into Chinese. Although Valignano in 1582 had directed Ruggieri to publish it, it still circulated only in manuscript form. In the summer and fall of 1584 a *hsiu-ts'ai* from the province of Fukien, assisted by Ricci who was giving him instructions in the faith, worked the text over, improving the literary style.[13] This was Ricci's first experience with the critical problem of finding Chinese words suitable for the expression of Christian ideas.

The translation was published in November, 1584, under the title *T'ien Chu shih-lu* (True Account of God). It was the first work of Christian literature to appear in Chinese. It discussed the existence of God, the attributes of God, His providence, man's knowledge of God, the immortality of the soul, the natural law, the Mosaic law, the Christian law, the incarnation of the Word of God, the sacrament of baptism, and similar topics.[14]

A legend has rather firmly fixed itself in historical writing that, concealing the character of his mission, Ricci did not discuss religious matters.[15] The contents of *T'ien Chu shih-lu* expose the legendary character of the charge. Even more conclusive is the evidence offered by a manuscript found in the archives of the Society of Jesus.[16] It is a Chinese-Portuguese vocabulary, prepared by Ricci during the Chaoching period of his life. Preceding the vocabulary are nine pages which Ricci had written as a memory guide for his own use. It summarizes the topics which he discussed with his scholarly visitors. It leaves no room for doubt that religion was the main subject of his discourse and that he presented his faith in full integrity.

In 1585 Duarte de Sande and Antonio d'Almeida joined Ricci and Ruggieri. Two years later the appearance in Canton of another group of friars, led by Martin Ignatius of Loyola who had already participated in one unsuccessful expedition to China, caused the usual repercussions. Officials in Canton wrote to Chaoching calling attention to the increased activities of foreigners and urging that Ricci and his companions be expelled. A series of incidents which emphasized the insecurity of their position forced Ruggieri and de Sande to return to Macao where d'Almeida had already preceded them. Ricci was left alone.

A group of one hundred influential Cantonese submitted a strong memorial to the imperial censor asking the expulsion of Ricci from Chaoching. The petition followed the regular channels of administrative procedure. The good friendships made by Ruggieri and Ricci now proved their worth. The support of the intendant, the prefect, the vice-prefect, and most of the other Chaoching officials was decisive. By September 8, 1588, the affair had been settled by the censor in favor of the Jesuit.

This incident prompted Valignano to despatch Ruggieri to Rome in an attempt to organize a papal embassy to the emperor of China for the purpose of obtaining imperial sanction for the unhindered preaching of the Gospel. Ruggieri sailed on November 20, 1588. The full weight of the mission now fell upon Ricci, aided by d'Almeida who had been able to rejoin him in the late summer.

Ruggieri, who had first breached the wall, never returned to China. He was older than Ricci when he encountered the Chinese language and, despite his best efforts, a not too retentive memory had prevented him from really mastering it. His struggles with the language and poor health had worn him out. Although he was not yet fifty years of age Ricci refers to him as "already old." The death of four popes in rapid succession, Sixtus V, Urban VII, Gregory XIV and Innocent IX, prevented him from accomplishing anything at the Holy See. In any event, wider experience and better understanding of the conditions which prevailed at the court in Peking revealed to Ricci the impracticability of a papal embassy. Ruggieri lived quietly in Italy until his death in 1607. To maintain its foothold in China the Church would have to look, not to papal embassies, but to Ricci's ability to win friends.

The mission had survived the regime of three successive viceroys;

but late in 1588 the incumbent died. His successor, Liu Chieh-chai, had hardly taken office when he took steps to expel the foreigners from Chaoching. Even Valignano seems to have lost heart and was ready to abandon the enterprise in favor of more fruitful soil. Ricci, on a quick trip to Macao, restored his failing courage. In a long contest of wits with Liu Chieh-chai in which Ricci showed how thoroughly he understood Chinese psychology he turned threatened disaster into major gain. Employing the intricacies of Chinese *politesse* with the finesse of a master parliamentarian manipulating the rules of order to achieve his ends he maneuvered Liu into such a position that to save face the viceroy compromised by permitting Ricci to settle in another city, recommending Shaochow. The two parted on friendly terms and in later years Liu Chieh-chai gave more than one proof of sympathetic interest and support.

On August 15, 1589, Ricci and d'Almeida took leave of their eighty Christians in Chaoching and set out for Shaochow which was situated in the north of Kwangtung province, at the junction of the Pe-kiang and Wu-shui rivers. Here they established themselves, "ready," as Ricci wrote to Valignano, "to serve seven more years for Rachel."[17]

In November his hand was strengthened by the arrival from Macao of two candidates for the Society of Jesus, (Sebastian) Chung Ming-jên and (Francisco) Huang Ming-sha.[18] Both would later render outstanding service as Jesuit lay brothers. Despite these reinforcements the years at Shaochow were filled with trials: the death of d'Almeida in October, 1591, and of Francesco de Petris, who had succeeded him, in 1593; the violent hostility of certain elements of the populace. Twice the residence was invaded by a mob. The second incident, in 1592, was serious and both Jesuit priests were wounded. The ringleaders were a group of young men, some belonging to prominent families, who, after a drinking bout in a nearby pagoda, stormed into the residence at midnight.

The handling of the affair by local authorities showed a high sense of duty and justice. Ricci vainly interceded for the culprits. The judge refused to grant clemency, remarking: "You do your duty as a Western religious; but I must do my duty as a Chinese judge."[19]

The judicial processes arising out of this incident led Ricci to Chaoching in the fall of 1592. From there he visited Macao. It was the last time he saw Macao and the last time he was to see Valignano.

Important decisions were reached, the nature of which can be judged from Ricci's future conduct.

Up to this time he had been absorbed in immediate problems: the mastery of the language, customs and psychology of the Chinese, the developing of friendly contacts. Now he applied himself, under the direction of a competent teacher, to the study of the classics. "In my old age," he wrote in pleasant exaggeration, "I return as a boy to school."[20]

It was through his studies during these years at Shaochow that Ricci came to distinguish between the original doctrine of the classics and the interpretations given to the text by commentators of the Chu Hsi school. These interpretations had determined the character of Sung neo-Confucianism, the accepted orthodoxy of the day. Convinced that the unrelieved materialism of contemporary Confucianism had been arbitrarily grafted on to the original doctrine, Ricci began to seek in the classical texts themselves points of contact for Christian ideas.

The scholarly traits of his mind reveal themselves in the care with which he formulated his conclusions. Modern scholarship may be able to add to his analysis of the main positions of original Confucian doctrine, but it is doubtful that it would disagree with it on any major point.[21]

It is easy to see how Ricci's method of apologetics grew out of his essentially correct analysis. If Christianity were to enter deeply into the life of China, it had to find points of contact with Confucianism. If it were to receive a sympathetic hearing Ricci would have to persuade the scholars that the metaphysics of Chu Hsi, thoroughly materialistic and utterly opposed to the Christian world view, were not an integral part of original Confucian doctrine. This he attempted to do by appealing to the original texts. He adopted the same attitude vis-à-vis Confucian thought that the early Fathers of the Church had adopted towards Greek thought: endeavoring to preserve all those elements of natural truth which it contained, to add other truths which it lacked in the natural order, and to introduce the whole new order of supernatural truth contained in Christian revelation.

Another important development which followed his last visit to Macao was a complete change in the style of dress which he and the other Jesuits would henceforth adopt. Until now they had dressed in the fashion of Buddhist monks. On the occasion of Ruggieri's second visit to Chaoching the vice-prefect had advised him that, if he wished to remain in China, he would have to follow the Chinese fashions in dress. In order to conform to this requirement and, at the same time, make clear the religious character of his mission, Ruggieri, with Valignano's approval, had adopted the Buddhist garb.

Many of the difficulties which had been encountered in the years that followed were due to the fact that in the public mind they were often identified with the Buddhists. In Shaochow Ricci's residence was near a Buddhist monastery. This enabled him to observe at close range the lives of the monks. His judgment of the low state of morals which generally prevailed explained the poor opinion widely current about Buddhist priests and intensified his distaste at the prospect of longer being confused with them. "Besides this reason," writes Ricci, in his account of this move, "it was necessary for ours to have a suitable garment of silk and the corresponding head piece for the visits of magistrates and other important persons who come to the house in their robes of ceremony."[22]

This question Ricci had discussed at length with Valignano in Macao in 1592. Valignano gave the matter long thought and consulted the Jesuits in Macao as well as Bishop Luis Cerqueira. When Lazzaro Cattaneo joined Ricci in Shaochow on July 7, 1594, he brought with him authorization to adopt the mode of dress followed by the scholars. Anyone who knows the Chinese and their sense of humor can well believe that, once the formalities of serious etiquette had been attended to, there was much joshing between Ricci and his scholarly friends the first time he and Cattaneo donned the robes and the formal and handsome head piece. "Our friends were pleased," wrote Ricci.[23] Probably no one could have been more pleased than Ricci himself who is on record as expressing regret that he could not change the cast of his eyes and the size of his nose the more completely to sinicize himself.

The most fruitful friendship which Ricci formed at Shaochow was with Ch'ü Ju-k'uei. He was the son of one of China's most distinguished and brilliant scholar-officials, Ch'ü Ching-ch'un. Although highly gifted, Ch'ü Ju-k'uei was not attracted to the rather sterile literary learning characteristic of the contemporary examination system. Hence he made no effort to pursue a career, but led a rather dilettante life, chiefly devoted to travelling about with his family, enjoying the hospitality of numerous highly placed friends.

In Shaochow he conceived a genuine affection for Ricci, a feeling warmly reciprocated. From the beginning Ch'ü was fascinated by the revelations of European science. Hitherto the scholar-officials whom Ricci had met, while curious to examine the products of European culture, had given no signs of a deeper interest. Ch'ü, on the contrary, displayed an eagerness to absorb all that Ricci could teach him. For a year he studied assiduously. Ricci taught him arithmetic, and explained Clavius' books on the sphere. He taught him the first book of the Elements of Euclid, how to make various sun-dials and how to measure heights and distances. Ch'ü was enthralled by the vistas which these discoveries opened to him. "He was enraptured," writes Ricci, "and seemed insatiable, passing day and night in study."[24]

In Ch'ü Ju-k'uei Ricci saw a type of Chinese humanist, forward looking, receptive to new ideas. Although the stereotyped, inbred classicism of Ming Confucian scholarship lay heavily upon the intellectual life of the country, there were fertile minds capable of freeing themselves from its stifling influence. This was the revelation which Ch'ü gave to Ricci. In the years that followed Ricci sought out and allied himself with this progressive element and directed his main effort to it.

Ch'ü Ju-k'uei constituted himself a herald. Through him Ricci established friendly relations with all the officials of Shaochow. Ch'ü introduced him to the neighboring city of Nanhsiung where he founded another Christian community and made a valuable friend in Wang Ying-lin, prefect of the city.

Ch'ü's interest was not limited to science. Ricci instructed him in the doctrines of the Church. He was not a mere passive auditor, but took notes of the instructions and proposed objections carefully worked out in writing. Ricci's admiration for the caliber of his mind was enhanced by the fact that the difficulties he raised were not superficial, but reached to the center of some of the gravest problems of theology. He was in the end convinced of the truth of Catholic teaching. However, although his wife had died, he could not bring himself to marry the concubine who held her place because she was of lowly social origin. Neither was he willing to dismiss her. "His baptism was deferred," writes Trigault, "until he could summon up as much courage to embrace the truth as he had light to recognize it."[25]

It was typical of Ricci's warmly human comprehension of the difficult problems rooted in *mores* hundreds, even thousands, of years old, that he did not permit such situations to interfere with friendship. In the case of Ch'ü Ju-k'uei, as in the case of many others, his patience and understanding were rewarded. Many years later, in 1605, having been presented with two sons by his concubine, Ch'ü "no longer hesitated to rank fecundity above blood," as Trigault put it, "and to accept the mother of his sons as his legitimate wife."[26] Ricci rejoiced that "our old friend . . . to whom all the first Fathers owed so large a part of the prestige which they had enjoyed in the beginning in Kwangtung, in Kiangsi, and in Nanking, and to whom they were greatly indebted for the residence in Nanking and the second and successful expedition to Peking . . . [was] within the fold of holy Church . . . [as] all had desired, as the best payment they could make to him for the good deeds which he had done."[27]

Ch'ü Ju-k'uei left Shaochow in 1592. Although some years elapsed before he saw Ricci again, his interest did not abate nor his affection cool. He kept up a correspondence with his Western friend and spread his fame wherever he went.

For some time Ricci had sought an opportunity to move further into the interior. The unhealthy climate of Shaochow, the unfriendly attitude of the people as a whole, and the fact that the intellectual life in the province of Kwangtung was sluggish compared to that in other provinces, all combined to suggest the urgency of establishing another foothold.

His opportunity came when Shih Hsing,[28] a member of the imperial Board of War, was summoned to Peking during the crisis provoked by the Japanese invasion of Korea. In the hope that he could cure his son of a profound depression into which he had fallen as a result of failure in the *hsiu-ts'ai* examination, he asked Ricci to accompany him and his family at least part of the way. Leaving Cattaneo in charge in Shaochow and taking with him two young Macaists known to us only by their Portuguese names as Juan Barradas and Domingo Fernandes, Ricci set out on April 18, 1595. His "service for Rachel" had lasted not quite six years.

NOTES

(1) For other examples of his affection for his family cf. *Opere storiche*, II, 122 f., 218 ff., 229.

(2) *Ibid.*, p. 13.

(3) The title "General" does not have the military connotation it might suggest to the reader not familiar with Latin. It is the English rendition of "superior generalis" which simply means the superior of the whole Society as distinguished from a "superior provincialis" or "localis" i.e., the superior of a particular province or particular house.

(4) *Ibid.*, p. 20 f.

(5) F. Colin and P. Pastells, *Labor evangelica de los obreros de la Compania de Jésus en las islas Filipinas*, ed. Pablo Pastells, S. J. (Barcelona: Henrich, 1900-1902), I, 529.

(6) *Monumenta Xaveriana* (Matriti: typis Augustini Avrial, 1899-1900), I, 158-188.

(7) Matteo Ricci, S. J., *Fonti Ricciane*, ed. Pasquale M. d'Elia, S. J. (Roma: Libreria dello Stato, 1942-1949), II, 87. Cf. bibliography for description of this invaluable work hereafter referred to as *FR*.

(8) Louis le Comte, *Nouveaux mémoires sur l'état présent de la Chine* (Paris: J. Anisson, 1696) and R. P. Gabriel de Magaillans [Magalhães], *Nouvelle relation de la Chine, contenant la déscription des particularitez les plus considerables de ce grand empire* (Paris: Claude Barbin, 1688).

(9) Le Comte, *op. cit.*, I, 368 f.

(10) Arnold H. Rowbotham, *Missionary and Mandarin, The Jesuits at the Court of China* (Berkeley: University of California Press, 1942), p. 250.

(11) Cf. reprint from the *Annual Report of the Librarian of Congress for the Fiscal Year Ended June 30, 1940, Division of Orientalia* (Washington: Government Printing Office, 1940), p. 167.

(12) *FR*, I, 211.

(13) The three degrees attainable through the examination system were the *hsiu-ts'ai*, the *chü-jen*, and the *chin-shih*, which the Jesuits not inappropriately translated bachelor's, master's, and doctor's degree respectively.

(14) For a description of this work, two copies of which are in the Jesuit archives in Rome, cf. *FR*, I, 197, n. 2.

(15) Cf. for example Rowbotham, *op. cit.*, p. 56.

(16) Pasquale D'Elia, S. J., "Il domma cattolico integralmente presentada da Matteo Ricci ai letterati della China. Secondo un documento cinese inedito di 350 anni fa," in *Civiltà Cattolica* anno 86 (Roma, 1935), II, 35-53.

(17) *Opere storiche*, II, 75.

(18) All of the early Chinese Jesuits were Macaists and had been given Portuguese surnames at their baptism. I have preferred to use the Chinese name wherever it has been possible to discover it, prefixing the Christian name in parenthesis. These two, the first Chinese Jesuits, are known in the records as Sebastian Fernandes and Francisco Martines. Both rendered distinguished service after being admitted to the Society as novices in 1591. The former died in 1621, the latter died a hero's death in 1606.

(19) *Ibid.*, p. 109.

(20) *Ibid.*, p. 118.

NOTES

(21) Cf. *FR*, I, 108-132, for Ricci's analysis of China's religions.

(22) *FR*, I, 337.

(23) *FR*, I, 338.

(24) *FR*, I, 298.

(25) Nicolas Trigault, S. J. *De Christiana expeditione apud Sinas suscepta ab Societate Jesu, ex P. Matthei Ricci ejusdem Societatis Commentariis . . .* (Augustae Vindelicorum: C. Mangium, 1615), p. 254.

(26) *Idem.*

(27) *FR*, II, 341.

(28) Cf. *ibid.*, I, 339, n. 1 on the identity of Shih Hsing.

Chapter III

Ricci Takes Charge

WHEN RICCI LEFT Shaochow he hoped to reach Peking or, that failing, to establish himself at Nanking.[1] The times were not propitious. In May, 1592, Hideyoshi, scarcely having completed the task of breaking the power of the feudal daimyo and unifying Japan, hurled an army of three hundred thousand men upon Korea. This he planned as the first step toward realization of a grandiose dream of a Japanese empire embracing China, India, the Philippines, and the Southwestern Pacific. Within six weeks his armies had overrun the entire Korean peninsula. A Chinese army of eighty thousand, sent to the relief of Korea, met defeat.

After its initial success, the Japanese army bogged down. The problems incidental to extended communications lines, made more difficult by a series of crushing naval defeats suffered at the hands of the brilliant Korean Admiral Yi Sun-sin and harrassment by Korean guerillas kept it pinned down; while the hostility of the populace, the inclemency of the weather, and the inadequacy of food supplies, gradually sapped Japanese morale. Nevertheless, the disasters in Korea and the continued presence there of Japanese troops deeply disturbed Peking court circles. The Wan-li emperor summoned to Peking all those who were supposed to have some competence in military matters to plan a campaign against the invaders.[2] Great levees of troops were being raised; extensive preparations for war were being made. The fears current in Peking communicated themselves to the nation. In a letter to Claudio Aquaviva of November 12, 1592, Ricci refers to the current wave of fear of the Japanese whom he describes as a "very bellicose people."[3]

In the feverish and uneasy atmosphere prevailing, Nanking officialdom was not disposed to welcome a foreigner in its midst. Ricci arrived in Nanking on May 31, 1595, after an exciting trip marred by tragedy when his boat foundered in the rapids appropriately known as *Shih-pa t'an* (Eighteen Currents) and he, who could not swim a stroke, was saved by the luckiest of chances while young Barradas, an excellent swimmer, was drowned.

Ricci was at first encouraged when he found the fifth son of Liu Chieh-chai, the viceroy of Chaoching, living in the southern capital. The "fifth Liu" was pleased to renew his friendship with the Jesuit. He entertained him at dinner and introduced him to a number of his friends who each in turn insisted upon playing the host. There is something deeply moving in the thought of these small and intimate gatherings where the cultures of West and East first revealed themselves to each other in an atmosphere of warm cordiality which did credit both to the broad humanism of the Italian and to the cultivated intelligence of his Chinese hosts.

Despite the confidence of his new friends that, inasmuch as he was thoroughly Chinese in dress, language, and manners he would meet little difficulty in Nanking, Ricci was soon disillusioned. Learning that an old acquaintance, Hsü Ta-jên, held an important post in Nanking, Ricci called upon him. When the Jesuit manifested his desire to remain in the city, the amiable friendliness with which Hsü had first received him gave way to something akin to panic. He feared to compromise himself and endanger his career by becoming the patron of a foreigner. He urged Ricci to leave, assuring him that, were it any place but Nanking, he would be willing to help him. To forestall suspicion of friendship with Ricci he haled before his tribunal the unfortunate keeper of the inn where Ricci was staying. Simulating high indignation he ordered him to get Ricci out of the city at once.

Although some of his friends urged him to ignore the storm, Ricci realized that to do so might endanger his plans for the future. Deeply disappointed, but without bitterness, he left Nanking June 17, scarcely more than two weeks after his arrival. "I am persuaded that he acted thus for my own good, as he said; but as far as I am concerned, so great was my desire to stay here that I should have preferred to be cast into prison rather than quit the city."[4] This was his charitable interpretation of the conduct of Hsü Ta-jên.

Ricci did not wish to retreat to Kwangtung province, so he resolved to try to establish himself in Nanchang, provincial capital of Kiangsi, and a city renowned for the large number of its scholars. En route by boat from Nanking he struck up an acquaintance with a fellow passenger who was employed in the offices of the viceroy of Kiangsi. Upon arriving at Nanchang on June 28, 1595, this new friend took him in charge. He found him lodgings and saw him safely installed.

Ricci's name was not unknown here. Ch'ü Ju-k'uei had sung his praises to his many friends in the city. Through a celebrated doctor of medicine, Wang Chi-lou, Ricci began to establish contact with cultivated society. At a dinner in his honor, given by Wang, where the guests included two members of the imperial family, his familiarity with the Chinese classics excited as much admiration as his knowledge of mathematics. From this auspicious beginning his circle of friends rapidly widened. The number of visitors who called to see him constantly increased. Many were drawn by a desire to see him give a demonstration of his truly prodigious powers of memory. The Chinese, whose examination system put a premium upon a highly developed memory, were astounded at the mnemonic feats of which Ricci was capable. He could at a single reading memorize over four hundred characters having no logical connection and repeat them in order forwards and backwards.[5] For the benefit of his admiring friends he wrote a small treatise on mnemonics entitled *Hsi-kuo chi-fa* (Western Memory Techniques).

The viceroy, Lou Chung-hao, after a preliminary investigation, summoned Ricci to an audience. Rumors that the viceroy had ordered an inquiry struck fear into the hearts of Ricci's landlord and his neighbors. The former wanted to turn him into the streets with all his belongings; but Ricci, assured by Wang Chi-lou who was the viceroy's personal physician, that Lou Chung-hao was well disposed, refused to be dislodged by force. He did, however, voluntarily move to the doctor's home.

Despite the reassurances of his friend Wang, Ricci approached the audience with misgivings. To his relief the viceroy treated him with the utmost courtesy, refusing to allow him to observe the custom of kneeling during the interview. He questioned him about the doctrine and the mathematics he taught. He embarrassed him by his praises and at the end of the interview urged him to remain in

Nanchang.

Ricci had been definitely accepted. The example of the viceroy dissipated the fears that had restrained many from showing a friendly interest in the foreigner. Ricci immediately made a round of formal visits to the important officials and met with a uniformly cordial reception. The number of his visitors multiplied and several months later he was so occupied that often he had to wait until night to read his breviary.

"I don't have time to eat until at least one o'clock in the afternoon," he wrote to Girolamo Costa on October 28, 1595. "Two or three times a week I am invited [to dinner] and some times to two places on one day, and I have to go to both of them. . . . One difficulty is that on fast days of the Church I have to fast all day inasmuch as these dinners don't start until night; but fortunately I have a good stomach. . . ."[6]

A particularly warm friendship developed between the Italian humanist and the famous Chinese scholar Chang Huang, then in his sixty-eighth year. Chang was a man of outstanding natural virtue. The history of the Ming dynasty describes him as a man who "from infancy to old age never uttered an improper word, performed an improper action, had improper friends, or read improper books."[7] His most important scholarly work, the *T'u-shu Pien* (Encyclopedia of Geography) in one hundred and twenty-seven *chüan*, confirms Ricci's account of his intimacy with its author and shows that the benefits deriving from the relationship were reciprocal.[8] There are numerous references to Ricci in the encyclopedia, especially in the sections which treat of astronomy and those which deal with cartography where a sketch of Ricci's world map is reproduced.[9]

Through Chang Huang, Ricci came into contact with a phase of contemporary Chinese intellectual life which was to have far-reaching effects upon the Jesuit apostolate. One of the most significant phenomena of the last half century of the Ming dynasty was the mushrooming of literary and philosophical societies or academies, as the Jesuits called them.

In Nanchang, Chang Huang presided over one of the earliest of these societies. It numbered over one thousand members. The scholars who belonged to it met, usually in small groups, to discuss literary and current problems.

The movement began unpretentiously enough when scholars

began to come together to "make friends by means of literature," in the phrase of the Analects, and to help each other prepare for official examinations. Out of such humble beginnings there grew a movement of nationwide social and political significance. These small groups coalesced to form societies numbering thousands of scholars. The most important of the larger societies became known as the Tung-lin society or, with emphasis upon its political side, the Tung-lin party.

During these years the real powers of government were largely in the hands of eunuchs who swarmed about the court in Peking and of the self-seeking and reactionary type of officials who were allied with them. The sinister influence of these two groups paralyzed the forces of good government and undermined the whole political structure. Their rule was chiefly responsible for the growing disorders during the first decades of the seventeenth century which prepared the way for the downfall of the Ming dynasty.

The more patriotic and incorrupt intellectuals looked on in anguish and anger. The Tung-lin society became their rallying point and in the first years of the seventeenth century transformed itself into a political party. The internal political history of China during the first four decades of the seventeenth century is largely the story of the bitter struggle between the Tung-lin party and the reactionary cabal for control of the government.

In the academies to which he was introduced in Nanchang Ricci found the elements which were deeply concerned about the cause of good government. Many were already in rebellion against the slavish conformity which dried up the springs of initiative and kept power in the hands of corrupt reactionaries. Whatever minds were not closed to fresh ideas came together here. Ricci recognized in this milieu the medium through which he might introduce new doctrines into China.

Much has been written about Ricci's alleged alliance with Confucianism as a means of facilitating the introduction of Christianity into China. The allegation, whether made in praise or in blame, is inexact. In Confucianism, purged of Sung materialism, he sought points of contact. If it is a question of alliance, it would be closer to the truth to say that he sought an alliance with the more progressive and potentially receptive elements of the scholar-official class incorporated in the academies. Their prestige, as he said, "might reassure those who would otherwise fear this novelty."[10]

Even in this connection, however, the term "alliance" is misleading. Ricci saw in the academies the medium through which the Christian ferment could be introduced into Chinese society. They might well become so many nuclei diffusing Christian ideas throughout the length and breadth of the land. There is no indication that Ricci hoped to make Christians of the academicians as a whole. It is erroneous to say, as writers continue to do, that the Jesuits sought to convert China "from the top down."[11] Naturally Ricci hoped "if possible," as he put it, "[to convert] some graduated scholars and officials," but more important, he aimed through them to develop an atmosphere increasingly favorable to Christianity.

It is no accident, but proof of the soundness of his judgment, that, during the last four decades of the Ming dynasty, all of the eminent Christian converts of the scholar class and the many non-Christian friends of Christianity emerged from the Tung-lin milieu. (Paul) Hsü Kuang-ch'i, (Leo) Li Chih-tsao, (Michael) Yang T'ing-yün, all of whom would play leading roles in the development of the Church in China, were academicians.[12]

The apostolate which Ricci ultimately inaugurated in these academic circles had both a scientific and a philosophic aspect, both directed to the goal of creating an atmosphere receptive to the Christian leaven. The prestige acquired by the missionaries in the sphere of science could not fail to affect favorably the fortunes of the Christian message. Many valuable friendships flowered from contacts first made as a result of the reputation of Ricci and other Jesuits as teachers of new scientific truths. Many a Chinese intellectual who would have been coldly indifferent to Ricci's reputation as a teacher of religious truth was irresistibly drawn to him by his renown as a master of science. Often enough, friendships which budded in a mutual interest in science flowered in a common faith. If this happy eventuality were not realized, at least a sympathetic patron and protector was won for the faith.

By the time Ricci was ready to move on from Nanchang in 1598 the main lines of his method had been laid down. Henceforth he would devote his principal efforts toward their further development. Up to this point he had been carefully feeling his way. He now felt sure that he had found the only feasible path through the wilderness.

His last years in Nanchang gave him valuable experience. He was a welcome participant in the discussions of the academicians which inevitably led to fundamental religious questions and to further inquiries. Some came out of curiosity, others because they hoped to learn from Ricci the secret of alchemy which, despite his protests, they believed he had; but most of his visitors came because they wished to learn more about the scientific, philosophical, and religious ideas which he held. "From morning to night," he reported, "I am kept busy discussing the doctrines of our faith. Many desire to forsake their idols and become Christians. . . ."[13]

In 1595 "as an exercise in Chinese letters," Ricci composed a small treatise on Friendship (*Chiao-yu lun*). It was a subject bound to interest Chinese scholars, never tired of discussing the "five human relations" which formed a central feature of Confucian moral doctrine. It was the first of a series of works which were to spread his fame into every corner of the empire. Ricci had established a genuinely warm friendship with the two princes of the imperial family resident in Nanchang. To one of them, Prince Chien-an, he dedicated his essay on friendship. Its success astonished even Ricci. Many scholars desired to make copies of it. One of them had it printed and published. Before long, references to it began to appear in other books. Three years later, writing from Nanking, Ricci could report:

> This *Amicitia* has won more credit for me and for Europe than anything else we have done; because the other things give us the reputation of possessing ingenuity in the construction of mechanical artefacts and instruments; but this treatise has established our reputation as scholars of talent and virtue; and thus it is read and received with great applause and already has been published in two different places.

In this same letter, to his friend Girolamo Costa, Ricci expressed his annoyance with an ecclesiastical censorship which seriously impeded his work. If his treatise had been published, it had been thanks to the unauthorized act of an anonymous scholar. As for himself, he writes, "I cannot publish it, because in order to publish anything I have to get permission from so many of our people that I cannot do anything. Men who are not in China and cannot read Chinese insist upon passing judgment."[14]

Some years later Ricci reported that his treatise on friendship had been published "many times." It is a testimony to its abiding influence that in May, 1914, three hundred and nineteen years after he had written it, the newspaper *Shên-chow jih-pao* published it again in serial form.

Ricci's *Chiao-yu lun* is a good example of how the Jesuits discharged their task as middlemen between East and West. Ricci made no pretensions to originality in writing this *opusculum.* Assuming that Prince Chien-an had asked for an explanation of European views on the subject of friendship, the dialogue undertook to satisfy his curiosity. The Chinese, accustomed to regard all other peoples as "barbarians," were no doubt surprised to discover that Europeans entertained such lofty notions on a subject dear to Chinese hearts. Their respect for European civilization immediately rose. It is for this reason that Ricci wrote that the work won credit not only for him, but for Europe as well.

At Nanchang Ricci resolved to practice greater reserve in the deployment of the external apparatus of his religious mission. In the summer of 1596, after successful negotiations, he bought a house to serve as a residence. This gave him the second foothold so ardently desired. He decided, in opening this new establishment, to abandon the practice, observed in Chaoching and in Shaochow, of opening a public chapel.

It may be said, popular legend to the contrary notwithstanding, that he was not inspired to take this step by any desire to disguise his religious character. Experience had, it is true, taught him that a certain discipline of the *arcana* was necessary. He was furthermore persuaded that the direct effort to hurry the movement of conversions must be postponed until the ground had been prepared, and, at this stage of his career, he still felt that extreme caution had to be observed until imperial sanction to preach the Gospel had been obtained. He therefore resolved, without denying or disguising his true character, not to thrust into the forefront of public consciousness the fact that his object was to propagate a new religion. In addition to this, conditions in China at the time made it extremely dangerous to gather crowds. The Japanese invasion of Korea had made China spy conscious. More important, official circles, not without cause, had a phobia of China's numerous secret societies, most of them revolutionary in character. Any gathering of people in considerable numbers was sure to provoke suspicion. It will be recalled that the assemblages of Christians in the early Roman empire aroused suspicion on the part of the official world that they were engaged in subversive conspiracies. The same situation existed in China. It has already been remarked that the members of the various academies met in small groups of nine or ten people. It will be seen later that the first deviation from Ricci's policy in this respect helped to provoke a violent persecution and that, in a recrudescence of this same persecution, the principal charge made against the Christians of Nanking was that they were members of the notorious White Lotus society.[15]

Ricci's principal motive, however, was identical with that which had moved him to abandon the Buddhist style of dress. The Jesuits were still being confused with Buddhist monks. He was less hesitant to take this step since he was convinced that, in the environment of Ming China, more could be accomplished through private conversations and small discussion groups than by public preaching. Two of his letters reveal his mind clearly. Writing to his friend Giulio Fuligatti in Rome, on October 12, 1596, he remarks, after telling about the acquisition of the new residence:

> I do not think that we shall establish a church, but instead a room for discussion and we will say Mass privately in another chapel, or perhaps use the reception hall for chapel; because one preaches more effectively and with greater fruit here through conversations than through formal sermons.[16]

Three days later, writing to Girolamo Costa, he states his chief motive: "As we have banished [from use in our regard] the name of bonze, which is equivalent among [the Chinese] to the word friar among us . . . we shall not in these beginnings establish either church or chapel, but conversational halls." Today they would be called seminar rooms.

The fact is that the public chapel in the residence had occasioned grave inconveniences both in Chaoching and in Shaochow. Buddhist temples had come to be regarded as more or less public property and it was a common custom for any group of citizens to appropriate them to their convivial uses. Some of them were more familiar with the sound of merrymaking around a festive board than they were with the chanting of Buddhist sutras. The local gentry saw no reason why the chapels opened in their cities by the foreign "bonzes" should not be put to the same good use. More than one incident resulted from the refusal of the Jesuits to allow their chapel to be converted into a banquet hall. When, in Chaoching they attempted to free themselves from this annoyance by locking the doors a minor riot resulted. Having by immemorial use acquired a kind of prescriptive right to free access to the Buddhist temples, the action of the Jesuits in closing their doors seemed to the partygoers somehow an infringement of customary law.

What finally determined Ricci's decision was another, and more serious, incident of this kind.[17] It occurred in Shaochow where Lazzaro Cattaneo was in charge. A group of *hsiu-ts'ai* from another city attempted to force their way into the residence late at night. They were under the influence of liquor. Repulsed by the domestic servants, they returned to the assault and subjected the servants to indignities. The next day to forestall possible action against themselves they lodged a complaint against Cattaneo alleging that they had been maltreated. They found a minor official to listen to them. He ordered two of Cattaneo's domestics beaten. When (Sebastian) Chung Ming-jên, the Jesuit brother, attempted to defend them he too was beaten and kept in the stocks in front of the official's tribunal throughout an entire day. The intervention of other officials restored justice to her throne. The offending official, who had been moved to act chiefly because he had been piqued by failure of Cattaneo to give him a watch he coveted, apologized and made reparation in the time-honored form of a banquet in Cattaneo's honor held in one of the pagodas of the city. It was to avoid repetition of such unhappy incidents that Ricci decided "in these beginnings" not to open public chapels or churches.

Nanchang offered the first opportunity for Ricci to set in motion what may aptly be called his apostolate by radiation. It was a city of scholars. More important, it was a city frequently visited by scholars from other parts of the empire. Furthermore, as metropole of the province, it was the scene of the provincial examinations. Every three years candidates for the *chü-jên* degree poured into the city from all over the province. In December, 1597, there were four thousand such candidates in Nanchang to take the examinations which lasted from December 19 to December 29. Ricci, writing the same month to his old professor of science Clavius, reported that he was overwhelmed with visits.[18] It was a type of apostolate which, on a broader scale, he was to carry on during the last ten years of his life in Peking, from where scholars would carry back into the provinces the memory of a sincere friendship and of stimulating conversation, a sympathetic regard for the religion which he professed, and an interest in its doctrines. Before Ricci left Nanchang he had friends in ten of the fifteen provinces of China; yet, except for his brief visit to Nanking, he had thus far set foot in only two of them, Kwangtung and Kiangsi.

Despite the fruitfulness of his work in Nanchang, he still had his eyes fixed upon Peking. On October 13, 1596, he writes to Aquaviva that he is anxiously waiting word from Rome of the outcome of Ruggieri's proposal of a papal embassy to the court of China. If Rome fails to act upon the suggestion, he is determined to try "with all his strength" to reach Peking himself.[19] He did not think it would be impossible to manage. In Nanchang he numbered among his friends members of the imperial family and many others who had relatives in important positions in the capital, among them the three sons of the prefect of Peking.

Letters from Japan bringing the report that the Japanese ambassador sent to Peking to negotiate terms of peace with the imperial court was "one Agostino, a good Christian," probably stimulated his anxiety to reach the center of the Chinese world. The Japanese referred to was Konishi Settsu-no-kami Yukinaga, a leading Christian daimyo and at this time one of Hideyoshi's most trusted lieutenants.[20]

In 1598 important administrative changes were made. Two years earlier Valignano, as a result of a personal appeal to the general to be relieved of the burdens of the office which he had held for twenty-two years, was replaced as visitor of India by Nicolau Pimenta. His hope of spending the rest of his life in the ranks was thwarted, however, when the general directed him to retain the post of visitor of Japan and China.

Valignano arrived in Macao in July, 1597, and remained there until July, 1598. Until now not Ricci, but Duarte de Sande had been superior of the mission. In 1583 Cabral, the rector of the College in Macao, had advised the general against appointing Ruggieri superior of the China mission. He evidently felt that a superior should have less of the dove and more of the serpent in his makeup for he wrote to the general that Ruggieri, although a man of virtue, was "more simple than is necessary."[21] The general had directed Valignano to appoint a more prudent man than Ruggieri and Valignano's choice had been de Sande. He had been appointed superior in 1585 upon entering China. Despite several attempts poor health had prevented him from ever remaining long. And in 1590 he had become rector of the College in Macao.[22] It was a clumsy arrangement. Ricci, although carrying nearly the full load of the mission, could not take any important step without de Sande's approval. Apart from the long delays entailed, de Sande was not in a position to judge the realities in the interior.

Valignano now ended this anomalous situation. Ricci was named superior of the mission and given broad discretionary powers. Manoel Dias, who had already been in the Indies for ten years during most of which he had held various offices, succeeded de Sande as rector of the College of Macao. In contemporary Jesuit accounts he is always referred to as Manoel Dias, Senior, to distinguish him from another Manoel Dias, Junior, who would also play a distinguished part in the mission. Dias' great attachment to the China mission was an augury of support in this quarter. Valignano then sent Nicolò Longobardo to join Lazzaro Cattaneo and João de Rocha in Shaochow. Since December, 1595, Ricci had João Soerio as companion in Nanchang.

All of these measures were calculated to facilitate Ricci's move upon Peking. Valignano now recommended to him that he attempt to reach "the court of Peking and the emperor." As presents for the emperor he sent a painting of the madonna and one of the Savior; a clock in bronze, gift of Claudio Aquaviva, and a similar clock sent by the bishop of Manila.

Ricci's first tentative explorations furnished him with another lesson in Chinese politics. He had overestimated the influence of relatives of the emperor. Emperors had more than once been overthrown and supplanted by members of their own family. The Ming rulers were familiar with history. To eliminate the danger of palace intrigues the fixed policy of the dynasty was to scatter the princes of the family to various parts of China. There they were provided with means of living an honorable and comfortable life, deprived of power and influence.

When Ricci approached Prince Chien-an to invoke his aid in reaching Peking he quickly learned that "not only does the emperor not govern through his relatives, he holds them in great suspicion." To have continued along these lines would, as Ricci later wrote, "not only not have served the mission, but would have been very dangerous, would have done great damage and possibly would have destroyed it."[23]

During his stay in Shaochow Ricci had established contact with Wang Hung-hui, a high official of the empire. At that time Wang, wearied of the intrigues of political enemies, had temporarily retired from office as president of the Nanking Board of Rites and was en route to his home in Hainan. Passing through Shaochow he met Ricci. The two had spent an entire day in conversation. Wang conceived the project of bringing Ricci to Peking to reform the national calendar. His motive was not entirely disinterested since he hoped, as a result of the credit which would accrue to him, to obtain the presidency of the Peking Board of Rites.

In 1598 he was summoned to return to Nanking to resume his office. Passing through Shaochow he inquired from Cattaneo as to Ricci's present whereabouts. Cattaneo agreed to hurry ahead to Nanchang and prepare Ricci for Wang's coming. He and de Rocha reached the provincial capital of Kiangsi on June 23, two days ahead of Wang. The latter proposed to take Ricci with him to Peking where, on September 17, he was to take part in the official audience honoring the emperor's birthday.

Joining Wang Hung-hui's flotilla of boats Ricci left Nanchang on June 25, 1598, taking with him Lazzaro Cattaneo, (Sebastian) Chung Ming-jên and (Manoel) Yu Wên-hui, a young Macaist preparing to enter the Society. The latter would become a Jesuit lay brother in 1605 and would be at Ricci's bedside when he died in 1610 in Peking. Like several of the first Chinese Jesuits, Yu Wên-hui, identified in the contemporary accounts as Manoel Pereira, was an artist of considerable talent. Some of the religious paintings from his brush were later hung in the chapel built in Peking. The excellent portrait of Ricci painted just after his death and which hangs in the Jesuit house of the Gesù in Rome is also his work.

De Rocha and Soerio were left in charge of the Nanchang residence. Longobardo assumed direction of the Shaochow mission. After sixteen years of patient waiting Ricci was at last en route to the Dragon throne.

NOTES

(1) The principal source for the events narrated in this chapter is Ricci's own account found in his memoirs, *FR*, I, 335-380, and in two long letters, one of October 28, 1595 to Girolamo Costa, the other of November 4, 1595 to Claudio Aquaviva, in *Opere storiche*, II, 177-187 and 182-213 respectively.

(2) A word of explanation of the method used to designate China's emperors: Before his accession to the throne an emperor had his personal and family name, as well as a princely title. Upon ascending the throne he assumed what can be called an imperial personal title. In addition to this a distinctive title was given to his reign period. Thus the Ming prince whose family and personal name was *Chu I-chün* (Chu was the family name of the Ming rulers), assumed the imperial name of *Shên-tsung*. To his reign period was given the title *Wan-li*. He may properly be referred to as Emperor Shên-tsung or as the Wan-li emperor. Western writers have habitually employed the reign title as though it were the emperor's name. Thus it has been the fashion to write of "Emperor Wan-li," which would be much like referring to Franklin Delano Roosevelt as President New Deal. In this book designation of the emperors is usually by reign title.

(3) *Ibid.*, p. 111.

(4) *Ibid.*, p. 201.

(5) Cf. D'Elia in *FR*, I, 360, n. 1.

(6) *Opere storiche*, II, 186.

(7) Quoted by D'Elia, *FR*, I, 371, n. 5.

(8) Note on the word *chüan* which I generally employ instead of the English word volume: The latter word is misleading inasmuch as it suggests to the western reader a much bulkier book than the facts sometimes warrant. The word *chüan* dates from the time when books were written in the form of scrolls. Each scroll — a section or sometimes a chapter of the book — was rolled up and tied in the form of a cylinder. This was the *chüan*.

(9) Cf. the *T'u-shu Pien* in the Library of Congress.

(10) *FR*, I, 382.

(11) An example is John J. Considine, M. M., *Across a World* (Toronto-New York: Longmans, Green and Company, 1942), p. 147. The passage referred to not only misconceives the precise nature of the Jesuit apostolate in China, but also misunderstands the apostolate of the early Church in Rome. From the first years in Rome there were converts from every level of society of which many of the ancient monuments in Rome give striking evidence, e.g., those associated with the memory of the Pudens family. The Church did not move from the bottom up. She diffused herself throughout society.

(12) That the reader may know what characters appearing in this story were Christians, I have inserted their Christian names in parenthesis. In the case of those whose names appear so frequently as to become familiar to the reader I usually drop the Christian name in order to retain as far as possible the authentic Chinese nomenclature. Perhaps it is not necessary to point out that in Chinese the personal name follows the surname, just the reverse of western usage. In some cases the Chinese personal name does not appear in the records available to me. In such cases I have employed the Christian name followed by the surname, e.g. Martin Ch'in.

(13) *Opere storiche*, II, 220.

NOTES

(14) *Opere storiche*, II, 243-250.

(15) On Chinese secret societies and officialdom's fear of them cf. A. Wylie, *Chinese Researches* (London: K. Paul, Trench, Trübner and Company, 1937).

(16) *Opere storiche*, II, 215.

(17) Ricci mentions the incident in his letter to Costa, *ibid.*, p. 230.

(18) *Ibid.*, p. 242.

(19) *Ibid.*, p. 225.

(20) On Kunishi Yukinaga cf. C. R. Boxer, *The Christian Century in Japan, 1549-1650* (Berkeley-London: University of California Press-Cambridge University Press, 1951), p. 181 *et al.*

(21) *Archivum Romanum Societatis Iesu*, Jap-Sin 9 II, f. 186r/v. These are the Roman archives of the Society of Jesus, hereafter referred to as *ARSI*. The Jap-Sin rubric refers to documents pertaining to the Japanese and Chinese missions.

(22) Cf. D'Elia in *FR*, I, 222, n. 1.

(23) *FR*, II, 7.

Chapter IV

Broadening the Base

ARRIVED IN NANKING en route to the capital Ricci found the atmosphere edgy with the same uneasiness which had aborted his first visit to that city. Hostilities had broken out again in Korea with the Japanese. Because of the prevailing nervousness he could not take lodging on land. He had no difficulty, however, visiting numerous friends resident in the city. His association with Wang Hung-hui led to new and advantageous contacts, notably with the viceroy of the province, Chao K'o-huai. In intelligence and in the art of government Chao K'o-huai was, in Ricci's words, "one of the most illustrious men in China. . . ."[1]

Chief factor in bringing together the viceroy and the Jesuit was Ricci's world map. Among the gifts showered upon Wang Hung-hui in felicitation of his resumption of office as president of the Nanking Board of Rites was a copy of Ricci's map, presented by the viceroy. The latter had received a copy of the map from Ricci's old friend, Wang Ying-lin, formerly vice-prefect of Nanhsiung and now prefect of Chinkiang in the province of Kiangsu. Chao K'o-huai in turn had it engraved on stone with a laudatory preface of his own composition. The discovery that the author of the famous map was in Wang Hung-hui's entourage created a minor sensation. Wang Hung-hui agreed that it would be discourteous for Ricci to refuse to accept the viceroy's insistent invitation to visit him in the city of Chüyung where he had established his seat of government. Accordingly, while Wang Hung-hui and his party set out for Peking by land and Cattaneo began the voyage to the north on the Grand Canal, Ricci went to Chüyung, a day's journey from Nanking. Here he spent over a week. The viceroy put aside his official business to engage Ricci in long conversations about mathematics and European civilization. In a gracious gesture he transformed a small room in his residence into a quasi-chapel where Ricci could retire to pray and to read his breviary, kneeling before the painting of the Savior which he was taking to Peking to present to the emperor.

Chao K'o-huai invited the notables of the city to meet his learned guest. Among others, Ricci thus made the acquaintance of Ch'ên Tzu-chêng, superintendent of the schools of the province and president of the local academy of scholars. Ch'ên later proved a valuable friend in Peking and, still later, in Fukien where he served as viceroy.

When Ricci left Chüyung, Chao K'o-huai presented him with a substantial sum of money to assist him on his journey; and, well aware of the conditions in Peking and therefore sceptical about the success of Ricci's mission, he offered him much sage advice. He then had him escorted to the Grand Canal and rowed to Huaian where Cattaneo awaited him.

The Jesuits arrived in Peking on September 7, 1598. Wang Hung-hui, who had preceded them, extended the hospitality of his home. However, it soon became clear to Ricci that there was no hope of immediately achieving his goal. For the first time, he came into direct contact with the real conditions of government in the capital. The bitter struggle between honest officials and those of the eunuch party had not yet flared into open violence, but, beneath the surface, the battle was already engaged. Wang Hung-hui, whose temporary retirement a few years earlier was due to a sense of frustration induced by the opposition of the party of corruption, now learned, to his disappointment, that his political enemies were as powerful as ever. As day succeeded day and the announcement of his appointment to the presidency of the Peking Board of Rites, which he confidently expected, was not forthcoming, he began to lose heart.

Excitement caused by renewal of hostilities with the Japanese made Peking an inhospitable place for a foreigner. Fearful of being compromised, many of Ricci's friends who now held office in the capital refused to receive him. Financial embarrassment added to the difficulties of his position. A bill of exchange drawn by Manoel Dias at Macao upon a Peking merchant could not be cashed. There was no such merchant in Peking.

Ricci's disappointment was great and elicited a judgment unusually severe for him:

> The cause [of the refusal of his former friends to receive him] is the great cruelty of the emperor, who often, for a trifle, causes eunuchs in his palace to be beaten to death.
>
> He does not interest himself with public affairs except where they offer him a chance to make some money; and the mandarins act in like manner, demanding money from all who come on business to the court from outside the capital, forcing the mandarins from outside to disgorge a portion of what they have stolen in the provinces; hence this city seems a real Babylon of confusion, filled with all sorts of sins, without any signs of justice, or piety, or a desire for salvation.[2]

It is not surprising that Ricci concluded that "the hour had not yet arrived to begin preaching here the holy Gospel." Early in November, 1598, he and his three companions forsook the capital and set out for the south.

The "assault" upon Peking had failed in its principal objective, but it had not been time wasted. Ricci came away much better informed about the functioning of the political system in the capital, more deeply convinced of the need for patience and prudence, and confirmed in his belief in the necessity of building up a network of reliable contacts. In addition there had been a gain of knowledge in other directions. En route to the north Ricci and Cattaneo made solar observations upon the basis of which they calculated the latitudes of the larger cities through which they passed. They also measured the distances in Chinese *li* from city to city. From information gathered in Peking, Ricci was convinced of the identity of China and Marco Polo's Cathay. Final proof of the correctness of his judgment in this celebrated and in Europe hotly debated question had to await the remarkable voyage (1605-1607) of Bento de Goes, the Jesuit lay brother.[3]

Out of this first trip to Peking there also came a notable bit of pioneering in the field of Chinese language studies. While their boat made its leisurely way along the Grand Canal, Ricci, Cattaneo and Chung Ming-jên devoted their spare time to constructing "a good vocabulary and drawing up orderly rules for the peculiarities of this language, with the aid of which it will henceforth be twice as easy to learn." Any Westerner familiar with Chinese language study will appreciate the important place in the history of sinology which this achievement merits. Ricci has himself described the trail-blazing effort:

> In this language, composed of monosyllabic words and characters, it is necessary to pronounce each word with its proper accent and, when it has one, aspiration; by this kind of pronunciation many words are distinguished which otherwise would sound the same; and this it is which makes this language more difficult to learn. Besides distinguishing carefully the words which are aspirated, they noted five different accents; Father Cattaneo, who knows music, was especially valuable in distinguishing and noting these differences. They determined a method of representing the five accents and the aspiration, which everyone may use in rendering Chinese words into our alphabetic forms: thus they established a uniform method of writing for all, and Father Matteo ordered that henceforth everyone was to observe this method, rather than, as had hitherto been done with consequent great confusion, each one writing as seemed best to him.[4]

Thus in the rather unusual surroundings of a navicular seminar there was carried out the first effort to establish a satisfactory system of Romanization for the Chinese language. Since no solution to this thorny problem satisfies everyone, Ricci's pioneering attempt has been often imitated, down to our own day, but probably never under like conditions.

Winter and frozen canals sent the voyagers into hibernation at Lintsing in the province of Shantung. Ricci was unwilling to lose four or five months. The memory of his cordial relations with the viceroy of the province and with others, on the occasion of his recent visit to Nanking, fostered a strong hope that he might establish a residence in that city or in its vicinity. Leaving Cattaneo and the others to guard the baggage, he set out by land for the south.

It was a grueling trip through winter snows. He arrived in the milder, but damper, climate of Soochow in the Yangtze valley in a state verging on exhaustion. Here, with delicate prodigality of attention, his friend Ch'ü Ju-k'uei nursed him back to health.

The Soochow that Ricci saw in the twilight of the sixteenth century was one of China's two loveliest cities. In giving his impressions of the city Ricci quoted the well known Chinese proverb: *T'ien shang t'ien t'ang, Ti shang Su Hang*, which does not have the same lilting melody either in his Italian version or in the English equivalent: "In heaven there's paradise, on earth there's Soochow and Hangchow." City of beauty, center of art, mecca for the intellectually alert, it seemed admirably suited for the work of penetration which Ricci was developing. Ch'ü Ju-k'uei and his friends urged Ricci to stay. Nanking was dangerous. "Powerful mandarins were so numerous," they pointed out, "that it was impossible to stand well with all of them all of the time and hence one easily risked expulsion."[5] Soochow, near enough to Nanking to enable Ricci's influence to reach it, was yet far enough removed to obviate the dangers attendant upon a misstep.

Ricci was persuaded and when, accompanied by Ch'ü Ju-k'uei, he set out for Nanking on January 7, 1599, it was only for the purpose of obtaining from Wang Hung-hui, who had returned from Peking, letters of introduction to the officials of Soochow. The two friends paused in Chinkiang where they celebrated the Chinese New Year with Wang Ying-lin. The holiday festivities past, Wang Ying-lin insisted upon sending them to Nanking on one of his official barks. They sailed up the Yangtse river and arrived in the ancient southern capital on February 6, 1599.

Those who have seen Nanking in the twentieth century may have difficulty appreciating the grandeur of the city as it revealed itself to Ricci's eyes.[6] When he passed for the third time through the great gates of the city walls almost two centuries had passed since Nanking had ceased to be the capital of the empire. Although shorn of the source of its political power, it had lost little of its grandeur or of its importance. It was at this period a more impressive city than Peking. Ricci reports that the Chinese "regard it as the greatest and most beautiful city in the entire world," and he confesses that there are, in fact, few cities in the world to which it has to yield the palm:

"It is," he writes, "filled with great and numerous public and private edifices, with many temples, pagodas, and innumerable bridges, and is famous for the fertility of its countryside, for its favorable climate, for nobility of talent, civility of manners, elegance of language, and finally for the multitude of its inhabitants. . . . It holds first place not only in China, but throughout the kingdoms of the Orient."[7]

Perhaps out of nostalgic regard for its splendid past, the Ming rulers maintained in Nanking all the external façade of an imperial capital. The seat of government had been transferred to Peking in 1420; but, although Nanking had no real political authority, all the principal agencies of government in Peking had their duplicates in Nanking.[8]

The highest governmental body in China was the *Nei Yuan* or *Nei Ko*, i.e., the Imperial Chancery or Grand Secretariate. Its members, whose number often varied according to the whim of the emperor, were known as *Ta Hsüeh Shih* (Grand Secretaries) or more familiarly as *Ko-lao*, i.e., elders of the *Nei Ko*. It is by this latter name that they are nearly always designated in the writings of the Jesuits of this period. Beneath the Grand Secretaries were six governmental ministries, each with a varying number of subordinate offices. These ministries were:

1) *Li Pu:* Board of Civil Offices, with jurisdiction over all the officials of the empire. The Jesuit, de Magalhães, writing in 1688, gave the number of civil officials as 13,647 and of military officials as 18,520.

2) *Hu Pu:* Board of Finance.

3) *Li Pu:* Board of Rites or Ceremonies. This is not to be confused with the Board of Civil Offices, the two *Li* having different ideograms. One of its subordinate boards dealt with problems involving foreigners and with foreign embassies. This is why the early Jesuit accounts show the missionaries frequently having to deal with the Board of Rites.

4) *Ping Pu:* Board of Military Affairs.

5) *Hsing Pu:* Board of Criminal Justice.

6) *Kung Pu:* Board of Public Works.

Each of these ministries was presided over by a president, assisted by two assessors or vice-presidents. All of these imperial offices had their counterparts in Nanking. As if this anomalous situation did not already people Nanking with a sufficiently large aristocracy of officials and eunuchs, the Ming rulers followed a policy of relegating to Nanking minor officials who had been cashiered for having submitted false denunciations or higher officials convicted of serious faults. Small wonder that Ricci's friends warned him of the dangers!

However, Ricci found a different atmosphere in Nanking than had existed there on the occasion of his previous visits. The Japanese threat in Korea had disappeared. Hideyoshi died in Japan on September 16, 1598.[9] On his deathbed, discouraged by the fruitless success of his Korean victories and feeling that there was no other leader ambitious enough to carry out his programs of conquest, he ordered Ieyasu and other military leaders to recall the entire Japanese army from the continent. The last battle of the war was fought on November 2, 1598. Although it resulted in an overwhelming Japanese victory in which the Ming army was routed after losing some thirty-eight thousand men, the Japanese proceeded to carry out Hideyoshi's orders. The last Japanese army left Korea in November, 1598. As it was sailing away the Chinese and Koreans attacked its rear guard, captured one ship and took two hundred and twenty-eight prisoners. China, then as always, a land more wont than most to magnify its victories, blew up this small triumph into an overwhelming defeat for the Japanese. In Nanking Ricci heard the report that "a great slaughter" had been inflicted upon the Japanese.[10]

The mood of general exaltation induced by reports of these events, real and imagined, was evident in the changed attitude of Nanking officials. The heavy air of fear, distrust and suspicion had lifted. Wang Hung-hui was prodigal in his demonstrations of regard for Ricci. He pressed him to establish himself in Nanking and, although the latter avoided committing himself, commissioned two of his subordinates to look for a house for his Western friend.

As Wang Hung-hui's guest Ricci attended a concert in the magnificent Temple of Heaven. Seated in the front row with Wang's sons and members of his entourage, he listened to a performance by an orchestra composed of Taoist monks, official musicians to the emperor. He did not appreciate Chinese orchestral music which "seemed entirely devoid of consonance, so much so that the Chinese themselves admit that, while still using the instruments, they have lost the art of harmony familiar to the ancients." He did, however, admire the architectural grandeur of the Temple of Heaven:

> There is something truly imperial in the grandeur and magnificence of its construction. The temple stands in a wood, surrounded by strong walls twelve miles in circumference. Although constructed for the most part of wood, the temple is well worth seeing. Of the five naves, four are lined with wooden columns, each so large that two men together could not embrace it, and high in proportion to its thickness. . . . The ceiling is decorated with well executed designs and covered with gold. Although over two hundred years have passed since . . . the emperor has come to Nanking to perform the sacrifice, the temple still conserves much of its beauty.[11]

Among others who entertained Ricci was the Duke of Wei.

Although no governmental authority attached to the hereditary title, the Duke, whose seat was fixed at Nanking, enjoyed a kind of imperial prestige and lived in what Ricci described as "truly regal palaces."

The aged chief eunuch summoned Ricci to the imperial palace. Ricci adopted an air of cold reserve, refusing to pay him the excessive deference he required. It was a courageous thing to do, inasmuch as this old creature, the head of several thousand eunuchs who swarmed about the imperial palace in Nanking, wielded great power. Ricci's attitude indicates that at this early date he had already taken his stand with the party of reform.

The commandant of the imperial troops in Nanking, Li Huan, Marquis of Fêng Chêng, established friendly relations with Ricci and amiably confessed to him that, on the occasion of his first visit to Nanking in May, 1595, he had him closely watched and would have had him arrested but for the fact that he was such a good friend of Wang Hung-hui.

During these months in Nanking Ricci was sought out by some of the most eminent scholar-officials in China. The relationship he established with them was rooted in mutual admiration and respect. It was warm, personal and easily bridged the gulf that separated East from West. Without exception these were friendships which endured. Yeh Hsiang-kao, at this time an assistant to Wang Hung-hui on the Board of Rites, proved in years yet to come a friend of inestimable value. In 1607 he became grand secretary in Peking, an office he held for eighteen years, during all of which he was a staunch supporter of the Jesuits. During the T'ien-ch'i reign (1621-1627), when the real ruler of the empire was the notorious eunuch, Wei Chung-hsien, Yeh was the leader of the Tung-lin party in its bitter struggle against Wei. His activities finally forced him into retirement in Fukien province where he assisted Giulio Aleni in introducing Christianity. One hundred and fifty years after his death an edict of the Ch'ien-lung emperor would praise him as "an upright man whom contemporaries greatly esteemed."[12]

Wang Ch'iao, the president of the Supreme Court and at the age of seventy-eight in the twilight of a distinguished career of public service, visited Ricci. Chao Ts'an-lu, subsecretary and later minister of justice; Chang Mêng-nan, minister of finance; Kuo Chên-yü, president of the Academy of Nobles, who later as minister of rites in Peking would be an ardent champion of Ricci; Yang Tao-ping, who the next year would be advanced to the Board of Rites in Peking where, like Kuo Chên-yü, he proved himself one of Ricci's best friends, were some of those whose durable friendship dated from these Nanking days.[13]

Another who was strongly drawn by Ricci's science was the celebrated doctor of medicine and erudite, Wang K'êng-t'ang, a son of Wang Ch'iao. He was living at the time in Chintan, some forty miles from Nanking. He wrote to Ricci expressing a desire to become his student. Fearing that Ricci would find it impossible to come to him and since he was unable at the time to come to Nanking, he sent a bright young man to take lessons in his stead. That the doctor profited well from the lessons he received through his intermediary is indicated by the books he wrote, which contain many evidences of Ricci's influence.[14]

In a different category was the brilliant, if eccentric, Li Tsai-chih. He had retired from a successful public career to devote himself to the study of Buddhism. Initially he thought to effect a marriage between Confucianism and Buddhism, but before long his severe criticism of Chu Hsi and the school of neo-Confucianism identified him in the minds of the orthodox as an enemy. When Ricci met him in Nanking in 1599 he was at the height of his fame. Perhaps it was their mutual dislike for the materialism of Sung neo-Confucianism that drew them together. At any rate, Li went out of his way to express his admiration for Ricci. He presented him with two fans upon which he had written poems in honor of the Western sage. He later included one of these poems in one of his books.[15] He also had copies of Ricci's treatise on friendship, the *Chiao-yu lun*, sent to some of his disciples in the province of Hupeh.

Li Pên-ku, a retired official of considerable erudition and a Buddhist with a reputation for wisdom, sought Ricci out. Their discussions were amicable, although Ricci saw little hope of winning him to Christianity. Li admitted quite frankly that Buddhism was like an apple half rotted away, but said he was content to throw away the bad part and hold on to the good that was left.

In one of the private discussion groups which he was accustomed to gather in his home Li Pên-ku found himself under sharp attack from Liu Kuan-nan, an official in the Board of Public Works, for his rejection of Confucianism in favor of Buddhism. In his pointed remarks about the defects of Buddhism Liu made free use of Ricci's name. As a consequence Li Pên-ku contrived to set up a meeting between Ricci and Huang Hung-ên, a Buddhist monk, better known by his religious name of San Hui. Described by Chinese sources as a man of "high forehead, brilliant eyes, square chin, large mouth and creamy complexion," San Hui was one of the most celebrated intellectuals of his day, an outstanding poet, and a true erudite of Buddhism.[16] It was no mean adversary that Li had picked for the Westerner.

The *mise en scène* was a dinner in Ricci's honor. The argument broke out before the dinner. When voices began to be raised, the nervous host moved San Hui away from Ricci's vicinity. During the dinner the discussion was resumed and with the dinner guests for audience Ricci and San Hui debated some of the most fundamental problems of philosophy: the nature of God, the nature of man, the problem of evil. Ricci quickly discovered, as others have often discovered since, the difficulty of arguing with a Buddhist, who is a philosophical idealist and who denies the principle of contradiction. However, if he was unable to move San Hui, he seems to have won the sympathy of the audience, which is probably the best one can hope to accomplish in a debate about religion. San Hui lost his temper, and to that extent the argument. The debate was discussed in intellectual circles all over Nanking and Ricci's reputation was greatly enhanced.

So much success caused both Ricci and Ch'ü Ju-k'uei to reconsider the decision not to stay in Nanking. Nearly all his new friends combined to urge him to establish himself in the southern capital. When Chu Shih-lu, a censor and probably the most important official in the city, added his voice to the chorus, there seemed no longer any reason to hesitate.

Wang Hung-hui offered to put at his disposal a residence reserved for his assistant but which was then unoccupied. Ricci declined and rented a house to serve until such time as he should be able to buy a permanent residence. The opportunity presented itself shortly before the arrival of Cattaneo from the north. Liu Kuan-nan offered him a residence which he had had constructed for the functionaries of the Board of Public Works but which, because of popular reports that it was the scene of ghostly apparitions, had stood empty for several years. It was admirably suited to Ricci's purpose. There were three buildings, one of which could serve as a reception hall, another as a chapel. The third had enough rooms to house nine or ten missionaries. When, around the middle of April, 1599, Cattaneo and his two companions arrived in Nanking, Ricci lost no time closing the deal with Liu Kuan-nan.

The safe arrival of Cattaneo was a relief to Ricci and to Wang Hung-hui. The war with the Japanese had exhausted the imperial treasury. In an effort to refill the emptied coffers the emperor imposed a two per cent sales tax on all merchandise. He entrusted the collection of this tax to eunuchs. A horde of these creatures, possessed of well-nigh unlimited powers and independent of civil officials descended like locusts upon the provinces. Ricci has no words severe enough for these parasites: "for the most part fools, barbarians, proud and without conscience or shame." They carried out their mission "with such cruelty that in a short time all China was in revolt and in a worse state than it had been in during the Korean war." For a boat to pass a toll gate was "equivalent to falling into the hands of highway robbers."[17] Less than a tenth part of all these exactions reached the imperial treasury. Officials in both Nanking and Peking showered the imperial court with memorials of protest, warning of the dangers inherent in the tumult which had arisen everywhere. Some courageous officials openly resisted the eunuchs. Their reward was to be thrown out of office and into prison.

Under these turbulent conditions, Wang Hung-hui was deeply concerned about the safety of Cattaneo. If he arrived in Nanking at all, surely it would be only after having been robbed of his baggage! When he arrived in April, unmolested, Wang was no less surprised and relieved than Ricci.

In July Cattaneo continued to Macao to raise funds for the new enterprise. Ricci had been able to pay only half the purchase price of the residence. The annual ship from Japan, upon which the prosperity of Macao in large part depended, was lost that year; but, thanks to the efforts of Dias and the generosity of the Portuguese merchants, Cattaneo managed to scrape together enough to provide for the upkeep of the three residences, and to pay off the debts incurred at Nanchang and Nanking. He immediately sent Ricci a bill of exchange for two hundred ducats, drawn on a Nanking merchant. Ricci searched in vain for the address and name of the assignee. The bill was worthless and Ricci was pained by his inability to fulfill his promise to Liu Kuan-nan. The latter was thoroughly understanding and made no difficulty about granting an extension of the time agreed upon for remittance of the second half of the purchase price of the residence. The Chinese merchant in Macao who had drawn the bill of exchange made good the two hundred ducats.

During Cattaneo's absence Ricci wrote a letter, August 14, 1599, to his friend Girolamo Costa in Rome which shows his usual ability soundly to evaluate the situation. He is fully aware of the great value of the contacts he has made in Nanking. "Our credit and reputation have so grown that it can be said that we have doubled our gains in China this year." Success had not, however, affected the soundness of his judgment nor altered his views about the pioneering nature of his work. He is realistic. Caution is still the order of the day. The time had not yet come when the gospel could be preached on the streets or to crowds gathered in the market place. "This is not the time for harvesting, or even for sowing, but for clearing the soil." He is also optimistic: "China is very different from other countries and peoples, inasmuch as the Chinese are an intelligent people, given greatly to letters and little to war, of great talent, and at the present time more than ever sceptical of their religion and superstitions; and therefore it will be easy, as I clearly see it, to convert an infinite multitude in a short time." Despite his frank recognition of the fact that many years of toil have not yet produced much in the way of tangible results, he is convinced that what has been accomplished "can be compared favorably [to the achievements of] other missions which seem to be doing wonders."[18] When this was written Japan numbered its Christians in the hundreds of thousands; the Moluccas had been the scene of mass conversions; India boasted an imposing façade of Christian centers, flourishing institutions, and numerous priests. Few things better reveal Ricci's calm confidence in the soundness and ultimate success of his methods.

When Cattaneo, in the first days of the year 1600 returned to Nanking, he brought with him a recruit to the mission, the Spanish Jesuit Diego de Pantoia. So numerous were the visitors during the ensuing months that Ricci's days were almost entirely given over to conversation. He has described the manner in which he aroused a sympathetic interest in Christianity by creating for his visitors a picture of Christian Europe:

> The hospices for the sick, for orphans, for abandoned ones, for incurables, for pilgrims, the *monti della pietà*: the confraternities of charity and of mercy which assist prisoners, widows, and other poor; the different religious orders devoted to seeking perfection and assisting others to live well; the feast days when everyone goes to the churches for the sacrifice of the Mass and to hear the word of God. . . . The generous alms which christians constantly give to the poor. . . .[19]

He made a particular point of stressing the monogamous and indissoluble character of Christian marriage, a law from which not even kings were exempt. His auditors were at one in "praising this to the skies" although "few desired to imitate it." Perhaps they were only being polite when they agreed with Ricci that the contrary custom was responsible for "many disorders . . . in China." They listened with grave respect when Ricci called attention to the ban on child-marriages in Europe. He described to them the episcopal organization of the Church. They were astonished to learn that the dignity of the pope was "superior to that of all Christian kings." In the annotations to his world-map Ricci took pains further to signalize the position of the pope. Thus, "suave modo," as he termed it, he prepared Chinese minds for one of the features of Roman Catholic Christianity to which imperial China would have extreme difficulty reconciling itself: the existence of a supreme spiritual authority, independent of the emperor, to whom Chinese Catholics would be expected to look as the final arbiter in matters of faith and morals. Ricci sensed that as in the days of the Roman empire the refusal of Christians to participate in the cult of the emperor had been at the root of the persecutions, so in China, the entire civilization of which gravitated around the throne of the Son of Heaven, the existence of a distinct and supreme spiritual power would prove the most delicate point in the rapprochement of Roman Catholicism and Chinese culture. Events long after his death proved the accuracy of his prevision.

The first baptized converts to Christianity in Nanking were members of the Ch'in family which, by perpetual grant descending from father to son, held a monopoly of the privilege of transporting to Peking the annual imperial levy of rice. The head of the family, who was seventy years old, took the Christian name of Paul at his baptism. His wife, son and grandson were also baptized. The son, who had won first honors in examinations for the military licentiate, took the name of Martin. As time passed he rendered many services to the mission.

Highly exaggerated reports of these conversions reached Europe by way of Manila. By the time the story reached Rome it had been blown up until these modest first fruits were represented as being two very important officials together with their entire families, numbering in all over one hundred persons. To add a fantastic touch it was even reported that the emperor of China had become a Christian! Manoel Dias, the Older, writing to Rome from Nanchang, November 22, 1604, tried to restore a sense of proportion: The two "important officials" are quite unimportant and the members of their household do not exceed twelve persons. As for the emperor's conversion, Dias comments: "Would to God it were true! But he is neither a Christian nor does he give any hope that he will become one."[20]

This was but the first experience of a kind frequently repeated. During the first decades of the seventeenth century the missionaries in China were embarrassed by exaggerated reports that circulated in the Philippines and from there reached Europe of resounding successes achieved. Other missionaries, their intemperate zeal already with difficulty held in check, would thereupon sound the tocsins for a general assault by missionary hosts upon the Chinese world. More than once the Jesuits in China, astounded by the proportions which reports of their achievements assumed between Macao and Manila and alarmed by the dreams of spiritual conquest which these tales inspired, felt it necessary to protest.

In a letter of July 26, 1605, to the general of the Society, Ricci attempts to correct such exaggerations by setting forth a picture of the true situation. Not unmindful of the importance of what has been accomplished and deeply grateful to divine providence, which alone could have overcome the humanly insuperable obstacles, he points out that, nevertheless, little more than a foothold has thus far been established.[21]

Despite their protests the Jesuits were never able to lay the ghost of these exaggerations. They have survived to our own day. C. Wells Williams writes that, when Ricci died, "there were churches in most of the provincial capitals and great cities; Christians were numbered in thousands."[22] René Fülop-Miller, with his customary insouciance for exactitude, states that "when Ricci died, there were already over three hundred Christian bells to be heard in the Chinese empire."[23] Not to be outdone by this vault of fantasy another author says: "Other Jesuits, formed by [Ricci], had spread through the provinces and, at his death (1610), affairs had advanced so well that three hundred Christian communities had been organized in the Chinese empire."[24]

If one cannot praise the cavalier attitude these authors show towards historical evidence, one can at least admire the casual ease with which they soar into the stratospheric regions of poetic fancy where limitless vistas are unobscured by unwelcome intrusion of facts. For those more concerned with fact than with fancy it should be pointed out that actually when Ricci died there were four Jesuit residences in the empire. Each had a small chapel fitted out in one of the rooms. In Peking a separate chapel, made possible by the generosity of (Leo) Li Chih-tsao, was being built. There were something over two thousand Christians in China, most of them grouped around these four residences. As for bells, there was not a single Christian church bell in the land outside of Macao. It would be many years before Christians could safely herald their liturgical gatherings with the ringing of bells.

During these months in Nanking Ricci had prepared a revised and augmented version of his world map. He did so at the insistence of Wu Chung-ming, at the time an official in the Board of Civil Offices. Wu, a mandarin highly esteemed for his integrity and who would later serve as governor of Kwangtung and in high national offices of state, had it engraved and published together with a laudatory preface written by himself. In it he said of Ricci:

> This Father is modest and asks for nothing; he finds his pleasure in practicing virtue and honoring heaven; every morning and evening resolving to guard his thoughts, words, and actions. Although his complicated mathematics on the relations of heaven and earth, moon and stars, are not easily understood, they seem to be well documented.[25]

These printings of Ricci's revised map generated new and wide interest reaching far beyond the confines of Nanking. They played an important part in drawing towards Christianity Hsü Kuang-ch'i (1562-1633), rightly regarded as the greatest glory of Chinese

Catholicism.[26] In proportion to her numbers the Catholic Church in China has known many outstanding men and remarkable women. Even the hostile critic S. Wells Williams admits that: "Few missions in pagan countries have been more favored with zealous converts."[27] Of them all Hsü Kuang-ch'i is unquestionably the greatest.

A native of Shanghai, Hsü at this time was not yet fairly launched on his brilliant career of public service which would eventually carry him, as grand secretary, to the highest office in the land. A man of great natural virtue and keen intelligence, his considerable studies of Buddhism, neo-Confucianism and Taoism had left him deeply dissatisfied. He had seen the first edition of Ricci's map in 1596 while tutoring in a private family in Shaochow and had then made the acquaintance of Lazzaro Cattaneo who planted the first seeds of faith in his heart.

In the following year in Peking he won the *chü-jên* degree, heading the list of candidates and leading his examiner, the celebrated scholar Chiao Hung in whose Nanking home Ricci had first met the brilliant eccentric Li Tsai-chih, to salute him as "a truly outstanding Confucian scholar."[28]

His interest in Christianity was renewed when a copy of Ricci's revised map reached him in Shanghai. He resolved to meet the author. In April-May, 1600, he came to Nanking. It was a hurried trip and Ricci was able to do little more than give him some fundamental ideas about the Christian concept of God. With that meager baggage, as Ricci remarks, God apparently wished to lead him to the light of the faith.[29]

Three years later Hsü Kuang-ch'i returned to Nanking to ask for baptism; but by then Ricci was in Peking. He took further instructions from João de Rocha and was baptized. In 1604 en route to Peking where he would win the coveted *chin-shih* degree he stayed for two weeks in the Jesuit residence in Nanking. Here he gave great edification. He attended Mass daily, had further instruction in the doctrines of the faith, and for the first time received the sacrament of penance. It was the beginning of a fervent and devout faith whose ardor only flamed higher with the passing years.

Kept as busy as he was by his constantly growing circle of friends, Ricci still found time during his stay in Nanking to construct many astronomical instruments: clocks, spheres, globes, quadrants and sextants. These activities and his knowledge of mathematics sent a wave of fear through the crowded ranks of the mathematicians attached to the imperial bureau of astronomy in Nanking. Well aware of their own ineptitude in the offices they held, they feared for their jobs. Ricci's friends assured them that he had no designs upon the bureau of astronomy. Their fears dissipated, they adopted a less unfriendly attitude.

Ricci was greatly impressed with the excellently designed and beautifully constructed astronomical instruments in the Nanking observatory. He had seen none better in Europe although they were, he judged, about two hundred and fifty years old. They were older than that. Nor were they, as Ricci surmised, "the work of some foreigner acquainted with our science." They had been constructed in the days of Khubilai Khan by the brilliant Kuo Shou-ching (1231-1316), at a time when Arab influence upon Chinese science was quite strong. The weakness of Chinese astronomy in Ricci's day was not due to any lack of instruments, but to the deterioration during the Ming period of their once rather remarkable astronomical science.

This is perhaps the place to say that it is equally erroneous to exaggerate or to minimize either the magnitude of the Jesuit scientific contribution to China or the deficiencies of Chinese science. Ricci and his successors made truly brilliant contributions. In Europe, however, dawn was just beginning to break upon the age of scientific discovery. Copernicanism had not yet triumphed. Although some of the Jesuits were convinced Copernicans, others were not.

In general, as might be expected, the Jesuits brought with them some of the limitations and errors of the Ptolomaic-Aristotelian world view. In the third volume of his monumental work on the development of the natural sciences in China, Joseph Needham gives a balanced view of the strengths and weaknesses of Jesuit and of Chinese science. In the end, he recognizes that, with its faults, the Jesuit scientific contribution "stands for all time nevertheless as an example of cultural relations at the highest level between two civilizations theretofore sundered. . . . [The Jesuits] successfully achieved a task which had proved beyond the powers of their Indian forerunners in the Thang [T'ang], namely to open communications with that world-wide universal science of Nature into which the Chinese achievements would also be built."[30]

With Cattaneo's return from Macao early in 1600, Ricci made plans for another move upon Peking. Prince Chien-an sent word that P'an Hsiang, a eunuch in charge of collecting the recently imposed sales tax in the province of Kiangsi, was willing to draw up a memorial to the emperor in Ricci's behalf. Cattaneo had brought back from Macao gifts to be presented to the emperor. These the eunuch wished to see and Chien-an urged Ricci to bring them to Nanchang where he could discuss the matter of the memorial with P'an Hsiang. Ricci, who deeply disliked and distrusted the eunuchs, declined with thanks.

Ch'ü Ju-k'uei came up to Nanking from Chinkiang where he was then living to discuss the Peking project. Together with Li Hsin-chai, a scholar esteemed for his literary compositions whose interest in furthering Ricci's affairs rivaled Ch'ü's own, Ch'ü Ju-k'uei and Ricci called upon Chu Shih-lu, the censor, to ask his advice. To their delight Chu offered to give Ricci a passport to the capital. This was more than they had hoped. To add to their joy Chu, as well as other Nanking officials, furnished Ricci with letters of recommendation addressed to important personages in Peking. The faithful Wang Hung-hui was no longer in Nanking. Displeased by his failure to receive a promotion to the Board of Rites in Peking, he had, towards the end of 1599, resigned his office and retired to his home in Hainan. Before leaving, however, he had given Ricci letters to friends in Peking.

Cattaneo, already well known, was to remain in Nanking in charge of the residence. De Rocha came on from Nanchang to reinforce him, leaving Soerio in charge of the residence in the Kiangsi capital. De Pantoia and Chung Ming-jên were to accompany Ricci.

In token of appreciation for his many kindnesses, Ricci presented Chu Shih-lu with a number of presents, among them a Venetian glass prism which the censor particularly liked. He in turn, and Ricci's other friends, presented the Jesuit at the moment of his departure with gifts: "as is the custom in China," observed Ricci. It is not out of place to remark that it is a custom which provides a striking illustration of how difficult it has been for the Jesuits in China to receive just treatment from writers unable to exorcise their imaginations of the scheming Jesuit of legend. Thus Arnold H. Rowbotham, an author not conscious of being unfair, remarks, *à propos* a similar incident in Ruggieri's experience: "Bribery by this form of gift soon came to be a common Jesuit practise."[31] What is bribery to Mr. Rowbotham was the act of a gentleman to the Chinese. It was by conforming to what he called the "style" in China, by observing the ritual of Chinese etiquette, that Ricci and his followers persuaded the Chinese that, unlike the first Europeans who had attempted to enter China in the sixteenth century, they were gentlemen and not barbarians. The presentation of gifts to the emperor fell into the same category. It was the custom in China. No foreigner could think of approaching the court without gifts. Nor did a foreigner ever leave the court without receiving gifts from the emperor in return.

A eunuch who was in charge of a small flotilla of ships bearing silk to the imperial court agreed to take the Jesuits to the capital. On May 18, 1600, Ricci with his companions left Nanking.

NOTES

(1) *FR*, II, 14; for a summary of Chao K'o-huai's career cf. D'Elia, *ibid.*, p. 13, n. 4.

(2) *Ibid.*, p. 30.

(3) For the story of de Goes' epochal journey cf. Ricci's account, *FR*, II, 391-445, or the modern account by Vincent Cronin, *The Wise Man from the West* (London: Rupert Hart-Davis, 1955), pp. 236-256.

(4) *FR*, *II*, 32 f.

(5) *Ibid.*, p. 37.

(6) Louis Gaillard, S. J., *Nankin d'alors et d'aujourd'hui, aperçu historique et géographique* (Shanghai: Mission catholique, 1903), p. 187, graphically describes Nanking in its hey-day.

(7) *FR*, I, 350.

(8) There is an accurate description of the structure of the central government of Ming China in Gabriel de Magaillans [de Magalhães], *op. cit.*, pp. 191 ff. Cf. also William F. Mayers. *The Chinese Government* (3d ed., Shanghai: Kelly and Walsh, 1897). Mayers says there were four Grand Secretaries; de Magalhães says the number was variable.

(9) The date of his death is given variously by different authors. D'Elia rejects the other dates in favor of September 16; cf. *FR*, II, 38, n. 9.

(10) *Ibid.*, p. 39, n. 2.

(11) *Ibid.*, p. 71.

(12) Cf. L. C. Goodrich, *The Literary Inquisition of Ch'ien-Lung* (Baltimore: Waverly Press, 1935), p. 75, n. 2. For a list of his literary works *cf. ibid.*, pp. 258 f. For biographical sketch cf. D'Elia in *FR*, II, 42, n. 1.

(13) Excellent biographical sketches of all these men are given by D'Elia in *FR*, II, 40, n. 8; 41, nn. 1, 2; 42, n. 1.; 43, nn. 1, 3.

(14) *Ibid.*, p. 53, n. 4.

(15) The Chinese text of this sonnet, with Italian translation, is given by D'Elia in *FR*, II, 68, n. 5.

(16) *Ibid.*, 75, n. 5.

NOTES

(17) *Ibid.*, 81 f.

(18) *Opere storiche*, II, 243-250 *passim*.

(19) *FR*, II, 94 f.

(20) *Opere storiche*, II, 479 f.

(21) *Ibid.*, p. 289.

(22) S. Wells Williams, *The Middle Kingdom* (rev. ed.; New York: Charles Scribner's Sons, 1883), II, 330.

(23) René Fülop-Miller. *The Power and Secret of the Jesuits*, trans. F. S. Flint and D. F. Tait (New York: The Viking Press, 1930), p. 245.

(24) A. Reville, *La religion Chinoise* (Paris: Librairie Fischbacker, 1889), p. 670.

(25) *FR*, II, 59, n. 5.

(26) There is a good biographical sketch of Hsü Kuang-ch'i in *Eminent Chinese of the Ch'ing Period (1644-1912)*, ed. Arthur W. Hummel (Washington: United States Government Printing Office, 1943), I, 316 ff.; hereafter cited as *Eminent Chinese*.

(27) S. Wells Williams, *op. cit.*, II, 295.

(28) *FR*, II, 250, n. 3.

(29) *Ibid.*, p. 253.

(30) Joseph Needham, F. R. S., *Science and Civilization in China* (Cambridge: University Press, 1959), III, pp. 457 f.

(31) Rowbotham, *op. cit.*, p. 44.

Chapter V

Reaching the Moon

THE AUSPICIOUS SIGNS under which Ricci's memorable journey to Peking began continued as far as the city of Tsining in the province of Shantung. The eunuch in charge of the flotilla in which the Jesuits travelled was delighted to have them with him because their presence facilitated his own passage.[1] The Grand Canal was a busy aqueous highway crowded with boats and with traffic problems worthy of the twentieth century. Right of way belonged to the often immense flotillas carrying provisions to the imperial court and to the smaller, but still considerable, flotillas carrying important mandarins on official business. At the numerous locks other ships had to stand aside to let these pass. The locks were worked by a primitive but ingenious system of blocking the passageway beneath a bridge with a wooden barrier until the water was raised to the desired level. This process and the size of the preferred flotillas often imposed delays of as much as four or five days upon those who stood lower on the priority list. The eunuch found in Ricci an excellent instrument to avoid these interminable delays. He invited the captains of the preferred flotillas to meet the Western sage and to examine the gifts he was bearing to the emperor. Their good will thus won, it was easy to persuade them to yield their precious right of way to the distinguished foreigner.

In Tsining Ricci and his companions received a royal welcome. Here he found his friend Li Tsai-chih, the poet of the fans, a guest in the splendid residence of Liu Tung-hsing, the imperial commissar in charge of the transport of rice to the capital. This was a highly important post, equivalent in dignity and authority to that of a viceroy. Liu Tung-hsing was a mandarin of distinguished ability and virtue who had filled with honor a long list of government positions.[2] In addition to the commissariat he currently held the title of Minister of Public Works and was also president of the Board of Censors.

Liu had heard of Ricci not only from Li Tsai-chih, but also from his son, who had been on friendly terms with the Jesuit in Nanking. When he learned of Ricci's arrival in the city he sent his sedan chair and porters to bring him to his palace and later the same day paid a formal visit in state to his boat, a striking gesture of courtesy which caused excited comment in the city. He left after examining with great interest the gifts destined for the emperor and extracting a promise from Ricci to visit him again the next day. Ricci must have long cherished the memory of that delightful next day which he spent surrounded by Liu Tung-hsing, his sons, and the amiable Li Tsai-chih, treated, so he wrote, "with such benevolence, that it seemed as though [he] were not at the ends of the earth and in the midst of the gentiles, but in Europe surrounded by devout Christians and intimate friends."[3]

Liu Tung-hsing was not satisfied with the tenor of the memorial drawn up in Nanking for presentation to the emperor. He prepared another and had the best calligraphers in the city work on it. As a final gesture he gave Ricci letters to certain people in Peking which were to prove of greater service than those with which his Nanking friends had furnished him.

Ricci took away with him a deep affection for these good friends and a hope that he might some day repay them by leading them to the faith. His hope was not to be realized. Liu Tung-hsing died the following year at the age of sixty-four and a year later Li Tsai-chih, in his seventy-sixth year, summoned to Peking and condemned on the charge of holding the "orthodox" neo-Confucian authors in contempt, committed suicide rather than accept banishment and further trial in his native province of Fukien.

Once away from Tsining and its pleasant associations Ricci's luck ran out. Arrived at Lintsing in the same province on July 3, 1600, he and his two companions fell into the clutches of Ma-t'ang, a notorious eunuch in charge of the collection of customs duty. In order to escape his usurious exactions the eunuch Liu abandoned the Jesuits to Ma-t'ang's mercies after telling him that they had valuable gifts for the emperor. Not entirely ungrateful, however, for the benefits he had derived from Ricci's presence on the voyage, he left behind, to help de Pantoia learn Chinese, a ten-year-old boy whom he had purchased from a famine-stricken family in Nanking.

Ma-t'ang was a dangerous man to have as an enemy. Even the military commandant of Lintsing, Chung Wan-lu, whom Ricci had known in Shaochow and whose friendship he had renewed in Nanking, warned him to handle the eunuch with extreme care. As he remarked, in a sad commentary upon the state of political affairs in the China of his day, "the eunuchs are the rulers of China; the emperor does nothing but what they advise, and not even the most prominent men in China can do anything against the injustices they commit."[4]

Six months of frustration followed. After a few weeks at Lintsing they were moved to Tientsin, there to await the imperial answer to a memorial Ma-t'ang had sent to Peking informing the emperor of the gift-bearing foreigners. During the first months they were treated with an external show of respect by the gross and unprincipled eunuch. A reply from Peking demanded a list of the gifts which Ricci carried. As weeks passed with no reply to Ma-t'ang's second memorial giving an inventory of the presents, the eunuch began to fear imperial displeasure. His attitude brusquely changed. The three Jesuits were moved into a pagoda inside the Tientsin fortress and kept under military guard day and night.

The situation became desperate when Ma-t'ang, under pretext that Ricci had not listed all the gifts in his possession, had the military commander of Tientsin at the head of a company of soldiers, drag out and examine all of Ricci's baggage. When they found a crucifix Ma-t'ang raised a great hue and cry. Clearly this figure of a naked man nailed to a cross, a bloody, gaping wound in his side, was a devilish charm by which these foreigners meant to effect the death of the emperor!

According to de Pantoia, Ma-t'ang was given a full explanation of the identity of the figure on the cross. When the eunuch demanded to know "what this was," says de Pantoia, "we told him that this was the true God, creator of heaven and of earth, whom all the world must adore; who, for our sins and to give us life, died and then, by his own power, rose from the dead and ascended into heaven."[5]

De Pantoia's "diximos" is undoubtedly an editorial "we." Inasmuch as he had been in China only a few months it is hardly likely that he spoke Chinese as fluently as this resounding proclamation of man's redemption would suggest. It is equally unlikely that he could understand what Ricci said to Ma-t'ang. With a flair for the dramatic de Pantoia evidently built the story up a bit for the benefit of the provincial of the Jesuit province of Toledo to whom he was writing.

Ricci had too much good sense and too much experience with how little the Chinese were prepared to understand straight off the doctrine of a crucified God, to pour this kind of inflammatory oil on the fire. Undoubtedly the correct version is that of Ricci himself: "Not wishing to say that this was our God, inasmuch as it seemed difficult in these circumstances to explain so profound a mystery to these ignorant people, especially as it would only be interpreted by the eunuch as an effort to deceive . . . [I] began little by little to explain to the *ping-pi-tao* [the commandant of troops] and to the others, that . . . this was a great saint who had wished to suffer for us the pain of the cross; and that for this reason we made sculptured and painted representations of him in order always to have him before our eyes so that we might be grateful for so great a benefit."[6]

The scandal was great. Ricci's explanation availed nothing. Everything seemed lost. (Sebastian) Chung Ming-jên, the Jesuit lay brother in the party, managed to slip away and reach Peking where he sought the intervention of Ricci's friends. Fearful of the power of the eunuchs these dared not compromise themselves. They advised the Jesuits to save themselves by making a gift of all their baggage to Ma-t'ang. A petition to the emperor was out of the question inasmuch as he did nothing except through the eunuchs. Ricci's friend, Chung Wan-lu, judged the party lost and urged them to flee to Canton. But Ricci and de Pantoia were unwilling, however desperate the situation, to abandon hope. "Seeing that there was no longer anything to hope from human auxiliaries," wrote Ricci, "they applied themselves more diligently to implore divine help and to prepare themselves for any eventuality. Willingly they desired to offer their lives for the cause which had provoked Ma-t'ang's persecution."[7]

They were delivered from their impasse when, against all expectation, there arrived an imperial order, issued January 9, 1601, to send the foreigners with their gifts immediately to Peking. The long ordeal was over, although other trials awaited them in the imperial capital.

Arrived in Peking on January 24, 1601, they found themselves caught in the vortex of political factionalism. According to administrative procedure foreigners fell under the jurisdiction of the Board for Foreigners, one of the four subsidiary offices of the Board of Rites. It was the function of this board to examine visitors on the purpose of their mission, to present their gifts to the emperor, and to advise the throne on the treatment to be accorded them. This procedure the eunuchs were determined to circumvent. They were motivated by the hope of sharing the rewards which they thought the emperor might bestow upon the foreigners and no doubt by a malicious delight in thwarting the officials of the Board of Rites.

Much nonsense has been written about the astute way in which Ricci insinuated himself into the court. The facts, although no less interesting, are quite different from the romanticized versions which certain writers have popularized. Consider the rare fantasies, with only a remote relation to fact, with which Fülop-Miller adorns his tale.[8] By the omission of all dates he so telescopes Ricci's first eighteen years in China as to create the impression that by some feat of legerdemain he reached Peking shortly after he reached China. He then describes his arrival in Peking:

> He established himself outside the capital and, after making the acquaintance of a high official, he requested the latter to take into the palace a present for the emperor; this present was an ingenious and beautifully embellished European clock.
>
> The Chinese official took the missionary's gift to one of the gates of the palace, and handed it to the court official on duty there. At first, the official hesitated for a long time whether he should pass the gift on, but, when he had examined the clock more closely, it filled him with such wonderment that he called his superior officer up and showed him the marvel. Ricci's clock thereupon passed through the whole hierarchy of officials in the palace up to the highest minister, and ultimately reached the emperor himself.
>
> Even the 'Son of Heaven' had never before seen a spring clock, and was filled with rapture by it. Of course, it was far beneath his exalted dignity to make even the suggestion of an inquiry about the mortal who had sent him this present. On the following morning, however, the clock suddenly stopped tick-

> ing. The emperor summoned one of his officials to set it going again, but all the efforts of the mandarin were in vain. The whole of the royal household in turn tried their skill, but not one among them could set the clock going again.
>
> At last, the emperor permitted himself to inquire who it was that had brought the clock to the palace, and the question was passed down through the whole hierarchy of officials to the keeper of the gate. [The king asked the queen and the queen asked the dairymaid!] The emperor could not rest until the stranger should be found, and the clock set ticking again.
>
> Thus it came about that, escorted by two mandarins of the court, the astute Doctor Li [Ricci] passed through the mighty portals of the imperial palace, mounted a marble staircase guarded by two copper lions, and proceeded along the bank of the stream that wound its way right through the whole palace.

There was nothing remarkably "astute" in Ricci's procedure. Fortified with letters of introduction to officials in Peking, he approached the capital with the plain intention of endeavoring to obtain permission to establish himself there and authorization freely to preach the gospel. His plans went awry when he fell into the hands of the eunuchs and for several months became a football of Peking politics, a pawn in the unceasing contest between eunuchs and mandarins. To keep him from the mandarinal officials, the eunuchs lodged him and his companions under guard in a house belonging to one of Ma-t'ang's creatures.

On January 27 the eunuchs presented Ricci's gifts to the emperor together with his memorial. There was nothing of monetary value among the gifts: a reproduction of the famous painting of the Madonna long attributed to the evangelist St. Luke, which was then and is still today the object of great popular devotion in the basilica of St. Mary Major's in Rome; another painting of the Blessed Mother with the infant Christ and John the Baptist; a Roman breviary; a reliquary in the form of a cross, but with the relics removed "because it did not seem wise," reasoned Ricci, "to put relics of the saints into hands of unbelievers"; two glass prisms, a spinet; two clocks, the smaller of which was more valuable, but the larger of which excited greater interest because it made more noise! There were a number of other items of similar nature.[9]

In the accompanying memorial Ricci stated that he was a foreigner who, drawn by the good name of China, had arrived in the Middle Kingdom after three years of travel; that he had spent fifteen years in Chaoching and Shaochow studying Chinese, and five years in Nanchang and Nanking; that he was a religious without wife or children and therefore seeking no favor; that, having studied astronomy, geography, calculus and mathematics, he would be happy to be of service to the emperor.[10]

The paintings astonished the emperor, as they did all the Chinese. As yet unfamiliar with the art of perspective which European artists had mastered, the paintings seemed alive to them. "This is a living God!" the emperor was reported to have exclaimed. A little fearful of having a "living God" too close, he sent the paintings of the Madonna to his mother, an exceptionally devout Buddhist. It was later put in the imperial treasury.

The emperor was especially interested in a clock which sounded the hours and, when it stopped, he sent eunuchs to bring Ricci to set it going again. Thus Ricci and de Pantoia entered the Forbidden City. Ricci asked that someone be designated to whom he could explain how to regulate the clock and keep it going. For several days he and de Pantoia were lodged in the college of mathematics within the Forbidden City while they gave a course in horology to four eunuchs appointed for the purpose.

Among the other gifts was a spinet. Four eunuchs were appointed to learn to play it. For a month de Pantoia went daily to the palace to give them lessons. This inspired Ricci to compose eight simple motets with lyrics inculcating lessons of Christian moral doctrine. They were later published by Li Chih-tsao in Peking in 1629 in his collection of Christian books and have been published several times since in other editions of the same work, the latest in Shanghai in 1938. In the late eighteenth century they were included in a list of the best literary productions of China.[11]

More than a month had passed when Ts'ai Hsien-ch'ên, director of the bureau which held jurisdiction over foreigners, indignant at the circumvention of his authority by the eunuchs, sent a squad of police who snatched the Jesuits from the hands of their eunuch guards. In a public hearing Ricci was kept on his knees for more than an hour while Ts'ai Hsien-ch'ên, who would later become a good friend, took him to task for not having submitted his gifts through his board rather than through the eunuchs.

Ricci's defense was not difficult to formulate. He pointed out that he had fallen into the hands of Ma-t'ang against whom even the most prominent mandarins were helpless and that he had been kept in custody ever since. He also laid claim to a kind of naturalized citizenship which should exempt him from the jurisdiction of the board for foreigners. He argued that, having lived for so many years in China, he should not be treated as a foreigner.

Ts'ai Hsien-ch'ên was mollified. He reassured Ricci that he had nothing to fear, promised that he would himself memorialize the throne in his behalf. He did not, however, approve of his staying in Peking. Meanwhile Ricci and his companions were moved into what Ricci euphemistically calls the "palace for foreigners." It was actually a huge enclosure with more than a thousand rooms; but these rooms were hardly more than stalls, without doors, chairs, benches or beds. Here were housed foreigners who came to Peking in the guise of ambassadors to seek an audience with the emperor. Actually they were nearly all merchants interested only in trade. Everyone was aware of this, but all by a kind of tacit agreement and to their mutual profit kept up the ambassadorial charade.

The charade had begun in the reign of the Yung-lo emperor (1403-1424) who, in an excess of vainglory, had sent emissaries far and wide to invite foreigners to pay tribute and homage to the emperor in his new capital. Merchants were only too glad of the opportunity and from then on a steady stream of tribute-bearing "embassies" flowed to Peking from every country in the Far and Near East. Their camels, their horses, their caravans were a common sight in the dusty streets of Peking, although their freedom of movement was strictly limited while in the imperial city.

Ricci found seventy or more Mohammedans from Central Asian countries in the enclosure. From his conversations with them he adduced more evidence to support his conviction that China and the mysterious Cathay of Marco Polo were one and the same.

Part of the charade was the imperial audience which was granted "ambassadors." Ricci and de Pantoia, a few days after being lodged in their new quarters, took part in one of these audiences. It was a colorful procession of richly robed mandarins and foreigners in ceremonial dress which, escorted by several thousand soldiers and led by lumbering elephants, made its way with the first streaks of dawn appearing in the eastern sky to the magnificent audience chamber capable of holding thirty thousand people. This had long been the scene of genuine audiences, but since 1585 the Wan-li emperor had shut himself off from nearly all contacts with the outside world. The game was played out in his absence, the gifts for the emperor presented, the ceremonial prostrations made to the empty imperial throne. Ricci could not but laugh at the gifts: battered iron swords, homemade breast plates, poor bony horses which arrived in Peking ready to lie down and die from hunger. The cost of vanity comes high. These "ambassadors" were all maintained in Peking by the imperial treasury, wined, dined, entertained and sent on their way with far better gifts than they had brought.

Ricci and his companions were well treated in the palace of foreigners. They were given special rooms, furnished with beds, chairs and tables, and a separate room in which they celebrated Mass. Ts'ai Hsien-ch'èn entertained them at dinner and was pleased when, in response to his request, Ricci constructed a number of mathematical instruments for him: a sphere, a quadrant and a celestial globe.

While Ricci was happy to have been delivered from the hands of Ma-t'ang, the contest between eunuchs and civil officials threatened to defeat his purpose, which was to stay in Peking. Chu Kuo-tso, the acting head of the Board of Rites was opposed to the idea. He sent a parade of notaries day after day to quiz the Jesuits on a variety of subjects, but especially about their reasons for coming to China. Because the question was juridically put, it received a forthright answer. "Orally and in writing," reports Ricci, "they replied that they had come by order of their superiors to China to preach the law of God: that, having lived so many years in his empire, they had come to Peking to present the emperor with gifts as a sign of their respect; that they desired neither office nor gifts, but simply to remain as hitherto in China or in Peking as the emperor should determine."[12] In reply to Chu's inquiry about the nature of the doctrine they taught, Ricci sent him a manuscript exposition of his teachings, probably a copy of his *T'ien Chu shih-lu*.[13]

Chu Kuo-tsu, in a memorial to the throne bitterly criticizing Ma-t'ang for usurping the functions which belonged properly to the Board of Rites, advised that Ricci and his companions, although they should be excused because being foreigners they could not be held to account for failure to observe the proper protocol, should nevertheless be sent to Canton and deported. When weeks passed without a reply Chu began to fear that he had overreached himself. He modified his attitude towards Ricci and allowed him to go about the city and to visit his friends, accompanied by servants attached to the Board of Rites. One of those who received him cordially was Ts'ao Yü-pien, who held the important office of censor of the Peking magistrates. Ricci had met him during his first month in Peking and from the first the two formed a close and enduring friendship. Ts'ao Yü-pien later figured as one of the interlocutors in Ricci's book *The Ten Paradoxes*.

Chu Kuo-tso sent five successive memorials to the throne advising that Ricci leave Peking. They were all much milder in tone than the first and instead of urging his deportation simply advised that he be sent back to the south. All of the memorials remained unanswered.

What prompted the emperor to tolerate the foreigners? A Chinese source says that he was flattered that they had come from so great a distance. Says the *Ming-shih Kao* (Draft History of the Ming Dynasty):

> Pleased that [Ricci] had come from so far away, the emperor gave him a lodging, a pension, gifts, and treated him splendidly in such wise that the leading personages and the mandarins of state all honored this man and established relations with him. Ma-t'ou [Ricci] then remained peacefully and did not again depart.[14]

His tolerance may also have been partly due to the pleasure he shared with the eunuchs in frustrating the officials. The Wan-li emperor, who had ascended the throne in 1573 as a child of ten, was thoroughly corrupt. Surrounded only by his harem and thousands of eunuchs he led a dissolute life of sensuality and drunkenness in the isolation of his palace from which he rarely emerged.

Since 1588 a bitter struggle had been waged between the emperor and the eunuchs on the one hand and, on the other, the patriotic scholar-officials over the question of the imperial succession. The officials insisted that he name his eldest son, Chu Ch'ang-lo. The emperor, supported by the eunuchs, wished instead to designate as heir a younger son whose mother was his favorite concubine. The courageous and unrelenting pressure of censors and ministers of state eventually forced the emperor to yield. On November 11, 1601, he declared Chu Ch'ang-lo heir to the throne, although he later attempted to reverse his decision.

At the moment of Ricci's arrival in Peking this long contest was in its critical stage. That the emperor was at the point of finding himself forced to capitulate could hardly have inspired him with feelings of good will towards the officials who were opposing him. It is not altogether unlikely that he welcomed this opportunity to nettle them.

In any event it is certain that he wished Ricci to remain in Peking. He preferred not to issue a decree to this effect unless, as protocol required, requested to do so by the Board of Rites. In the absence of any such request he adopted the strategy of ignoring the repeated memorials.

It was an impasse from which Ricci's friends finally delivered him. They protested vigorously to Chu Kuo-tso against keeping Ricci in the enclosure for foreigners. Ts'ao Yü-pien angrily demanded that he be released and given the freedom of the city.

Under the pressure of these protests and of his mounting concern that the silence of the emperor indicated displeasure, Chu Kuo-tso, whose animus all along had been directed chiefly at Ma-t'ang's presumption in usurping the functions which properly belonged to the Board of Rites, yielded. The ordeal of the Jesuits ended on May 28, 1601, more than a year after their departure from Nanking.

Thus after two decades of patient and persevering effort Ricci achieved the goal which he had set for himself. "Never was an apostolic enterprise undertaken with greater audacity, pursued with more tenacity and astuteness, mundane diplomacy, and devotion to a great cause," writes one historian.[15] This judgment creates a false image which the record does not support. What the record does support is a profile of high courage, good judgment, imperturbable patience, serene faith and great charity.

NOTES

(1) Research has failed to establish with certainty the identity of this eunuch whom Ricci calls Liupusié. It is not improbable that his name was Liu P'o-hsi. It was not an uncommon practise to adopt the name of some historical personage. Liu P'o-hsi was a famous actress of the Yüan period. In view of the fact that he was a eunuch it is less improbable than one might be inclined to suppose, as D'Elia piquantly observes, that Liu should take the name of a woman; *FR*, II, 101, n. 2.

(2) Cf. *ibid.*, p. 103, n. 2 for an account of his career.

(3) *Ibid.*, p. 105.

(4) *Ibid.*, p. 109.

(5) Diego de Pantoia, S. J., *Relaçion de la entrada de algunos padres de la Compania de Jesus en la China, y particulares sucessos que tuvieron, y de cosas muy notables que vieron en el mismo reyno* (Valencia, 1606), pp. 41 ff.

(6) *FR*, II, 116.

(7) *Ibid.*, p. 119.

(8) Fülop-Miller, *op. cit.*, pp. 242 ff.

(9) De Pantoia, *op. cit.*, pp. 33 ff., gives a list of the gifts. A number of items he lumped together under the rubric "things of less importance." A more detailed list is given by D'Elia, *FR*, II, 123, n. 5.

(10) The text of the memorial is found in a collection published in Fukien province in 1638 by Giulio Aleni. It is summarized by D'Elia, *id.*

(11) *Ibid.*, p. 134, n. 6, gives the title and theme of each of these motets.

(12) *Ibid.*, p. 146.

(13) Cf. *supra*, p. 29.

(14) *FR*, II, 151, n. 4.

(15) A. Reville, *op. cit.*, p. 665.

Chapter VI

The Grain of Wheat

THE LEGEND HAS somehow persisted that Ricci was on intimate terms with the Wan-li emperor. Ricci actually never saw the emperor. He himself has recorded the origin of the legend. Not long after his release from the foreigners' enclosure something went wrong with the now famous clock. The four eunuchs charged with its care brought it to the house where the Jesuits were living to be repaired. During the few days it was there many of Ricci's mandarin friends came to see it. The emperor, hearing of this, gave orders that in the future the clock was not to be removed from the palace. Should it need repair, the Westerners were to be summoned to the palace to attend to it. "From this," writes Ricci, " there arose a report of the emperor's great benevolence towards the fathers, and it was said that he took great delight in talking to them, and thus a false report, not easily laid to rest, spread through China, that the emperor frequently spoke on terms of familiarity with the fathers, whereas important mandarins could not even see him."[1]

If he had succeeded in reaching the imperial city, as he had so long desired, his first-hand observations of political realities there caused him to make an important revision in his strategic views. As has been seen, he had for years been persuaded that it was essential above all else to obtain imperial sanction to preach Christianity in the empire. This would shelter the nascent Church from destruction at the hands of unfriendly officials. Once this authorization was obtained it would be possible to stimulate the movement of conversions. But now he had seen with his own eyes the true situation of the emperor. The Wan-li emperor was not an autocrat, but the corrupt and weak ruler of a decaying dynasty in the hands of a horde of eunuchs.

De Pantoia estimated the number of eunuchs as 16,000. In 1602, 3,000 out of 20,000 applicants were selected to swell the ranks of the emasculated army which swarmed through the imperial palaces in Peking.[2] Most of them were ignorant and stupid, but there were always some who were intelligent and, because of their generally low moral standards, all the more dangerous. Some attained positions of great power. A few were capable of virtuous lives. Among these latter were some who became exemplary Christians in the last years of the Ming dynasty. Most notable of these was P'ang T'ien-shou (always identified by the missionaries in their letters as P'an Achilles), who distinguished himself by his virtuous life and by his loyalty to the Ming dynasty.

P'ang T'ien-shou and others like him were distinguished exceptions to a general pattern of vicious corruption. Ricci realized the futility of trying to obtain an edict of religious freedom from an emperor so much the tool of his eunuchs, and hence the necessity for a different strategy.

The fact of residence in Peking, which everyone knew was impossible without the acquiescence of the emperor, would itself serve as an implied sanction of Christianity. Inasmuch as the emperor tacitly accepted this situation, the missionaries should do the same. In China more could often be accomplished by indirection than by frontal attack. To insist upon explicit imperial approval would confront the emperor with an issue which, for fear of arousing opposition, he might be unwilling to resolve affirmatively. The political organization of China was and is not the only one in which it is often better to interpret tacit acceptance of a situation as permission than to provoke refusal by demanding formal commitment on the part of superiors.

Henceforth the strategy would be to intensify, in and from Peking, the intellectual apostolate, thus building up throughout the empire a network of friendly contacts and developing ever broadening Christianizing masses. Accompanying this campaign, and indirectly served by it, the work of evangelization, of "making Christians," should be carried on both in Peking and in the provinces. This should be done along the lines laid down, following the methods of pacific penetration and cultural adaptation. Europeanism was to be shunned. Contact with Europeans, specifically with the

Portuguese in Macao, should be reduced to a minimum. Measures should be taken to obtain income property in China to provide for the mission's support. Meanwhile, as long as recourse to Macao for funds remained necessary it should be resorted to "as cautiously and as little as possible." While there could be no question of compromising Christian doctrine, needless conflicts with Chinese prejudices and suspicions should be avoided. The apostolate should be carried on "prudently, without fanfare, and with good books and reasoned arguments, proving to the scholars the truth of our doctrine, which not only works no harm, but on the contrary serves the cause of good government and peace in the empire." Emphasis should be placed upon procuring *good* Christians rather than *many*.

This is the conception of methodology systematically formulated by Ricci in a letter of February 15, 1609, to the vice-provincial, Francesco Pasio.[3] These are his mature views, the fruit of years of experience. It may be surmised, however, that they had been established in his mind from the first months in Peking, inasmuch as his apostolate from 1601 on is an expression of this program.

Certain critics of Ricci's methods have reproached him for excessive reliance upon "human" or "natural" means. The reproach is unjustified. Ricci had a sound and balanced view. His memoirs and his correspondence reveal him as a man of profound and transparently simple faith. To him it was evident that divine action alone could achieve the supernatural ends of the Christian mission. Hence it was always to divine providence, the interventions of which at times seemed to him miraculous, that he attributed whatever success he achieved. At the same time, he was by no means an unrealistic fanatic. He realized that grace does not operate in a vacuum. It makes use of human instrumentalities; it moves in a thousand mysterious ways "its wonders to perform." It is the duty of those instrumentalities to put no obstacle in the way of the operation of grace, and to scorn no means, provided in itself good, which might serve, by whatever winding ways, to carry grace and inspiration to human souls. Thus he did not judge even the composition of motets for a spinet improper to his calling.

Far from being unmindful of the role of supernatural grace in the apostolate, it may be claimed that Ricci's awareness of it was far deeper than that of his later critics. It was his understanding of the manifold and subtle ways in which grace operates which gave him his imperturbable confidence in ultimate victory. He had none of that impatience for immediate and tangible results which characterized so many of his contemporaries in the mission field, precisely because he was so sure that in God's own time the fruits would mature. He did not demand an immediate and crystal-clear solution — the *solution simpliste* — to every perplexing and difficult problem. In this too he was strikingly different from his later critics. Here again his attitude was rooted in a deeper faith and confidence. None of the problems which were later to torture the consciences of missionaries and split them into two camps and ultimately bring ruin to the mission was lost upon him. The difference was that Ricci, realizing their complexities, was content, when the immediate solution was not clear, to abide with confidence the directives of a divine providence which does not operate under the pressure of time.

The letter referred to above provides a characteristic example of this attitude. It was occasioned by a letter from Pasio urging that he endeavor to obtain from the emperor explicit authorization for the missionaries to preach the gospel freely in China. Ricci in reply explains why this cannot be safely attempted and then, by way of showing that it was not now necessary, sets forth his considered views on methodology. After indicating that the ideal should be to strive to make "good Christians rather than multitudes" of indifferent Christians, he adds that eventually "when we have already a goodly number of Christians, then perhaps it will not be impossible to present some memorial to the emperor asking at least that the right of Christians to practice their religion be accorded, inasmuch as it is not contrary to the laws of China; but Our Lord will make known and discover to us little by little the appropriate means for bringing about in this matter His holy will." These words reveal at once the deep trust in divine providence which characterized the man and supply a key to an understanding of his approach to the problems of the apostolate. They also, when read in the light of later events, are another proof of his remarkable prevision. In 1692, eighty-two years after Ricci's death, when there were a "goodly number" of Christians in China and when the leaven of Christianity had penetrated deeply into the body of Chinese society, such a memorial was presented to the K'ang-hsi emperor, who thereupon promulgated an edict of toleration of the Christian religion.

The last nine years of Ricci's life, all of which were spent in Peking, were the most fruitful and productive of his career. In all their main lines his views had been formed by 1601. As the result of nineteen years of experience he had worked out his program. From then until his death he devoted himself to giving to it as full a development as possible.

As superior of the mission he directed and inspired the labors of the Jesuits stationed in the other residences. On all major questions of policy he reached no decision without the approval of Valignano. His work in Peking absorbed so much of his time that, from 1602 on, he was relieved, through the appointment of Manoel Dias, Senior, as vice-superior directing the activities of the residences in the south, of a considerable part of the burdens of this office.

Most of his time was given over to the sort of apostolate which he had carried on in Nanchang and in Nanking, but with broader developments. Scarcely had he, after being released from the "palace for foreigners," set himself up in a house of his own when the influx of visitors poured in upon him. Friends whom he had known in the south, prominent officials to whom his Nanking friends had recommended him, no longer feared to come forward. Often throughout the day the street in front of his residence was congested with the carriages and palanquins of distinguished callers.

Within a few months he had established amicable relations with the more prominent officials of the chief governmental offices. Ts'ai Hsien-ch'ên, who had given Ricci an uneasy hour on his knees at their first meeting, entertained him in his home and treated him with singular courtesy. He jovially remarked that Peking was large enough to make room for one more foreigner.

Many of Ricci's callers became bound to him with hoops of closest friendship. Ts'ao Yü-pien, whose strong representations to Chu Kuo-tso had had much to do with his release from limited detention, was among his most frequent visitors. Another was Shên Yi-kuan, who had been *Ko-lao* or Grand Secretary since 1594. In 1603 he became the leading *Ko-lao*, or Prime Minister. During the five years he held this office he was always a staunch friend and protector of Ricci and his Jesuit companions.

Shên Yi-kuan was one of the outstanding leaders of the official group which stood firm against the intriguers who were attempting to set aside the heir apparent, Chu Ch'ang-lo, in favor of the favorite concubine's son. This it was which forced him out of office and into retirement in 1608 when an anonymous pamphlet charging the emperor with again planning to carry out this design infuriated the ruler. His frantic efforts to discover the author of the pamphlet drove Shên from office, led many innocent persons to prison, and struck fear into every heart in Peking.

Wang Ju-shun, whom Ricci had known in Nanking, was now a secretary of state in the Ministry of Justice in Peking. He had a deep interest and considerable talent in mathematics and was Ricci's great friend. Through him the Jesuit met both Hsiao Ta-hêng and Fêng Ch'i. The former had served for twenty years as governor of Ninghsia, near the Mongolian border. He afterwards became successively Imperial Censor, sub-Secretary of War, Minister of War, and Minister of Justice. In 1602 his eighteen-year-old nephew, with his uncle's blessing, became a Catholic, taking the name of Michael, but he unfortunately died a few months later.

Fêng Ch'i was another who was cut down by an early and unexpected death. He was a great loss to Ricci who had had high hopes of his conversion. He was Minister of Rites in 1601 when he became a close friend and developed a deep interest in Catholicism. He hoped to introduce Christian doctrine into the schools. He was widely respected for his learning and his integrity. His death in 1603 at the age of forty-four, when he was very close to conversion, was a severe blow. In his book, The Ten Paradoxes, published in 1608, Ricci used the substance of some of his conversations with Fêng Ch'i as the material for one of his chapters in which Fèng himself figures as the interlocutor. The discussion centers on the problem of evil and the theme that man's true home is not on earth but in eternity, an appropriate subject in view of Fêng's imminent demise.

Another who became a close friend at this time and who would also later figure in a chapter of the same book as interlocutor, was Li T'ai-tsai, the Minister of Civil Offices. Next to the position of *Ko-lao* or Grand Secretary, this was the most powerful office in government, inasmuch as it controlled all governmental appointments in the empire. Li T'ai-tsai often had Ricci to his house where they spent many hours discussing religion. In the chapter of Ricci's book which features Li T'ai-tsai the subject of their conversation is the brevity, and therefore the preciousness, of time. *Carpe diem quia tempus fugit.*

Friends from Nanking days also helped widen the circle of his acquaintances. Wang Hung-hui, former Minister of Rites and Chang Mêng-nan, former Minister of Finance, when visiting Peking confirmed their old friendship. Kuo Chên-yü and Yang Tao-ping were both now stationed in Peking in the Ministry of Rites. They were frequent callers at Ricci's home and both defended him against critics of his religious teaching.

These were but a few of the many eminent personages, including relatives of the emperor and the empress, whose visits filled Ricci's days so that sometimes he did not have time to eat. On ordinary days as many as twenty cards were left at his door. On special occasions such as the New Year the number was never less than one hundred. Elementary requirements of politesse obliged him to return these visits.

Despite the fatigue which this imposed and the long hours of conversation entailed, he found it a highly valuable form of apostolate. All who came to see him were brought into contact with Christianity. Admitting, in a letter to his brother, that in all probability most of his visitors were drawn out of curiosity, it was still true, he said, that "without going out of the house we preach to the gentiles, some of whom are converted, and as for . . . the majority of our visitors who do not renounce their false religion, which grants them greater license, little by little through the contacts which they establish with us God softens their hearts."[4]

It was not only Peking which thus came to know Ricci and his message. From the parlor of his residence his quiet voice and influence reached out into almost every part of the sprawling empire. Peking was the mecca which every year drew thousands of scholars, both those already holding office and those who, through the crucible of the examination system, were preparing for official careers. Ricci has left a description of this feature of life in Peking and its effect upon his work:

> In some years, besides the imperial audiences, doctoral examinations, both civil and military, are held. In other years there are examinations for the civil and military licentiate. Other years bachelors are selected for certain offices. And then one month every year is appointed for officials from the provinces to visit Peking to congratulate the emperor on his birthday; another month is set aside for appointments to certain

> offices, another month for appointment to other offices, etc. Among the thousands who thus flock here from the provinces, there are many who either already know the Fathers in Peking or in other residences, or who have heard of us and our teachings, or have seen the books which we have published. As a result, we have to spend the entire day in the reception hall receiving visitors. Although the fatigue is great, we try always to welcome cordially all who come, thus rendering them benevolent. To all we speak of the things pertaining to our holy faith.[5]

Ricci's accounts do not indicate the high esteem with which he was regarded by innumerable officials from all parts of the empire who had learned, in these intimate gatherings in the Peking residence, to appreciate his qualities of mind and heart. His fellow missionaries were aware of it. Alfonso Vagnoni, writing from Nanking in 1605 to Europe, remarks:

> Incredible is the reputation which good Father Matteo Ricci enjoys among the Chinese, and the extent to which he is visited by important personages and esteemed throughout the whole empire of China. . . . They say that there cannot be another man in Europe equal to him. And when we say that others are more gifted than he, they cannot believe it. In truth . . . he captivates everyone by the graciousness and suavity of his manners, by his conversation and by the solid virtue which his life exhibits.[6]

The phrase "throughout the whole empire" is not simply a rhetorical expression. Thus Kuo Tzu-chang, governor of Kweichow, one of the provinces farthest from Peking, published an edition of Ricci's world-map. In his introduction he defends, against possible detractors, Ricci's qualifications as a geographer. To those who object to receiving lessons in geography from a foreigner, he cites the authority of Confucius who saw nothing incongruous in the Son of Heaven enlisting foreigners in his service. And in any case, he concludes, "Ricci has been so long in China that he is no longer a foreigner, but a Chinese."[7]

Ricci and his teachings were talked about in every province. A certain indication of this was that every year an increasing number of books, published in widely separated localities, spoke of him and his doctrines, both favorably and unfavorably. It was such a book that led to the important discovery of the existence of an ancient Jewish community in China. A Chinese Jew, Ai T'ien, reading about Ricci and Cattaneo and realizing that they were neither

Mohammedans nor pagans, concluded that they must share his Hebrew faith. He sought Ricci out in Peking in June, 1605. Some of Ricci's most interesting pages describe this touching encounter: the first impression, created by Ai's familiarity with Biblical figures, that he was a Christian; the gradual realization, as it became clear that he was acquainted only with characters of the Old Testament, that he was of the Jewish faith; the discovery of the small Jewish community in Kaifeng.[8]

Thus his apostolate by irradiation from his center in Peking was beginning to achieve the twofold end to which it was directed. Christian influences were gradually being diffused throughout the intellectual world, creating an atmosphere propitious to the slow transformation of society and preparing the way for an expanding movement of conversions. At the same time, numerous friends were being won in every province whose authority was calculated to ward off from the not yet deeply rooted Church the dangers of persecution and destruction. From the outset he had resolved to have no recourse to the support of European arms to defend Christianity in China. Not European arms, but Chinese friends were to constitute the main defense of the Church against the attacks of prejudice and ill-will which must inevitably come. It was an enlightened, liberal, humanitarian, Christian, and courageous policy. That it should have been attacked by partisans of Europeanism is not surprising. That it has been made the object of disparaging commentary by those who pride themselves upon their liberalism is at once curious and sad.

Professor Rowbotham provides an interesting example in point. He is drawing a comparison between the Jesuits and the later Protestant groups in China in the nineteenth century. After giving deserved praise to the achievements of the latter, he gratuitously adds:

"What success they had certainly did not come through truckling to officials." The implication is that the success of the Jesuits did come in this fashion. By way of extenuation Rowbotham adds: "But the Protestants had behind them the forceful and organized support of their governments. The Jesuits were pioneers and had to rely upon themselves alone to establish their position in the empire."[9]

The extenuating circumstance is correctly described; but actually there is nothing to extenuate. Ricci and those who followed him tried to break through the wall of prejudice and establish amicable relations with officials. Should they have been truculent in order to avoid being charged with truckling? Ricci endeavored to make friends and he was successful to an amazing degree. He made them with no tricks and no truckling, but simply because he was, by Chinese as well as Western standards, a gentleman, and a man of great personal charm, intelligence, kindliness and sympathy. The evidence on this point is *luce clarius*. If it had depended upon Ricci alone, there never would have arisen those conflicts between civilizations which have written so much unhappiness into the history of the relations of West and East.

An equally important feature of Ricci's apostolate during these years was his literary activity. He had often called attention to the fact that in China, more than in any other country, the pen was the most potent of weapons. In February, 1605, writing to his Jesuit friend Ludovico Maselli, after describing the power of the pen, he concludes:

> If I, who have had to work alone and with no one else to help me, have caused so great a stir in the schools of this country, it is easy to see how much could be accomplished by one less occupied with other matters and of greater talent than I. . . . For this reason I recommend to all our fathers that they devote themselves to the study of Chinese letters as to an affair upon which depends in large measure the conversion of China.[10]

Writing to the general of the Society on August 15, 1608, he expressed the wish that he could be relieved of the office of superior of the mission in order to devote more time to writing books.[11] And to his friend Costa two years later, haunted by the same preoccupation, he wrote: "How much can be done in China through the publication of books."[12] And the next year to the general again: "In China more can be done with books than with words."[13]

In view of his strong convictions on the subject it is not surprising that he applied himself with the collaboration of a small group of talented friends to the multiplication of books. Among those who assisted in this work none is more interesting, considering the circumstances of his collaboration, then Fêng Ying-ching. One of the most high-minded scholar-officials of his time, he presided over the tribunal of criminal justice in Hukuang when the plague of eunuchs swarmed out across the provinces in 1599 to collect the special taxes imposed by the emperor. Already noted as "an enemy of avarice, a friend of the common good and of works of charity, a protector of widows and of the poor," he now distinguished himself by his courageous opposition to the exactions of the eunuchs.[14] He did not hesitate to release the victims of their rapacity when jailed because of inability to meet the demands made upon them. He carried the cause of the people to the imperial court itself, thrice memorializing the emperor and denouncing the excesses of his unscrupulous agents. For his pains the Wan-li emperor ordered him removed from office. He was brought to Peking and thrown into prison. His martyrdom for justice's sake only enhanced his reputation among the people.

While still in Hukuang, Fêng had heard of Ricci. He had sent one of his disciples to Nanking to study mathematics under the direction of the Jesuit; but Ricci had already departed for Peking. Shortly afterwards Fêng himself was brought to the capital. One of the first visitors whom Ricci received after emerging from "the palace for foreigners" was a messenger from Fêng Ying-ching. Ricci, who was aware of the reputation for integrity enjoyed by the prisoner, immediately called upon him. They spent one hour together. Ricci did not see Fêng again during the three years or more of the latter's incarceration in Peking. Immediately after this visit the terms of confinement were made more stringent and Fêng was not allowed to receive visitors. Nevertheless, this one hour together was enough to establish a lasting and intimate friendship. During the next three years the two remained in constant and close contact through the exchange of letters and messages. From his prison cell Fêng gave Ricci valuable advice and encouragement. At his own expense he published a new edition of the treatise on Friendship to which he added a preface of his own composition. He also published "with elegant prefaces" a treatise by Ricci on the four elements, "and other questions pertaining to mathematics, with two small world-maps, together with whatever else he had been able to gather together of our teaching."[15]

He published Ricci's *Er-shih-wu-yen* (Twenty-Five Sentences), a short exposition of essential Christian moral doctrines.[16] In his preface Fêng took pains to point out the superiority of the doctrine it contained to that of the celebrated Buddhist work *Ssu-shih-erh-chang ching* (The Sutra of Forty-two Chapters). Hsü Kuang-ch'i also contributed a preface.

Fêng greatly encouraged the publication of Ricci's master work, the famous *T'ien Chu shih-i* (Treatise on the True Idea of God). It is not possible to list the number of editions this work has known. Its influence reached across the years and across frontiers. It was the reading of this book which induced the great K'ang-hsi emperor to issue his edict of religious toleration on March 22, 1692. It is reviewed in the *Ssu-k'u ch'üan-shu tsung-mu*.[17] It was translated into Japanese, Korean, Indo-Chinese, Mongolian. Almost two centuries after its first appearance François Bourgeois, missionary in China, reported that there were Chinese scholars in his day who read it repeatedly for its literary style.[18]

Yet it is chiefly this work which has led certain critics to place the most fantastic interpretations upon the teaching of Ricci. Thus one writes: "Ricci limited himself to teaching pure deism . . . He mentioned neither the Trinity, nor the Incarnation, nor the Redemption . . . It is probable that his Chinese friends saw in it only a special kind of Buddhism."[19] Another writes: "[Ricci] presented Christianity as a completion of Confucianism."[20] It is as though from a reading of the treatise De Deo one were to conclude that St. Thomas Aquinas was a deist! It is a curious sort of criticism which demands that every time Ricci took brush in hand he should set forth the entire panoply of Christian doctrine.

The *T'ien Chu shih-i* is chiefly a treatise in theodicy and represented in its final form the fruits of ten years reflection and experience. It was directed towards the refutation of opinions with regard to the existence and nature of God and the soul which, from his discussions, he knew constituted fundamental obstacles among intellectuals of the time to the acceptance of Christian revelation. It were futile to talk about the seven sacraments to an adherent of Sung materialism or Buddhist monism. The work is directed towards the remote preparation of the unbelieving mind for the gospel message.

Ricci himself explained as well as anyone could the purpose of the *T'ien Chu shih-i*. After mentioning its publication, he says:

> This does not treat of all the mysteries of our holy faith, which need be explained only to catechumens and Christians, but only of certain principles, especially such as can be proved and understood with the light of natural reason. Thus it can be of service both to Christians and to non-Christians and can be understood in those remote regions which our Fathers cannot immediately reach, preparing the way for those other

> mysteries which depend upon faith and revealed wisdom. It treats of such truths as that there is in the universe a God, who has created all things and continually conserves them in being; that the soul of man is immortal, and will receive from God in the next life remuneration for its good and evil works; that the transmigration of souls into the bodies of other men and of animals is false, and similar things. . . . If it does not propose to refute directly all the errors of the sects in China, it destroys at the roots, with irrefragable arguments, the opinions of the Chinese which contradict those truths. . . . Towards the end it explains something about the coming of Christ our Redeemer into the world to save and teach men, and it urges the Chinese to seek from the Fathers the true doctrine which is taught in greater detail in other books.[21]

So far was it from being regarded as only a "special kind of Buddhism" that it excited lively attacks from Buddhist quarters. Certain influential Buddhist partisans in Peking, not content with publishing polemics against Ricci's theses submitted several memorials to the emperor attacking the missionaries and Christianity.

Ricci had written the first draft of this work in 1593 in Nanchang and as early as 1597 had submitted it to Luis Cerqueira, bishop of Japan resident in Macao, and to Valignano for approval. In Peking he had reworked the entire manuscript, adding his debate with the Buddhist bonze San Hui in Nanking and the gist of his discussions in Peking with Huang Hui, brilliant Buddhist scholar and tutor to Chu Ch'ang-lo, heir to the throne.[22] Fêng Ying-ching read it in manuscript form and corrected the style, being careful, as Ricci wrote Longobardo on September 6, 1602, not to change "the least word without first consulting me."[23] He was impatient to publish it, but Ricci was obliged to await permission from the Inquisition in Goa. Because he found it difficult to explain to his friend the reasons for the long delay — he found it hard to understand himself — he held him off by alleging that the style still needed to be improved. Whereupon Fêng made the pointed observation that, in his opinion, China, from the moral point of view, was in a dangerous condition and only this book could save her. A doctor called to prescribe for a person who is on the point of death would hardly say: "Wait a little: I want to phrase this prescription as elegantly as possible."[24]

Ricci lost this invaluable collaborator when, as a result of the persistent efforts of the highest mandarinal officials in Peking, he was finally released from prison by the emperor and sent back to his home near Nanking. He wanted to receive the sacrament of baptism, but during the two or three days he was in Peking before leaving for the south, his every minute was taken up receiving the stream of mandarins who wished to pay their respects. Ricci was able to see him only briefly. They decided that he should wait until arriving home when one of the priests in Nanking would visit him, complete his instructions, and baptize him. Unfortunately, before one of the priests in Nanking was able to visit him, death unexpectedly struck him down. His Jesuit friends found consolation in the hope, expressed by Ricci, that, "in view of his services to us and of his great desire to aid and further our holy faith and to follow it himself, [God would grant] that this desire for baptism would take the place of actual baptism and win for him the salvation of his soul."[25]

It was during these same years that Ricci met Li Chih-tsao. Born in 1565 in Hangchow, he had received his *chin-shih* degree in 1598 and was appointed an assistant department director in the Board of Public Works in Nanking. He was thus a subordinate of Ricci's good friend Liu Kuan-nan, but does not seem to have met Ricci until after the latter's arrival in Peking where Li had been transferred in 1599. It was probably his keen interest in geography that first attracted him to Ricci. In his youth he had drawn up a description of China with maps of the fifteen provinces, which he regarded as a map of the world. Ricci's world map was a revelation to him. Possessed of an eager and open mind and conscious of the shortcomings of his own knowledge, he immediately undertook under Ricci's direction the study of geography and of Western sciences in general. It was the beginning of a close association which would endure to the end of Ricci's life. Ricci admired the keenness of his intelligence. He would later say that of all the Chinese he knew Li Chih-tsao and Hsü Kuang-ch'i were the only ones who succeeded in acquiring a perfect understanding of Euclidian geometry.

In 1602 he published a new edition of Ricci's revised world map, embellished with poems by a number of scholars. The following year he was in Fukien supervising the provincial examinations, but upon his return to Peking and to a higher office, he resumed his studies. He collaborated with Ricci in writing the *Yüan-jung chiao-i*, a short treatise on geometry not published until 1614, four years after Ricci's death. Another work which bears the impress of his collaboration is Ricci's *T'ung-wên suan-chih*, a translation of Clavius' practical arithmetic, likewise published in 1614 in eleven *chüan*.[26] He also worked with Ricci on the two *chüan* treatise on the stereographic projection of the celestial sphere, published in 1607 under the title of *Hun-kai t'ung-hsien t'u-shuo*, a work which was copied into the *Ssu-k'u* library.[27]

In 1606 Li Chih-tsao, angered by a demotion, retired from public office and returned to his home in Hangchow. He was one of several thousand officials who were deprived of office or reduced in rank in a bureaucratic holocaust. The wholesale lopping of heads was the work of the eunuchs and their partisans. It probably was the immediate occasion for the formation of the Tung-lin party. The charge against Li was that he was too often at the banquet table and too much given to gambling. Both charges may well have been true, but these were common failings in his milieu and obviously no more than pretexts. While in retirement Li published a new edition of Ricci's masterly *T'ien Chu shih-i* with his own preface. He also published another edition of the treatise on Friendship. In 1608, yielding to the importunities of Ricci and other friends, he returned to Peking and resumed his official career.

Li Chih-tsao, unlike Hsü Kuang-ch'i, was not a saint. He was in many respects like Ch'ü Ju-k'uei: a man possessed of a lively intelligence, a forward looking mind, and an engaging personality, but with strong attachments to the good things of life. The chief obstacles to his baptism, which he sought as early as 1603, were concubines. As for many another Chinese the Christian doctrine of monogamy was a "hard saying." Some of Ricci's confrères were critical of his continued friendship with Li. No doubt de Pantoia, always a thorn in Ricci's side, was one of the critics. "It did not seem right to some," reported Trigault, "that the good old man (sic!) should give him so much of his time, giving him a lesson in mathematics every day."[28]

As usual Ricci's intuitions and kindly impulses were not deceived. In March, 1610, less than two months before his own death, Ricci had the consolation of receiving Li Chih-tsao, ready at last to take the plunge into monogamy, into the Church. Most of his family had already preceded him. His baptism worked a transformation in his manner of living and made him indefatigable, throughout the remaining twenty years of his life, in his zeal for the propagation of the faith and in his valorous defense of the missionaries.

In 1604 Hsü Kuang-ch'i successfully passed his doctoral examinations in Peking. Martin Ch'in, who accompanied him to the capital, passed the military doctoral examinations and immediately afterwards received an appointment in the province of Chekiang. In the examinations for civil office, Hsü Kuang-ch'i was among the twenty-four new *chin-shih* admitted to the Han-lin Academy. This necessitated his remaining in the capital for three years to undergo a series of twenty-four supplementary examinations which led to special distinction for the twelve highest ranking candidates, of which he was one.

During these three years in Peking Hsü Kuang-ch'i worked continuously with Ricci, translating works on mathematics, hydraulics, astronomy, and geography. One of the most influential of these translations was Euclid's *Elements*, published under the title *Chi-ho yüan-pên*, in six *chüan*. It was written by Hsü at Ricci's dictation and, after several revisions, published in 1611.

Hsü Kuang-ch'i and Ricci were kindred spirits. Highly spiritual, possessed of a perfectly balanced temperament, sound judgment, profound faith, unaffected humility, a courageous readiness to sacrifice his career in defense of Christianity, he became, after Ricci's death, the chief support of the Church in China. He was like Ricci too in the inerrancy of his judgment on matters of policy. The missionaries learned from experience that they could ignore his counsel only with cost to themselves and their work.

In 1606 Hsü Kuang-ch'i's father, Hsü Ssu-ch'êng, came to Peking, where he received baptism. Hsü Ma-chi, Hsü Kuang-ch'i's only son, was also baptized taking the Christian name Jacob. In 1607 Hsü Kuang-ch'i became a corrector in the Han-lin Academy. Shortly thereafter his father died. At the funeral services held in Peking, he carefully excluded any rites that were "contrary to what Christianity allowed, consulting the Fathers on every point."[29]

Hsü Kuang-ch'i resigned his office and returned to his home in Shanghai to observe the three-year period of mourning. He returned to Peking to resume his office as corrector of the Han-lin Academy in 1610, a few months after Ricci's death.

One of the most widely read of Ricci's works, written during this period, was his *Chi-jên shih-p'ien*, (Ten Paradoxes or, more exactly, Ten Truths Contrary to Common Opinion). Published in two *chüan* in Peking in 1607, by the summer of 1608 it had gone through several reprintings, including one in Nanking and another in Nanchang. Ricci was moved to write this work by the advice of friends. The *T'ien Chu shih-i* had, by its direct attack upon Buddhist beliefs, excited such strong reaction that some of his friends suggested the advisability of avoiding for the time being frontal assault upon Buddhism. Why not write, in the style of the widely admired *Chiao-yu lun*, upon certain Christian views of life? The *Chi-jên shih-p'ien* was the result of this suggestion.

The ten treatises dealt with such subjects as the value of time, the problem of evil, the advantages of reflecting upon death, preparing for the judgment to follow death, the wisdom of silence, the rationale of fasting and abstaining, the benefits of self-examination and self-improvement, the necessity of sanctions in a next life, the folly of seeking to know the future, the miserable state of the avaricious rich man. As Ricci remarked in a letter to Aquaviva, these doctrines seemed to the Christian more *catadoxa* than *paradoxa*. But to the Chinese, and he regarded this as a proof of the unhappy state of thought among them, they were indeed paradoxes. The wide vogue enjoyed by the work indicates that Ricci was right. Even he was surprised at the wide interest this book aroused in intellectual circles. "It is difficult to believe," he wrote.[30] And a few months later he reported that, while all of his books had been well received, none had attracted as much attention as the *Paradoxes*.[31]

Ricci's efforts were not confined exclusively to these two principal features of his apostolate. There was a constantly, if slowly, growing community of Christians to care for. De Pantoia seems to have devoted most of his time to this work, but Ricci was also active. He baptized his first two Peking converts on June 10, 1601. In a letter of May 9, 1605, he gives the number of Christians in Peking as over a hundred.[32]

The first Christians of Peking were few, but they were outstanding and reflected great credit upon the faith. They were from all levels of society. The first convert was from the common people. His Chinese name is not recorded. He took the Christian name of Benedict and led an exemplary life until his death in 1624 at the age of eighty-four. Other converts included mandarins holding office, two sons of the emperor's personal physician, the husband of a sister of the empress.

Perhaps, the most zealous and edifying of these first converts was (Paul) Li Ying-shih. Keenly intelligent, but much addicted to astrology and to *fêng-shui* superstitions, he was not easily converted. Attracted to Ricci first by the appeal of science, he put up a stubborn battle of the intellect against the arguments in behalf of Christianity. Once his last intellectual defenses fell his conversion was complete. On the day of his baptism he laid on the altar a written profession of faith. This was no doubt the first observance of a custom which was thereafter universally followed.[33]

Ricci's success in Peking prompted Valignano to reorganize the administration of the mission. In 1601 he replaced Manoel Dias as rector of the college in Macao with Valentim Carvalho and sent Dias to visit the four houses in China. He spent two months with Ricci in Peking, bringing with him (James) Ni Yi-ch'êng, a candidate for admission to the Society as a lay brother.

In 1603 Valignano removed the Chinese mission entirely from the jurisdiction of the rector of Macao, an arrangement which had never been satisfactory. The line of command henceforth was to run directly from the superior of the China mission to the vice-provincial of Japan and from him to the provincial of India. Ricci had long urged this. He had also urged that he be relieved of command. Unwilling to grant this, Valignano appointed Dias as superior of the three southern houses, Nanking, Nanchang and Shaochow, but subordinate to Ricci. He also recommended to the general, after consultations both in Japan and in Macao, the establishment of a Japan-China province separate from India.

The financial support of the missions in Japan and China was always a grave problem. Organizations, such as the Propagation of the Faith, which today sustain the foreign missions of the Church, did not then exist. The missions had to rely chiefly upon the generosity of the king of Spain (and Portugal) and of the pope. And these proved slender reeds indeed. C.R. Boxer, in this connection, quotes the Spanish proverb: "Socorro de España o llega tarde o nunca," (Help from Spain arrives late or never).[34] Promised papal subsidies materialized as seldom as the royal promises. Valignano never ceased urging that the Japanese mission be endowed with landed income property to meet its needs, which were great. By 1590 there were 136 Jesuits in Japan, 170 catechists, a caretaking and domestic staff of 300, to support. There were over 200 churches, a mission press, schools, hospitals, and seminaries to maintain. In an effort to adopt a rational plan to meet the difficulty Valignano in 1578 made an agreement with the Macao trading community permitting the Jesuits to invest in the Macao-Nagasaki silk trade.[35] Each year a cargo of 1,600 piculs of silk was shipped to Japan in which each local merchant had a share. The Jesuits were allowed to invest in a total of 100 piculs. This arrangement was approved by Pope Gregory XIII, ratified in 1582 by the viceroy of India and in 1589 by the senate of Macao.

No one pretended that this was an ideal way to support the missions. Francis Borgia, general of the society, had earlier expressed distaste for resorting to trade as a prop for the missions. His successor Claudio Aquaviva, although approving it as a necessity, was not happy about it. The large number of letters on the subject from various Jesuits in Japan which are found in the Roman archives of the Society reveal clearly that many of them had misgivings about it.[36] The greedy Macao merchants who begrudged yielding any part of the trading profits to the missions complained to king and pope. One of the striking characteristics of the mission history of this period being the large number of religious filled with holy zeal to cast the mote from their brother's eye, it comes as no surprise to learn that in Manila Fray Martin Acerca bitterly attacked the Jesuits in print. Valignano published an unimpassioned reply, a simple statement of the facts.[37]

This was an age in which commercial enterprise had not yet achieved a full status of respectability. The better people did not indulge in trade. They lived off their landed estates or their benefices or their inherited riches. This perhaps explains some of the concern about the Jesuits' involvement in trade. For this was not a black market operation. It was a legitimate trade from which everyone benefitted, the Chinese who supplied the silk, the Japanese who bought it, the Portuguese who acted as middlemen.

In the modern world in which trade is king the cry of scandal is less easy to understand, particularly in view of the fact that the minimal annual expenses of the Japanese missions amounted to 12,000 ducats, whereas the total annual profit from their participation in the silk trade brought the Jesuits between 4,000 and 6,000 ducats. The reply of Valignano to criticism seems beyond reproach. It was a question of trade or of closing down the thriving missions in Japan. As soon as pope or king or someone else provided the necessary funds the Jesuits would gladly withdraw from the silk trade.

The China enterprise was also largely dependent upon these revenues which, however, often failed entirely when the silk-bearing ship fell victim to typhoons or to Dutch piracy. Such was the case in 1604 and the disaster was a rude blow to Valignano's plan to reinforce the China mission personnel and to strengthen its financial position. The annual cargo of silk had already been stowed aboard the Great Ship which lay at anchor at Macao ready to sail for Japan. Officers and most of the crew were ashore when two Dutch corsairs and a brigantine, under the command of Captain Cornelius van Veen of the fleet of Admiral Wijbrand van Waerijck, swooped down like birds of prey. The Dutch seized the ship and, after transferring the silk to their own holds, burned her and sailed off to Holland with a cargo of stolen silk valued at two million Chinese dollars in which the Jesuits had an investment of 15,000 ducats.[38]

Valignano, who had experienced similar disasters before, had to modify his plans to suit the emergency. The Macao Jesuits, always quick to advise retrenchment in China, strongly urged him to close the Shaochow and Nanchang residences. This he refused to do, but he had to trim the budget projected for the four residences already established. The missionaries, who were already on a diet of rice and water with a little meat added once a week, tightened their belts and perhaps added more water to the rice. Despite this blow Valignano was able to send eight more priests into China in 1604 and 1605. Ricci was moved to tears of joy.

The loss of the ship to the Dutch had prevented Valignano from providing the six or seven hundred *scudi* needed to buy a house in Peking, but with the help of Hsü Kuang-ch'i and other friends a loan was negotiated and on August 27, 1605, the Jesuits moved into their own house. A chapel was fitted out large enough to accommodate all the Christians in Peking.

The number of Christians was growing. In 1605 de Pantoia began to visit villages in the region about Paoting, a city south of Peking. Gaspar Ferreira succeeded him in this work and by 1607 there were some one hundred and fifty Christians in this area. Writing to his brother in Macerata on August 24, 1608, Ricci reported that there were "already more than two thousand Christians, among them many scholars."[39]

This number represented the immediate fruit of twenty-six years of patient labor. But the prescience of Ricci saw in it only reason for hope. He knew the dynamic potentialities contained in the seed now planted in Chinese soil. In all fifteen provinces of China he had friends sympathetic to him and to what he represented. He knew, of course, that clumsy hands could destroy the tender plant before it reached maturity. Hence to the end of his life he adhered to the policy of laying firm foundations:

> We desired [he wrote] to build something solid, so that converts would answer to the name of Christian and, in these beginnings, spread the good odor of our faith. For this reason the number of baptized is not as great as might be wished.[40]

In his last letter from Peking, written on February 17, 1609, he insists upon the importance of sending to China men who are not only "good, but also men of talent, since we are dealing with a people both intelligent and learned."[41]

Ricci's work was done. The circumstances of his last months indicate that he sensed the end approaching.[42] Inasmuch as he was not yet sixty years of age and was apparently in good health this seems curious. Nevertheless, he had several times predicted that he did not have a long old age to look forward to. The labors which he had borne had been crushing. All the contemporary accounts mention this. The months immediately preceding his death had been especially difficult. It was the year of doctoral examinations in Peking. The constant flow of visitors was so great, says de Ursis, that Ricci often did not have time to eat. From morning to night he was busy receiving callers.

Strongly suggesting that he sensed these to be the last months of his life, he completed his memoirs, burned his letters, put his papers in order, drew up directives to be followed in the affairs of the mission in case of his death, named Longobardo his successor. His companions also noted that he spent a longer time in prayer in the evenings than had been his wont. He was heard to remark on several occasions that he thought the greatest service he could now render the advancement of the faith among the Chinese was to die. "Unless the grain of wheat fall to the ground. . . ." Evidently he felt that *his* task had been accomplished. The soil was cleared. The time had come for the planting.

On May 3, 1610, he suddenly became seriously ill. Li Chih-tsao, himself ill at the time, sent the best doctor in Peking to attend him. His prescriptions were unavailing. A consultation of six doctors resulted only in disagreement and produced three different diagnoses.

Christians and personal friends flocked to see him in such numbers that the "house was filled," de Ursis says. With his habitual graciousness Ricci had himself moved to a more commodious room so as to be able to receive his visitors. On May 9 he received viaticum, insisting upon getting up from his bed and kneeling down. The same day he became delirious. The next day, his mind clear again, he asked for the sacrament of extreme unction. Throughout that day and the next he conversed freely with de Pantoia and de Ursis and with the Christians who crowded into his room.

As the evening of May 11 approached he smilingly gave his blessing to his fellow Jesuits. At seven o'clock he quietly turned on his side and gently slipped off into eternity. A constant stream of visitors, including most of Peking officialdom, came during the two days following his quiet death to pay their respects to this priest who, a foreigner, was no alien and who had so greatly appealed to Chinese minds and hearts. Immediately after his death Li Chih-tsao drew up a memorial addressed to the emperor requesting that, in view of the great merits of Li Ma-t'ou, the Westerner become Chinese, a worthy burial ground be assigned to receive his body. The Board of Rites added its own memorial approving the request. Yeh Hsiang-kao lent the full weight of his prestige and authority to bring the affair to a successful conclusion.

The request was granted. An imperial rescript gave the Jesuits title to a plot of land, the property of a eunuch, situated near one of the gates of the western wall of Peking. On November 1, 1611, Ricci's body was entombed. He had not been wrong in his premonition that his death would serve the interests of Christianity. The imperial grant served both as official recognition of the accepted status of Ricci and as a protection for the religion which he had taught.

Several years later Ricci's old friend, Wang Ying-ling, become governor of Peking, issued an official proclamation to be carved in stone and erected at his grave.[43] Against the background of the sober text sketching his career, the extraordinary and far-reaching impact which Ricci had upon Chinese society stands out in sharp relief;

for here are mentioned, as though in passing, only a few of the noted scholars and scholar-officials with whom he stood on terms of intimate friendship:

Wang Hung-hui, Minister of Rites; Chu Shih-lu, Censor; Chang Mêng-nan, Minister of Finance; Fêng Ch'i, Minister of Rites; Li T'ai-tsai, Minister of Civil Offices; Ts'ao Yü-pien, Censor; Hsü Kuang-ch'i, Academician; Li Chih-tsao, Director in Ministry of Public Works; Kung Tao-li, Assistant Governor of Kwangtung Province; Chêng Yi-wei, Director of Education to the Heir Apparent; P'êng Wei-ch'êng, Censor; Chou Ping-mu, Academician and Assistant Minister of Rites; Wang Chia-chih, Academician; Hsiung Ming-yü, Censor; Yang T'ing-yün, Province Director of Education, P'êng Jui-wo, Provincial Censor; Fêng Ying-ching, Assistant Provincial Judge; Ts'ui Ch'ang, Secretary of Ministry of Civil Offices; Ch'ên Liang-ts'ai, Assistant Provincial Judge; Liu Yin-ch'ang, Sub-prefect; Wu Tao-nan, Acting Minister of Rites; Huang Chi-shih, Governor of Peking. As Henri Bernard has well said:

> It is Chinese society in mourning for him whom it had so completely adopted, the Doctor of the Occident, Li-Ma-t'ou. [44]

NOTES

(1) *FR*, II, 159 f.
(2) De Pantoia, *op. cit.*, p. 117.
(3) *Opere storiche*, II, 377-388.
(4) *Ibid.*, p. 375 f.
(5) *FR*, II, 353 f.
(6) *Opere storiche*, I, 499, n. 1.
(7) Pasquale D'Elia, S. J., "Due amici dal P. Matteo Ricci ridotti all'unità", *Archivum Historicum Societatis Jesu*, VI (Roma, 1937), pp. 303-310.
(8) *FR*, II, 315-325; on Judaism in K'ai-fêng-fu cf. Jerome Tobar, S. J. *Inscriptions juives de K'ai-fêng* (Shanghai: Mission catholique, 1912).
(9) Rowbotham, *op. cit.*, p. 63.
(10) *Opere storiche*, II, 257.
(11) *Ibid.*, p. 301.
(12) *Ibid.*, p. 336.
(13) *Ibid.*, p. 343.
(14) *FR*, II, 163.
(15) *Ibid.*, p. 165 f.
(16) *Ibid.*, p. 287, n. 3.
(17) This imperial catalogue compiled by order of the Ch'ien-lung emperor, chiefly between the years 1772-1788, purported to have as its object the preservation of all worthy literary works. To be excluded, however, was no proof of literary demerit, for the catalogue was also used as an instrument of reprisal against those scholars who had been hostile to the Manchus. Cf. L. C. Goodrich, *op. cit.*, pp. 258 ff. For more details on this famous catalogue cf. *Eminent Chinese*, I, 120-123.

NOTES

(18) Cf. also D'Elia's excellent note, *FR*, II, 293 n. 1.
(19) Reville, *op. cit.*, pp. 669 f.
(20) H. Boehmer, *Les Jésuites*, tr. by G. Monod, 2 ed., (Paris: Armand Colin, 1910), p. 166.
(21) *FR*, II, 292.
(22) *Ibid.*, p. 180, n. 6.
(23) *Ibid.*, p. 292, n. 1.
(24) *Ibid.*, p. 301.
(25) *Ibid.*, p. 168.
(26) Cf. D'Elia's analysis of this work, *FR*, II, 175, n. 2.
(27) Cf. *Eminent Chinese*, I, 452 f., and *FR*, II, 174, n. 1.
(28) *Litterae Societatis Jesu a regno Sinarum annorum MDCX et XI ad R. P. Claudium Aquavivum eiusdem Societatis praepositum generalem; auctore P. Nicolao Trigautio, eiusdem Societatis* (Augustae Vindelicorum: Christophorus Mangium, 1615), p. 24; hereafter cited as *Lit. X-XI*.
(29) *FR*, II, 361.
(30) *Opere storiche*, II, 343; and cf. D'Elia, *FR*, II, 302, n. 1.
(31) *Opere storiche*, II, 360.
(32) *Ibid.*, p. 263.
(33) *FR*, II, 263 f. gives the text of the profession.
(34) C. R. Boxer, *op. cit.*, p. 119.
(35) Cf. *ibid.*, pp. 117 ff.
(36) Aquaviva's view is stated in a letter of Feb. 19, 1582, found in *ARSI*, Jap-Sin 9 I, f. 81. Numerous letters by Jesuits in Japan, indicating the amount of soul-searching that went on, are in *ARSI*, Jap-Sin 8 I, 9 I-II, 10 II, 11 I, 12 I, 14 I, 15 I-II, 16 II, 17, 18 I, 20 I. In a letter of March 21, 1613, Jap-Sin 56, f. 159, the future martyr Carlo Spinola worried about a tendency of some local superiors to engage in a little extra-curricular trade to help meet the demands of their own mission house; but in a letter of October 8, 1618, Jap-Sin 36, f. 193, this abuse having been corrected, he finds nothing wrong with the way the trade is conducted.
(37) Valignano's reply is found in Colin-Pastells, *op. cit.*, II, 682-692.
(38) Valignano's letter of Jan. 21, 1604 from Macao to the Portuguese Assistant tells of the disaster, *ARSI*, Jap-Sin 14 ff. 156 r/v.
(39) *Opere storiche*, II, 376.
(40) *FR*, II, 347.
(41) *Opere storiche*, II, 390.
(42) There are a number of accounts of Ricci's last days. There is the eye-witness account of Sebastiano de Ursis written on May 20, 1610, less than two weeks after Ricci's death, in *ibid.*, pp. 483-488; Trigault adds further details, *FR*, II, 530 ff., and *Lit. X-XI*, pp. 31 ff.
(43) The full Chinese text with Italian translation is given by D'Elia, *FR*, III, 9 ff.
(44) Henri Bernard, S. J., *Le père Matthieu Ricci et la société chinoise de son temps* (1552-1610) (Tientsin: Hautes Etudes, 1937), II, 374.

Chapter VII

Storm Warnings

As HE LAY DYING in the gathering shadows of his room Ricci had remarked to de Ursis: "I leave you before a door open to great merits, but not without numerous dangers and much labor." Not once during his twenty-eight years in China had he deceived himself about the pioneering nature of his work. Eleven years before, he had described his task as one of clearing the soil. "*Aprire i boschi fieri,*" was how he had put it in his native tongue. In the last hushed moments of his life he was conscious of having accomplished his task, although, evidently with St. Paul's text in mind *(ostium mihi apertum est magnum et evidens: et adversarii multi)*, he had changed the metaphor.

The door was open, but there were many dangers still to be faced and it would require great virtue and much labor to keep the door open. Ricci was in no wise deceived on this point. He might have been pardoned if, in his last moments, yielding to the satisfaction of a task well done, he had exaggerated the extent of his gains. But the abhorrence for hyperbole and the sobriety of judgment which had distinguished him throughout life were with him to the end. Almost his last words sounded a warning against excessive optimism. The Church was still far from being deeply rooted. Prudence could not be thrown to the winds. It was still necessary to proceed, as he had long before observed, "*à piè di piombo.*"

Not all of Ricci's confrères shared his attitude of restraint. One who shared it least was his successor as superior of the mission, Nicolò Longobardo. Longobardo was a man of indefatigable zeal and exemplary virtue. He was one of the true giants of the China mission. Laboring without remiss almost to the moment of his death, on December 11, 1654, at the patriarchal age of 95, his phenomenal career was an epic of devoted service. His virtues had been fully recognized by Ricci who wrote to the general of the order urging that Longobardo be made a professed member of the Society and who named him, subject to the approval of the provincial for Japan, his successor.[1]

It is nevertheless true that Longobardo in his first years as superior was excessively optimistic. This optimism was, in fact, evidenced from the very beginning of his apostolate in China. He arrived in China in 1597 and less than a year later wrote a long letter to Europe filled with naive extravagances of judgment and unrealistic appraisals of the factual situation.[2]

If Longobardo were to be believed, Plato would find in China the perfect realization of his ideal Republic. Virtue flourished on every hand. The Chinese were assiduous in almsgiving, in supporting hospitals, caring for the poor! They highly praised monogamous marriage! (He overlooks the fact that they did not widely practice it.) They examined their conscience, did penance, fasted, and gave themselves to contemplation "like the ancient Fathers of the desert!"

The China that Longobardo described never existed. Since he was an honest man his enthusiastic picture can be explained only by the fact that he was less than a year in the country when he wrote this letter and had as yet been nowhere but to Shaochow.

He certainly could not have read Chinese with any great facility at that time and his speaking knowledge was still quite limited. Perhaps a Chinese whom he had employed to tutor him in the language was indulging in a bit of fanciful romancing about his country, and Longobardo accepted literally everything he said.

The nearly always correct Bartoli has accused Longobardo of scorning Ricci's intellectual apostolate and other writers have accepted this judgment. "Longobardo . . . in the beginning held views entirely contrary to those of Ricci," Bartoli says, "and wrote of him as though he were pusillanimous, lacking in confidence, or at least excessively cautious, and he laughed at and ridiculed his efforts to win the mandarins to him through mathematics; afterwards taught by the unhappy result of his fervor, which brought him to the brink of being thrown out of China along with all the others who were there, if the favor enjoyed by Ricci with the mandarins had not saved him, he became wise at his own expense, and abandoning his badly inspired opinion from then on faithfully followed the road marked out by Ricci. . . ."[3]

The letters of Longobardo in the Jesuit archives do not reveal any such attitude, unless one reads sarcasm into a casual reference in one of his earliest letters from China to "glass prisms and similar objects" to which he does not seem to attach much value as tools of the apostolate.[4] This is rather insubstantial evidence upon which to build a serious case. It is probable that Bartoli was prejudiced by adverse reports of Macao Jesuits who bitterly opposed Longobardo's attempts to win independent status for the China mission and who bombarded Rome with letters attacking him. Bartoli wrote with these letters before him and they undoubtedly affected his judgment.

Actually Longobardo seems to have been fully aware of how greatly the direct apostolate depended upon the indirect apostolate of Ricci. In his first letter to the general of the Society after taking over Ricci's job, he left no doubt about his realization of how much the mission owed to his predecessor. "With the death of Father Ricci," he wrote, "we are left orphans, as your Paternity can imagine; for his authority and fame served as a shade and a shield for all of us. Let us hope that from heaven he can help us even more."[5] It is interesting that when Valignano died five years earlier Ricci had made the same comment. "We are left as it were orphans," he had written.[6]

That Longobardo did not undervalue the importance of the intellectual apostolate is proved by the fact that one of the important tasks he entrusted to Nicolas Trigault when he sent him off to Europe in 1613 was to gather all the good books he could. He wanted every residence in China equipped with a library. While his own early writings were entirely devotional in character, he later, in 1624, published a treatise on earthquakes entitled *Ti-chên-chieh*. In the field of philosophy he wrote a one *chüan* work which bore the title *Ling-hun tao-t'i shuo* (Treatise on the Substance of the Soul). And in 1642, in the genre of Ricci's best apologetic work, he published a small treatise in which he undertook to answer the difficulties of a pagan scholar on such questions as the first cause, the Incarnation, eternal life, the cult of spirits, chastity, polygamy, and other subjects.[7]

It is impossible, therefore, to infer from the evidence that Longobardo did not wholeheartedly agree with the wisdom of Ricci's methods. The only difference lay in Longobardo's excessively optimistic appraisal of the situation. Ricci too was optimistic, but he knew that caution was still in order. The door was open, but there were dangers lurking across that threshold. Longobardo underestimated these dangers. He had worked out a thesis to prove that there was no longer any danger of expulsion from China.[8]

It cannot be denied that the developments in the years immediately preceding and following Ricci's death seemed to justify an optimistic view. New foundations, one in Shanghai in 1608 and one in Hangchow in 1611, added to the growing sense of security. Events in both Peking and Nanking encouraged roseate hopes for the future. The successful entry into China of several more Jesuits, some of whom were destined to figure prominently in the history of the mission was a happy augury.

At the request of Hsü Kuang-ch'i, Lazzaro Cattaneo was sent to Shanghai in September, 1608. The zeal of Hsü Kuang-ch'i was chiefly responsible for the progress of this new center. Within two years there were more than two hundred Christians in Shanghai. These promising beginnings naturally raised the question of making it a permanent post. However, Shanghai was at that time a city of minor importance. While the question was being discussed, Li Chih-tsao, passing through Nanking en route to his home in Hangchow, urged that a residence be established in the latter city rather than in Shanghai. Hangchow was the capital of a province. It was easy to reach Shanghai from there, thus assuring that the Christian community in that city would not be neglected. Hsü Kuang-ch'i supported this view.

The decision was made. In the spring of 1611, Cattaneo, Nicolas Trigault, who had arrived in China a few months earlier, and (Sebastian) Chung Ming-jên went to Hangchow. Li Chih-tsao lodged them in his country house until he could find a place for them in the city. There they celebrated Mass for the first time on May 8, 1611.[9]

During his first months in Hangchow Cattaneo made a conquest which ranks in importance with the conversion of Hsü Kuang-ch'i and Li Chih-tsao. The winning to the faith of Yang T'ing-yün completed the triumvirate which was to become known as the *K'ai-chiao san-ta chu-shih* (The Three Pillars of the Early Catholic

Church).[10]

In 1611, after a distinguished career as scholar-official, Yang was living in retirement in Hangchow where he had organized a philosophical society known as the *Chên-shih shê* (Truth Society). Like many Confucian scholars of his day he was deeply interested in Buddhism. He made large contributions to the monasteries in Hangchow and associated with priests of the Ch'an (Zen) sect. He met Cattaneo in the home of his relative, Li Chih-tsao. Interested by Cattaneo's discussion of the existence and nature of God he invited the Jesuit to his villa. For nine days, sometimes talking far into the night, the two men discussed the Christian argument.

Yang T'ing-yün was not one easily persuaded. A man of considerable acumen he disputed every foot of the ground. The doctrine of the Incarnation was the greatest stumbling block on the level of dogma. Only after the battle had swayed back and forth across the whole field of discussion, covering the economy of man's supernatural destiny, his fall and redemption, did Yang T'ing-yün at length give way.

It is interesting that this particular difficulty was one of those most frequently encountered by the Jesuits. More than one Chinese intellectual, otherwise strongly attracted to the faith, felt that there was an essential incompatibility between the notion of the Incarnation and the majesty of God. This was what prevented Yeh Hsiang-kao, for so many years a good friend, from becoming a Christian.

This perhaps reveals something of the psychology of the Chinese. This is certainly a more nobly inspired objection than most of the objections to the Christian faith common in the West, but it reveals a limited understanding of the nature of love. To love is to give oneself. To love infinitely is to give oneself without limit. If Yeh Hsiang-kao and others grasped, perhaps better than many Christians, the implications of the Incarnation, they underestimated the infinite capacity for love proper to divinity.

In the moral order Yang's principal difficulty was also one he shared with many another Chinese intellectual: he had two wives. For a man of his sensibility the exigencies of Christian moral doctrine on this point were excruciatingly painful. It seemed to him "a manifest offense against the natural law, and against the first principles of Chinese honor, to repudiate one who was not only innocent of all fault, but who had merited well of him."[11] Only at the end of a severe struggle with himself was he able to overcome his scruples and, after providing generously for her, to dismiss his second wife.

The story of his conversion and the motives conducing to it were later told by Giulio Aleni in an essay entitled *Yang Ch'i-yuan hsien-shêng ch'ao-hsing shih-chi* (The Spiritual Odyssey of Yang Ch'i-yuan). Ch'i-yuan was Yang's literary name. Aleni, one of his closest Jesuit friends, had the story from Yang himself.

In his full official ceremonial dress Yang T'ing-yün received the sacrament of baptism on Easter Sunday, 1613, taking the Christian named Michael. His entire family took instructions in the faith. Some thirty baptisms, including those of his father and mother, followed. Yang's wife was the last to yield to the arguments of Christian apologetics. The fact that it had removed from contention a rival claimant to her husband's affections did not prejudice her in favor of the faith. Not until 1615 did she accept it. Following her baptism her husband, in thanksgiving, purchased the house which Cattaneo had been renting in Hangchow and presented it to the Jesuits. He also bought a piece of property outside the city to serve as a cemetery for poor Christians.

Yang T'ing-yün became an ardent Christian. With friends and relatives, converted largely through his efforts, he organized a society devoted to self-improvement in the understanding and practice of Christian doctrine. He wrote and published, with a preface by Li Chih-tsao, a tract explaining the tenets of Christianity. In 1615 he gathered together and published, under the title *Chüeh-chiao t'ung-wên chi*, sixty-seven miscellaneous items relating to Western science, geography, philosophy and Christianity, which had appeared in Chinese since the advent of Ruggieri. In one of the two prefaces which he wrote to this work he defended the essential unity of the human race.[12]

Some time after 1615 Yang returned to official life. He served as vice-governor of the metropolitan area of Peking. In 1620 he again retired, in time to escape the intrigues and persecutions of Wei Chung-hsien. The last years of his life were devoted entirely to furthering the cause of Christianity. In numerous articles he argued the superiority of Christianity to Buddhism. He devoted two works to the incompatibility of the two: his *T'ien-shih ming-p'ien* (A Clear Differentiation Between Christianity and Buddhism) and his *Hsiao-lüan pu-ping-ming shuo* (The Owl and the Pheasant Cannot

Harmonize). In 1623 he collaborated with Giulio Aleni to produce the *Chih-fang wai-chi*, descriptive notices in five *chüan* of the then known countries of the world. This work was later copied into the *Ssu-k'u* library. The foundation for this treatise consisted in the explanatory notes which de Pantoia and de Ursis had written, in compliance with an imperial order, to the World-map (*the K'un-yü wan-kuo ch'üan t'u)* which Ricci had presented to the throne in 1601.

Yang T'ing-yün, like Ch'ü Ju-k'uei, Hsü Kuang-ch'i, Li Chih-tsao, and many others, belonged to that group of forward-looking, open-minded intellectuals who refused to be chained to the narrow provincialism of Sung orthodoxy. Men of vision, cosmopolitan by instinct, they sensed the fruitful potentialities which a rapprochement between the cultures of East and West offered to China. In a preface, written in 1623, to Aleni's work *Hsi-hsüeh fan* (General Survey of Western Knowledge), Yang T'ing-yün remarked: "Some seven thousand titles of western books have come to this country from overseas, all of which ought to be translated. . . If I had ten years to collaborate with a score or more persons of like ambition we together could complete the task."[13]

Developments in Peking after the death of Ricci also encouraged fond hopes for the future. In December, 1610, the astronomers of the imperial college erred in predicting an eclipse. They defended themselves by attributing the error to faults in the traditional system of calculation which they were obliged to use. Hsü Kuang-ch'i persuaded the Board of Rites to petition the emperor to entrust the correction of the system and the emendation of the calendar to the Jesuits.

This démarche led to a discussion among the Jesuits as to whether such work was appropriate to the purpose which had brought them to China. They decided, in view of the indirect benefits to the faith, to accept the commission should they be ordered to do so.

The emperor handed down an affirmative response to the petition of the Board of Rites. De Ursis and de Pantoia immediately set to work. De Ursis, with the aid of Hsü Kuang-ch'i and Li Chih-tsao translated into Chinese a treatise on planetary theory (Hsü Kuang-ch'i wanted the Jesuits to translate not only their books on mathematics, but everything that had been written in Europe on every kind of science; an impossible task, but a splendid dream!). By means of a comparative study of observations of a series of lunar eclipses observed in China, India, and Europe, de Ursis determined the longitude of Peking. Meanwhile de Pantoia calculated the latitude of most of the chief cities of the empire from Canton to Peking.

The undertaking did not get beyond these preliminary stages. The jealousy of mathematicians attached to the imperial college proved an insurmountable obstacle. News that the European missionaries had received an imperial mandate to reform the calendar had been published throughout the empire. The enhanced prestige which thus accrued to the Jesuits was extremely beneficial to the cause of Christianity, but it sat ill with the discredited members of the imperial college. In order to "save face" they demanded that they be raised in dignity and that their salaries be doubled. Supported by intrigants among the eunuchs and by old guard reactionaries, they threatened to stir up a tempest. The emperor, unwilling to face the issue courageously, ordered the project abandoned.

With the abandonment of calendar reform, de Ursis turned his talents to the construction of hydraulic machines. They created a sensation. Officials of every rank: the grand-secretaries, governors, intendants, prefects came to see them. Hsü Kuang-ch'i persuaded de Ursis to write a treatise on hydraulics. The result was a six *chüan* work published in 1612 under the title *T'ai-hsi shui-fa* (Western Hydraulics). De Ursis wrote the work in the vernacular. Hsü Kuang-ch'i translated it into elegant literary style. He included it in his monumental sixty *chüan* treatise on agriculture entitled *Nung-chêng ch'üan-shu* (Complete Work on Agricultural Administration) which later formed the basis for a similar work, entitled *Shou-shih t'ung-k'ao* begun by imperial order in 1737 and completed in 1742.[14]

So many prominent officials wrote prefaces for de Ursis' treatise that many of them had to be omitted. Four were included, the most important of which was from the pen of the chief monitor of the emperor. One of the other prefaces, written by a celebrated official, extolled Christianity as a doctrine which taught the knowledge of the one true God and of eternal salvation. When the book was published de Ursis presented copies to the most important officials at court, including the grand secretaries, who received him with courtesy, each of them sending a member of his household to return the visit the following day.

Further symbolizing the constantly increased recognition which the Jesuits were winning, and encouraging a deceptive feeling of security, was an imperial request, transmitted through the eunuchs, for a map describing "the four parts of the world, each separated from the other."[15] Pantoia, who had been trained by Ricci, prepared the map. The Chinese Jesuit lay brother and artist (James) Ni Yi-ch'êng decorated it and illuminated it with golden letters. Hsü Kuang-ch'i stylized the geographical and historical description. This section included an explanation of the Roman Catholic faith, and the number of nations which professed it.

If these developments encouraged optimism, other events of fairly recent occurrence should have suggested that the environment still called for a policy of circumspection. There had been a terrible massacre of Chinese in Manila in 1603.[16] This event aroused excitement in Peking. Feeling ran high against the Spaniards. It had seemed almost a miracle to Ricci that the resentment of the Chinese against this savage manifestation of Western barbarism did not vent itself upon the Jesuit missionaries in the empire. In any event it did not render easier the delicate task of effecting a rapprochement between East and West.

Then, in 1606, Canton had been the center of a storm which might well have proved disastrous. Though not without its comic aspects, it was a serious, and in at least one of its consequences, a tragic affair. It had its origin in one of the innumerable disputes among religious which disfigured the history of Macao.[17] Most of these disputes had their origin in nationalism, in the attitude of Portuguese merchants who looked upon every attempt by Spanish religious to establish themselves in Macao as a prelude to an invasion by Spanish commercial interests. The union of the Crowns of Spain and Portugal in 1580 intensified Portuguese fears as well as Spanish ambitions.

In addition to this there was a psychological factor of utmost importance at the root of many of these disputes. Historians who overlook it will never write the real story. The inhabitants of Macao, lay and religious, suffered from claustrophobia. Forbidden to pass the wall shutting off the Chinese mainland, they were literally imprisoned, month after month, year after year, on their tiny peninsula. Inevitably they got on one another's nerves. Clashes of temperament, differences of opinion, small jealousies, were magnified, creating smouldering resentments which often grew into volcanic proportions. Men adrift for weeks on a raft or thrown together in the confinement of a prisoner-of-war camp experience the same psychological phenomena. Mole-hills become mountains, mutual distrust crops out, suspicions are easily aroused, prejudice supplants reason. The Europeans at Macao were perpetually marooned on a stationary raft. The results were similar.

After the death of Bishop Leonardo de Saa, in 1597, the archbishop of Goa named Michele de Santis administrator of Macao. It was an obviously ill-advised choice. De Santis had been expelled from the Society of Jesus and had then become an Augustinian. It was hardly likely that he would entertain friendly feelings towards the Jesuits. The latter frequently found themselves at odds with him.

In 1606 a priest, attached to de Santis' party, mistreated a Franciscan friar in the administrator's presence. The friar, Francisco Pinto, demanded that Valentim Carvalho, rector of the Jesuit College be appointed to represent him in a canonical hearing through which he sought vindication of his honor. De Santis refused to grant the canonical hearing or to recognize Carvalho's right to defend the friar. An explosion followed. Carvalho, as apostolic delegate and apostolic judge, excommunicated the administrator; the latter in turn placed the entire city under interdict. Macao was divided into two camps.

Certain unscrupulous adherents of the de Santis faction concocted a sensational story of a plot by the Jesuits to attack and conquer China with the aid of the Portuguese, the Dutch, and the Japanese. They passed this fable on to some Chinese. Lazzaro Cattaneo was pointed to as the leader-designate of the forces of invasion and the future ruler of a conquered China! Cattaneo was a man of imposing physique. His confrère, Alvarõ Semedo, remarked of him that "those who do not know him would think him better cut out to shoulder a pick-axe than to read a breviary."[18] He was often seen in Macao where he was frequently driven to seek rest and treatment for his painful arthritis. These facts plus his knowledge of Chinese and familiarity with conditions in the empire made him the logical choice of the rumor-mongers.

It was a fantastic story, but it spread like wildfire and found ready credence. The grisly tragedy enacted in Manila had not been forgotten. Panic seized the Chinese inhabitants of Macao who precipitately fled the city. The governor of Kwangtung ordered the authorities in Canton to take suitable measures to put the city in a state of readiness. A special council of war was held. Despite the efforts of more level-headed officials to restore a sense of balance, the council decided upon severe measures: the arrest of Christian missionaries, the arming of the people, the razing of some hundreds of private dwellings outside the walls of the city in order to deprive an attacking force of cover.

At this juncture the Jesuit lay-brother (Francis) Huang Ming-sha arrived in Shaochow. He brought from Nanking a passport which authorized Valignano to visit the residences of the Society in China. Learning that Valignano had died, Huang stayed in Shaochow, instead of continuing as planned, to Macao. An apostate Christian from Macao, angered by his failure to extort money from the Jesuit brother, denounced him to the authorities, charging that he was a spy from Macao.

Towards the end of March, 1606, Huang, together with several Christians with whom he was staying, was arrested, taken to Canton, and thrown into prison. He was subjected to torture in an effort to force from him an admission that he was involved in the supposed conspiracy of the foreigners to overthrow the state. The Chinese Jesuit bore his sufferings with admirable patience and was firm in his protestations of innocence. On March 31 he died while being carried back to his prison cell after receiving an unusually severe bastinado.[19]

Longobardo was at the time in charge of the residence of Shaochow. He made every effort to free Brother Francis and his companions. A memorial to the viceroy brought a decree declaring Huang innocent and excoriating the criminal judge responsible for his incarceration. But the verdict was too late to help the victim of the calumny.

Repercussions of this affair did not end here. Certain elements in Shaochow, relying for support upon the popular excitement which had been aroused, lodged a charge of adultery against Longobardo. Like the conspiracy against Susanna, the plot fell to pieces. The supposed witnesses, stooges of the conspirators, admitted that they had been bribed to give false testimony. The sub-prefect wished to hush the matter up, but Longobardo insisted upon a public hearing. A verdict establishing his innocence and imposing a fine upon the conspirators was handed down.

It was the influence of Ricci which finally restored calm to these troubled waters. The maritime intendant of Canton, who had been completely taken in by the reports of the plot, was replaced by an official who came directly from Peking where he had been on friendly terms with Ricci. He accorded an amiable reception to Longobardo and sent an agent to Macao to investigate on the spot the truth or falsity of the reports of preparations for an invasion of the empire. After a searching examination of the establishments there he submitted a report which ended the fantasy.

The Christians who had been imprisoned were restored to liberty. The apostate who had accused the Jesuit brother of espionage escaped a sentence of death by flight. In the following year the official visitor from Peking dismissed from office the two Canton officials who had been most active in stirring up popular excitement. The affair thus officially ended.

The mission in Shaochow never really recovered. Seizure of a messenger bearing letters from Macao revived the old suspicions of a Portuguese plot and led in 1611 to the imprisonment of the Jesuit brother (Dominic) Ch'iu Liang-pin. The fact that no Chinese could read European languages made it impossible to convince suspicious officials of the innocent character of the letters. When the case came before the local tribunal the Jesuits were ordered to leave the city. Gaspar Ferreira, Manoel Dias and two brothers left Shaochow on April 25, 1612, and moved to Nanhsiung, a large and wealthy city on the northern border of the province. Although Longobardo, now superior of the mission, managed a few months later to obtain a revocation of the edict of banishment, the residence in Shaochow was not reopened.

These disturbances of still recent memory did not seem to dampen the mood of optimism which prevailed. In 1611 en route to Peking Longobardo saw the other residences for the first time. The favorable impression which he then received probably tended to thrust into the background the impelling reasons for a continuing policy of caution. The annual letter of Trigault for this year reflects the prevailing mood. He gives a glowing report on the state of the mission and explains why the missionaries are no longer in danger of being expelled.

Longobardo seems to have made some move towards petitioning

the emperor for an edict of full religious liberty. Friendly officials advised strongly against such a démarche which, they insisted, would do more harm than good. Apparently Longobardo did not insist.[20]

Nanking, where Vagnoni was in charge, seemed the most promising of the missions. In the number of conversions it held first place. In the esteem enjoyed by the fathers and in the excellent opinion held of the faith, so Longobardo argued, it was at least on a par with the residence in Peking.

Vagnoni thought his position sufficiently secure to undertake the building of a church. Until then a large room in the residence had served as chapel. He lacked the necessary funds since he had to share his rather slim subsidy with the residence in Hangchow. The Chinese came to his aid. Li Chih-tsao bought the site. Other friends, Christian and non-Christian, contributed generously to the building fund.

The building was rapidly completed. On the feast of the Holy Cross, May 3, 1611, in the presence of a large crowd, Vagnoni officially opened the church. In solemn procession the Christians carried the furnishings from the old chapel to the new edifice.

During the years that immediately followed, the Nanking mission seemed to justify the optimistic hopes of the Jesuits. In 1612 among the numerous converts were three men of more than ordinary prominence. One of these was a scholar named Hsü who came to Nanking from Sungkiang to study geography. This was in all likelihood the future father-in-law of Candida Hsü, granddaughter of Hsü Kuang-ch'i. Candida was to marry Hsü Yüan-tu, a native of Huating, Kiangsu; but Huating is an old name for Sungkiang where Candida lived after her marriage.[21] In 1612 Candida was five years old. It is easy to imagine the devout Hsü Kuang-ch'i, anxious that his granddaughter marry a Christian, arranging a marriage with the son of the man in whose conversion he played an important part. It would accord entirely with Chinese custom.

The fervor of the Nanking Christians was unmatched by any other Christian community in the empire. They abounded in works of charity and of mercy. Vagnoni divided the city into three sections and assigned to Christians of each section their days of reunion at the church. In addition, each section had a meeting place where the Christians assembled for prayer and instruction.[22]

The more fervent formed a congregation dedicated to the Blessed

Virgin. The members of the congregation followed a rule of life which encouraged them to strive to be more than "pedestrian" Christians. To this congregation Vagnoni attributed a large share of the credit for the flourishing state of Christianity in Nanking. To him it seemed that the Nanking Christians, in their charity, fervor, and zeal, and in the way they vied with one another to help the poor, the widowed, and the orphaned, had recreated the spirit of the primitive Church. Their charity to impoverished sick, who were taken into Christian homes and cared for, was a source of wonder to non-Christians.

The example of Hsü Kuang-ch'i and Li Chih-tsao, who frequently visited Nanking, was an invaluable aid to Vagnoni in stimulating the zeal of the Christian community. On one occasion Hsü Kuang-ch'i found Ch'ü Ju-k'uei, Ricci's old friend, slipping away from his former fervor. Ch'ü was growing old. He was a man who had immensely enjoyed living. It is not surprising that the thought of approaching death was unwelcome to him. The habits of a lifetime are not easily broken and Ch'ü in his fear of the inevitable event, had taken up certain superstitious practices which promised the prolongation of life. Hsü Kuang-ch'i directed him through the spiritual exercises of St. Ignatius. Ch'ü Ju-k'uei abandoned superstition and returned to the ways of a devout Christian. Not long afterwards he died an edifying death in his native city of Changchow.[23]

During these years a number of Jesuit priests, most of whom were destined to play outstanding roles in the history of the mission, successfully entered the empire. In 1610 Manoel Dias, Junior, and Nicolas Trigault; and, in 1613, Giulio Aleni, Francesco Sambiasi, Alvarõ Semedo and Peter van Spiere, reinforced the small band of Jesuits dispersed in the five residences.

Aleni and van Spiere had attempted to enter China from Macao a year earlier. They were seized and sent back to the Portuguese city. It was another of the straws which showed that not all winds were favorable. They had better luck on their second effort, this time accompanied by Sambiasi and Semedo. Van Spiere stopped at Nanchang. Aleni and Sambiasi went to Peking. There they found everything contributing to a feeling of confidence. In 1614 de Pantoia published in seven *chüan* a work on the seven capital sins. *Ch'i-k'o ta-ch'üan* (The Seven Triumphs Over Sin, Complete Collection),[24] which enjoyed extraordinary success among scholars and aroused a lively interest in the faith. Conversions in the imperial city were numerous. Even some of the eunuchs showed a less hostile attitude. Many of them had visited the residence to see the hydraulic machines made by de Ursis. Some of them became quite friendly. De Ursis gave them copies of the *T'ien Chu-shih-lu* and thus, for the first time, an exposition of Christian doctrine entered the palace. In 1614 the Jesuits in the capital witnessed the obsequies of the empress dowager who died in her eightieth year on the 9th Day of the Second Moon — March, 1614. In their letters to Europe, they described in considerable detail the extraordinary pomp of the funeral rites.

In this full flood of success it was easy to forget that whether in Peking, or Nanking, or elsewhere, the freedom of action enjoyed by the missionaries rested upon the friendship of scholars and scholar-officials, and that this in turn was the fruit of Ricci's wise methods of indirect apostolate. Significant in what it reveals of the tendency to overlook or minimize this relationship was the interposition, in 1615, of Valentim Carvalho, the provincial of Japan, who, because of the persecution raging in that nation, had been forced to transfer his headquarters to Macao in 1614. Hardly had he made this move when, without ever having set foot in China proper, he promulgated a severe edict proscribing the methods employed by Ricci. The teaching of mathematics and philosophy was to be abandoned. The fathers were to concern themselves exclusively with the preaching of the gospel. They were to refuse to have anything to do with the emendation of the calendar even if expressly ordered by the emperor.[25]

Such lack of understanding on the part of the provincial superior stupefied not only the Jesuits in China, but Hsü Kuang-ch'i, Li Chih-tsao and Yang T'ing-yün as well. It is no exaggeration to call Carvalho's attitude, shared by so many of his contemporaries, one of total incomprehension of the missionary function of the Church. It is a reflection of the notion that the sole purpose of the missionary is to "make Christians," and that this is done only by preaching the gospel.

It seems somehow scandalous to this kind of mind that missionaries should take part in discussions of ethics and metaphysics with Chinese scholars, that they should teach and publish books on astronomy, geography, mathematics, and other sciences.

Georges Goyau, a distinguished French scholar and writer, has shown deeper insight:

> If one regards the building of a Christianity as the final cause of the mission, one will more easily understand the long labors of approach of certain apostles. Why did the Jesuits in seventeenth century China spend a large part of their time working as astronomers, engineers, watchmakers, and artists, instead of devoting themselves exclusively to the obscure task of baptizing dying infants? Why are Jesuits and Benedictines in China, Marianists and Jesuits in Japan and in India, French Jesuits at Trichinopoly, at Palamootah, and at Loyola, German Jesuits at Bombay, absorbed in the scientific work of universities and university colleges instead of gathering, at the bedside of the dying or among the newly born, what is called a rich harvest of souls? Because the interests of a Church which wishes to establish herself required in the seventeenth century an effort of intellectual penetration even in the court of Peking, and requires in the twentieth [century], in the countries where she wishes to implant herself, a persuasive contact with the high spheres of learning.[26]

These had been Ricci's views. He recognized as clearly as anyone that the making of conversions was an essential objective of the mission. "As for what you tell me about the desire to hear of a great movement of conversions in China, know that I and all the others who reside here do not think of anything else day or night; and it is for this purpose that, having left our country and our dear friends, we are here, clothed and shod in Chinese style, speaking, drinking, eating, and living according to the customs of China."[27] So he wrote in 1599. But he was also a realist and acutely aware that the position of the infant Church was precarious and that indiscreet zeal to hasten the movement of conversions would place it in jeopardy; ". . . we should risk suddenly losing the few we have, should we yield to the impulse of wanting to make Christians."[28] So he had written in 1596.

He opposed the long view to the short view. His vision was of a quiet, slow growth, Christianity first firmly planting itself, then thrusting its roots more deeply into Chinese soil, then pushing upward through the surface, finally with growing vitality and self-assurance lifting itself towards the sky, spreading forth its branches, entering into full maturity. It was the vision of the mustard tree.

He fully shared the view expressed by Ruggieri:

> This mission is a new and tender plant, and it would take but a breath of wind to destroy it; for this reason it is necessary that it be handled in these beginnings with great suavity and delicacy, and receive in due time cultivators who will cultivate rather than destroy it.[29]

Carvalho was obviously not such a cultivator. Fortunately he was not in office long enough to destroy the tender plant upon which he laid such violent hands and his incredible edict was revoked. The storm which was soon to break exposed the folly which inspired it.

In Nanking Vagnoni, carried away by the success of his mission, threw restraint aside and gave full publicity to the preaching of the gospel. Services were conducted in the church with the full panoply and pomp of the liturgy. The Christians were, of course, happy about it. Many non-Christian scholar-officials, whose sympathetic interest reached back to the effulgent days of Ricci's stay in Nanking, were not displeased. Some, both in Nanking and in other cities to which the fame of Nanking's dynamic Christian community reached, were edified and drawn closer to the faith. But there were others in Nanking who looked on with jaundiced eye. There were the numerous Buddhist monks who saw in this young and vital movement a threat to their position. Vagnoni's attitude did not tend to appease their natural antipathy. He regarded most of them as what some of them no doubt were, frauds, preying upon the credulous people. He did not hesitate to manifest his contempt. Vagnoni was a zealous and talented man. According to Bartoli, next to Ricci there was no man in the mission so universally loved or widely esteemed by pagan and Christian alike.[30] He had his faults, however, if the judgment of his confrères is to be trusted. Longobardo, in a confidential report, after recognizing his splendid gifts of mind and heart, his prudence, and the prestige he enjoyed, remarks that at the same time a certain asperity and arrogance in his manner caused him sometimes "to be hated."[31] Longobardo could have been somewhat prejudiced, since Vagnoni was his most formidable opponent in the long debate about Christian terminology which marked these years. However, a catalogue of 1626, summarizing the opinions which his colleagues had of Vagnoni, after listing his many virtues and talents, mentions that he had "a more than moderately" hot temper and that he would make a good superior of the vice-province "if he could show more mildness."[32]

These were dangerous faults to have in the milieu in which he was living. He would have better served his cause had he had more of Ricci's tolerance. The Buddhist priests were far from powerless. They had influential friends among the Confucian reactionaries who had their own reasons for disliking Christianity. They watched with smouldering resentment Christian activities in Nanking. Ricci and, following him, de Rocha, Cattaneo, and Vagnoni, had made many friends in the southern capital. Hence for a time these hostile elements were forced to remain inactive. They were biding their time. They needed a pretext for action and a leader influential enough and courageous enough to attack. Vagnoni, by his abandonment of the policy of quiet advance, furnished the pretext. Shên Ch'üeh, vice-president of the Nanking Board of Rites, supplied the leadership.

NOTES

(1) Juridically the vice-province of Japan became a province on December 9, 1608, when patents were signed in Rome naming Francesco Pasio visitor and Valentim Carvalho provincial. However, these patents did not reach Japan until July 31, 1611, when the change effectively took place.

(2) Published in a collection by P. J. Hay, S. J., *De rebus Japonicis et Indicis epistolae recentiores* (Antverpiae: Martini, 1605), pp. 913-934.

(3) Daniello Bartoli, S. J., *Del'istoria della Compagnia di Gesù. La Cina. Terza parte dell'Asia* (Ancona: Giuseppe Aureli, 1843), III, 233.

(4) To Giovanni Alvarez, November 4, 1598; *Opere storiche*, II, 469-476 (extract quoted on p. 475.)

(5) *Ibid.*, p. 490.

(6) *Ibid.*, p. 299.

(7) Louis Pfister, S. J., *Notices biographiques et bibliographiques sur les Jésuites de l'ancienne mission de Chine 1552-1773* (Shanghai: Mission catholique, 1932), I, 65.

(8) Bartoli, *op. cit.*, III, 45 f.

(9) The account given here of the Hangchow events is based upon Nicolas Trigault's report in *Lit. X-XI*, 209 ff.

(10) Cf. *Eminent Chinese*, II, 894 f.

(11) Bartoli, *op. cit.*, III, 97 f.

(12) *Eminent Chinese*, II, 894.

(13) *Ibid.*, p. 895.

(14) *Ibid.*, I, 318.

(15) Bartoli, *op. cit.*, III, 59.

(16) Ricci refers to this macabre event in his letter to Maselli of February, 1605; *Opere storiche*, II, 258. He reports the Peking estimate of the number of slain as 20,000. Official Spanish documents published in Colin-Pastels, *op. cit.*, II, 432-441, give the number of victims as about 15,000.

(17) *FR*, II, 372 ff.

NOTES

(18) Quoted by Pfister, *op. cit.*, I, 52, n. 1.

(19) Ricci reported this sad news to Aquaviva in his letter of August 15, 1606; *Opere storiche*, II, 301.

(20) Pfister, *op. cit.*, I, 104, erroneously says that de Ursis obtained an edict of religious toleration.

(21) Cf. G.M.H. Playfair, *The Cities and Towns of China* (2d ed.; Shanghai: Kelly and Walsh, 1910), under "Sungkiang."

(22) On the state of the Nanking mission, cf. *Lit. X-XI*, pp. 178 ff., and Bartoli, *op. cit.*, III, 73 ff.; 227 ff.

(23) *Lit. X-XI*, pp. 193 ff. tells of his death and recalls with affection the indebtedness of the mission to Ricci's old friend "Ignatius."

(24) Cf. Pfister, *op. cit.* I, 71 f. This work which has had many printings, the last in 1922, was reviewed in the annotated bibliography of the *Ssu-k'u* library, one of eight books by Jesuits so honored.

(25) Bartoli, *op. cit.*, III, 232 ff.

(26) Georges Goyau, *Missions et missionaires* (Paris: Libraire Bloud et Gay, 1931), pp. 238 ff.

(27) *Opere storiche*, II, 246.

(28) *Ibid.*, p. 225.

(29) *Ibid.*, p. 422.

(30) Bartoli, *op. cit.*, IV, 758.

(31) Quoted by D'Elia, *FR*, II, 277, n. 4.

(32) *ARSI*, Jap-Sin 134, f. 305 .

Chapter VIII

Typhoon

In 1615, the most prosperous year the Christian mission in China had experienced, Shên Ch'üeh arrived in Nanking from Peking to assume the office of vice-president of the Board of Rites in the southern capital. He proved to be an implacable foe of Christianity.[1]

Shên Ch'üeh never fully explained the reasons for his hatred. People do not usually admit their prejudices, much less analyze the reasons for them. Speculation, therefore, enters into any effort to assign motives to his persecution of Christianity. Camillo di Costanzo, writing from Macao on January 15, 1618, gives four reasons for Shên's hostility: (1) One of Shên's closest friends, a Buddhist priest, had published an attack upon Christianity to which Hsü Kuang-ch'i is said to have responded so effectively that the Buddhist died of chagrin. The unfortunate conclusion to this incident hardly seems plausible, although, in view of the extreme mental disturbance which grievous "loss of face" can provoke in an Oriental, it is not impossible. (2) Shên had himself been worsted by both Hsü Kuang-ch'i and Yang T'ing-yün in several disputations in Peking on the subject of religion. (3) His resentment, caused by these encounters was deepened by the sponsorship by Hsü and Yang of the proposal to entrust the calendar reform to the Christian missionaries. (4) He had his eye fixed upon the high office of grand secretary, which post he hoped to attain by acquiring, through his exposure of the supposedly subversive character of Christianity, the reputation of a zealous and fearless defender of the state. Alvarõ Semedo, one of the chief victims of Shên's animosity, is in substantial agreement with di Costanzo.[2]

Neither di Costanzo, nor Semedo, seems to have perceived the deeper issue involved. Whatever personal motives may have contributed to Shên's hostility, his opposition had its roots in Sung orthodoxy. The persecution which he led represented the first large-scale counterblow of the school of orthodox reactionaries against innovation. The evidence on this point comes from Shên himself. The ultimate source of his animus and the real character of this persecution are revealed in the official documents which he published as *pièces justificatives* at the conclusion of his campaign. They were published again in 1639 by one Hsü Chang-chih, forming the first two *chüan* of his eight *chüan* attack on Christianity entitled *P'o-hsieh-chi* (Collection Exposing Heterodoxy).[3] It is the voice of official Confucianism which speaks in these pages. What it resents in Christianity is its novelty, the fact that it is not found in the classics of Confucian literature; that it does not recognize the emperor as the supreme spiritual authority; and that it asserts a moral system superior to and more comprehensive than that embraced in the classical five relationships of Confucianism.

Shên Ch'üeh was a member of a bureaucracy which, as the result of a struggle lasting hundreds of years, had won a superior place in the state. The continued dominance of his class depended upon the maintenance of an examination system which limited learning to the sterile type of literary dilettantism into which Sung orthodoxy had degenerated. Revelation of new horizons in either the intellectual or the religious sphere threatened to break down the barriers of that system. Reactionary bureaucrats guarded against outcroppings of new ideas. They labored assiduously to maintain the fiction that Sung orthodoxy had said the final word on truth and virtue, and that any suggestion that there were other truths, or sources of truth, was not only heresy, but treason. There is no reason to doubt that they were sincere in identifying the interests of state and society with a system of thought in the maintenance of which they had a deeply vested interest. Neither is there doubt that the defense of this vested interest played a large, if subconscious, part in their opposition to innovation. An indication of this may be seen in the fact that, on the whole, no scholars were so fiercely reactionary as the younger ones who had passed the *hsiu-ts'ai* examinations. They had passed the first milestone on the road which led to a successful official career. Both their prestige and their hopes for the future depended upon preserving the closed system of learning in which they had been trained. Initiates to the fraternity, their determination to defend its and their privileged position led them inevitably into the camp of reaction. Most of the annoyances which Ricci had endured at Chaoching and later at Shaochow had been inspired by young *hsiu-ts'ai.* In 1607 three hundred *hsiu-ts'ai* in Nanchang had signed a petition demanding the expulsion of the missionaries and the proscription of Christianity.

In Nanking the *hsiu-ts'ai* gave Shên Chüeh the encouragement he needed to launch his campaign. A group of them submitted a petition demanding the exclusion of foreigners from the realm as persons pernicious to the public good and inimical to the state. It was alleged that several times a year, under pretext of religious solemnities, men and women met during the night in the church, dispersing before dawn. One is reminded of the suspicions and fears aroused in bureaucratic circles in the Roman empire by the liturgical assemblies of the early Christians. It was further charged that all who became Christians were given five pieces of silver by the missionaries who possessed the secret of alchemy; that the neophytes were enrolled under foreign and unknown names; that they were taught the sign of the cross to be used as a password in the revolution which was contemplated; that the house of the foreigners was stocked with arms.

In May, 1616, Shên Ch'üeh opened his attack with a memorial to the throne in which he demanded that the missionaries and their converts be condemned to death. He charged the Jesuits with having entered the empire secretly. He mentioned de Pantoia and de Ursis by name as being located in Peking, and Vagnoni, Dias and others as being in Nanking. He was mistaken about Dias. The older Dias was in Macao, the younger in Nanhsiung. Others, he declared, were stationed in the capitals of other provinces. He probably had Hangchow and Nanchang in mind, but was not prepared to say so. Shên Ch'üeh's home was in Hangchow. He certainly knew that the missionaries in that city were supported by Yang T'ing-yün, but Yang had many friends and considerable prestige. It was better not to attack him directly. Similarly, it is likely that Shên knew that the Jesuits in Nanchang numbered among their friends certain members of the imperial family.

This memorial was secretly presented to Peking, but the missionaries and the Christian officials had too many friends in court circles to permit the secret to be kept. They soon knew what was afoot and lost no time trying to ward off the storm. Yang T'ing-yün wrote to Shên and to several other officials defending the missionaries and their teachings. This defense he enlarged into an *Apologia* which he sent to Li Chih-tsao who was in Kaoyu, a city two days distant from Nanking. Li added an essay in praise of Christianity and of the Jesuits and had it published.

Meanwhile the missionaries in Nanking encouraged the Christians to prepare to suffer for the faith.[4] One of the Christians, John Yao, made four standards each bearing his name, place of origin, and a proclamation of his Christian faith, which he proposed to carry with him as symbols to animate the courage of the faithful. Yao was a stouthearted fellow whose ardor to suffer proved somewhat confusing to those charged with carrying out the ensuing judicial processes against the Christians. Not knowing quite what to make of him, they treated him with considerable deference, probably to Yao's disgust. In this early stage, before an overt act had been committed by Shên, the fathers found it necessary to restrain his impetuous ardor, there being no sense in supplying Shên with fire for his powder box.

Shên impatiently awaited a response to his memorial. None was forthcoming. If it had reached the emperor that august person gave no sign of it. Nothing daunted by the pointed silence of the court, Shên Ch'üeh returned to the charge. Three months after the presentation of his first petition he submitted a second. He complains that his first petition has elicited no response and that its contents have leaked out. New charges against Vagnoni are joined with accusations contained in the first memorial:

> He has established a residence before the Gate of the Rising Sun, to the west of the mountain of the founder of the dynasty. . . . In his church he suspends portraits of barbarians, and persuades the ignorant people to accept his doctrine. To each follower he gives three ounces of silver. He inscribes in a book their name, their family, their age, and gives them a new name which they must not forget. Every month he designates four days on which his followers are to assemble at his house. He calls these congregations. There are at those meetings at least fifty men, sometimes as many as two hundred. . . . Within the

> city Vagnoni has also established a residence in front of the palace of the founder of the dynasty. Outside the city walls he possesses a country house. It is situated directly in face of the tomb of the same founder of the reigning dynasty. There a hill was chosen as the home of the Imperial Dragon. Can one permit these contemptible rats to pollute its soil! these barbarian dogs to enter there!

Shên deplores that these doctrines "are already so widespread that a man from the common people has already shown himself in the streets of Nanking carrying a small yellow banner which proclaims that he is a Christian and that he wishes to die for the Lord of Heaven." John Yao was clearly not pouring oil upon the troubled waters. Warning that revolution might break out at any moment, Shên demanded permission to take preventive measures aimed at Vagnoni and "all those who live with him, and all those who profess to be adherents of the religion of the Lord of Heaven."

The president of the Board of Rites in an accompanying memorial supported the demands of Shên. These two documents were presented to the court on August 15. The contents of the memorial submitted by the president of the Board of Rites were published in the government *Gazette*. Hsü Kuang-ch'i immediately presented a counter-memorial defending the Jesuits against the charges. It is valuable for the light it throws upon this stalwart Christian's character. It is couched in terms of dignified respect, but without obsequiousness. He states that he is a Christian who from years of intimate association knows that the accused "are not only in deportment and in heart wholly free from aught which can excite suspicion, but that they are indeed worthies and sages; that their doctrines are most correct; their manner of life most strict; their learning most extensive; their hearts most true; their views most steady. . . ."

After pointing out the virtues of Christianity and analyzing the deficiencies of Buddhism, he calls attention to the fact that Buddhism, Taoism, and Mohammedanism are all tolerated in the empire. He urges that the same degree of toleration be granted Christianity. " Let [Christian missionaries] be allowed the exercise of their appropriate functions . . . allowing them to influence and guide whomsoever they please."

Hsü tells the emperor that before he knew the missionaries he had heard the same charges made against them that were now brought forward by the president of the Board of Rites and he too had regarded these foreigners with suspicion. "But after years of careful examination and inquiry . . ." he is positive that there is not the "smallest reason for entertaining suspicions regarding these men. . . ."

He proposes three modes of examination by which the emperor can determine whether or not the allegations are well-founded:

1—Let the Jesuits named in the rescript of the president of the Board of Rites be called to Peking, there to translate the standard works they have brought with them from the West: works on religion, natural and moral philosophy, civil government, astronomy, mathematics, physics, medicine, agriculture, political economy, and so forth. Let them then write a treatise on each subject. If a commission appointed by the emperor should judge, after examination, that these writings contain anything subversive, then let the missionaries be expelled from the empire, "and your majesty's servant will willingly abide the punishment appointed for those who aid and abet deceivers of your majesty."

2—Let the accused Jesuits engage in a debate with the most qualified representatives of Buddhism and Taoism. If the Jesuits are not judged victors in the debate, let them be expelled "and let your majesty's servant be punished with them."

3—Let the Jesuits draw up a compendium of their religious doctrines. If the emperor, after himself examining this compendium together with some thirty books on the Christian religion which have already been written in Chinese, should judge unfavorably of their teachings, let the missionaries be expelled and appropriate punishment be visited upon Hsü Kuang-ch'i.[5]

This memorial is a monument to Hsü Kuang-ch'i's Christian faith. The quiet courage of this future chancellor of the Chinese empire conjures up the image of another chancellor of another kingdom, St. Thomas More, almost a contemporary.

Five days after presenting his memorial to the throne, the president of the Board of Rites, without waiting further for the emperor's response, despatched couriers to the provinces with orders that the missionaries be arrested and imprisoned. At midnight, August 30, a messenger arrived at the residence in Nanking bringing word from the Jesuits in Peking of these developments. Longobardo, Aleni, Semedo and Vagnoni were in Nanking. At daybreak Longobardo and Aleni set out for the north. Semedo and Vagnoni on the same day were visited by three officials sent by the president of the Nanking Board of War to inform them that he and Shên Ch'üeh had been charged with the task of expelling them from the empire. These emissaries, who were, says Semedo, "very good fellows," expressed regret at the turn events had taken. They expressed their conviction of the innocence of the missionaries, but advised that they yield quietly and depart without resistance. The president of the Board of War would see that they suffered no vexations on their voyage. One of them added the hope that the priests would be able to return as soon as their innocence had been established.

That night a guard of police, sent by Shên, surrounded the residence. At dawn three officers appeared who were charged with arresting the missionaries and searching the premises. They presented Vagnoni with a letter in which apologies were offered for the orders which were being carried out. Their moderation made things easier for the two Jesuit priests, and contrasted sharply with the harshness manifested by Shên Ch'üeh.

Leaving Semedo, who was ill, under guard in the residence, they ordered Vagnoni carried off in a sedan chair to jail. In China, as elsewhere, the sight of a squad of policemen attracts a crowd. In China, too, rumor and report are equipped with swifter wings, perhaps, than in any other clime. By the time Vagnoni was carried from the residence the street was thick with people. The police, laying about freely with their batons, cleared a path.

En route to the jail the procession stopped at the home of the intendant of circuit, who was related to Shên Ch'üeh. For two hours Vagnoni was left seated in his chair in the street. During this time the foreign priest was surrounded by a hooting and jeering mob. However, it seems to have been a typical Chinese crowd, which is to say that, while seeming to give vent to a lot of sound and fury, actually it was merely having a good time. In every Chinese crowd there are a number of wits, and no people appreciate wit more than do the Chinese. That the present instance was no exception may be guessed from Vagnoni's account in which he describes himself as unable to restrain his laughter. One is glad he thought to mention this. It puts the scene in a natural setting. It is true that Vagnoni ascribes his laughter to a special grace which gave him a "particular joy and gaiety, which made me burst out laughing, unable to restrain myself." Without denying the special grace, the suspicion remains that his laughter was not unrelated to comments from the spectators. Spiritual consolation does indeed produce a feeling of joy and even of gaiety, but rarely moves to uncontrollable laughter.

Upon emerging at length from the intendant's the officers were apologetic for the long delay. Arrived at the prison they turned Vagnoni over to the jailer with recommendations that he be treated with the consideration due an innocent man. Imprisoned with him were two Chinese domestics, one of whom, Chang Ts'ai, had been with the Jesuits for three years. He had voluntarily come forward and asked to be allowed to share Vagnoni's lot.

When word of Vagnoni's imprisonment got about, a number of Christians hurried to the residence, forcing their way by the guards. They were led by John Yao, gallantly flaunting his yellow standard. Asked by the soldiers what he wanted, Yao replied, "To die a Christian and to shed my blood for the faith of Jesus Christ." Willing to accommodate him, within the limits of their office, the guards bound his hands, put a rope around his neck, and led him off to the tribunal. Here the officials seem to have been rather dazed by Yao's ardor. He was, apparently, far more anxious to suffer persecution than they were to inflict it. They ordered him unbound, offered him a chair, and soon released him.

Shên Ch'üeh was angered by the tendency of his subordinates to treat the accused with consideration. On the next day, September 1, he ordered Semedo and all others found at the residence locked in jail with Vagnoni. Imprisoned with Semedo were the Jesuit lay-brother (Sebastian) Chung Ming-jên, a twenty-one-year-old Macaist, Louis Paris, who was a candidate for admission to the Society, four servants, and four Christians who happened to be at the residence on the morning of the arrest. Shên also sent a party to search the garden, used by the Jesuits as a place of recreation, outside the city walls. There he expected to find arms, but was disappointed.

The Nanking Christians sent word of developments to Longobardo. He and Aleni were with Li Chih-tsao at Kaoyu. The three men decided that Longobardo should continue to Peking while Aleni took refuge with Yang T'ing-yün in Hangchow. Li supplied Longobardo with money for his journey to the capital. He also gave him letters to Peking officials. Despite the warning of friends and relatives that unless he abandoned his public defense of the missionaries he would jeopardize both fortune and career, Li was indefatigable in their behalf. He even sent the messenger back to Nanking with money and clothing for the imprisoned Jesuits.

Longobardo reached Peking to find de Pantoia and de Ursis seeking by every means to obtain a hearing for their cause. Longobardo tried to persuade officials to intervene with the emperor. Shên Ch'üeh, who was well supplied with money, had shut off all avenues of approach.

Hsü Kuang-ch'i wrote a tract in defense of the missionaries and of the Christian religion. It was little needed in Peking where, except for the president of the Board of Rites, the official world did not take Shên's charges too seriously. Consequently Longobardo sent (John) Chung Ming-li to Nanking with instructions to publish it and circulate it there.

With the assistance of Ignatius Hsia, a Christian relative of Li Chih-tsao, Chung found six printers who were willing to undertake the job. They worked in the house of a convert who lived outside the city walls. The first copies of the *Apologia* were barely finished when the printers were betrayed. A neighbor informed Shên Ch'üeh. The printers and the Jesuit brother were seized.

Shên subjected Chung Ming-li to the bastinado and brought Semedo and Vagnoni before the officials of his own board for a grueling examination of six hours. The line taken may be judged from the few questions which Semedo records: "What is the law you profess? How did you enter China? Who feeds you? How do you govern yourselves? What relations do you maintain with the foreigners at Macao?"

Thanks to one of the members of the Board of Rites, to whom Hsü Kuang-ch'i and Li Chih-tsao had written, no punishment was inflicted at the end of the examination. Yielding to the pressure of the furious Shên, the board sent the case to a higher tribunal which was asked to deal severely with the accused. Instead, the tribunal found, after a short hearing, that no crime had been committed. As a sop to Shên's feelings, it ordered the Christian who had allowed his home to be used for the printing of the *Apologia* to receive twenty blows and ordered an additional twenty blows meted out to Chung Ming-li.

It is clear from the attitude exhibited by other officials in the course of these hearings that but for the tenacity of Shên Ch'üeh the affair would have been dropped. Shên's fellow officials obviously regarded his campaign as an unnecessary tempest in their teapot. Their sympathy for the accused was evident. But Shên was not to be diverted. He redoubled his efforts in Peking. Several memorials to the throne brought no response, but finally a petition dated the 12th Moon of the 44th Year of Wan-li (January, 1617) brought the desired result. It was submitted for Shên by the vice-president of the Peking Board of Rites together with an edict needing only the emperor's signature. Semedo gives the following version of this document:

> Having been fully informed by the vice-president of the third Board of Peking of the presence of certain foreigners in this court and in the realm; upon the humble prayers and remonstrances which our officials have made to us, that we issue an order to all the provinces, that Vagnoni and de Pantoia, with their companions, be sent back to their own country, for having preached an unknown doctrine, and for having, under pretext of religion, troubled the tranquillity of our people, and conspired to cause a revolt among our subjects and a general uprising against the state, for these reasons we order the Board of Rites of Nanking to notify the officials of our provinces that these foreigners, wherever found, are to be escorted under a strong guard to the province and city of Canton, and from there let them return to their own land, leaving China in peace. And although last year, upon being advised that these foreigners had entered our realm to be of service to us, and that de Pantoia and his companions were well qualified to accomplish the correction of our calendar, we aggregated them to the order of mandarins; we desire and ordain that notwithstanding this aggregation, they be dismissed, and returned to their own land. This is our pleasure. Let this sentence be returned to the Board of Rites. . . .[6]

This edict received the imperial signature on February 14, 1617. Shên Ch'üeh's persistence finally had its reward. All that had been accomplished through thirty-five years of tedious, painful, patient labor faced imminent destruction. Ruggieri's "tender plant" was feeling the tempest's breath. Ricci's prophecy of danger lying ahead was coming true all too soon.

In whatever way it had been brought about, the edict was a *fait accompli* and was promulgated throughout the empire. Had the realities of Chinese government corresponded to surface appearance its promulgation must have spelled the end of the Jesuit adventure in China. Fortunately for the Jesuits, China, whatever the theory, was not in practice the "oriental despotism" so often described. Theoretically all power flowed from the Son of Heaven: his authority was absolute. Actually, the authority of the emperor was hedged by many limitations, good and bad. Thoroughly bad was the power of the eunuchs who, by their control of many approaches to the throne, and by their intimate contact with the emperor, were able to weaken the imperial authority. A healthy check upon despotism lay in the discretionary powers enjoyed by the officials throughout the empire who were charged with the execution of imperial decrees. These were couched in the language of autocracy "Tremble and obey!" Administrative officials in the provinces rarely trembled and often enough did not obey, since they enjoyed wide latitude in determining the extent to which the decrees should be enforced in their respective jurisdictions. It was, of course, possible to remove and punish officials who were guilty of dereliction of duty. Through the system of censors, monitors, and visitors, a check was maintained. Frequently officials were cashiered, but usually not because they had failed to execute imperial decrees, but because they were charged with excessive severity towards their subjects. Deeply ingrained in Chinese consciousness is the concept of the official as the father of his people. One of the tests of a good official is whether his people find him a *hao fu-mu*, a "good father and mother." Such a criterion could have no meaning in a system in which the function of the superior is simply to execute the law in its cold and bloodless literalness. The discretionary powers exercised by administrative officials were not, therefore, arbitrary and unconstitutional usurpations of authority. They were an essential part of the Chinese political system and were rooted in Chinese political theory.

That officials owe obedience only to those imperial orders which are just was a doctrine taught by both Confucius and Mencius.[7] In Confucian political theory, the official is a mediator between the ruler and his people.[8] Few Westerners have understood this central feature of the Chinese political system. Journalists and writers of fiction have perpetuated the legend of imperial China as a highly integrated despotic autocracy. Much of the friction which seriously disturbed the nineteenth-century relations between Western powers and the Chinese empire had its roots in the inability of the Westerner to see beneath the phenomenon of centralized autocracy the noumenon of a wide dispersal of responsibility and decentralization of authority.

The edict took the Jesuits in Peking by surprise. There were in the city four priests, Longobardo, Sambiasi, de Ursis, and de Pantoia, and two brothers, probably (James) Ni Yi-chêng and (Manoel) Yu Wên-hui. Efforts to appeal to the emperor were unavailing. Shên Ch'üeh's agents effectively barred approach to the throne. On Palm Sunday, March 18, 1617, after celebrating Mass in the crowded church, distributing palms to the faithful and exhorting them to stand firm in their faith, the Jesuits took leave of the Chinese community founded by Ricci in the shadow of the imperial throne.

Neither Longobardo nor Sambiasi nor the two brothers had been named in the edict. The officials charged with its execution in the capital therefore blandly ignored their presence. The two priests found refuge in the Peking home of Hsü Kuang-ch'i, while the brothers retired to Ricci's burial ground outside the western wall of the Tatar city. Instead of confiscating the church and residence the same officials allowed one of the Peking Christians to take charge of them. De Ursis and de Pantoia, however, passed through the massive gates of the capital under escort en route to Canton. No doubt they turned more than once to look back upon the walls of the imperial capital where de Pantoia had lived for sixteen years, de Ursis for eleven. They were never to gaze upon them again, for both would die in exile in Macao.

In Nanchang the edict was carried out with extreme moderation. The two priests stationed there were allowed to withdraw to the city of Kienchang. The Jesuit Brother (Pascal) Ch'iu Liang-hou remained undisturbed in charge of the residence.

The forced departure of the priests from Nanchang was a blessing in disguise. De Rocha had already visited Kienchang and made converts there. He and van Spiere were now received with the greatest of charity by a member of the first family of the city who is identified in the accounts only by his Christian name Stephen. Stephen lodged the priests in a house, near the city walls, which contained four rooms in addition to a kitchen and a large hall which served as chapel. Visited at first only by the few Christians of the place, the Jesuits gradually began to receive increasing numbers of callers. Many were converted. When Semedo was there two years later he attended a Mass sung before a large gathering of people. Twenty years later Semedo was able to report:

> It is now one of our best residences, with a large number of well instructed Christians, and two annexed churches in the neighboring province of Chinceo [Chekiang], sufficiently near to Kienchom [Kienchang] to be visited by one of the fathers every year.[9]

Gaspar Ferreira and Manoel Dias, Junior, who had been chased from Shaochow in 1612 were still in Nanhsiung. The local officials when informing them of the imperial edict told them that they need be in no hurry to leave the city, but might await the arrival of de Ursis and de Pantoia. Instead, the fathers sold their residence and set out to join the others who were assembling in Hangchow under the protection of Yang T'ing-yün. Cattaneo, Ribeiro, and Aleni were already there. Others followed. During the ensuing years, while the shadow of Shèn Ch'üeh lay athwart the mission, Yang's home in Hangchow was the center of Christian hopes in China. There was no secret about the presence of the Jesuits in Yang's home. Shèn himself was well aware of it. While galled by the knowledge that his fellow townsman was frustrating his desire to rid China of Christianity, the prestige of Yang T'ing-yün was such that he dared not attack him openly. The Hangchow officials, out of respect for Yang, never promulgated the expulsion edict.

Only in Nanking was the imperial order executed with full measure of severity. Three documents in the collection later published by Shèn Ch'üeh testify to the zeal with which he applied himself to the affair. The three bear one date, the Second Moon (March), 1617.

The first is an order of the Nanking Board of Rites directing its agents to examine the prisoners. In this it is stated that Vagnoni had admitted that he is a barbarian. The agents are instructed to examine Semedo with a view to determining whether he, too, is a barbarian. They are also to ascertain if Manoel Dias has returned to Europe. They are to inquire into the history of (John) Chung Ming-li and (Sebastian) Chung Ming-jèn, and of the other prisoners.

The second document is a *procès-verbal* drawn up by the secretary of the Board of Rites. He has examined the prisoners and reports, in part, as follows:

> As for Vagnoni, he has a red face, white eyebrows, large blue eyes, a long and pointed nose, yellow hair. He claims to be fifty years old, to be a European, to have studied in his youth the books of the barbarians, to have undergone several

examinations, to have succeeded therein; he claims that his grade corresponds to that of doctor in China, that he has not desired to become a mandarin, that he voluntarily entered a religious congregation, that he entered China with da Silva and others to preach religion, when he was thirty years old, on the order of his superior Claudius Aquaviva. With da Silva and Dias, he boarded a ship in Europe and, after a voyage of two years and four months, in 1600, the 7th Moon, he arrived at Macao. He remained there about five months. Leaving Manoel Dias there, he and da Silva spent some days in Shaochowfu, then four months at Nanchangfu in Kiangsi. In 1611 at the 3rd Moon, he came to Nanking where Ricci, de Pantoia, Cattaneo, de Rocha and others, at present dispersed, had been established for ten years (sic). Ricci went to Peking to offer gifts to the emperor. De Rocha took his place at Nanking, soon giving way to Vagnoni, who labors there to establish the Christian religion. He has a little more than two hundred followers. He assigns them days of reunion, etc.

As for da Silva: in 1613 at the 6th Moon, he fell ill and died. His coffin is still in the church.

As for Dias: He is in Macao. In past years he was at Nanhsiung. Some months ago he came to Nanking and spent two weeks with Vagnoni. He also went to Peking. At the 12th Moon of 1615 he returned to Nanhsiung.

As for the money which Vagnoni dispenses, he receives it from Europe. It is brought to Macao on the trading ships. He thus receives each year about six hundred ounces of silver. When he has to build some edifice the annual amount reaches as much as one thousand ounces of gold. This money is shared with de Pantoia and the others who propagate their religion.

As for Semedo: he has a red face, white eyebrows, a long and pointed nose, large ears, has no ambitions to become a mandarin, joined his friends for purposes of study, came by sea to Macao about three years and six months ago. According to this, and in view of his great resemblance to Vagnoni, there is no doubt that he also is a barbarian. As for Dias, although he has not returned to his own country, he is said to be at Nanhsiungfu and is no longer in this jurisdiction.

Conclusion: The two criminal barbarians, Vagnoni and Semedo, the latter at present ill, having been examined and clearly identified, should be conducted to Canton, and turned over to the proper authorities to be sent back to the Occident.

The third document is an order of the Board of Rites to the Board of Censors to take the necessary measures to have the two Europeans conducted to Canton and there turned over to the proper officials to be sent back to Europe. It refers to the petition approved by the emperor and to the *procès-verbal:* in conclusion, it sets forth the judgment of the Board of Rites. The judgment was written by Yên Wên-huei and was approved by his colleagues on the Board. Its tenor leaves no doubt that the principal factor in the attack launched by Shên was the hostility of Confucian "orthodoxy" to Christianity.

On March 6 Vagnoni and Semedo were brought before Shên's tribunal. Semedo was so weak from illness that he had to be carried on a plank. Vagnoni was led, after the fashion with criminals, with a rope around his neck. For two hours they were interrogated by an official of the Board of Rites. During this time Vagnoni was forced to remain upon his knees. Semedo, unable to kneel, lay upon the ground. At the conclusion of the examination Shên had them brought before him. He declared that although they merited death for having taught a new doctrine in China, the bounty of the emperor spared their lives. They would instead be sent back to their own country. For his own part he ordered that a bastinado of ten blows be administered each of them. The serious illness of Semedo saved him from this punishment. Vagnoni was not spared. He was so beaten that his wounds were a month in healing.

"When, after a month, my wounds were closed," writes Vagnoni, "Shên Ch'üeh sent three minor military officers and two of his agents to conduct another and more rigorous search of the residence; I was obliged to assist them. The books, manuscripts, holy pictures, mathematical instruments were sorted out, confiscated, and carried off to Shên Ch'üeh. The furniture was left for me to dispose of as I wished, and I was then taken back to prison."

It was on this occasion that the coffin of da Silva was opened. The officers hoped to find treasure in it. According to Vagnoni, da Silva's body was found in a state of perfect conservation. The superstitious fear aroused by this discovery was intensified when a sudden thunder storm broke upon the city. The officers precipitately ended their search of the premises. Shên Ch'üeh ordered da Silva's body thrown into a field outside the city. The Christians retrieved it and gave it burial.

On April 30, 1617, Vagnoni and Semedo were taken from prison and carried in cages ordinarily used only for criminals condemned to death to one of the tribunals. Here the presiding officer pronounced final sentence upon them. Thereupon an imperial seal was affixed to the cages. The officers of the guard received their orders.

Thus the procession started out, the two Jesuits in cages, with heavy chains suspended from their necks, their hands in irons. Their hair and beards had not been trimmed in months. Their clothes were in tatters. The streets were packed with people. But, strangely for a Chinese crowd, the procession passed through the streets amidst a profound silence. Three placards, carried at the head of the procession, described the prisoners as evil men, disturbers of the public peace, teachers of a new doctrine, and forbade anyone to speak to them or to have contact with them.

The original plan had been to send them by boat. Certain Christians had organized means of providing for the comfort of the two prisoners en route to Canton. Shên Ch'üeh circumvented this charity by sending them by land, under guard, and prohibiting any intercourse with them.

Not until the fourth day were they allowed to leave their cages, and then for a short rest only. By that time they were so weak they could not stand. The worst of the ordeal ended when they reached the city of Nanhsiung. Nanking Christians accompanied the procession all the way to Nanhsiung, but had been prevented from approaching the prisoners. In the later stages of the journey, however, many scholars and scholar-officials, with whom the guards did not dare interfere, visited the Jesuits. Usually they presented them with bits of verse "as a sign of their affection, and a souvenir of their visit, the visit of good friends filled with compassion for their misfortunes," writes Vagnoni.

The prefect of Nanhsiung released them from their cages, dismissed the guard, and sent them by boat to Shaochow. Here their reception was less cordial. They were led from one tribunal to another, harshly treated, and finally shipped off to Canton which they reached on May 20, one month after leaving Nanking.

In the southern metropolis they were thrown into a wretched prison. It was "small, damp, pestilential, and so crowded with prisoners," writes Vagnoni, "that it was impossible to stretch out on the ground without putting one's feet on top of one's neighbor." The intercession of friendly officials effected their transfer to a less unpleasant prison. Here they were joined by de Ursis and de Pantoia, whose journey from Peking had been made under conditions quite different from those experienced by Vagnoni and

Semedo. De Ursis and de Pantoia had had an escort the first day only out of Peking, then, upon pledging their word that they would go to Canton, they had been allowed to make the rest of the trip alone and unmolested.

After a month's confinement in jail the four Jesuits were released by the prefect of Canton who seemed to regard their persecution as a personal vendetta of Shên Ch'üeh. He established them in a pagoda and provided for their maintenance. Early in 1618, some seven months after their arrival in Canton, the prefect had them honorably conducted to Macao. This was the end of their sufferings.

Meanwhile the officers of the guard which had conducted Vagnoni and Semedo to Nanhsiung reported to Shên Ch'üeh that their mission had been completed. The report is included in the *P'o-hsieh-chi.* It is dated the 8th Moon (September), 1617, and states that Vagnoni and Semedo had been conducted, under good escort, to Canton, with all the marks of imperial benevolence; that they had been given two ounces of silver a month for their sustenance; that they had been turned over to the officials of Canton; that they had been joined by de Ursis and de Pantoia; that they had been conducted to Macao, and there turned over to the barbarian dogs. It concludes by stating that it is the duty of the officials of Kwangtung province to see that they do not re-enter China. The officials of Kwangtung province were presumably little inclined to take instructions from Shên Ch'üeh or his agents on the responsibilities of their office. Both Vagnoni and Semedo re-entered China, the latter in 1620, the former in 1624, and both rendered distinguished service to the mission.

The Christians whom Vagnoni and Semedo had left behind in the prisons of Nanking had been released after receiving a bastinado of seventy blows. The two Jesuit lay brothers (John) Chung Ming-li and (Sebastian) Chung Ming-jen, were more severely dealt with. The former was condemned to three years at hard labor pulling boats on the canals. The latter was condemned to servitude to the stone masons working on the Great Wall. Actually Sebastian escaped this fate. An heroic Christian, identified only as Mathew, substituted himself; and he in turn was released through the intercession of Hsü Kuang-ch'i with the commander of the section of the Great Wall to which he had been sent.

Shên Ch'üeh had both the church and the residence in Nanking razed. The land was sold for one hundred and fifty *taels* to one Li Ch'êng. The money realized from the sale was turned over to one Shang Yuan-hsien, a sub-prefect, to be used for needed repairs to his offices. The small garden owned by the Jesuits outside the city was sold for fifteen *taels* to a eunuch named Wang Ming.

In what he evidently regarded as the official conclusion of the affair, Shên Ch'üeh issued in the name of the Board of Rites, in the 8th Moon, 1617, a solemn proclamation to the people of Nanking. It is directed against those "who falsely claim to be of the religion of the Lord of Heaven and who lead the ignorant people towards revolution." This religion is prohibited in China. The people are solemnly forbidden to honor "Jesus, whom the barbarian preachers of this religion claim to be the Lord of Heaven become man," to receive baptism, to assemble on Sundays and feast days. China must preserve the cult which has been handed down by her ancestors.

If in Shên's ears this proclamation sounded like the grand finale, actually it was but the end of the first movement. His triumph was complete only in Nanking and even there it was not lasting. Only four of the missionaries had been driven to Macao, and two of these returned. The others, thanks to the courageous loyalty of their Chinese friends, remained in the empire. Although, for some years, they had to restrict their freedom of movement, at no time was their work brought to a halt.

However regrettable the attack launched by Shên Ch'üeh there is this to be said: Whether compared with their contemporaries in other lands or with their latter-day descendants in communist China, the Chinese of seventeenth-century Ming China appear as almost paragons of civilized behavior. At this very time Japanese Catholics were being put to death amid great torment for their faith; and for a long time European Christians had been torturing and killing each other in the name of religion. And today foreign missionaries have been pitilessly jailed and relentlessly driven from the land to which they had given their lives, Chinese priests languish in prison cells, and everywhere the Church lies prostrate under the cruel hand of a despotism unrelieved by the urbane moderation that was once the mark of Chinese culture.

NOTES

(1) This chapter is based mainly upon the first-hand accounts of principal participants. The best is the unpublished report of Vagnoni, *ARSI*, Jap-Sin 161 I, ff. 1-26. Semedo's account, written more than two decades after the events and in unimportant details inaccurate, is in Alvarô Semedo, *Histoire universelle de la Chine* trad. nouvellement en français (Lyons: H. Prost, 1667). From the other side there is the collection of official documents issued by the Nanking tribunals which dealt with the case, cf. *infra*, n. 3.

(2) Di Costanzo's long letter to the general telling of the persecution is in *ARSI*, Jap-Sin 114, ff. 99-139; and cf. Semedo, *op. cit.*, p. 407.

(3) There is a copy of the *P'o-hsieh-chi* in the Zikawei library in China. The extracts quoted or referred to in this chapter are taken from the manuscript of Auguste M. Colombel, S. J., *Histoire de la Mission du Kiang-nan* (lithographed, Zikawei: Shanghai, 1895-1905), I, 204-234.

(4) Semedo, *op. cit.*, p. 309.

(5) The Chinese text of Hsü Kuang-ch'i's memorial with English translation by E. C. Bridgman is in *The Chinese Repository*, XIX (Canton, 1850), pp. 118-126. It is dated the 44th year, 7th month, of the Wan-li reign, which Bridgman erroneously translates as the year 1617. The Chinese date corresponds to August, 1616, which leaves no doubt that the rescript of the president of the Board of Rites mentioned by Hsü as having appeared in the government *Gazette* is the memorial of August 15, 1616, referred to in my text. On the concordance of dates cf. P. Hoang, *Concordance des chronologies néoméniques chinoise et europée ne* (Variétés sinologiques No. 29, Shanghai: Mission catholique, 1910).

(6) Semedo, *op. cit.*, p. 326.

(7) Cf. *Analecta*, XV, 8; XIV, 13.

(8) On this whole subject cf. Elbert Duncan Thomas, *Chinese Political Thought* (New York: Prentice-Hall, Inc., 1927), pp. 172-195.

(9) Semedo, *op. cit.*, p. 334.

Chapter IX

Riding the Storm

When Shen Ch'ueh issued his solemn proclamation in August, 1617, there remained in China fourteen Jesuits of whom eight were priests, the others lay brothers. The priests were Europeans, the brothers Chinese. Driven under cover, their religion proscribed, their cause seemed forlorn. Yet one looks in vain for a pessimistic note in their letters.[1] A soberer and more balanced view had replaced the excessive optimism of the past, but of despair there was no sign. These fourteen men seemed to share a firm confidence in the ultimate triumph of their cause.[2]

Most of the Jesuits were gathered in Hangchow. Here, under the direction of the scholarly Yang T'ing-yün, they prepared themselves by intensive study of Chinese literature and language for a more effective apostolate when the storm should have passed. Giulio Aleni, Yang's favorite pupil, acquired during these years of semi-retirement so great a mastery of Chinese literature and customs that, during his later apostolate in Fukien province, he was widely known as the "Western Confucius." Nor did Vagnoni waste the years of his exile in Macao. He devoted his time to writing works in Chinese, improving his literary style, and deepening his knowledge of the classics. The fruits were extensive and lasting. Vagnoni would later do some of the most effective writing of any of the Jesuits. Certain of his works are still read.

There is much that is inspiring in the spectacle of this handful of men carrying on in the face of the apparent ruination of so many years' work. How much patient effort and how many toilsome years had Ricci devoted to winning a foothold in Shaochow, in

Nanchang, in Nanking, and in Peking! Now all the gains seemed wiped out overnight. Only stout hearts could face a situation such as this with equanimity, but stout hearts these men had. No time was lost in brooding over temporary retreat. No recriminations took place, no assessing of blame. Certain criticisms went to Rome, but they were even-tempered. Longobardo had been too optimistic; Vagnoni had been indiscreet. That much was admitted and wisely dismissed. With unity of purpose preparations were made for the morrow while, as far as circumstances permitted, the apostolate of the moment was continued.

As often as possible the priests visited the Christian communities now deprived of their regular pastors. Despite difficulties, they were able to register 277 new converts in 1619 and to report the enrollment of many catechumens. This was enough to prove Shên had failed in his effort to destroy Christianity.

In this same year four of the Jesuits undertook a mission to the distant province of Shensi at the invitation of (Philip) Wang Chêng who lived in the city of Chingyang. Wang had won his *chü-jên* degree in 1594, but would not successfully pass the *chin-shih* examinations until 1622, after nine previous failures. The examination papers which finally won him the doctorate are still preserved in the Shensi provincial library at Sian, whether because of their brilliance or as a testimony to his perseverance it is difficult to say. In any event, his frequent trips to Peking to undergo the examinations had made him well acquainted with the Jesuits and had led to his conversion. His efforts to introduce the faith to his native province in 1619 failed, the echoes from Nanking and the edict of expulsion making the times unpropitious. A few years later when Wang was in a position to render more effective assistance the effort was renewed with success.

Also in 1619 van Spiere and Brother Chung Ming-jên managed to visit Nanking. Received with joy by the Christians, they encouraged them to keep the flame burning. Semedo pays high tribute to the constancy of the Nanking Christians.[3]

In 1621 a mission center was established in the city of Kiating, near Shanghai. (Ignatius) Sun Yüan-hua, a Christian scholar-official, was responsible for this move. Sun had studied Western mathematics under Hsü Kuang-ch'i, an association which led to his conversion. In 1621 he wrote to the Jesuits in Hangchow, inviting them to visit him. When the letter arrived, Cattaneo and Sambiasi were on the point of leaving for Shanghai. Sambiasi went on to Kiating where he found that Sun had prepared an apartment in his home, complete with chapel.[4] Sambiasi's labors were fruitful: within a short time it was necessary to build a larger chapel. Four years later Semedo, who had quietly left Macao in 1620, visited Kiating and was able to report:

> I can say in truth that I found there a goodly number of Christians as fervent in the faith, the men and women no less than the children, as assiduous in assisting at Mass, listening to the word of God, going to confession, and frequenting the august sacrament of the altar, as the most devout Christians in Europe.[5]

A small and pleasantly situated town, Kiating was admirably suited for a house of studies. Young Chinese from Macao, candidates for admission to the Society of Jesus, were brought here to study Chinese letters while being trained in the spiritual discipline of the novitiate. As recruits arrived from Europe they too were sent to Kiating to begin their Chinese language study. Four priests newly arrived in the mission were studying Chinese there in 1622.

Hsü Kuang-ch'i was in retirement in Shanghai from 1621 to 1627. His presence was a boon to Cattaneo who soon found the number of catechumens so great that he had to call upon the Jesuits in Hangchow for help. Despite the protection afforded by Hsü's prestige, precautions had to be observed. In 1622, to avoid gathering large crowds, Cattaneo still observed the rule of allowing the Christians to assist at Mass in groups of no more than five. Before Hsü Kuang-ch'i re-entered public life in 1627, however, he found it necessary to build a larger church in Shanghai, the old structure having grown too small to accommodate the flourishing community.

The annual letter of 1620 reports 268 conversions for that year: 20 in Peking, 105 in Hangchow, 25 in Nanking, 20 in Shanghai, 98 in Kienchang. In 1621 there were 40 conversions in Peking, some 300 in Hangchow, 12 in Nanhsiung, 72 in Shanghai, 60 in Kiating, 52 in Nanking, 46 in Nanchang. In 1622 Peking reported 31 converts, Kiating 70, Hangchow 191, Shanghai 86, Nanchang and Kienchang 50.

Measured against the difficulties, the harvest was encouraging. At this time the missionaries did not have a single residence of their own in China, and they had but one church, that in Shanghai. They lived in the homes of loyal Christians: with Hsü Kuang-ch'i in Shanghai, with Sun Yüan-hua in Kiating, with Stephen in Kienchang, with Yang T'ing-yün in Hangchow, and with Martin Ch'in and a Christian scholar, identified only as Dr. Nazarius, in Peking.

In 1621 Shên Ch'üeh, now removed from office in Nanking, was living in retirement in Hangchow. His temporary eclipse gave renewed hope to the missionaries. Trigault, writing to Europe, reported that the storm seemed to have passed. Most of the Jesuits were living at the home of Yang T'ing-yün under the very eyes of their arch-enemy. On feast days as many as one hundred persons gathered at one time to assist at Mass. Trigault was puzzled by Shên's silence. The explanation is not far to seek. For the moment he was in no position to reassume the offensive. He had not had a change of heart. He made this plain by ignoring Yang T'ing-yün's invitation to meet the Jesuits.

With Shên's retirement the situation in Peking improved. Prudence was still required, but once a month Christians gathered in groups in designated houses for instruction. Five or six times a year they met in church for confession, a sermon and Mass. The feast of Christmas, 1620, was celebrated with considerable solemnity, not excepting Chinese-style music.

A notable conversion in 1621 led not only to the establishment of a Christian center in Yangchow, the city once governed by Marco Polo, but also to the first successful mission to the provinces of Shensi and Shansi. Ma San-chih, a scholar-official of wide reputation, held a position in the government of Shensi province. As a result of a meeting in Peking with the Jesuits, he became interested in the study of Western mathematics. He asked Hsü Kuang-ch'i to persuade one of the Jesuits to visit and tutor him in the positive sciences. Giulio Aleni was selected for the mission. He joined Ma San-chih at his home in Yangchow and gave him lessons in mathematics and other sciences. At the same time, he succeeded in converting Ma to Christianity. He was baptized on the Feast of the Annunciation, 1621, taking the Christian name Peter. Baptized with him was his son. Many of his relatives became catechumens. Van Spiere later established himself in Ma's home in Yangchow, continuing the work begun by Aleni and broadening the foundations of another important Christian center in the empire.

When his convert set out for Shensi Aleni accompanied him. The journey to Ma's seat of government in the city of Shangchow lasted twenty-nine days. Here Aleni spent five months, often accompanying his friend on official visits to the nineteen cities which lay within his jurisdiction.

While in Shensi Aleni experimented successfully with winemaking. His discovery that the grapes of Shensi made good wine was important, inasmuch as the problem of obtaining Mass wine from Europe had been a vexing one. Earlier efforts to make wine in China had failed. It either turned to vinegar or refused to ferment.

When Ma San-chih was transferred to the province of Fukien, Aleni went to Shansi province at the invitation of (Stephen) Han Yün, member of a family of scholar-officials, who with his brother (Thomas) Han Lin, had been converted in Peking. As in so many cases these conversions were due to the influence of Hsü Kuang-ch'i under whose tutelage the Hans studied mathematics and military science. Both brothers became zealous Christians; Han Lin, the younger, later achieved fame as a bibliophile.

In 1621 when Aleni visited the Han home in Chiangchow, Shansi, Han Lin was away. At the age of twenty, he had just passed his *chü-jên* examination in Peking. Before returning home he spent nine years traveling in Chihli, Shantung, Kiangsu, Chekiang, and Kiangsi, collecting books. Aleni found at home the older brother Han Yün. referred to in contemporary missionary accounts as Dr. Stefano. Han Yün had been instructing many of his friends and relatives in the tenets of Christianity. After completing their instruction Aleni baptized eighteen of them. Ten years later Chiangchow became one of the most promising of the Christian communities in China. At this time, however, Aleni could do no more. The visitor of the province, a friend of Shên Ch'üeh, issued a manifesto against Christianity. Aleni rejoined Ma San-chih who was waiting for him in Honan. Together they returned to Yangchow, whence Ma, after a visit with his family, left to take up his post as viceroy in Foochow.

In 1622 there were thirteen Jesuit priests in China, five more than there had been when Shên issued his proclamation five years before. In 1621 Semedo had re-entered China with Nicolas Trigault. The next year Rodrigo de Figueredo, Wenceslas Pantaleon Kirwitzer, and Johann Adam Schall von Bell followed them.

A new flare-up in Nanking in 1621 and the return to high office, this time in Peking itself, of the arch-enemy threatened again to destroy the foundations for missionary hopes. The new setback was intimately related to the internal political situation in China.

For years the patriotic elements in Chinese officialdom had been waging a losing battle against the eunuch party. The growing power of the latter had driven many capable administrators from public life. Those who remained found it increasingly difficult to operate effectively.

The deplorable condition of politics within China contributed to the ever-growing menace of the Manchus beyond the Wall. While China, during the long Wan-li reign (1573-1620) was increasingly torn by factional disputes and party strife, the Eastern Tatars, or Manchus, had been developing greater unity and strength.

The transformation of the disunited tribes of Eastern Tatary into a united nation constituting a major threat to China, was the work of Nurhaci (1559-1626), who from a minor chieftain in an obscure tribe became the leader of a united people. Nurhaci was born in the Aisin Gioro clan which held the chieftainship of a Ju-chên tribe. The Ju-chên people lived north of Korea and east and northeast of China's Liaotung territory. In the twelfth century they founded the short-lived Chin dynasty (1115-1234). Conquered by the Mongols in the thirteenth century they were divided into three main tribes: the Chien-chou, Hsi-hsi, and Yeh-jên. Nurhaci was a member of the Chien-chou tribe, in which, following the violent death of his father, Taksi, he became a minor chieftain.

From then on his story is the saga of a rapid expansion of power and growth in prestige. He established his authority first over his relatives and tribesmen. By 1601 he had conquered all the neighboring tribes in Eastern Tatary with the exception of the Yehe. In this same year he organized his people into four units, known as banners. Changed in 1615 into eight banners, the system transformed the state into a powerful military machine.

In 1608 he signed a treaty with the Ming generals on the Liaotung border fixing the boundaries of his domain. But as his military power grew, he began to develop a hostile attitude towards the Ming court and ceased paying tribute to China in 1609.

On February 17, 1616, Nurhaci proclaimed himself emperor with the reign title T'ien-ming. He named his dynasty the Chin or Hou-Chin (Later Chin) so signify that it was a continuation of the twelfth century dynasty of that name. Twenty years later the dynastic name was changed to Ch'ing.

In 1618 Nurhaci led an army to invade China. In doing so he published a list of seven grievances against the Ming. Probably the one which rankled most and which, together with his own vaulting ambition, really motivated him, was the fact that Chinese authorities in Liaotung, disturbed by Nurhaci's growing power, had been giving military assistance to the Yehe. Sweeping into Liaotung he captured several cities, including Fushun.

The fall of Fushun alarmed the Wan-li emperor. He appointed Yang Hao vice-president of the Board of War and sent him to Liaotung to head an anti-Manchu campaign. It would have been difficult to make a worse choice. As a result of his own indecision and mismanagement, Yang Hao in 1598 had suffered a disastrous defeat at the hands of the Japanese in Korea.

On April 5, 1619, Yang Hao despatched four armies against the Manchu stronghold of Hsingching. The plan called for them to converge from four directions on April 15. Instead, the first army, which arrived on April 14, was annihilated. The second army was overwhelmed at Senggiyan on the following day; on April 17 the third army, with its Korean auxiliaries, was destroyed at Dungge. Only by a rapid retreat to Shênyang was Yang Hao able to save the fourth army. The losses suffered by the Chinese in four days of fighting were enormous.

Disgusted with the ineptitude of government in Peking, Hsü Kuang-ch'i, on August 7, 1619, petitioned the emperor to send him to Korea as a special envoy to advise the Korean government in the struggle against the Manchus. He was motivated not only by the desire to organize assistance for China, but also by the hope of introducing Christianity into Korea. For this purpose he intended to take with him Sambiasi, who at this time was living in Hsü's home in Peking. His proposal, although approved by the Board of War, was rejected by the emperor. Instead of going to Korea, Hsü was sent to Tungchow, east of Peking, to take charge of a training center for recruits to the army. It was another experience in frustration. Unable to obtain from Peking the funds needed to support the troops, he was forced to appeal to Li Chih-tsao and Yang T'ing-yün for contributions.

On August 18, 1620, Emperor Shên-tsung, more commonly

known by his reign title Wan-li, died after an illness of two months. He had occupied the throne of China with disastrous consequences to the empire, for almost forty-eight years. He was succeeded by his son Chu Ch'ang-lo, under the reign title T'ai-ch'ang.

Chu Ch'ang-lo had been born in 1582 to a lady-in-waiting in the palace of the empress. Although recognized by the empress as the legitimate heir, his father, the emperor, wanted to name as his successor Chu Ch'ang-hsün, a younger son whose mother, surnamed Chêng, was his favorite concubine. Although, in 1601, after a struggle of fifteen years' duration, the emperor yielded to the pressure of the ministers of state and named Chu Ch'ang-lo his successor, the intrigues continued. It was largely out of this struggle that the Tung-lin party arose. Although the immediate issue centered on the question of succession, what was really involved was a struggle by the forces interested in good government to break the grip of the eunuchs, the concubines, and their corrupt satellites upon the government.

In 1615 a nameless assassin, armed with a club, gained access to the palace of the heir-apparent whom he attempted to beat to death. At his trial, the would-be assassin was pronounced insane. Although political factionalism succeeded in beclouding the issues, it was generally believed that the attempt upon the life of the crown prince had been inspired by the eunuch party supporting the concubine Chêng.

In 1619 upon the death of the empress, Chêng became chief consort of the emperor. When the emperor died in the following year, he left instructions that she should be raised to the rank of empress dowager. During his father's last illness Chu Ch'ang-lo was prevented by Chêng from seeing him. Fearful that a palace *coup d'état* was being prepared by the mother of Chu Ch'ang-hsün, a group of ministers, led by the intrepid Yang Lien demanded and obtained an audience at which the emperor confirmed the succession of Chu Ch'ang-lo. The same group of ministers succeeded, after the monarch's death, in blocking the attempt to raise his consort to the rank of empress dowager which would have given her a commanding position over the new emperor.

Chu Ch'ang-lo ascended the throne on August 28, 1620. The Jesuits viewed his accession to power with great hopes. They saw in him a man of ability and integrity who might rescue the country from the morass into which corrupt government had led it. That their judgment was well-founded is indicated by the bitter battle which honest officials waged to assure his succession and by the fact that he immediately began a reorganization of the government. No one will ever know how far the reform movement might have gone under his direction, because it was stopped in its tracks. Nine days after mounting the throne, the emperor became suddenly ill. Medicine given him a few days later by a eunuch attached to the concubine Chêng aggravated his illness. His condition further deteriorated after the ministrations of a doctor who claimed to have wonder-working medicine. Yang Lien protested, in a series of memorials, against the inexpert medical treatment provided for the ruler.

Meanwhile the emperor's favorite concubine, Hsi Li, installed herself in his apartments. This move intensified the fears of Yang Lien and his associates that the palace janissaries were preparing to establish a joint regency of the consorts Chêng and Li in the event of death.

On September 26 the emperor died. The Jesuits in Peking shared the common opinion that he had been poisoned. Immediately upon receiving word of his death, Yang Lien led the ministers of state to the imperial palace. The eunuchs attempted to prevent their entry, but Yang Lien overawed them. He and his companions took possession of the person of Chu Yu-chiao, the oldest son of the deceased emperor, carried him off to the coronation hall and proclaimed his accession. They then refused to allow him to return to the imperial palace until the concubine had moved out. Bitter quarreling ensued between Yang Lien and his supporters on the one side and the eunuchs and their henchmen on the other. The eunuchs hoped to maintain their hegemony through the control which the concubine Hsi Li would exercise over the policies of the young emperor. The deadlock was broken on the fifth day when Hsi Li was ejected from the imperial palace.

It was an empty victory for the Tung-lin party although one must admire Yang Lien's zeal and courage. In putting Chu Yu-chiao, who ruled under the reign title T'ien-ch'i, upon the throne, he had rendered no service to the cause of reform. But he had little choice in the matter. Chu Yu-chiao was the legitimate successor. Had he been shunted aside in favor of Chu Ch'ang-hsün the ascendancy of the eunuch party, working through the concubines Chêng and Li, would have been assured. As it turned out the eunuchs won anyway. The reign of the T'ien-ch'i emperor (1620-1627) was disastrous. During this seven-year period the actual ruler of China was the notorious Wei Chung-hsien, one of the most powerful eunuchs in the history of the empire.

Wei Chung-hsien, as a youth, had had himself made a eunuch and entered the service of the palace in order to free himself from difficulties arising out of his gambling debts. Ambitious, unscrupulous, and able, he pushed himself forward in the entourage of Chu Ch'ang-lo's concubine mother. Collaborating with him in his intrigues was Chu Ch'ang-lo's wet nurse, K'ê-shih.[6]

One of the first decrees which emanated from the new emperor conferred high rank upon the eunuch and upon K'ê-shih. Abandoning power entirely into the hands of Wei Chung-hsien, the young emperor retired into his carpenter shop to devote most of his time to carpentering, the one passion, other than unrestrained sexual indulgence, which he seems to have had. It was rumored about the palace that the emperor called Wei Chung-hsien "father," "a monstrosity of affection," as Bartoli ironically remarks, "no less unseemly from the point of view of decorum than impossible from the point of view of nature."[7]

Wei Chung-hsien drove most of the capable men out of the government. Hsü Kuang-ch'i was one of many who found his tyrannous misrule intolerable. Scarcely had the eunuch taken over effective control of the government when Hsü Kuang-ch'i was ordered to reduce the number of troops he was training at Tungchow to forty-six hundred men. After fruitless efforts to arouse Peking to the necessity of organizing effective forces under capable leadership to resist the Manchus, Hsü Kuang-ch'i resigned and retired to his farm at Tientsin.

The year 1621 showed clearly that China was headed towards disaster. In that year Nurhaci, having finally conquered the Yehe tribe, turned his attention again to the Celestial Empire. His forces swept through Liaotung, capturing its two most important cities, Shênyang and Liaoyang. In Liaoyang Nurhaci established his new capital and made it his principal base of operations.

Following this disaster Hsü Kuang-ch'i was recalled to the capital. Once more he petitioned to be sent as envoy to Korea, no doubt convinced that more effective resistance to the Manchus could be organized in that quarter than in Peking where every constructive effort was paralyzed by the satellites of Wei Chung-hsien. Ts'ui Ching-jung, president of the Board of War, strongly opposed his petition.

When, shortly after this, Shên Ch'üeh was appointed to high office in Peking, Hsü Kuang-ch'i again retired, this time to his home in Shanghai. Perhaps as a symbol of disillusionment with the world of affairs, he there wrote, from Sambiasi's dictation, a two *chüan* treatise on the soul, published in 1624 under the title *Ling-yên li-shuo*.

Hsü Kuang-ch'i had long been persuaded that the Manchus could be checked only by the development of a new instrument of defensive warfare. He saw in cannon-fire, with which neither the Manchus nor the Chinese were familiar, the instrument which could checkmate the innovations of the Manchu leader. Hence he had repeatedly endeavored to persuade controllers of governmental policy to turn to the Portuguese in Macao for aid. While in command of the training center at Tungchow, he had sent his own unofficial mission to Macao. His envoys were two Christians, Michael Chang and Paul Sung. They were well received by the Portuguese authorities. Although reluctant, in view of the imminent threat of a Dutch attack upon Macao, to deprive themselves of artillery or men, the Portuguese sent four cannon and a small squad of cannoneers. Local officials in Kiangsi kept the cannon and sent the cannoneers back to Macao.

Shortly before Hsü Kuang-ch'i went to Shanghai in 1621, Li Chih-tsao, who since 1616 had been living in retirement in Hangchow, was called to Peking to become concurrently sub-director of the Banqueting Court and head of the Department of Waterways and Dikes in the Board of Public Works. In the latter capacity he memoralized, in the fifth moon of 1621, proposing that Hsü Kuang-ch'i's initial move be further exploited by sending an official mission to Macao to solicit assistance. The petition met with the approval of the Board of War. Orders were sent to the Kiangsi officials to send the four cannon to Peking. Michael Chang and Paul Sung were given official rank and again sent to Macao where they received a royal welcome. The Portuguese were not unmindful of the fact that it was the first time they had received any sign of official recognition from Peking. The fact, too, that the Chinese representatives were

Christians whose attitude during a solemn Pontifical Mass was one of extreme reverence and devotion added to the stir aroused by their mission.

Meanwhile Captain Lopo Sarmento, returning from a voyage to Japan, reported that the Dutch were at the moment not in sufficient strength in the China seas to attack Macao. The Macao authorities, anxious to meet the request of the Chinese, agreed to send artillerymen to man thirty cannon which the Chinese had salvaged from an English vessel wrecked on the coast, together with a force of one hundred musketeers under the command of Captain Lorenzo de Lis Veglio.

The mission of Chang and Sung seemed crowned with success. The Jesuits and their Christian friends had particular reason to rejoice. Inasmuch as they had used their good offices in the negotiations at Macao it appeared possible that the success of the project might lead to the quashing of the edict of expulsion. At this juncture, however, Shên Ch'üeh reappeared upon the scene and succeeded in sabotaging the entire undertaking.

With the advent of Wei Chung-hsien to power, Shên, who had retired to Hangchow after his dismissal from office in 1620, found his star once more in the ascendancy. Michael Chang and Paul Sung were just completing their negotiations in Macao when Shên was summoned to Peking to assume the office of grand secretary. Before leaving Hangchow he made a show of hostility by demanding that the viceroy provide him with an escort of five hundred men to protect him from the Christians! The viceroy refused the request. Arrived in Peking, Shên immediately undertook to undo the work of Chang and Sung by arousing fears in official circles of Portuguese conquest of the empire. The Portuguese offer of men was refused.

Before long two of the four cannon in Peking, manned by inexpert Chinese artillerymen, exploded and killed several Chinese. This accident resulted in Li Chih-tsao's forced retirement from the court. Li returned to Hangchow where, in the seclusion of his garden, he devoted himself to writing and to assisting the missionaries in their studies.[8]

Meanwhile Shên Ch'üeh seized upon the accident as a pretext for renewing the persecution of Christianity. An uprising in Shantung which occurred at this time played directly into his hands. The long years of misrule, oppression, and general governmental ineptitude were reflected in growing unrest in the provinces. Exactions of the eunuch party impoverished the people. Mismanagement of the war with the Manchus, marked by mass levees of men for the army and by disastrous military reverses, contributed to popular dissatisfaction. The annual letters of the Jesuits written during these years consistently report growing unrest and disturbances.

In this state of popular ferment the secret societies, never long dormant in China, became increasingly active. In 1622 a large band belonging to the notorious *Pai-lien-chiao* (White Lotus Society) led an uprising of the populace. They seized imperial ships en route to Peking with the annual rice levy. Emboldened by success they then attacked several well garrisoned centers and captured a large city. The rebellion was finally put down, but its effects were felt in neighboring provinces.

Orders issued from Peking to provincial authorities to hunt down every member of the society. In Nanking a Christian went to the defense of a neighbor who was being manhandled by the police. He was seized and his home searched. A painting of the Savior identified him as belonging to the religion of the Lord of Heaven, which certain Nanking officials alleged was but another name for the *Pai-lien-chiao*.

The Christian artist who had painted the picture was arrested. Under torture he named forty other Nanking Christians. Thirty-four of these were seized. They readily admitted that they were Christians, but despite torture, steadfastly denied that they had any connection with the *Pai-lien-chiao*. All but eight of them were released. The eight were those in whose homes the Christians were accustomed to assemble for prayers. Forced to run the usual gamut of tribunals, they were severely treated, and given several bastinados. One of the Christians, a carpenter by trade, in whose home van Spiere celebrated Mass and administered the sacraments upon his secret visits to Nanking, died in prison as a result of the beatings he received. John Yao, whose militant courage had puzzled officials in the persecution six years earlier, had lost none of his ardor. Disappointed because in the arrest of the thirty-four he had been overlooked, he presented himself before the authorities, declared himself a Christian, and demanded to share the fate of his fellows. Apparently the officials still found this desire to suffer rather mystifying and refused to arrest him.

The presiding magistrate in Nanking handed down a judgment condemning Christianity. After recalling the memorials of Shên Ch'üeh and the edict of expulsion, he sentenced the prisoners to a month's imprisonment and ordered confiscation of their books, pictures, and other articles relating to their cult.

Meanwhile a Nanking Christian carried word of these developments to the Jesuits in Hangchow. Yang T'ing-yün immediately wrote to the officials in Nanking, defending the Christians. Hsü Kuang-ch'i composed another defense of Christianity, enumerating fourteen ways in which Christianity differed essentially from the *Pai-lien-chiao*, and sent copies to key officials in Nanking. His intervention had no effect as most of the Nanking officials at the time belonged to the eunuch party and were anxious to ingratiate themselves with Shên Ch'üeh who as grand secretary was one of the most powerful officials in the empire. The magistrate who had passed sentence upon the Christians replied to Hsü Kuang-ch'i in a letter, the disdainful tone of which was rarely used in writing to one of Hsü's standing. In China even bitter hostility usually cloaks itself in polite forms. The magistrate stated bluntly that the Christian sect was absolutely one with the *Pai-lien-chiao* and accused Hsü Kuang-ch'i and Yang T'ing-yün of making a profession of disobedience to the emperor, his laws, and his ministers.

On September 15, 1622, word reached Hangchow that Shên Ch'üeh had fallen. Before being called to Peking to assume the office of grand secretary he had already made many enemies. His own brother was among those who had lodged complaints against him. During the short time that he was in Peking protests against his ambitious intrigues and high-handed injustices multiplied. Not even his powerful allies in the eunuch party could save him.

Active persecution was at an end. Although they still had no residence or public church in the land, the missionaries began to enlarge the scope of their activities, but with circumspection. There could be no gathering of crowds, no preaching in the street, no ecclesiastical processions. They would not repeat the indiscretions into which the excessive optimism of the years 1611-1615 had led them.

There had been no official abrogation of the edict of expulsion. The missionaries still had no legal sanction in China. The sanction which they had enjoyed prior to the edict, that of official recognition of their presence in Peking, they no longer enjoyed. So long as Wei Chung-hsien wielded power their position was in grave danger. These were the darker shadows in the picture. But the removal of Shên Ch'üeh from the scene compensated for a great deal. When their old enemy died at his home in Hangchow on April 19, 1624, the Jesuits probably said a prayer for his soul; but perhaps they also felt a degree of satisfaction in the thought, since they did not believe in ghosts, that his power to injure their cause was at an end.

NOTES

(1) Chief sources for this chapter are:
   a) The annual letters by Dias, Kirwitzer, and Trigault, in *Relatione delle cose più notabili scritte ne gli anni 1619, 1620, 1621 dalla Cina* (Roma: Zannetti, 1624); hereafter cited as *Relatione 1624.*
   b) Semedo's *Histoire universelle.*
   c) A letter of Trigault's written from Hangchow on August 15, 1622, in *ARSI*, Jap-Sin 114, ff. 274-296; and the annual letter for 1622 written by Semedo in *ibid.*, ff. 344-367.
   d) Annual letter by Dias for 1625, in *Histoire de ce qui s'est passé es royaumes d'Ethiopie, en l'année 1626, jusqu'au mois de Mars 1627. Et de la Chine, de l'année 1625 jusques en Fevrier de 1626 . . .* (Paris: Sebastien Cramoisy, 1679). Hereafter cited as *Histoire 1625.*
   e) *Eminent Chinese*, I, 176, 190, 316 ff., 452 f., 594 ff.; II, 846 f., 885 f., 892 f.

(2) Cf. Longobardo's letter from Hangchow, October 27, 1618; *ARSI*, Jap-Sin 17 f. 187.

(3) Semedo, *Histoire universelle*, p. 335.

(4) Trigault confuses Semedo with Sambiasi in his account. Semedo himself says that it was Sambiasi who made the first trip to Kiating.

(5) Semedo, *op. cit.*, p. 337.

(6) *Eminent Chinese*, II, 847.

(7) Bartoli, *op. cit.*, IV, 69.

(8) *Eminent Chinese*, I, 453. Semedo gives a somewhat different account. He says the cannon exploded at Shanhaikuan, but that a powder depôt in Peking, ignited through carelessness, blew up killing twenty-one people; *op. cit.*, p. 153.

Chapter X

Who Killed Cock Robin?

When Nicolas Trigault re-entered China in 1621 he brought to an end a notable mission to Europe and left two mysteries for future historians to puzzle over. He had sailed from Macao in February, 1613, under orders from Longobardo who had decided, probably without authority to do so, to send him to Rome to seek definitive answers to many problems, to try to obtain independent status for the China mission, and to solicit additional personnel and financial support. Trigault, a native of Douai in the Low Countries, had only had two years' experience in the mission; but he was both brilliant and enterprising and no less persuasive in propagating his ideas than he was fecund in conceiving them. That is probably why Longobardo selected him.

Most of the problems for which he was to seek answers were of an administrative character, as is clear from the fifty *postulata*, i.e., requests for policy directives, which Trigault submitted to the general of the Society in Rome.[1] Actually, Vitelleschi, the general, simply transmitted many of them back to the visitor of the mission for a solution. There were, however, two requests, radical in nature and of far-reaching importance, with which only the Holy See could deal. One was that priests in China be permitted to keep the head covered while celebrating Mass. The other was that China be allowed her own liturgical language.

The former permission Valignano had petitioned for some years earlier, but had been informed by the general that it was contrary to canon law and that only the Holy See could grant the exemption. In China it was regarded as disrespectful for a man to remove his hat. For a priest to stand bareheaded at the altar seemed incongruous in Chinese eyes and out of keeping with the dignity of the function he was performing. Europeanism, always confusing ends with means and giving to the latter absolute values which belong only to the former, would have insisted upon the observance of European custom. Longobardo understood, as had Valignano, that the end to be sought was respect for the divine mysteries. A social observance which in Europe symbolized respect, but which in China had the opposite connotation, should be discarded in favor of the Chinese custom.

Another argument made by Trigault may have brought a smile to the face of the pope when he read it in the *supplicatio* submitted to him.[2] In China men cultivated their hair, "not otherwise than women." Only the bonzes shaved their heads. The Jesuits, in order not to be confused with the latter, observed the common custom. "It can easily be seen," remarks Trigault, "how indecent it is for priests to approach the altar with horrible womanish coiffures, especially among a people who so abominate an uncovered head."

The question of a liturgy in the Chinese language is shrouded in a double mystery. Who was responsible for the genesis of the idea? Who was responsible for its death?

When Trigault sailed from China he carried with him written instructions from Longobardo about the questions which he should raise in Rome. These instructions are in the Roman archives of the Society of Jesus, and, although among them is the question of the head-piece to be worn during the celebration of Mass, they say nothing about a Chinese liturgical language.[3] Because of this some historians have concluded that the idea was Trigault's own.[4] Others, however, think it incredible that Trigault would have taken it upon himself to propose a matter of such grave importance without the prior approval of his superior.[5] Given the character of Trigault this negative argument is far from conclusive. Trigault was a man whose mind was extremely fertile in ideas which he was never loath to urge. On the other hand, a comparison of the two documents shows that nearly all the fifty *postulata* submitted to the general by Trigault are based at least substantially upon the written instructions of Longobardo. It would seem likely, therefore, that there was some sort of understanding between Longobardo and his agent in the matter of the liturgy. The most plausible solution would seem to be this: Longobardo would hardly have included a formal petition for a Chinese liturgy in his written instructions because it was forbidden to ordain Chinese to the priesthood at all. Replying to an inquiry by Valignano and no doubt influenced by the negative reports of many Jesuits in the Far East, especially in Japan, the general of the Society had in a letter of December 12, 1606, directed that Chinese were not to be ordained, upon the ground that they were too young in the faith.[6] Longobardo had consistently and vigorously opposed this policy, arguing that the Chinese brothers had given complete satisfaction in every respect and that Chinese were no less fit for the priesthood than either Japanese or Europeans.

Longobardo felt so strongly on this subject that it is highly unlikely that he would have sent Trigault off to Europe without commissioning him to work for the removal of this interdict on Chinese priests. In urging this upon Trigault orally, he may also have told him, if successful in this, to sound out the possibility of raising candidates to the priesthood without a knowledge of Latin. In fact Trigault did attack the interdict and successfully. With this obstacle removed he also raised the question of a liturgy in the Chinese language.

The promptitude with which the Holy See acted reveals clearly where the sympathies of the pope lay. Trigault reached Rome in October, 1614, during the pontificate of Paul V. Claudio Aquaviva was in the last months of his long term of office (1581-1615) as general of the Society of Jesus. He immediately submitted Trigault's requests to the Jesuit theologians on the faculty of the Roman College. On January 6, 1615, they reported favorably. Trigault presented them to Pope Paul V who referred the matter to the Holy Office. One influential member of this congregation was Cardinal Robert Bellarmine, whose lectures Ricci had attended as a student in Rome. The cardinals wasted no time. In what must almost be a record for an institution noted for its prejudice against precipitate action, the Holy Office, in a meeting held on January 15, 1615, in the presence of Paul V in the Quirinal, granted the concessions asked for, namely, permission for priests to wear a head-piece while celebrating Mass; permission to translate the Bible into literary Chinese; permission for Chinese priests to celebrate Mass and recite the canonical hours in literary Chinese.

Evidently some uncertainty remained as to the exact terms of the concessions, for the same subject was taken up again in another meeting of the Holy Office, held on March 26, also in the presence of the Holy Father. This time Bellarmine was chairman of the board of six cardinals. A new text was drafted and approved. It was substantially the same as the earlier decree, but with some important qualifications added. It was made clear that the permission to adopt the head-piece was granted to all missionaries in China. As for the liturgy it specified that while Chinese could be used as the liturgical language, the Roman rite was still to be followed; nor was the permission to prejudice episcopal jurisdiction if and when bishops were constituted in China. To give the highest possible authority to this decree of March 26, 1615, Pope Paul V promulgated it by the Brief *Romanae Ecclesiae Antistes*, issued on June 27, 1615.

The permission for priests to wear a head-piece while celebrating Mass was acted upon. With the assistance of some of their Chinese friends the Jesuits in China designed a special head-piece, modelled after the ceremonial hat worn by scholars in ancient times. The wearing of this hat, known as the *chi-chin*, during the celebration of Mass was for a long time a feature of Catholic liturgical practice in China. It is no longer observed. The changes which many Chinese sociocultural attitudes have undergone make it no longer necessary.

The permission to adopt Chinese as the liturgical language was not acted upon, a fact which has mystified and confused historians ever since. In 1683 Cardinal Franciscus Albitius, a former secretary of the Holy Office, stated that both the decree of March, 1615, and the papal brief, although drafted, were withheld and never given to the Jesuits. Pope Benedict XIV in the next century stated that the decree was never sent to China.[8]

Many authors have accepted these statements. Both the cardinal and the pope were mistaken. Authenticated copies of the decree, made by the Holy Office notary with seal, are in the Jesuit archives in Rome.[9] Other copies were immediately despatched to China by Trigault, as is proved by an unedited letter of his of December 31, 1615.[10] In this long report to his confrères in China on his activities in Europe, Trigault tells them that he has obtained permission to wear the *chi-chin* and to say Mass in Chinese, and that he has already sent them three copies of the papal document and will bring two more copies with him when he returns.

Other writers have stated that Paul V's successor revoked the permission. This too is erroneous. The Holy See has never revoked the permission. Others have blamed Mutio Vitelleschi, Aquaviva's successor. They have theorized that Vitelleschi, a more timid man than his predecessor, thought the innovation too audacious and, inasmuch as the decree was not mandatory but permissive, decided not to apply it. This is also a mistaken view.

A possible, but by no means certain, explanation is that the real roadblock lay in differences between the Jesuits in Japan and their confrères in China and that the project was definitely killed by Francisco Vieira, the visitor. There is no doubt about the existence of these differences, nor is there much doubt that Vieira would have killed the project had he been asked for a decision.

The Jesuits in Japan were strongly opposed to all the objectives of Trigault's mission. In October, 1614, the first congregation of the Japanese province met in Nagasaki, Japan, and after discussion which lasted fifteen days adopted policy positions which on almost every point squarely contradicted the purposes for which Longobardo had sent Trigault to Europe. One of the delegates to the congregation, Gabriel de Matos, was selected to carry a statement of these positions and a summary of the reasons for them to Rome. To make sure that they reached their destination another Jesuit, Pedro Morejon, was sent with another copy of the documents by way of Mexico. De Matos arrived in Rome in May, 1617, and submitted to the general of the order the Nagasaki proceedings which revealed how far apart were the views of the two groups of Jesuits.[11]

The Jesuits in Japan were opposed to the idea of a native clergy. They recommended against the ordination of Japanese to the priesthood or the admission of Japanese, even as lay brothers, to the Society. Five of them signed an accompanying memorandum describing the Japanese as secretive, lacking a desire for perfection, wanting in zeal and in the purity of intention required for a religious vocation. This was a harsh judgment to pass upon a people many of whom would in the next twenty years suffer martyrdom, some of whom had already died bravely for the faith.

It is undoubtedly true that among a people to whom the faith is new, where time and tradition have not had a chance to develop a deep understanding of the severe demands of priestly life, the problem of a native clergy is much more difficult than some have on occasion recognized. Not many years after the Nagasaki conference the first vicars apostolic in Cochin-China learned this to their cost when, filled with enthusiasm for the cause, they ordained catechists who were wholly unsuited for the disciplined and celibate life of the priesthood. More cockle than wheat resulted from their indiscriminate sowing.

If one wonders why the problem should have been more difficult in these mission lands than it was in earlier centuries in Europe when the faith was new, the answer obviously lies in celibacy. This was the rub. As St. Thomas Aquinas points out, a life of celibacy is not a natural life. To resist the demands of nature requires discipline, training, a rather intensive supernatural life, and strong motivation. These conditions are less likely to be generally encountered where the ideal of a celibate priesthood has not had time to strike deep roots. In the early centuries in Europe when the faith was young the problem did not exist because celibacy was not demanded of the priesthood.

It is not surprising then that there had been unfortunate incidents in Japan where Japanese had been admitted to the priesthood. There was no justification for concluding from this, as the Nagasaki conferees did, that the Japanese were unfitted for religious or sacerdotal life. As one of a dissident minority of Japan Jesuits pointed out in a letter of October 11, 1618, it was not valid to conclude from the failure of some to the incapacity of all.[12] The source of the trouble, besides the newness of the faith, lay with faulty screening and inadequate training. In the hectic conditions of a young, rapidly growing, and persecuted mission, institutions which could offer proper training and testing did not exist. What is surprising is not that some fell by the wayside, but that others were martyrs and saints.

It is difficult not to see at work here the influence of Europeanism, the deeply ingrained notion that the non-European is by nature unsuited for the high demands of the priesthood. It is an expression of racial and nationalistic pride which is not easily exorcised. Well into the twentieth century there could be found some who looked on with jaundiced eye when Pope Pius XI elevated Chinese priests to the episcopacy.

The record both then and since of Japanese priests and religious is abundant proof of how wrong was the judgment made at Nagasaki. To his credit, the general of the Society, Mutio Vitelleschi, rejected that judgment. Because of the financial straits of the mission he agreed that for the time being admissions to the Society should be strictly limited; but he expressed the hope that the doors would never be closed to the Japanese who, as he pointedly reminded the fathers, had already proved their nobility of character by the supreme test of martyrdom.

The pejorative opinion formulated at Nagasaki was also applied to the Chinese. Here too, the outstanding record of devotion, zeal and even heroism on the part of the first Chinese Jesuit brothers, most of them men of considerable talent, one of whom had died heroically for the faith eight years earlier, as well as the later record of Chinese priests, disproves the Nagasaki thesis.

Because the Nagasaki Jesuits opposed the idea of a native clergy, de Matos, their spokesman, reasoned that they would also oppose the idea of a native liturgy, the whole purpose of which was to facilitate ordination to the priesthood. So when he discovered what Trigault had been up to in Rome he interposed his objection. "There seemed no necessity," his *postulatum* reads, "for this privilege." Since the privilege had already been granted he urged the general to leave to the visitor the decision as to whether it should be acted upon. Vitelleschi agreed to do this and his succinct reply absolves him of the charge of having withheld the permission. "Let them see to it there [in China]," he wrote, "and let the visitor decide, it being a matter of such importance."[13]

From the point of view of proper administration Vitelleschi's decision was unquestionably the correct one. Far from the scene and dealing with a matter of fundamental importance about which so strong a division of opinion existed, he placed responsibility for deciding the question in the hands of the superior on the spot. It was not then Vitelleschi who killed cock robin. Does the name of the visitor supply the answer to the mystery?

Francisco Vieira, while serving as provincial of India, had been appointed visitor of the Japanese province in 1615 and had arrived in Macao in July, 1616, to take up his duties. There is no doubt that he shared the views of the Nagasaki men on the subject of the liturgy. Furthermore, he had two grievances which were not apt to dispose him favorably towards the China mission.

Vieira was Portuguese. He had strong feelings of nationalistic loyalty and he looked upon the Trigault mission, one of the purposes of which was to persuade the general to raise the China mission to the status of an independent province, as a move by Longobardo to set up an Italian preserve in opposition to traditional Portuguese rights. He could not very well express himself along these lines to the Italian general, Mutio Vitelleschi, but he minced no words in writing to Nuno Mascarenhas, the Portuguese assistant to the general.[14] What Thyrsus Gonzales, one of Vitelleschi's successors, later in the century would refer to in exasperation as that "damned spirit of nationalism" (*maledictus spiritus nationalis*), ill served the cause of Christianity in the East.

Intensifying Vieira's complaints was the fact that in sending Trigault to Europe Longobardo had violated the rules of administrative procedure. Longobardo was subject to the jurisdiction of Valentim Carvalho, provincial of Japan. Apparently taking advantage of the fact that the death of Pasio had left the office of visitor vacant, Longobardo, without consulting Carvalho, had sent Trigault off to Rome on his own authority. Longobardo must have felt that it was useless to expect to get the cause of China properly presented in Rome by going through channels. Vieira and Carvalho both protested this breach of procedural rules.[15] In Rome Trigault said that Pasio had sanctioned the trip before his death. This seems doubtful inasmuch as Longobardo in a letter of February 2, 1613, to Aquaviva described how when he arrived in Nanhsiung en route from Peking to Macao to bring Pasio back on a tour of the missions, he learned of the latter's death and shortly thereafter despatched Trigault to Rome.[16] In any case the persuasive Trigault evidently convinced Aquaviva that circumstances extenuated Longobardo's *coup de main.*

These facts make it reasonable to conclude that had the matter been put to Vieira his decision would have been negative. This supposition is reinforced by the fact that Vitelleschi had similarly delegated to him the authority to decide whether or not China should be delivered from control of the Japanese province and here his decision was negative.

The jurisdictional ties with Japan had always been irksome to the men in China. The obstructive attitude of many of the Jesuits in Macao, the administrative center of the Japanese province, must often have made the handful of missionaries in the Celestial Empire feel that their mission was regarded as an unwanted stepchild. And so it was. The Japanese province resented diverting men and money from Japan to China. One of the *postulata* submitted by de Matos reflected this enduring attitude.

Trigault proposed, as directed by Longobardo, to tour Europe and to recruit some fifty Jesuits for the China mission. De Matos registered a strong protest against this proposal on the ground that the recruitment of non-Portuguese, chiefly Germans and Belgians, would be offensive to the Lisbon authorities who were very jealous of their *Padroado* over the missions in the Far East; and on the further ground that the China mission had neither places to put these men nor funds with which to support them. Some of the Nagasaki conferees, so de Matos reported to the general, even advised strongly that Trigault himself not be permitted to return to the Orient! He counterproposed that the general send some thirty Jesuits to be put at the disposition of the visitor who would assign them as he saw fit to either Japan or China, no doubt being quite sure that few of them would see China.

Before the Japan missionaries are condemned for selfishness they must be judged in the real context of the time. Looked at from the vantage point of Macao or of Japan the demands of the China mission must have appeared extremely unreasonable. During all the years that China's door had remained fast shut and during all of Ricci's laborious efforts to establish a small foothold in China the Japanese mission had been flourishing and developing at an extraordinary rate. There was good reason to hope for the conversion to Christianity of the entire people. It is impossible to determine with exactitude the number of Christians in Japan. The number both of Catholics and of martyrs has been greatly exaggerated. Some writers speak of one million Christians and of hundreds of thousands of martyrs.[17] These figures are far out of line. The number of well documented martyrdoms is somewhere between four and five thousand. The most conservative, and probably more nearly correct, estimate puts the total number of Catholics in Japan in 1614 at around three hundred thousand. In 1582, the year that Ricci entered China, there were already one hundred and fifty thousand Japanese Catholics.[18]

The demands of the rapidly growing Church in Japan taxed the resources of the province to the utmost, but the fruits of these efforts were tangible. In contrast the tangible fruits in China appeared negligible. There was a harvest to be gathered in Japan. Small wonder then that those devoted to the enterprise resented diverting manpower to what appeared the unrewarding task of clearing brush in unresponsive China. The most that can be said against them is that they lacked the vision of a Valignano. They were prudent men.

It was because of this sense of frustration which the China mission had felt ever since Ruggieri's day that Longobardo was persuaded that the only solution was to free China from its subordination to Japan and make it a fully autonomous and self-supporting province. The main object of Trigault's mission was to achieve this juridical status of independence and to raise funds and recruit men for the new province.

Trigault was successful with Aquaviva, but before the latter had juridically established the new province, he died on January 21, 1615. In view of the strong opposition from Japan Vitelleschi felt it wise to move cautiously. He decided for the time being to give it the status of an independent mission, whose superior would have the powers of a provincial, but to let the visitor decide whether it should be given vice-provincial status. Vieira informed the assistant of Portugal that the demands of the China missionaries were exaggerated and that he had decided not to give it this status.[19]

One can easily imagine that the irritation of the members of the Japanese mission must have suddenly expanded into a small atomic bomb of sulphurous wrath when they learned later that the brash Trigault had not only asked for provincial status for China with its few thousand Christians, its handful of priests, and its less than a handful of residences, but had also blandly proposed that Macao itself, the pride of the Portuguese Jesuits, the center of Christianity in the East, be handed over with its college and its churches to the new China province. He had calmly added a generous proviso, which must only have increased their anger, to the effect that the China province would allow members of her sister province to continue to live in Macao, though without any jurisdiction.

In December of 1619, during the last weeks of Vieira's life, the not easily defeated Trigault, who had returned to Macao from Europe only a few months earlier, succeeded in wringing from the ailing visitor the concession which he had previously refused. Notified of this the general in 1621 named João da Rocha, who had succeeded Longobardo as superior of the mission, the first vice-provincial of China. Da Rocha died in Hangchow, however, on March 23, 1623, before word of his appointment reached him.

Manoel Dias, Junior, who had been named as next in line to provide for such an eventuality, became effectively the first head of the vice-province of China.

There was very little, if anything, about Trigault's mission that Vieira had liked. Three years before the Belgian's return to Macao he had written that the idea of a Chinese liturgy was "so great a novelty that it would be many years before it could even be discussed." And of Trigault's request for a bishop for the China mission he had remarked in sarcastic hyperbole that it was "ridiculous to want a bishop for four Chinese Christians."[20]

From all this it seems clear that Vieira would have vetoed the liturgy project had it been submitted to him. There is no direct evidence in the archives that he did so and other factors in the situation make it improbable that the China missionaries ever confronted him with the necessity of making such a decision. Having obtained the permission, they were in no position to use it.

When Trigault got back to China persecution was raging. The missionaries were living virtually in hiding while fully occupied in trying to keep the mission alive. They could hardly take up the ambitious project of the liturgy or the training of candidates for the priesthood. Nor were such candidates at the moment available. The Chinese Jesuits, most of whom had originally entered the Society with the question of whether they would become priests or brothers left open, were by this time firmly settled in their vocations as brothers.

Before the permission could be implemented the missal, breviary, and books of ritual had to be translated into elegant Chinese. This was a monumental task. It was eventually accomplished by Ludovico Buglio, one of the best Jesuit sinologists of the seventeenth century, but it took Buglio twenty-four years (1654-1678) to complete his work of translation. Buglio did not even enter China until almost twenty years after Trigault's return.

In the voluminous correspondence which made its long way from China into the Roman archives during the years immediately following Trigault's return there is not a word about the liturgy. The only one who touches even indirectly upon the subject is the older Manoel Dias, and that is to say, in a letter of 1637 to the general, that it will be impossible for a long time, perhaps to the end of the century, to institute a Chinese clergy.

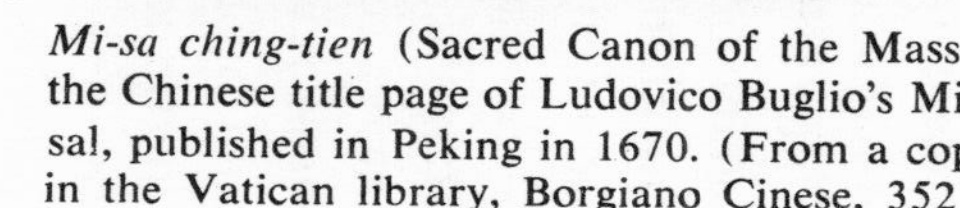

Mi-sa ching-tien (Sacred Canon of the Mass), the Chinese title page of Ludovico Buglio's Missal, published in Peking in 1670. (From a copy in the Vatican library, Borgiano Cinese, 352).

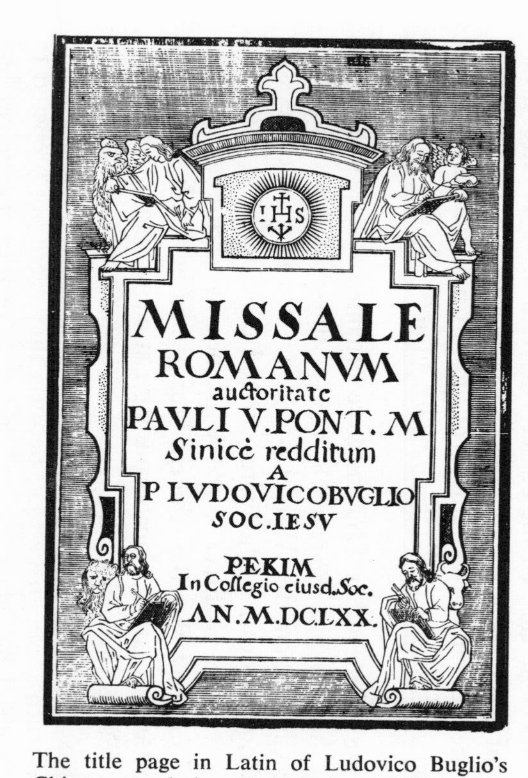

The title page in Latin of Ludovico Buglio's Chinese translation of the Roman Missal, published in Peking in 1670. (From a copy in the Vatican library, Borgiano Cinese, 352).

Dias was excessively pessimistic. The first Chinese Jesuit ordained to the priesthood was Chêng Wei-hsin (1633-1673) who went to Rome where he entered the Society of Jesus in 1651. After a full course of Jesuit seminary training he was ordained in 1664 and two years later set sail on his return voyage to China where he was to give devoted service until cut down by an untimely death in Peking in 1673.[21]

In 1688 three other Chinese were ordained in the priesthood, among them Wu Li (1632-1718), one of the great artists and poets of the Ch'ing period.[22] Wu Li was converted in middle age and, following the death of his wife, entered the Society at Macao in 1682 at the age of fifty. It was with men of mature age such as Wu Li in mind that the Chinese liturgy had been asked for; and during his six years in Macao studying Latin and theology in preparation for his ordination the Jesuits were making earnest but vain efforts to revive the privilege.

The truth seems to be that, because they were not prepared to use the privilege when granted, the missionaries themselves had simply pigeonholed the decree and forgotten about it. During those years there is no evidence that the missionaries themselves were anxious to develop a native clergy. Either because they thought the time inopportune, the mission too young, or because not all of them were immune to the virus of Europeanism, they tended to undervalue its importance. It took the persecution of Yang Kuang-hsien which broke out in 1664 and led to their imprisonment in Canton to jolt them out of their complacency. They then took up the matter of a Chinese liturgy again.

At least five attempts were made to obtain from the Holy See a renewal of the permission. Juridically speaking, it is doubtful that such a renewal was necessary inasmuch as the permission had never been revoked. However, because it had not been used at the time and probably because there were always some who were opposed to the idea, it was judged more prudent to renew the concession. In 1671 Prosper Intorcetto arrived in Rome with a memorial prepared by the Belgian Jesuit Frans de Rougemont. With the approval of the general of the order the request was presented to Pope Clement X. Unfortunately for the cause of the liturgy the Congregation *De Propaganda Fide* had been established in 1622 and given jurisdiction over all foreign mission affairs. The pope turned the matter over to *Propaganda* where it was pigeonholed.

This was the rock upon which the Chinese liturgy was wrecked. Not even the support of popes was able to carry the day. Both Alexander VII and Innocent XI favored the idea and recommended it to *Propaganda*, but neither was prepared to override the decisions of the congregation. In 1678 an impressively reasoned paper by Ferdinand Verbiest, one of the greatest of Jesuit missionaries; in 1686 a memorial presented by Philip Couplet, coming to Rome as procurator of the mission; in 1698 a memorial written by Anthony Thomas, another prominent Peking Jesuit, all met the same fate. The latter had been written at the urging of the Jesuit General Gonzalez who, following the failure of Couplet's effort, had at length, with force and with optimism urged the China Jesuits to renew the assault and pointed out the principal objections which their memorial should be prepared to dispose of in advance.[23] The last attempt seems to have been made in 1726 by the then general of the order, Tamburini. The decision of *Propaganda* was again negative.

There the matter still rests. In none of these appeals, which include one made by the first *Propaganda*-appointed vicars apostolic in 1673, was the permission revoked. It was, of course, effectively nullified by the negative decisions of the tribunals appealed to, so that it could not again be acted on without an explicit favorable decision of the same tribunals.

During his long voyage to Rome from China Trigault had translated Ricci's memoirs into Latin. Published for the first time in Rome in 1615, under the title *De Christiana expeditione apud Sinas suscepta ab Societate Jesu, ex P. Matthaei Ricci ejusdem Societatis Commentariis*, it was the most authoritative work yet to appear on China, her people, customs, laws and government. It was a resounding success and aroused great interest everywhere in Europe.[24]

The Jesuit historian Bartoli is extremely severe in his judgment of Trigault for the manner in which he published this work. He virtually accuses him of having deliberately thrust Ricci into the background and taken credit for a work which was not his. The Jesuit sinologist, Pasquale D'Elia, though less severe than Bartoli is also quite critical.[25] It is true that the title would lead one to believe that it was Trigault's work, written from notes left by Ricci, instead of being, as it actually was, simply a translation from the Italian of Ricci's completed memoirs. One result of this was that Ricci's original manuscript lay unnoticed in the Jesuit archives for almost three hundred years until brought to light in 1911 by Tacchi-Venturi. Not until 1942-1949 was it competently edited in D'Elia's work of monumental scholarship.

In Trigault's defense it must be said that he did not deny Ricci's authorship. In an introductory note (but in very small type, D'Elia points out) he explicitly acknowledged it. It must also be said that Trigault's translation, in the literary language common to all Europeans of the day, brought Ricci's achievements to the attention of the Western world.

After completing his work in Rome, Trigault spent more than two years traveling about Europe stimulating vocations and seeking financial aid for the mission.[26] In France, Marie de Medici gave him splendid Flanders tapestries to present to the emperor of China. In Brussels, Isabel of Spain presented him with rich church ornaments and valuable paintings. The archbishop of Trêves gave him a reliquary. He visited his family in Antwerp where his brother, Elie, a nephew, Michel, and a cousin, Jean Alberic, obtained permission to return with him to China. Trigault was a persuasive man.

In Munich he met William V, living in retirement in a monastery, and his son Maximilian, the chief figure in the Catholic League. They gave him gifts for China and promised an annual subsidy of five hundred florin.

Towards the end of 1617 Trigault reached Madrid. Philip III promised him subsidies sufficient to establish fifteen residences and to support three hundred missionaries. This opened vistas upon the future for Trigault. It must be remembered that he had left China upon the high wave of Longobardo's optimism. He knew nothing of the disaster which had befallen the mission in China. Not until he landed at Goa, on his return voyage on October 4, 1618, did he learn of Shên Ch'üeh's persecution and the edict of expulsion. He did not have to wait until then, however, to be disillusioned. When he reached Lisbon, after leaving Madrid, he discovered that Philip's promises were illusory. Portugal and Spain were united under one crown, but their mutual jealousies had become only the deeper because of it. Philip, as sovereign of Spain, had been motivated less by religious zeal than by a desire to use missionaries as a wedge through which to introduce Spanish influence into the Portuguese sphere of commercial domination in Chinese waters. At least, so the

Drawing by Rubens of a Jesuit missionary in China. This sketch, which is in the National Museum in Stockholm, very probably depicts Nicolas Trigault. In January, 1617, both he and Rubens were in Anvers. Jean Faber, doctor and botanist to the pope, was a close friend both of Rubens and of Terrenz, who was travelling with Trigault at this time.

Portuguese thought. Trigault and his party could not sail for China except "via Lisbonna," which carried with it the obligation of accepting the Portuguese *Padroado*. Before he could obtain permission to sail he had to renounce the promises made by Philip!

Vitelleschi, forewarned by de Matos — correctly as it turned out — of opposition by the Portuguese authorities to the introduction of foreign missionaries into the field in large numbers, had intervened energetically to moderate Trigault's zeal. The latter, during his tour of northern Europe, had recruited a formidable number of young Jesuit volunteers for the mission and had persuaded their provincial superiors to let them go. Despite Vitelleschi's actions Trigault still arrived in Lisbon with more than the number of non-Portuguese whom the authorities had reluctantly agreed to let sail. In the end many had to be left behind.

On the eve of departure the ship which carried most of the gifts Trigault had collected for China had to be scuttled to keep it from falling into the hands of Dutch pirates; while another ship carrying the alms given by Marie de Medici for the mission was pirated by the Dutch at the mouth of the Tagus river. Five ships made up the fleet which set sail for the Far East on April 16, 1618. With Trigault were the twenty-two Jesuits, ten of them Portuguese, whom he had salvaged. Their ship, the *Nossa Senhora de Jesus*, carried 635 men, "packed like herring among the ship's cargo, the baggage and the supplies."[27] Among the twenty-two was the brilliant Johann Terrenz Schreck, always referred to by his contemporaries by his middle name. Another member of the party was Johann Adam Schall von Bell who was destined to step into Terrenz' shoes when death cut down the noted mathematician before he was fairly launched on his Chinese career. Schall would go on to become a high official in the empire and an intimate friend and adviser of China's first Manchu emperor. On another ship in the same fleet, with ten Jesuits destined for Japan, sailed Gabriel de Matos who had done his best to defeat the purposes of Trigault's mission.

Actually only eight of the twenty-two recruits for China ever worked in the empire. Five of them, including Trigault's cousin Alberic, died en route when a contagious fever swept through the ship as it beat its way down the west coast of Africa. Without doctors on board, the Jesuits, directed by Terrenz, organized the medical work and by unsparing efforts kept the death list down to forty-five. Two more of the party, one of them Trigault's brother Elie, died in Goa where the party landed on October 4, 1618.[28]

When Trigault sailed from Goa for Macao on May 20, 1619, only four of his earlier companions were with him. The others stayed behind, either because of sickness or to complete their studies. Trigault and Terrenz landed at Macao on July 22. Schall, Kirwitzer, and Furtado, who had sailed on a different ship, had landed a week earlier.

One thing that Trigault had not lost to storm or piracy was a letter written by Robert Cardinal Bellarmine to the Christians of China, expressing his joy and that of Pope Paul V and the Roman Curia over the progress of Christianity in China and extending his best wishes. The letter touched a responsive chord in the hearts of the Christian scholars. Nearly all of them wanted to answer. It was decided, in view of the strict control exercised at Canton, that it would be dangerous to send too many letters abroad. If they fell into the hands of suspicious officials it might revive the old hysteria which had caused such a furor in 1606. Hsü Kuang-ch'i in the name of the Church in China indited an answer to the Roman cardinal. It was written from Peking in 1621. Hsü expressed gratitude for the Cardinal's letter, describing the joy which it had brought to the Church in China. He spoke of the persecution, expressed hope for the future, asked for prayers, and concluded with best wishes for Bellarmine's health and happiness.[29]

There is something truly touching in this sympathetic exchange across a not yet shrunken world between these two great Christian humanists, both eminent scholars, the one a trusted official in the government of China, the other a prince of the Roman Church. There was an affinity between the two men deeper than they knew. The spiritual outlook and the keen insight of Hsü Kuang-ch'i were cast in the Bellarminian mold.

Trigault's notable trip to Europe is a curious mélange of scintillating success and over-all failure. If bold, he was also brilliant and far-seeing. He made proposals to the pope for the organization of mission activity which are astonishingly in advance of his time. He urged establishment of an episcopal hierarchy in the East; the organization of centers in every European city to raise funds for the support of the missions, a project today realized in the activities of the Propagation of the Faith; the preparation and wide utilization of maps marking the various mission fields in different colors, today a commonplace. He also urged upon the Holy Father the establishment of a Roman commission with jurisdiction over the missions. Six years later *Propaganda Fide* was established for this very purpose.

He obtained from the general and from the Holy See most of what he had asked for. His tour of Europe to enlist recruits and raise funds had been a triumphal march. But the funds promised did not materialize and the alms given were for the most part lost to shipwreck or piracy. The extraordinary liturgical concession granted by the Holy See was never used. Relatively few of his recruits reached China, though those who did performed brilliantly. And the independence won for the mission may have been a pyrrhic victory.

With the closing of Japan by persecution and self-imposed isolation a few years later the resources both in men and money which had formerly gone every year to support the extensive works of the mission in that country could have been transferred to China. Because China no longer formed part of the province of Japan, these resources were diverted to Tonkin and to Cochin-China. The men in China may sometimes have wished that Trigault had argued less brilliantly the case for the separation of their mission from the Japanese province. No doubt it was this disappointment that led Alvarô Semedò, as valiant a defender of the rights of the China mission against Macao critics as anyone, though himself a Portuguese, to say a quarter of a century later that the idea of separation was entirely Trigault's and was against the wishes not only of the fathers of Japan, but of those of China as well.[30] Semedo was wrong. The idea was Longobardo's and, whatever their afterthoughts may have been, was probably shared by the men in China.

NOTES

(1) *ARSI*, Jap-Sin 100, ff. 10-17r.

(2) *ARSI*, Jap-Sin 150, ff. 10r/v.

(3) *ARSI*, *Jap-Sin* 113, ff. 265-281.

(4) Pasquale D'Elia, S. J., "Daniele Bartoli e Nicola Trigault," *Revista storica italiana*, XVI (June 30, 1938), 77-92.

(5) Dr. Joseph Jennes, C.I.C.M., "A propos de la liturgie chinoise," *Neue Zeitschrift für Missionswissenschaft*, II (1946), 241-254.

(6) *ARSI*, Jap-Sin 3, f. 25r.

(7) Cf. his letter of November 25, 1610, *Opere storiche*, II, 492 f.

(8) Cf. Jennes, *op. cit*., p. 249, nn. 48, 49.

(9) That of January 15, 1615, in *ARSI*, Instit. 175, f. 7r; that of March 26, 1615, *ibid*., f. 9r/v. All authors have hitherto assumed that there was but one decree, with much confusion over the dating of it. Francis A. Rouleau, S. J., has recently established in an article to be published that these are two separate decrees issuing from two different meetings of the Holy Office.

(10) This letter is in the archives in Lisbon: Biblioteca de Ajuda (Lisboa), Jesuitas na Asia 49-V-5, ff. 160v-171v. In the 1740's seven Chinese scribes, directed by Brother João Alvarez, made transcripts of all the documents in the Jesuit archives in Macao and sent them to Lisbon. This is how Trigault's letter got there. It has long been assumed that the original Macao documents were destroyed when the Jesuits were driven from Portuguese possessions by the Marquis Pombal. Recently Josef Franz Schütte, S. J., discovered a large part of the originals in Madrid. They evidently got there by way of the Philippines. Cf. Josef Franz Schütte, S. J., "Wiederentdeckung des Makao-Archivs," *Archivum Historicum Societatis Iesu*, XXX (1961), 92-124.

(11) These key documents, the *Acta Primae Congregationis Provinciae Japoniae* 1614 *Nangasqui, in oppido et portu Japoniae*, and the *responsa* of Vitelleschi to De Matos' *postulata* are in *ARSI*, Congr. 55 (Cong. Provinc. 1612-1626), ff. 270-286v and ff. 288r-295v respectively.

(12) *ARSI*, Jap-Sin 17, f. 99.

(13) *ARSI*, Congr. 55, 295v.

(14) *ARSI*, Jap-Sin 17, ff. 63-64.

(15) Cf. letters of Vieira in *ARSI*, Jap-Sin 17, ff. 41-42, 63-64, 84-86; a milder complaint by Carvalho in *ibid*., ff. 67-68.

(16) *ARSI*, Jap-Sin 113, ff. 215-264.

(17) Cf. e.g. Yoshi S. Kuno, *Japanese Expansion on the Asiatic Continent* (Berkeley: University of California Press, 1937), II, 79.

(18) Johannes Laures, S. J., *The Catholic Church in Japan* (Tokyo: Charles E. Tuttle Company, 1954), pp. 173, 174, 179. For the number of Catholics cf. p. 177.

(19) *ARSI*, Jap-Sin 17, ff. 63-64.

(20) *ARSI*, *Jap-Sin* 17, ff. 42-43 and f. 84v.

(21) Cf. Francis A. Rouleau, S. J., "The First Chinese Priest of the Society of Jesus," *Archivum Historicum Societatis Iesu*, XXVIII (January-June, 1959), 3-50

(22) *Eminent Chinese*, II, 875 f.

(23) Gonzalez' memo is in *ARSI*, Congr. 84 ff. 299-304r. Its length, in sharp contrast to the terseness of most memos issuing from Jesuit headquarters. indicates his intense interest in the project.

NOTES

(24) Trigault's Latin version has been translated into English by Louis J. Gallagher, S. J., *China in the 16th Century, the Journals of Matthew Ricci 1583-1610* (New York: Random House, 1953).

(25) Cf. D'Elia, *loc. cit.*

(26) The authoritative study of Trigault's activities during these two years is by Edmond Lamalle, S. J., "La propagande du P. Nicholas Trigault en faveur des missions de Chine (1616)," *Archivum Historicum Societatis Jesu*, IX (Roma, 1940), 49-120.

(27) Alfons Väth, S. J., *Johann Adam Schall von Bell, S. J.* (Köln: J. P. Boehm, 1933), p. 40.

(28) Trigault described the costly voyage in a letter written in Goa: *ARSI*, Jap-Sin 121, ff. 92-115.

(29) Bellarmine's Latin letter and a Portuguese translation of Hsü's reply are in Furtado's annual letter from Hangchow, August 24, 1621: in *ARSI*, Jap-Sin 114, ff. 234-261, the letters in ff. 243-245.

(30) In a letter to the visitor, Manoel de Azevedo, December, 1645: *ARSI*, Jap-Sin 161-II, ff. 224-226v.

Chapter XI

Nova Et Vetera

THE YEARS IMMEDIATELY following Shên Ch'üeh's dismissal from office were marked by definite improvement in the fortunes of the mission. This turn for the better was related to the temporary setback suffered by the eunuch party. Disastrous reverses at the hands of the Manchus led to the return to office of certain capable and patriotic leaders who had been driven into retirement by Wei Chung-hsien. In 1621, following the loss of Shênyang and Liaoyang, Hsiung T'ing-pi, a capable general and outspoken critic of the eunuch party, was reinstated and charged with the defense of Shanhaikuan, the eastern terminus of the Great Wall and the pass through which any large-scale invasion of China had to be directed. The eunuch party, however, succeeded in balancing this appointment by naming Wang Hua-chên military administrator of the Liaotung area. Hsü Kuang-ch'i predicted that his appointment would inevitably lead to the loss of the province to the Manchus. His prediction was verified the following year when Wang's rejection of Hsiung's views on strategy resulted in disaster at Kuangning. His army suffered a crushing defeat in March, 1622. Although Hsiung T'ing-pi was not responsible for the defeat and consequent loss of the province, the unscrupulous Fêng Ch'üan, one of Wei Chung-hsien's prominent satellites and a bitter enemy of Hsiung's, succeeded in bringing about his arrest and, some time later, his execution.[1]

Despite his efforts to make Hsiung T'ing-pi the scapegoat for the disaster which lost the entire Liaotung territory to the Manchus, the eunuch party could not evade responsibility. It dared not resist, therefore, when Yüan Ch'ung-huan came out of retirement and demanded to be entrusted with the defenses of the strategic passes. In September, 1622, the party of reform won another victory when Sun Ch'êng-tsung, a competent scholar-general, became president of the Board of War and at the same time a grand secretary. The close collaboration of Yüan and Sun during the next three years turned back the Manchu threat.[2]

Sun Ch'êng-tsung took personal command at Shanhaikuan. He and Yüan steadily pushed the Manchus northward, fortifying recaptured cities and establishing military colonies. A considerable part of their success was due to their adoption of suggestions made by (Ignatius) Sun Yüan-hua on the defense of the frontiers with the aid of cannon. Sun Yüan-hua, after the fall of Shên Ch'üeh, had been appointed to a post in the Peking Board of War and in this capacity had submitted a memorial again urging the project of using "foreign guns" for national defense.

Sun Yüan-hua had the advantage of dealing with men who did not share the prejudices of the eunuch bureaucrats. Another factor which probably contributed to the success of his proposal was the impression made upon the Chinese by the successful defense of Macao a few months earlier. A Dutch fleet of thirteen vessels, with two allied English vessels standing by, under the command of Admiral Cornelis Reijersen attacked the poorly defended Portuguese city on June 23-24.[3] After a preliminary bombardment which drove the force of sixty Portuguese and ninety Macaists out of the earthworks guarding the beach, the Dutch put ashore a formidable landing party of eight hundred men in thirty-two launches and five barges. Virtually unopposed, except for relatively ineffective musket fire from the badly outnumbered defenders, the invasion troops were marching triumphantly upon the city when disaster fell upon them from an unexpected quarter.

Father Bruno, acting superior of the Jesuit college, on his own initiative and according to Jesuit accounts in the face of the ridicule of Lopo Sarmento de Carvalho, doughty commandant of the garrison, had had four dismantled cannon hauled up and mounted on the hill upon which the college was situated. With the Jesuits Bruno, Rho, and Schall directing the fire the cannon opened up upon the Dutch. A lucky hit from the cannon served by Rho blew up a powder cask in the midst of the invading force spreading havoc and confusion. With most of their powder lost in this disaster and harassed by the small arms fire of a party of Macaist and negro sharpshooters, the Dutch retreated towards the beach. Spurred on by Sarmento's rallying cry "Saint James and at them!" the people of Macao, "Portuguese soldiers, Macaonese citizens and negro slaves to say nothing of armed friars and Jesuits to boot took up the cry and hurled themselves at the Hollanders."[4] In panic the Dutch overran their reserves on the beaches and took to the boats. Many drowned in the effort to escape.

This victory, in which half a handful of Jesuits and a few cannon played a decisive part, was important not only to Macao but to the mission in China. With Macao in the hands of Dutch Calvinists access to China would have been cut off and the mission ruined.

The authorities at Canton congratulated the Portuguese on their victory and granted them permission to fortify the city. Their refusal hitherto to permit fortifications had made the defense of Macao virtually impossible. Armed with this authorization, the Portuguese began construction of defenses which, when completed in 1626, rendered the city impregnable from the sea.[5]

Sun Ch'êng-tsung adopted Sun Yüan-hua's proposals and, for the first time, "foreign guns" were employed against the Manchus. By the summer of 1625 the Manchus had been pushed back more than one hundred miles northeast of Shanhaikuan. On November 6 of that year Sun Ch'êng-tsung, who had repeatedly protested against the misgovernment of Wei Chung-hsien, was relieved of his post. His successor, an appointee of the eunuch, ordered abandonment of the northern defenses and called for a general retreat to Shanhaikuan. Yüan Ch'ung-huan refused to obey. When, on February 19, 1626, Nurhaci, at the head of his Bannermen, crossed the Liao River and attacked Yüan at Ningyüan, he suffered the greatest defeat of his career. The blow to his pride was so great that it probably contributed as much to his death seven months later as did the slight wound he received in the battle.

The decisive factor in Yüan Ch'ung-huan's great victory was the firepower of a battery of cannon. It was a conclusive demonstration of the effectiveness of the measures so long advocated by Hsü Kuang-ch'i, Li Chih-tsao and others. If the potentialities of the new weapon were not further exploited, it was because of the obstructionist tactics of the eunuch party. In 1627 Wei Chung-hsien, at the height of his power, forced Yüan Ch'ung-huan into retirement.

Before his retirement in 1625 Sun Ch'êng-tsung helped reinstate the Jesuits in Peking. The missionaries could not resume their public ministry as long as they lay under the ban of the edict of expulsion. Either it had to be recalled or it had to be neutralized by some form of official sanction of their presence in the capital.

Following assumption of office by Sun Ch'êng-tsung in 1622, friends of the missionaries, in reviving the project of obtaining artillery from the Portuguese, urged that the Jesuits be invited to establish themselves again in Peking as expert advisers in military matters. A memorial to the throne argued that they were men of virtue, learning, and ability and that they were excellent mathematicians who were probably familiar with certain instruments of war which could be used to advantage against the Manchus. When informed of the project the missionaries protested, insisting that they were ignorant of the military art (although Rho had practiced it not badly against the Dutch in Macao) and were in China for another purpose. According to Semedo, Li Chih-tsao "who was one of the chief actors in this comedy," brushed aside their objections. They were not to take seriously the fact that they had been represented as military experts. "You will use this title as the tailor uses his needle. He uses it only to draw the thread through the cloth and when the sewing is done he throws it aside, having no further need of it. Once you have obtained imperial sanction for your presence in the empire, it will be easy to put aside the sword in favor of the pen. . . ."[6]

The project had the support of the members of the Tung-lin group who held office in Peking. Yeh Hsiang-kao was still a grand secretary and used his influence to further the scheme. No less active in behalf of the missionaries was another grand secretary, Chang Wên-ta, whose baptized son, Paul, later co-operated with his friend (Philip) Wang Chêng, in Christianizing Shensi. Chang Wên-ta, besides holding the office of grand secretary, was also president of the Board of Civil Offices.

The Board of War, dominated by Sun Ch'êng-tsung, placed its stamp of approval upon the project. Wei Chung-hsien did not feel strong enough at the moment to defy such powerful officials. The memorial received imperial approval and orders were issued to institute a search for the Jesuits and to bring them to Peking. "As a matter of fact," Semedo remarks, "it did not take much searching to find them, inasmuch as those who had charge of the search knew perfectly well where they were."[7]

The Jesuits were in Peking. Manoel Dias, the younger, had been there since 1621. Longobardo, no longer superior of the mission, having been succeeded in 1621 by da Rocha, had arrived in Peking, accompanied by Adam Schall, on January 25, 1623. They established themselves in the house which had been acquired by Ricci in 1605 near the southwestern gate of the North City.

Longobardo and Dias were brought before the Board of War. Members of the Board asked if they thought Portuguese cannon could be obtained and if they were experts in their use. They responded affirmatively to the first question and negatively to the second, stating that they were masters of religion, not cannoneers. They gravely added, however, that they could exhort the Portuguese artillerymen to do their duty!

This satisfied the Board which granted them permission to reside in Peking. Apparently no one had taken seriously the suggestion that the Jesuits were military experts. One has the feeling that Sun Ch'êng-tsung and his associates had tongue in cheek when questioning them. The sequel confirms this: The Jesuits re-established themselves in their old residence. They repaired the church, at the expense of Ignatius Ch'in, who held, at the time, a post in the Board of War. "And there," writes Semedo in 1635, "they still reside in peace and honor, without anyone ever having said another word to them about cannons, wars, or Manchus."[8]

Semedo was right. The whole affair was a gracious comedy in which Yeh Hsiang-kao, Chang Wên-ta, Sun Ch'êng-tsung, Li Chih-tsao and other prominent Chinese statesmen collaborated to restore the Jesuits to their position in Peking and in China. The most delightful aspect of the comedy was the seriousness with which the actors played their roles to final curtain-fall.

Comedy though it was, it was a signal victory for the mission. It meant the tolling of the bells over Shên Ch'üeh's efforts to extirpate Christianity. The missionaries again held a quasi-juridical status in the empire. Equivalently the edict of expulsion had been revoked.

The recall of the Jesuits to the capital was reflected in missionary activities in the provinces. In 1623 Giulio Aleni established a Christian community in Changshu, Kiangsi. The city was the home of Ricci's old friend Ch'ü Ju-k'uei and it was upon the invitation of the latter's son that Aleni visited Changshu. Here, during the course of several months he made a considerable number of converts, the most notable of whom was Ch'ü Shih-ssu who was later to play an heroic role in the struggle to restore the Ming after they had been driven from Peking in 1643-1644.[9] Ch'ü was a nephew of Ricci's friend and, like Ch'ü Ju-k'uei, came from a family of noted officials and scholars. His grandfather, Ch'ü Ching-ch'un had been vice-president of the Board of Ceremonies, chancellor of the Hanlin Academy, and chief editor for the second transcription of the *Yung-lo ta-tien*, an enormous Ming encyclopedia of 11,095 manuscript volumes.

Ch'ü Shih-ssu had become a *chin-shih* in 1616, and, two years later, had been appointed magistrate of Yung-feng in Kiangsi. Here his administration was so highly esteemed by the populace that when, in 1621, he was transferred to Chiangling, Hupeh, the move was protested. He had retired to Changshu to mourn the death of his father when he met Aleni and became interested in Christianity. Ch'ü wrote a preface to Aleni's eight *chüan* religio-psychological study *Hsing-hsüeh ts'u-shu* which was published in the year of his conversion.

Ch'ü Shih-ssu spent most of the next two decades in retirement, a victim of the political factionalism which rent China. Only after the Manchu conquest of northern China did he emerge to become, during the last six years of his life, the outstanding supporter of the Ming pretenders. In contemporary Jesuit accounts he is referred to as "Dr. Thomas."

It was in Fukien that Aleni accomplished his greatest work. His achievements here win for him a place among the greatest of the early Jesuits. In 1625 he introduced Christianity into this province which he entered at the invitation of Yeh Hsiang-kao, whose friendship for the European missionaries had never wavered since his contacts with Matteo Ricci in Nanking in 1600.

For eighteen years Yeh had held office as a grand secretary in Peking. There he was on intimate terms with the Chinese Jesuit lay-brother (Pascal), Ch'iu Liang-hou, one of the best educated and most accomplished men in the city. When Shên Ch'üeh reached Peking in 1622, and, as grand secretary, resumed his intrigues against Christianity, Yeh Hsiang-kao openly opposed him. It was Yeh who, through Ch'iu Liang-hou, kept the missionaries informed of what was going on. After Shên's fall, Yeh gave his support to the effort to reinstate the Jesuits in the capital. As a leader of the Tung-lin party, and an outspoken opponent of Wei Chung-hsien, however, his days in Peking were numbered. Wei and his minions succeeded in forcing him to retire in 1624.

While in Hangchow en route to his home in Fukien, Yeh and Aleni became close friends. The latter's exhortations to Yeh to embrace the faith interested the ex-grand secretary and, in December, he insisted that Aleni accompany him to the borders of his province. Although they travelled by boat, they had little time for discussion, inasmuch as most of Yeh's time was taken by official visitors who came aboard to pay their respects and remained to travel part of the way with him.

When they parted Yeh urged Aleni to visit him in Fukien in the following spring, promising that he would assist in establishing Christianity in his province. In April, 1625, Aleni set out for Fukien and reached Foochow, capital of the province, after a voyage of twenty-one days. Here he met initial disappointment. Wei Chung-hsien had filled the provinces with spies who reported to him the activities of his political opponents. Yeh Hsiang-kao, who in Peking had so often withstood the eunuch, seemed to have become a victim of fear once he returned to his native province. In Peking, Wei's persecution of the Tung-lin party was moving toward the climax which in the following year would result in the cashiering of hundreds of loyal officials and the execution of six of the most prominent officials in the capital. Yeh Hsiang-kao, whose opposition had already cost him his official position, feared that Wei's long arm would reach into Fukien, confiscate his possessions and drag him off to Peking in chains should he learn that the former grand secretary was lending support to foreigners in his province.

Moreover, the activities of the Dutch, hovering off the coast where they preyed upon Chinese commerce, added to Aleni's difficulties. The viceroy and the people in general tended to identify Aleni with the Dutch. All foreigners looked alike to them. The fact that the Dutch had recently seized a small island near the Fukien coast and fortified it as a base of operations strengthened anti-foreign sentiment already rampant in the province.

Dutch sources confirm the fact that their depredations had aroused intense bitterness among the Chinese. Writes Dr. Sonck, who succeeded Cornelis Reijersen as commander of the Dutch fleet in the

China seas:

> Our proceedings on the coast of China have so embittered the whole of China against us that we are looked upon as no better than murderers, tyrants, and pirates. Our dealings with the Chinese have indeed been very hard and cruel.[10]

Aleni's mission was not made easier by the fact that a local scholar celebrated his arrival by publishing a bitter tract against Christianity. Nevertheless, Aleni succeeded in renting a small house in which he celebrated Mass on the feast of Pentecost. A few days later there arrived in Foochow a Christian scholar whose intervention on Aleni's behalf proved decisive and effected a complete change in the atmosphere.

Melchior Chu was a man of "prodigious talent."[11] Because he had been innocently involved in a fraud in the doctoral examinations, he had been disqualified for life from receiving official rank. In the metropolitan examinations, a fellow candidate had submitted as his own one of Chu's compositions. The paper won him first place among the three hundred candidates, one of the greatest distinctions a man could win in China, but when the fraud was detected both the guilty man and Chu, not a party to the deception, received identical sentences of perpetual disqualification.

Despite his misfortune Chu was held in high esteem; but because of it he had to abandon thought of a public career. He had, accordingly, accepted the position of tutor to Yang T'ing-yün's grandchildren and, in this capacity, had become acquainted with the Jesuits. In 1623 he had received the sacrament of Baptism.

Chu, a native of Fukien, was on friendly terms with most of the important people in the province. Aleni had been in Foochow but a short time when Chu arrived from Hangchow. He immediately set to work to win for Aleni the favor of leading scholars and officials. Most important he recaptured the support of Yeh Hsiang-kao.

The former grand secretary was living at his villa thirty miles from Foochow, partly in the hope of escaping the notice of Wei Chung-hsien's spies, or possibly like Diocletian he really liked his villa and his cabbages. Chu visited him and revived his courage. As though in expiation of his temporary timidity, Yeh entertained Aleni and Chu at dinner. In addition, he deputed one of his nephews to accompany Aleni on his return to Foochow and there to recommend him to the local representatives of the Board of Rites.

A little later, Yeh made three public visits to Aleni's home in Foochow. On one of these occasions, he presented the Jesuit with a silken scroll in praise of the missionary and his teaching. In the balanced phrases of classical Chinese style, the scroll stated that Aleni had a twofold persuasiveness upon him: the one vocal, by the efficacy of his reasoning; the other silent, by the sanctity of his life; and both the one and the other were a testimony to the truth which he proclaimed.

The effect of these actions was far-reaching. It was difficult to maintain an attitude of hostility in the face of the unreserved approval openly manifested by one whose prestige was unequalled in the province. Yeh's example was imitated by others. The president of the local office of the Board of Rites, through one of his assistants, presented Aleni with a similar scroll. Other officials followed suit, Soon the author of the anti-Christian tract was attempting to collect as many copies of his pamphlet as possible in order to destroy them. In the presence of Yeh he apologized to Aleni for his diatribe excusing himself upon the ground of ignorance of the real nature of Christianity.

Aleni now began to receive a stream of visitors which included the most distinguished scholars and officials of the province. The visitors learned that Melchior Chu had exaggerated neither the learning nor the personal charm of the missionary. Aleni was schooled in the Ricci tradition; in addition to which he had profited from being Yang T'ing-yün's favorite pupil. Through his years of close association with Yang he had acquired an extraordinary mastery of Chinese culture. It is related that he never failed to observe in minute detail the ritual of cultivated society. This genial acceptance of the usages of the land endeared him to the hearts of most of those who met him.

Aleni's first field of apostolate was an academy of scholars in Foochow. Its president, to whom Aleni had presented a summary of the principles of Christianity, invited him to address the academy at its next meeting. The priest was received by the members of the group with every courtesy. After the accustomed inclinations in the direction of the name of Confucius, written in large gold letters at one end of the room, all were seated while an instrumental aria was played "in a grave tone calculated to free the soul from all distractions and to put the mind in a receptive mood." One of the academicians read a text from one of the Confucian classics. The president of the Academy called upon Aleni to discuss the text. The latter, familiar with the requirements of courtesy, excused himself, alleging that he was incompetent to lead a discussion among so many learned men. The president met his every protestation of unworthiness with an equally gracious assurance that none was so competent as he. In this contest, no less charming because part of a recognized ritual, Aleni, as was expected, finally allowed himself to be overcome. His discourse made his reputation and led to the first conversions in the capital of Fukien province. Soon Aleni had received twenty-six converts into the Church, most of them students, three of them *hsiu-ts'ai.*

After four months in Foochow Aleni set out on a tour of the province. He spent the next eight months moving from city to city, visiting officials whose interest had been aroused by Yeh Hsiang-kao's patronage. Most of them, he discovered, admired the sanctity of Christian teaching, many of them expressed a desire to embrace the faith before death; but few had the courage to free themselves from what Bartoli calls the "strong noose" of a plurality of wives. Nevertheless friendly contact with these men was an inestimable gain. Through them a better understanding of the character of Christian teaching reached a large number of intellectuals who, ill-informed, might easily have worked against Christianity. More than fifty scholar-officials, some of high rank, wrote eulogies of Christianity and of Aleni.[12] Some later contributed prefaces to his books.

During his first year in the province, Aleni was chiefly concerned with building a broad foundation of friendly contacts. Like Ricci, accustomed to taking the long view, he was content to gather little fruit for the present in expectation of ample harvests to come. The friends he made during these months showed how well he accomplished his task. But he left, nonetheless, a goodly number of converts and catechumens in most of the cities. He prepared the soil and planted the seed. The next ten years brought forth an astonishing harvest.

These same years witnessed establishment of missionary centers in the provinces of Shansi and Shensi. In 1624, Nicolas Trigault, at the invitation of the brothers Han, went to Chiangchow, Shansi,[13] where he spent the better part of a year. In 1625 Vagnoni, who had re-entered the interior from Macao the year before, replaced him. Vagnoni established a Jesuit residence in Chiangchow and for the next fifteen years labored with remarkable success in the province.

With the arrival of Vagnoni, Trigault, at the invitation of Wang Chêng, moved over into the neighboring province of Shensi. Writing on October 20, 1624, to the Elector of Bavaria from Chiangchow, he remarked: "I am waiting from day to day the arrival of a companion who is to carry on the work here in Shansi. I must then move on into another province at the invitation of certain prominent men."[14] The companion was Vagnoni. The prominent men were Wang Chêng and, apparently (Paul) Chang Chung-fang. Wang had just retired from the prefectural judgeship of Kuangping, Chihli.

Trigault spent five or six months in Wang's home convalescing from a serious illness. During this time the retired judge studied Latin under his direction. It is probable that he assisted Trigault to work out his key to the pronunciation of Chinese characters, a work which was edited and published by Wang Chêng and Han Yün in 1626 under the title *Hsi-ju er-mu tzu* (Western Scholar Aid to Ear and Eye). The printing of this work was financed by Chang Wên-ta and his son (Paul) Chang Chung-fang.

After recovering his health, Trigault accompanied Wang Chèng and Chang Chung-fang to Sianfu. Some time before this, an event notable in the annals of archeology had occurred near that ancient capital of the empire, the discovery of the Nestorian monument.[15] During the course of excavations in the subprefecture of Chowchih, some forty miles to the southwest, a monument was uncovered which had been erected on February 4, 781. One of its inscriptions was a beautiful specimen of T'ang calligraphy. Another inscription was in Syriac.

Since there exists an extensive literature on the subject, it is not necessary here to describe the Nestorian tablet.[16] Suffice to say that it revealed, for the first time in this age, that Nestorian Christianity had entered China under the T'ang in the seventh century, that it had received the patronage of several emperors, and that it had enjoyed a period of considerable prosperity.

The monument aroused great interest among the Chinese, who hold antiquities in the highest honor, and was brought to Sian by order of the prefect of that city. Scholars flocked to see it, but none was able to understand the inscription. Probably the first Christian to see it was Chang Kêng, a native of Fukien, then living in Shansi. An old friend of Ricci, he had been baptized by Aleni in 1621. Chang, suspecting that the inscription related to Christianity, made a copy and sent it to Li Chih-tsao at Hangchow.

"I was living in the country near Ling-chu [his villa near Hangchow]" writes Li, "when my friend Chang Kêng of Chiyang had the goodness to send me a copy of the monument of the T'ang, saying: 'Recently in excavating at Changan it was discovered. It has for a title: Monument Eulogizing the Propagation in the Middle Kingdom of the Illustrious Religion. One has not hitherto heard of this religion. Is it the same as the holy religion which Ricci came from the extremities of the Occident to preach?' "[17]

Li and the Jesuits in Hangchow had no difficulty in recognizing that the "Illustrious Religion" was, indeed, Christianity. Although replete with nebulous phrases, obscured by expressions of Taoist and Buddhist tincture, the inscription contained clear references to many Christian doctrines. There was no doubt that the mission, headed by the monk O-lo-pen, which according to the inscription had in 635 by the special favor of the reigning monarch made a "public and glorious" entrance to the capital, was a Christian mission. It could hardly have entered the minds of Li Chih-tsao or of the Jesuits that it had been a Nestorian mission, Nestorianism having long before faded into obscurity in Europe. They naturally tended at first to identify the "Illustrious Religion" of the monument with "the holy religion which Ricci came . . . to preach." Nevertheless, they did not lose their critical sense. One must admire the scrupulous honesty and scholarly caution with which they handled the subject. In their reports no extravagant claims were made. Manoel Dias, the older, writing on March 1, 1626, from Kiating to the general of the Society in Rome, announced the discovery: "There [in Sianfu] an ancient monument has been discovered which proves that there were once preachers of the Holy Gospel in China." After describing how Chang Kêng had sent Li Chih-tsao a copy of the inscription he indicates that the text offers difficulties: "It contains many equivocal expressions, a number of terms which are of pagan provenance and very difficult to understand, to say nothing of metaphors and literary allusions." After giving a good translation of the opening passages of the inscription, he adds:

Until now we have determined only the general sense of the

> inscription. Father Trigault has been ordered to the spot to examine the stone, because the Doctors have omitted certain details which we must have. We hope that he will obtain an exact copy of the inscription. When we have received it we will send it immediately to Your Paternity.[18]

In this wise the Jesuits in China reacted to an epoch-making discovery. Yet, for the next two hundred and fifty years, they were denounced as frauds and impostors by "scholarly" dilettantes in their homelands who saw in the Nestorian monument a gigantic Jesuit hoax. "A piece obviously faked," wrote Mathurin Veyssiere de Lacrozs in 1724. "A ridiculous fake . . . an absurd lie . . . a pious fraud," sneered Voltaire and ridiculed the Jesuits in satirical verse which does not seem particularly brilliant when read today but which no doubt convulsed Paris salons in his day:

> Ah! du moins Bonze que vous ètes
> Puisque vous me voulez tromper,
> Trompez-moi mieux que vous ne faites.

Ridicule was still the vogue as late as 1855 when Ernest Renan echoed the charges of fraud. He had the honesty eight years later to admit that he had been mistaken and that the objections to the authenticity of the monument had disappeared.[19] Today its authenticity is universally recognized: research in dynastic records and archeological discoveries of the past eighty years have confirmed the data given in the inscription itself.

The Jesuits in China were fully aware of the worth of the discovery. To them its chief importance lay in its effect upon their apostolate. One of the objections which the Chinese had constantly raised against Christianity was its novelty. In China more than anywhere else in the world a high value attaches to what is old. With their sense of history the Chinese are little inclined to attribute importance to anything which has no roots in their past. The younger Dias, in his commentary on the monument, describes the common experience of the missionaries:

> 'Without doubt,' visitors to the missionaries are wont to say, 'we have reason to be grateful for the teachings which you have brought to us from so far off; but why were they not brought to our ancestors as well, why have they reached us so tardily? This is what we cannot understand. . . .'

And Li Chih-tsao in the brief account which he published in 1625 of the discovery refers to the same objection:

> For more than thirty years our scholars in China have been familiar with the doctrine and example of the learned men from the West. There is no one who has not proclaimed the excellence of this doctrine and held it in honor; nevertheless, many have still been sceptical because they regarded it as something new.

Now the basis of their scepticism has been destroyed:

> Who could have believed it? Nine hundred and ninety years ago this doctrine was preached [in China]; amidst the constant vicissitudes of the world, the ever unchanging providence of God raised up wise men who knew no obstacle. Now this holy stone so providentially preserved has suddenly come to light. . . . Buried for so many years, this treasure seems to have waited only the propitious moment.

It had been difficult to answer the objection of the Chinese. Ricci had endeavored to do so by putting the blame for the late arrival of the Christian message in China upon geography. While he was correct, the Chinese were not satisfied with the explanation. That was one reason why Ricci and his successors had been anxious to find indications that Christianity had earlier reached China. Ricci's Jewish friend from Kaifeng gave him reason to think that there had been Christian communities in China but the thread of hope had not led to the prize. In 1619 Longobardo, accompanied by Brother Chung Ming-li had travelled from Hangchow to the province of Honan to search for these "Christians of the Cross."

Kaifeng, center of the Jewish community and source of these reports, exercised a strong attraction upon the Jesuits. That is probably why Trigault, before going to Shensi in 1623, spent some months there in a vain effort to establish a residence. Where Trigault had failed, Sambiasi succeeded a few years later. But the vague rumors about traces of an old Christian community could not be substantiated. The Jesuits could not advance them as an argument to their critical inquirers. But the monument of Sianfu offered incontrovertible evidence that Christianity was not new in China, as the scholars had supposed, and that, during one of the most splendid periods of China's history, it had received signal marks of favor from some of the greatest emperors.

Small wonder that Li Chih-tsao lost no time in publishing a notice of the discovery and its significance, or that his pamphlet was widely read. Manoel Dias, the younger, wrote a scholarly commentary of the inscription which he published under the title *Ching-chiao pei-ch'üan* (Commentary on Nestorian Monument) at Hangchow in 1644. In addition to seven pages giving the entire Chinese part of the inscription, there are forty-nine pages of comment.[20]

Chang Kêng might be said to have been the first Chinese investigator of Christian archeology. The part he played in bringing the Sianfu monument to the attention of the world must have stimulated his interest in the subject. In the province of Fukien, in 1638, he discovered a cross cut in stone, of which many others have since been found. They were Christian relics. Chang wrote a short account of this discovery which Manoel Dias included in his *Ching-chiao pei-ch'uan*. "This ancient stone of the cross," he wrote, "was found in the territory of Tung-p'an-ch'iao of Chüanchowfu. It is not known how long it has been there. No passerby had remarked it. It was in the spring of 1638. While my mind was turned to God, and led by His inspiration, I, together with some friends of the prefecture, discovered it. I asked the priest to erect it in his church at Yungchow. Chang Kêng leaves this record of the event."[21]

NOTES

(1) Cf. *Eminent Chinese*, I, 308 f., and II, 823.

(2) For these and later incidents in which Yüan and Sun played a part cf. *idem*, II, 670 f., 686, 954 f.

(3) The primary sources for this episode are: on the Dutch side, William Ysbrantsa Bontekoe, *Memorable Description of the East Indian Voyage 1618-1625* (New York: Robert McBride and Company, 1929), 85 ff.; on the Portuguese side, the official report found in the Macao archives and published by Aders Ljungstedt, *An Historical Sketch of the Portuguese Settlements in China; and of the Roman Catholic Church and Mission in China* (Boston: J. Munroe and Company, 1836), 75 ff. A colorful and accurate account based on primary sources is that of C. R. Boxer, *Fidalgos in the Far East 1550-1770* (The Hague: Martinus Nijhoff, 1948), 72-93.

(4) Boxer, *op. cit.*, p. 82.

(5) *Voyages et missions du père Alexandre de Rhodes de la Compagnie de Jésus en la Chine et autres royaumes de l'Orient; nouv. ed., par un père de la même Compagnie* (Paris: Julien, Lanier, etc., 1854), p. 72.

(6) Semedo, *Histoire universelle*, pp. 349 ff.

(7) *Ibid.*, p. 350.

(8) *Id.*

(9) On Ch'ü Shih-ssu cf. *Eminent Chinese*, I, 199 ff. See also Fr. Jäger, "Die Letzten Tage des Ku-shih-si," *Sinica*, VIII (1933), 197 ff., and Paul Pelliot, "Michel Boym," *T'oung Pao* (1934), 95 ff.

(10) Bontekoe, *op. cit.*, p. 15.

NOTES

(11) Bartoli, *op. cit.*, IV, 54.

(12) In 1942 Mr. Wang Chung-min, then with the Library of Congress, allowed me to examine his photostatic copy of a collection of such eulogies written by distinguished scholars of Fukien in honor of Aleni. It showed that the missionary annals exaggerated nothing in their accounts of Aleni's success.

(13) An account of Trigault's work in Shansi and Shensi is found in his letter to the Jesuit provincial of the Low Countries. The original is in the Jesuit college at Anvers. It is reproduced in C. Deshaisnes, *Vie du Père Nicholas Trigault de la Compagnie de Jésus* (Tournai: Casterman, 1865), Appendix, 280-284.

(14) Latin original in the Library of Bourgogne, Brussels; reproduced in Deshaisnes, *op. cit.*, pp. 275-277.

(15) The most scholarly treatment of the subject is that of Henri Havret, S. J., *La stèle chrétienne de Si-ngan-fou* (3 vols., Shanghai: Mission catholique, 1897). The exact date of the discovery is a matter of dispute. It is most likely that the stone was discovered in 1623, as stated by Manoel Dias, and moved to Sianfu in 1625; cf. P. Y. Saeki, *The Nestorian Documents and Relics in China* (Tokyo: Toho Bunkwa Gakuin, 1937), pp. 26-30.

(16) For a survey of the literature cf. Havret, *op. cit.*, II, 343-374. Since the publication of Havret's work the literature has further increased.

(17) *Ibid.*, II, 38, n. 1 gives the Chinese Text.

(18) *Histoire 1625*, pp. 186 ff.

(19) Ernest Renan, *Histoire générale et système comparé des langues sémitiques*. 3d ed. (Paris: Imp. impériale, 1863). It was in the first edition of the same work that he had made the charge of fraud.

(20) Dias' *Ching-chiao pei-ch'üan* also published in an Appendix the account written by Li Chih-tsao. The quotations I have given in the text are from a photostatic copy loaned to me by Mr. Wang Chung-min.

(21) The Chinese text is in Havret, *op. cit.*, II, 96, n. 4.

Chapter XII

Ebb and Flow

WITH NEW ESTABLISHMENTS in Shansi, Shensi, and Fukien, the Jesuits now had nine permanent residences located in seven of the fifteen provinces of the Chinese empire. The mission personnel comprised eighteen priests and six Chinese lay-brothers.[1] There were also ten young Macaist Chinese scattered in the residences where they were receiving intellectual and spiritual formation with a view to entering the Society of Jesus.

Extreme caution was still the order of the day. Although the shadow of Shèn Ch'üeh had lifted, that of the potentially more dangerous Wei Chung-hsien loomed ever more menacingly above the mission. Wei had peopled the country with spies who kept close watch upon the activities of the missionaries. Assemblies however small were strictly prohibited. The eunuch professed to see in them foyers of rebellion.

The fact was that the cause of Christianity had become linked to the internal politics of the realm. The orientation which Ricci had given the mission made the Jesuits the natural allies of the party of reform. Inevitably they shared the fate of their friends. Their fortunes ebbed and flowed in counter-rhythm with the rise and fall of the power of the eunuch party. Thus, when in 1622 the disasters suffered at the hands of the Manchus forced the reactionaries into partial retreat, the Jesuits were recalled to Peking. Adam Schall, whose scientific talents were already attracting attention, was especially effective in making new friends. Most notable of these was the president of the Board of Finance.

A lunar eclipse was expected on October 8, 1623. When Schall's predictions proved accurate, the enthusiastic finance minister begged him, in Chinese fashion, to accept him as his pupil. The following year, in preparation for an eclipse expected in September, Schall wrote a two *chüan* treatise graphically describing the stages of the eclipse and discussing the related astronomical questions. It is his first astronomical work. The Jesuit brother, Ch'iu Liang-hou, an accomplished stylist, was responsible for its literary merits. Hsü Kuang-ch'i presented it to the Board of Rites.

A note in the Jesuit archives in Rome tells us what his immediate superiors thought of Schall at this stage of his career: "Talent good. judgment good; prudence mediocre; experience limited; progress in letters good. Temperament: naturally good, sanguine, gay, not yet wholly mature. He knows how to deal with people, but as yet not suited for the position of superior."[2] Inasmuch as this is the confidential opinion of a Portuguese (Dias) and an Italian (Longobardo) about a German (Schall), it must be said that Schall emerged well from the scrutiny.

Schall watched the September eclipse from the finance minister's home. When his calculations again proved faultless, the minister and others wished to renew the old demands for calendar reform and to urge that the Jesuits be entrusted with the task. Although the brilliant Johann Terrenz arrived in Peking from Hangchow shortly after this and began to write astronomical works, the times were not propitious for such an undertaking. The reversals of 1622 had by no means destroyed the power of Wei Chung-hsien, but had served chiefly to feed his hatred of the Tung-lin party which he was now bent upon destroying. His struggle with the progressive elements of the scholar-official class now reached new heights of intensity and unprecedented depths of bitterness.[3]

His first move was to humiliate them. Deputed by the T'ien-ch'i emperor to pay a state visit to the Ming tombs, he surrounded himself with pomp and ceremony such as only an emperor had hitherto received. The entire route, twelve miles long, was covered with yellow sand. Preceded by an imposing column of troops, a forest of banners, and stringed orchestras, the eunuch, surrounded by an armed guard, was carried in the imperial sedan chair. The first officials of the court, presidents of imperial tribunals and councillors of state, were obliged to descend from their own palanquins, kneel in the dusty road, and *k'o-t'ou* as he passed. They were then ordered to follow him to the tombs on foot.

The Tung-lin academicians did not submit without a struggle. They were far from poltroons. Their recognized leader in the capital was Yeh Hsiang-kao. His courageous opposition to Wei Chung-hsien brought him down in 1624 and forced him to retire to Fukien, as already described.

Other leaders in the fight were Ch'ên Ch'i-yü, Tso Kuang-tou, Huang Tsun-su, and Yang Lien. Frequent conferences were held in the home of Huang Tsun-su, an imperial censor, to plan the Tung-lin counter-strategy against the eunuch. In 1624 Yang Lien, as senior vice-president of the Censorate, bitterly denounced Wei Chung-hsien in a memorial enumerating "twenty-four crimes of Wei Chung-hsien." The memorial received no answer. Silence was a customary way of indicating imperial displeasure, although with the strict control maintained by Wei Chung-hsien it was never certain that memorials reached the emperor. Yang Lien, never short of courage, presented a second memorial, couched in even stronger terms than the first. It provoked no reply. Inasmuch as Yang Lien had acted as their representative in this démarche, a large number of academicians felt that they, no less than he, were touched in their honor by failure to receive a response. Some of them resolved to resign their posts and retire from public life rather than submit longer to the intolerable regime of Wei Chung-hsien. They presented a joint memorial to the throne asking that their resignations be accepted and that they be permitted to retire to their homes in the provinces. It was Wei Chung-hsien who read the memorial to the emperor. He played his cards cleverly. Assuming an air of humility he asked the emperor to dismiss him, since his loss to the throne could not compare with the loss of so many capable officials. As he had anticipated, the emperor was furious at the petitioners. Instead of granting them permission to retire with honor to their provinces, he ordered them to do so. Stripped of all prerogatives, they were reduced to the commonalty. The penalty extended to all members of their families.

It was a sweeping victory for the eunuch who lost no time in exploiting his advantage. He filled the vacated offices with his own sycophants. It was at this time that the unscrupulous Fêng Ch'üan became a grand secretary. As the henchman of Wei he played a leading role in the violent measures taken against the Tung-lin party.

Peking was sharply divided. Unprincipled careerists vied with one another in currying favor with Wei Chung-hsien. Against them stood the members of the Tung-lin party, steadfastly refusing to compromise in their firm stand against the corrupt regime of the eunuch. From 1624 to 1626 the contest swept rapidly towards a climax.

The Tung-lin academy in Peking had its own building, recently erected. This meeting place of his enemies was the focal point of Wei's wrath. He refused to regard it as an academy of scholars, insisting that it was a congregation of rebels. Against it Wei Chung-hsien set up a contra-academy composed of his own satellites. From this latter, hundreds of furious memorials, filled with calumnies against the Tung-lin academicians, were showered upon the emperor. These constituted part of a campaign to create the appearance of popular backing for measures contemplated by Wei.

On July 29, 1625, the eunuch had Yang Lien committed to prison on the false charge of accepting bribes from Hsiung T'ing-pi. This was the signal for a full-scale attack upon the progressives. Imprisoned with Yang were most of the more active leaders of his party. Yang survived imprisonment less than a month. He died on August 26, 1625, as a result of floggings received every two or three days. Five other distinguished leaders of the Tung-lin party were put to death that same year. These were Wei Ta-chung, Tso Kuang-tou, Ku Ta-chang, Yüan Hua-chung, and Chou Ch'ao-jui. With Yang Lien they are honored in Chinese history as *Liu-chün-tze* (The Six Heroes).

They were not the only victims. Others committed suicide. Nearly all adherents of the Tung-lin were swept out of office in a purge which extended into the provinces. Here some three hundred and thirty scholar-officials were stripped of titles and reduced to the rank of the commonalty. In the capital the holocaust was complete, reaching as it did to the highest offices of the realm. Three grand secretaries who attempted to intercede for some of the victims were deprived of offices and titles. Hsü Kuang-ch'i and Li Chih-tsao were living in retirement and were not directly affected. Yang T'ing-yün, who only the year before had been appointed vice-governor of Peking was obliged to retire in April, 1625. He returned to his home in Hangchow.

By 1626 the eunuch had driven large numbers of his opponents into retirement. Others he had silenced by measures which did not stop short of death. He now undertook to distort history in order to brand his enemies with the stigma of rebellion. Under his direction the *San-ch'ao yao-tien* was compiled to discredit the Tung-lin party. It purported to be the official version of the famous *causes célèbres* around which the long conflict between the liberals and the reactionaries had polarized. These three cases, long the subject of acrimonious dispute, were: the *T'ing-chi an* ("The Club Case"), referring to the attempt upon the life of the crown prince in 1615; the *Hung-wan an* ("The Red Pill Case"), referring to the mysterious medicine alleged to have caused the T'ai-ch'ang emperor's death in 1620; the *I-kung an* ("The Removal Case"), referring to the ejection of the concubine Hsi-li from the late emperor's quarters in 1621. Lack of objectivity was guaranteed by the appointment of Fêng Ch'üan as chief editor of this version.

In the same year Wei Chung-hsien's megalomania, fed by triumph over his enemies, developed into a form of egotheism. He instigated a movement to erect temples in his own honor throughout the empire. The first petition, from the governor of Chekiang, asked that a temple be erected on West Lake in Hangchow. Similar petitions poured in from officials who were Wei's creatures. The emperor consented. Viceroys and governors vied with one another in erecting the most lavish temples in honor of the eunuch who insisted that the solemnities observed in them be in no way inferior to those accorded Confucius!

Early in 1627 (Philip) Wang Chêng was in Peking. He collaborated with Terrenz in producing a book on mechanical principles, illustrated by himself, entitled *Ch'i-ch'i t'u-shuo* (Illustrated Explanation of Rare Instruments). Some of its terminology has become a permanent part of the Chinese language.

Wang Chêng urged that Schall be sent to his native province. Wei Chung-hsien was now at the height of his power. The fact that superiors thought that Schall could be spared from Peking reflects the unfavorable conditions prevailing in the capital. In the summer of 1627 he was transferred to Sianfu to replace Trigault.

The reception accorded Schall in that ancient capital indicates how the work of the missionaries in the provinces was directly affected by the prevailing political currents in Peking. He found the atmosphere of Sianfu heavy with hostility. Semedo, who joined him some months later, said that he had found the dungeons of Nanking more tolerable. Despite the zealous aid of Wang Chêng little was accomplished and Semedo was transferred to Kiangsi, leaving Schall alone.

The triumph of Wei Chung-hsien was not of long duration. His regime of tyrannical misgovernment was at its peak when, on September 30, 1627, the T'ien-ch'i emperor died, leaving no sons. Next in line of succession was his younger brother, Chu Yu-chien. It was common report in Peking that Wei Chung-hsien, whose ambition knew no limits, hoped to seize the throne himself. After keeping the news of the emperor's death for some days, he is said to have called a conclave of some of the leading officials who owed their positions to him. After announcing the monarch's death, he made it clear that he would not refuse should they wish to declare him emperor. The prospect of a eunuch occupying the Dragon Throne was too much even for his satellites to stomach. They told him that there was no question about the succession. Wei, putting on a bold front, went himself in state to announce to the sixteen-year-old Chu Yu-chien his accession to the throne and to conduct him to the imperial palace.

The new emperor, who gave to his reign period the title Ch'ung-chên and who was fated to ring down the curtain on the Ming dynasty, was endowed with good sense and natural virtue. "Very talented, but very unfortunate," is the way Adam Schall summed him up.[4]

His accession to the throne marked the end of Wei Chung-hsien's tyranny. He was determined to get rid of the eunuch, but in a way that would not seem arbitrary. He first issued an edict forbidding any temples to be erected in honor of anyone without his consent. In the same decree he promised that complaints to the throne would receive a fair hearing. It was clear that the edict was directed against Wei Chung-hsien, who was in no doubt as to the way the wind was blowing. Within a week he attempted to resign.

Relying upon the imperial assurance, two officials immediately memorialized the throne against Wei. Several grand secretaries, among them Fêng Ch'üan, who knew that the fall of the eunuch would bring them down too, attempted to prejudice the emperor against the petitioners. They were soundly rebuked. When word of this got around, a flood of memorials attacking Wei poured into the palace.

The emperor restored to their rank and dignity the officials who had been degraded in the purge of 1625-1626. Many of Wei's creatures were thrown out of office, Desperately, Wei Chung-hsien attempted to divert the gathering storm by asking the emperor to degrade his relatives for whom he had wangled titles and sinecures from the former ruler. The emperor did so, but did not allow this move to distract him from the arch-culprit. Two months after the inauguration of the new regime, Wei was ordered to retire to his native village. He was declared guilty on three counts: of attempting to seize the imperial power, of unjustly putting to death or driving to suicide worthy officials, and of looting the imperial treasury. Arrived in his native village, the captain of the guard handed him a small box containing a cord: this was the imperial command to commit suicide. After his death the emperor ordered the destruction of his memorial temples, statues and images. The officials who had raised them were castigated. The engraved blocks of the *San-ch'ao yao-tien* were burned and "Wei Chung-hsien remained in the records of China only as a symbol of infamy."[6]

A harsher fate met Wei's female accomplice, K'ê-shih. During Wei's regime she had ruled the palace as tyrannously as the eunuch had ruled the empire. She treated the empress, whose father she banished from court, like a servant. The new emperor ordered her cudgeled to death in the presence of the empress-dowager.

The fall of Wei brought many progressive and patriotic men back into office. One of these was Hsü Kuang-ch'i who in 1629 became senior vice-president of the Board of Rites.

The turn in the wheel of fortune came too late to restore to public life two other scholars who, in different ways, had greatly served the cause of Christianity. Both Yeh Hsiang-kao and Yang T'ing-yün died in 1627. It was a matter of deep regret to the missionaries that they had not succeeded in bringing the former to the Church.[6] More grievously felt, however, was the loss of Yang T'ing-yün. With his close friends, Hsü Kuang-ch'i and Li Chih-tsao he had been in the words of Semedo, one of the "bulwarks of the faith in the kingdom of China."[7] He deserved the tribute paid him by Bartoli:

> With the possible exception of Doctor Paul [Hsü Kuang-ch'i], the Society did not have in this realm a more loving father, or the faith a more generous defender, or Christianity a

more perfect exemplar of every virtue.[8]

Yang shared with the Christian scholars of this period a deep interest in the contributions to knowledge, scientific and philosophical as well as religious, which the Jesuits brought with them. In liberal, humanistic interest in truth and in their desire to break the barriers to thought established by the narrow classicism of the age, these men were alike.

In 1627 Yang undertook to build a church, with residential quarters for the missionaries attached, inside the Wu-lin gate in Hangchow. Despite his age, he insisted upon helping the laborers. He overexerted himself, fell ill, and, on December 31, died. He was seventy-one years old.

It took some time before the political changes in Peking made themselves felt in the provinces; but by 1629 the atmosphere began to clear. Again Sianfu serves as a barometer. When Schall began to build a chapel he received encouragement and even financial assistance from some non-Christian officials. Even those who had been most inimical showed a friendly attitude. The chapel, surmounted by a cross, was completed without opposition. It was the first time since the construction of the church in Nanking in 1611 that it had been possible to raise the cross on top of a church with impunity.

The viceroy sent two officials to leave his card and present the missionary with a gift. He wrote a eulogy of Western science and of the learning of the Jesuits, ordered the governor of the city to have it embossed in gold letters upon a tablet and presented to Schall in a public ceremony. This about-face on the part of officialdom did not leave the populace unaffected. Their hostility disappeared. Schall, able for the first time freely to preach the Gospel, soon had made fifty converts.

Sianfu was the terminus of the caravan trails from Central Asia. Once every five years a major caravan and once in three years a smaller caravan were permitted, under the guise of tribute- bearing embassies, to go to Peking. Meanwhile, Sianfu served as the caravan headquarters. In 1628 a major caravan was due to visit Peking. Schall called upon Mirjudin, its leader. A genuine friendship developed. The two men, Christian missionary and Mohammedan caravan leader, exchanged more than twenty visits before Mirjudin left for Peking. They conversed in Chinese. Schall was interested in learning all he could about the land routes from Central Asia.

This was a subject which always interested the Jesuits. The sea route took a heavy toll of lives. Of the 323 ships which sailed from Lisbon for Goa between 1580 and 1640, 70 were lost at sea. Of the passengers on the ships that reached their destination, a large percentage died en route.[9]

Schall checked the information he got from this native of Balkh with other members of the caravan. In the end he wrote a careful memoir on the subject which is in the Jesuit archives in Rome.[10] He describes in detail, and accurately, the route followed by the caravan, the distances covered, the protocol regulating its passage through the Great Wall, the articles brought to China, those carried away.

He mentions two other land routes through Central Asia, one towards northwest India, the other through eastern Tibet into Bengal. But it is the northern route, from Bokhara to Suchow, which he describes in detail. It had been in Suchow that Bento de Goes, the Jesuit brother, had completed his arduous and memorable four-year journey and there had died on April 11, 1607, after sending word to Ricci of his arrival. Schall confirmed again de Goes' findings, still doubted by a few, that Marco Polo's Cathay and China were the same. He pointed out that the old maps had located Cathay too far to the north and, as had Ricci, insisted that Polo's Khanbaligh and Peking are the same.

Thirty years later the general of the Society, Goswin Nickel, would send two priests, Albert D'Orville and Johann Grueber to explore one of these routes mentioned by Schall. They chose the second. Leaving Sianfu in June, 1661, they crossed the desert to Tibet, scaled the Himalayas, passed through Nepal and Bengal, and arrived at Agra two hundred and fourteen days later. There d'Orville died and Grueber continued alone to Rome with his reports.[11]

The housecleaning which began the Ch'ung-chên reign seemed to augur well for the future; but the emperor, despite good intentions, was handicapped by indecision and timidity. Although he removed some of the more vicious officials, he lacked the courage to drive from public life all the corrupt elements which had pullulated during the regime of Wei Chung-hsien. The fact that so notorious a scoundrel as Fêng Ch'üan was able to escape punishment, shows that the reforms were incomplete. The day for half-measures had passed. Only drastic action could have saved the empire; but of this the emperor was incapable. He temporized and compromised. Many competent men, members of the Tung-lin party, were reinstated in office. Eunuch control was broken, but eunuch influence was not crushed.

Many of Wei's sycophants continued in office. Their influence remained strong to the end of the dynasty. How strong was indicated by the fact that in 1628, less than a year after Wei's fall, they were able to block the appointment of Ch'ien Ch'ien-i, one of the most distinguished poets, essayists and historians of his time, to the position of grand secretary. Their candidate, Wên T'i-jên got the post. Ch'ien Ch'ien-i was dismissed from office as vice-president of the Board of Rites. (Thomas) Ch'ü Shih-ssu, who in 1628 went to Peking to assume the office of Junior Metropolitan Censor, played a prominent role in this political struggle. He was an intimate friend of Ch'ien's. When the latter retired from office Ch'ü was obliged to go with him. As late as 1637 both men, who had been living quietly in Changshu, Kiangsu, were imprisoned for a short time upon a trumped-up charge.

This episode reveals how far short the emperor fell of destroying the influence of the eunuch party. It explains why he was permanently unable to form a strong government. Between 1621 and 1644 the presidents of the six ministries changed one hundred and sixteen times.[12] Nothing could better indicate the chaotic state of government in the last years of the Ming.

Incomplete as were the reforms of the emperor, the return to Peking of many friends of the Jesuits was a great gain for the mission. The Church had weathered another storm. The missionaries could move freely about the capital to resume open propagation of the faith.

Hsü Kuang-ch'i, as vice-president of the Board of Rites, was in an advantageous position to press once more the project of entrusting calendar reform to the Jesuits. After long discussion with Hsü, Terrenz gave approval to the plan. A solar eclipse was to occur on June 21, 1629. Calculations were made by adherents of the three schools of astronomy: the Chinese, the Mohammedan, and the European. The predictions of the first two schools were erroneous. Terrenz' calculations were correct. The Board of Rites made public the results of the competitive test. Again a demand arose for revision of the calendar.

The emperor demanded an explanation of the errors shown in the calculations by the two traditional schools. A careful check by mathematicians of the imperial college and by members of the Board of Rites, showed that there had been no mistake in the calculations. The rules had been exactly followed. The only conclusion was that both the Mohammedan and the Chinese systems were unreliable.

Hsü Kuang-ch'i in a carefully prepared report exonerated the mathematicians. Not they, but the systems they were obliged to follow, were at fault. These systems, followed for centuries, had been substantially reliable in the beginning, but in the course of time their inherent weaknesses had grown into errors of major proportions. The only remedy lay in scientific correction of the entire Chinese calendar.

The report was read in a meeting of the Board of Rites, approved, and sent to the emperor in the form of a memorial. The emperor gave his approval to the project and appointed Hsü Kuang-ch'i to take charge. A new Calendrical Bureau, the *Li-chu*, was established.

In a second memorial Hsü declared to the emperor that he could not carry out calendar reformation without the aid of the European missionaries. They were, he said, excellent mathematicians and, through long study, were thoroughly familiar with Chinese astronomy. The Board of Rites, fearful that the emperor would be angered by a proposal to entrust so important an undertaking to those who had been banished from the empire by his grandfather, hesitated to approve Hsü's request. In the end his arguments overcame their fears and the memorial was presented in the name of the Board.

In an edict dated September 27, 1629, the emperor approved employment of the Jesuits in the work of the Calendrical Bureau. The publication of this edict throughout the empire was of great help to the faith. The signal mark of favor enhanced the prestige of the missionaries and went far toward erasing memory of the edict of 1617. Both in Peking and in the provinces the Jesuits received congratulatory visits from scholar-officials.

Hsü Kuang-ch'i appointed (Leo) Li Chih-tsao, (Philip) Wang Chêng, Nicolò Longobardo and Johann Terrenz to the Calendrical Bureau. The two priests were to be paid their living expenses out of the imperial treasury and were to be supplied with a shop for the fabrication of astronomical instruments.

Fortunately there were several Jesuits in China competent in mathematics and astronomy. Their library was also well stocked with the best books on the subject, brought from Europe by Trigault in 1619. For both these advantages the mission was indebted to the foresight of Ricci. Twenty-four years earlier, on May 12, 1605, in a letter to João Alvares, assistant to the general for Portugal, he had emphasized, in a tone which leaves no doubt as to the importance with which he viewed the matter, the need for an astronomer and for astronomical books:

> ... I want to request from Your Reverence a thing which I have demanded for many years, but without ever receiving an answer. Nothing could be more advantageous than to send to Peking a father or brother who is a good astronomer. I say astronomer, because as far as geometry, horology, and astrolabes are concerned, I know them well enough and have all the books I need on these subjects. But [the Chinese] do not make so much of these things as they do of planetary phenomena, the calculation of eclipses, and especially of one who can make up a calendar. The emperor maintains, I think, more than two hundred persons at great expense to prepare the calendar each year. In addition there are two colleges: one follows Chinese canons and despite the fact that its publications are certainly erroneous, is more esteemed; the other, of lesser standing, adheres to the Mohammedan system and, although more exact in its predictions of eclipses, is not made much of. These two colleges are outside the imperial palace. There are two others, composed of eunuchs, within the palace. In Nanking are two more colleges, to which many scholar-officials belong. Yet none of them is capable of doing anything except to follow in a thoroughly unscientific manner their rules. When their predictions turn out badly they can only fall back upon the excuse that they have followed the rules laid down by their predecessors.
>
> Because of my world-map, my clocks, spheres and astrolabes and the other things I do and teach, I have gained the reputation of being the greatest mathematician in the world. And, although I have no book on astronomy, I am able, with the aid of certain Portuguese calendars and periodicals, to predict the eclipses more accurately than they do. When I tell them that I have no books and do not wish to undertake the emendation of the calendar, they do not believe me. Therefore I say, that if this mathematician of whom I speak should come, we should be able to translate our tables into Chinese, which I write with facility, and thus undertake the task of correcting the calendar. This would enhance our reputation, give us freer entry into

China, and assure us greater security and liberty.
I wish your reverence would take this matter up with father general as a thing of great importance for China, and, whatever their nationality, send one or two [astronomers] directly to China, and to Peking, since elsewhere they would be of little use. Let them bring with them the necessary books. They cannot rely upon Goa or any other place, because our colleges in India do not have this kind of books and if they did they would not give them to other houses.[13]

With the publication of the imperial edict of September 27, 1629, the dream he had dreamed at least three decades earlier materialized. The aggregation of Terrenz and Longobardo to the Calendrical Bureau in 1629 marked the beginning of the most romantic episode of the Jesuit saga in China. Assistants in the bureau at first, they were in fact the real directors of the work. Under Schall, who rose to a rank and to a position of influence which no other foreigner attained in the history of the empire, they were made titular as well as actual heads of the department. Some of the greatest names in the history of the mission headed the bureau. With the exception of a brief interlude (1664-1669) when the malevolent charlatan Yang Kuang-hsien brought about the downfall of Schall, a Jesuit remained in charge until 1775 when the Society of Jesus was dissolved in China by publication of the Brief of Suppression issued by Pope Clement XIV in 1773. The last Jesuit to head the Bureau of Astronomy and Mathematics was Augustine de Hallerstein who held the post from 1746 until the shock of learning of the suppression of the order to which he was deeply devoted resulted in his death on October 29, 1774.

During these years the work of the Jesuits in the astronomical office played a decisive part in the propagation of the faith throughout the empire. As Ricci had foreseen, the prestige acquired and the contacts made facilitated the more directly evangelical labors of the missionaries in the provinces. While during the dark years of decline precipitated by the banning of the rites, particularly during the long reign of the Ch'ien-lung emperor (1739-1796), only the work of the priests in the Calendrical Bureau and in similar services to the empire preserved any vestiges of the prestige formerly enjoyed by Christianity.

NOTES

(1) Väth, *op. cit.*, p. 70, n. 11.

(2) *ARSI*, Jap-Sin 134, f. 15.

(3) Most of the information on the pages which follow about the court struggle is taken from *Eminent Chinese*, I, 148 f., 240 f.; II, 892 f.

(4) Väth, *op. cit.*, p. 94, n. 15.

(5) *Eminent Chinese*, II, 847.

(6) Bartoli, *op. cit.*, IV, 232 f.

(7) Semedo, *Histoire universelle*, p. 362.

(8) Bartoli, *op. cit.*, IV, 211.

(9) Cf. Manuel de Faria e Sousa, *Asia Portuguesa* (Lisboa: H. Valente de Oliveira, 1666-1675), for a list of all the sailings from Portugal to Africa and Asia from 1412 to 1640. There is a list of all the Jesuits who sailed from Lisbon for the Orient from 1541 to 1603 in Jeronimo P. A. da Camara Manoel, *Missoes dos Jesuitas no Oriente nos seculos XVI e XVII. Trabalho destinado a X sessao de Congresso Internacional dos orientalistas* (Lisboa, 1894).

(10) *ARSI*, Jap-Sin 143, ff. 1-8 and ff. 9-20.

(11) Grueber's account of their journey is in Melchisédech Thevenot, *Relations de divers voyages curieux* (nouv. ed.; Paris: T. Moette, 1696), I, No. 7. 1-23.

(12) *Eminent Chinese*, I, 191.

(13) *Opere storiche*, II, 284 f.

Chapter XIII

Pillars Fall

THE MISSION SUFFERED a serious loss in the death of Nicolas Trigault on November 14, 1628, at the age of 52. A certain mystery surrounds his death. Bartoli, writing thirty-five years later, reported that he had died as a result of a mental breakdown. D'Elia blames Bartoli for having permitted his prejudice against Trigault to color his historical judgment.[1] It must be said, however, that Bartoli was not writing without evidence. In the Jesuit archives there is a letter of December 20, 1629, from the visitor, André Palmeiro, to Vitelleschi which contains in code the message that Trigault had hanged himself and that Cattaneo had predicted that his intense concentration upon the disputed problem of Christian terminology would kill him.[2] This is probably the clue to what happened. His mind gave way under excessive strain.

Trigault was one of the most ardent promoters of the apostolate of the pen. In Chiangchow and in Sianfu he had founded the first Christian printing establishments in China. Superiors were anxious to exploit his literary talents and for this purpose they withdrew him from the evangelical field and ordered him to apply himself exclusively to works of the pen. He overdid it. He had a prodigious memory and a voracious appetite for hard study. He is said to have limited himself to three hours sleep a night in order to have more time for his Chinese researches. It proved not to be enough.

In the spring of 1630 another severe blow hit the mission. Johann Terrenz, who had scarcely begun his work in the Calendrical Bureau, died on May 13. At the moment his loss seemed irremediable. Terrenz was a man of brilliant attainments. A native of Switzerland, he had achieved fame throughout Europe as a physician, philosopher, and mathematician, before his entry into the Society of Jesus at the age of thirty-five. Besides his own language he spoke fluent French, English, and Portuguese, and was well versed in the Semitic languages. It was Terrenz who first translated the Syriac inscription on the Sianfu monument.

En route to the Orient with Trigault he had collected on the shores of Goa, in Bengal, Malacca, Sumatra, and Cochin-China, plants, stones, animals, fish, reptiles, and insects and had made first-rate drawings to accompany his descriptions. He also made serious studies of the climate and the inhabitants of the countries which he visited.[3] He left unpublished two volumes *in-folio* containing these studies and the further fruits of his observations and studies up to the year of his death.

Terrenz had been a friend and fellow academician of Galileo. Galileo had been the sixth and Terrenz the seventh member elected to the Cesi Academy in Rome. For eight years, directly before leaving Europe and through various mutual scientific friends after reaching China, Terrenz tried to enlist the help of Galileo in the reform of the Chinese calendar. He was especially anxious to have Galileo's calculus of solar eclipses. He was quite unhappy about the injunction of the Holy Office of April 6, 1616, forbidding Galileo to defend the Copernican theory. It does not reflect credit upon the noted Pisa savant that Terrenz' repeated pleas for his solar calculations were ignored and finally rebuffed.[4] More rewarding was his friendship with Kepler, another famous European savant, with whom he carried on a correspondence from Peking and to whom he explained the Chinese method of calculating solar eclipses.

Terrenz' funeral services were the first to be solemnly celebrated in Peking since the edict of expulsion. Many non-Christian scholar-officials, anxious to honor his memory, contributed to the expenses of the obsequies.

Terrenz had been a man of proven ability and established reputation. Superiors looked upon his loss at this moment as a major catastrophe. Hsü Kuang-ch'i immediately named Adam Schall and Giacomo Rho to take his place on the Calendrical Bureau. Fortunately the thirty-nine-year-old Schall and Rho, his junior by two years, were to prove brilliant choices.

Schall had been in Sianfu since 1627. Rho was in Shansi with

Vagnoni. The emperor on June 29, 1630, approved their appointment to the Calendrical Bureau and issued orders to the officials in Shensi and Shansi provinces to facilitate the journey of the two men to Peking. After the dark years, Christianity had again won a recognized and honorable place in the empire.

For the first time in thirteen years the missionaries were able openly to carry on their work. The immediate results of their new freedom can be seen in the province of Shansi. In 1630 Vagnoni, assisted by Rho until the latter's departure for Peking, registered five hundred conversions. In 1631 Vagnoni, unaided, made seven hundred, and in 1632, eleven hundred conversions. When it is remembered that in 1625, the year Wei Chung-hsien's campaign against the Tung-lin party had moved to its climax, there were only six hundred and seventy-three conversions in the whole empire, the significance of these gains is evident. The missionaries in the other provinces reported similar increases.

In 1629 the Manchus, successfully repulsed by Yüan Ch'ung-huan, who had been restored to his command, moved westward. In the winter of that year, in a surprise move, they broke through the Great Wall from Mongolia and appeared in the neighborhood of Peking. Yüan Ch'ung-huan rushed from Ningyuan to defend the capital. Although he was in no way responsible for the Manchu breakthrough, partisans of the late Wei Chung-hsien succeeded in poisoning the mind of the emperor against him. On January 13, 1630, in the midst of an interview with the emperor, Yüan was seized. Charged with being in league with the enemy, he was cut to pieces in the marketplace.[5]

Imperilled by the Manchus, the emperor commissioned Hsü Kuang-ch'i and Li Chih-tsao to train troops on the European model. Again Hsü and Li raised the question of obtaining Portuguese assistance. On February 14, 1630, the emperor approved. Macao sent two cannon, a few muskets and five or six artillerymen, led by Gonzales Texeira Correa. A Jesuit, João Rodriques, accompanied them as interpreter. He did not belong to the China mission, but to Japan where he was known to the Japanese as "the interpreter." He was a brilliant linguist who had served for many years as interpreter to Hideyoshi and to his successor Ieyasu, but had been expelled from Japan in 1612.[6]

The small troop arrived in time to play a decisive role in lifting the Manchu siege of Chochow, a city not far from the capital. The Portuguese artillery and firearms drove the Manchus into retreat. Texeira, inflamed by his success, petitioned the emperor to be allowed to lead three hundred men from Macao, promising that with them he would drive the Manchus out of the empire and inflict upon them such crushing defeat that they would curse the day they had invaded China. Texeira's fiery confidence was probably due to the fact that he had not tested the prowess of the Manchus in combat. Inasmuch as they were not prepared to cope with artillery fire the Manchus had retreated from Chochow without serious fighting.

The Board of War recommended acceptance of Texeira's offer. Rodriques was deputed to bring the reinforcements from Macao. Two hundred men enlisted, of whom the majority were Macaist Chinese trained by the Portuguese. They were good soldiers and expert gunsmiths. Each soldier was accompanied by a servant. Well supplied with funds from the imperial treasury, they outfitted themselves superbly with uniforms and arms. Under the leadership of Captain Pedro Cordier and Captain Antonio Rodriques del Capo the little army set out for the north.

It got no further than Nanchang. Semedo, who was stationed in that city at the time, gives an eyewitness account of the episode.[7] The officials of Nanchang treated the troops generously. Semedo remarks that they "approved and praised everything about them, except the style of their clothes." They did not, however, permit them to continue their journey, but after a long delay sent them back to Macao.

Portuguese trading privileges were limited to the port of Canton. This limitation gave Cantonese merchants a monopoly of foreign trade. They saw in the Portuguese expedition to the north a serious threat to this source of rich profit. Success of the expedition might win for the Portuguese the privilege of trading freely anywhere in the empire and put an end to the Cantonese monopoly. With generous bribes the Cantonese merchants enlisted the help of some of the reactionary clique still holding office in the capital. These men persuaded the emperor that, with the withdrawal of the Manchus, there was no need for additional aid. They obtained from the indecisive ruler an order directing the expedition to return to Macao.

The abortive expedition had not been without advantage to the mission. Five Jesuits had entered the empire from Macao with the small expeditionary force. It was the first substantial reinforcement the mission personnel had received in eight years. The soldiers turned back from Nanchang, but the five missionaries advanced to the posts to which they had been assigned: Pietro Canevari, to Hangchow; Etienne Le Fèvre to Shansi where he joined Vagnoni; Tranquillo Grassetti stayed in Nanchang; Bento de Mattos to Fukien; Michel Trigault, Nicolas Trigault's nephew to Sianfu.

The year 1630 was one of both gain and loss for the mission. On the Feast of All Saints, November 1, Li Chih-tsao died in Peking. The second of the "three pillars of the Catholic Church in China" had fallen. It was thirty-one years since Li's meeting with Ricci. During all of this time, but particularly during the twenty years since his baptism, he had given invaluable aid to the missionaries.

As he lay dying in his home in Peking, surrounded by a small group of Jesuit priests, he took Hsü Kuang-ch'i by the hand and with tears in his eyes committed the mission to his care:

> I die content because with my own eyes I have beheld our fathers re-established and strongly supported by your authority. I would not presume to commend them to you, knowing well the place they hold in your heart. My sins made me unworthy to have part in this work in which you have done me the honor of taking me for an associate. If after the conclusion of this affair [the calendar reform], my name can contribute towards anything which concerns the glory of God and the spread of our holy faith, do me the honor of using it. I put upon your shoulders the Christianity of China.

(Leo) Li Chih-tsao was a Christian gentleman, an apostle of learning; and an evangelist of the faith. It would be difficult to improve upon Semedo's epitaph: "His memory will live eternally in the hearts of the members of our Society while the example of his virtues will never die in the generous souls of the noble people of China."[8]

Two years later, on September 7, 1632, the Jesuits lost another staunch friend and prominent Christian, Sun Yüan-hua, who was executed in the prisons of Peking, victim of his own high sense of honor. In 1630 he had been made governor of Têngchow and Laichow in the Shantung peninsula.[9] After the fiasco of the Macao expedition, Texeira Correa and his small squad of Portuguese soldiers with their artillery joined Sun in Tengchow.

The troops under Sun's command were Manchurians fighting on the side of the Ming. Sun was a Christian, a member of the Tung-lin party, and a *chü-jên* holding an office ordinarily reserved for a *chin-shih*, three reasons why the appointees of Wei Chung-hsien who still held many offices in Peking looked upon him with jaundiced eye. More interested in political revenge than in saving the empire, they proceeded to sabotage his position. Sun found himself isolated. His appeals for provisions and munitions disappeared into the great silent bureaucratic sea. His troops went for months without pay. Repeated and urgent messages to the capital were never answered. On January 19, 1632, the inevitable mutiny broke out. A detachment of troops, led by two of Sun's subordinates, Kêng Chung-ming and K'ung Yu-tê, rebelled. They pillaged the surrounding countryside. Sun, loyal to his trust, attempted to restore order. It was later charged that by his efforts to bring the mutineers back into the fold he had lost the opportunity to put down the revolt. Possibly knowing better than anyone else how far they had been goaded by wilful politicians in Peking, he was unwilling to use force against them if it could be avoided. At any rate, his efforts to bring about a peaceful settlement failed. On February 22 the rebels stormed and took Têngchow. Texeira fell while directing the defense from the city wall. Only three of his Portuguese soldiers survived. The Jesuit emissary, João Rodriques, made his way to safety by leaping from the high wall into deep snowbanks and fleeing to a neighboring village. Sun Yüan-hua was captured. The mutineers bore him no ill will. They were well aware that he was the victim of Peking politics. Consequently Kêng Chung-ming and K'ung Yu-tê, who planned to lead their men into the service of the Manchus, attempted to persuade him to join them. Although aware of the fate that awaited him in Peking, Sun steadfastly refused. His captors released him and, together with (Michael) Chang Tao who had been serving on his staff, he returned to the capital to face court-martial.

Hsü Kuang-ch'i had just risen to the exalted position of grand secretary. He moved heaven and earth to save his two friends; the opposing forces were too strong and too well organized. Against him, too, was the weight of the Chinese concept of political responsibility. The local official is charged with full responsibility for whatever happens in his jurisdiction. The system provided excellent coverage for the unscrupulous bureaucrats in Peking. By their machinations they had deliberately created an explosive situation. Sun Yüan-hua was helpless to checkmate them. Moral responsibility for what followed rested upon them. But there was no redress against them. Legally Sun was accountable. Over the strong protests of Hsü Kuang-ch'i, he and Chang were condemned and executed. While they sat in their cells awaiting execution, Adam Schall disguised himself as a petty coal merchant and, with blackened face and sack of coal on shoulder, managed to get into the prison and bring the two men holy viaticum.[10] It was a tragic, but not unheroic end for (Ignatius) Sun Yüan-hua, generous founder of the Jesuit establishment in his native town of Kiating, and for (Michael) Chang Tao, who in 1621 had been received with high honors in Macao as the first official envoy of the Ming court to appear in the Portuguese settlement.

A third prominent Christian was involved in this tragedy. Upon the recommendation of Sun Yüan-hua, (Philip) Wang Chêng had been appointed intendant of the Liaohai circuit with headquarters at Têngchow. He took up his post on August 17, 1631. When, six months later, Têngchow fell to the mutineers, Wang escaped. He returned to his home in Shensi. The following year he was sentenced to exile for his part in the failure to keep Têngchow out of the rebels' hands. Pardoned shortly afterwards, he never returned to public life. His remaining years he devoted to writing and to lending all possible aid to the Jesuit missionaries in his province. Despite the injustice which he, and especially his friends Sun and Chang, had suffered he remained loyal to the Ming. When Li Tzu-ch'eng took Sianfu in 1643 he urged Wang to join him. Wang spurned the invitation, declaring that he would rather take his life than support the rebels. Like many another patriotic official he gave to the regime from which he had suffered gross injustice a loyalty which it was far from deserving. He is said to have committed suicide after learning that Peking had fallen to Li on April 25, 1644.[11] If this is true, he acted contrary to the code of his Christian faith; but he is not to be judged too harshly. A devoted Ming loyalist, the collapse of the dynasty turned his world upside down. Under great emotional stress it is not surprising that the forces of a sanctioned, even honored, social custom with deep roots in his cultural past reasserted themselves in such strength as to submerge one of the canons of the new code which he had accepted with his Christian faith. There is evidence that this was not the first time, though it was surely the last, that Wang Chêng, though a good and sincere Christian, wavered in his allegiance to his newly accepted code of morals. After his retirement from public life he had taken a concubine. In punishment he was excommunicated by the missionaries, probably by his good friend Vagnoni. He repented of his fault and in 1635 wrote an humble avowal of his sin and asked pardon. He got rid of the concubine and was restored to the good graces of the fathers.[12] He was posthumously honored by the Ch'ien-lung emperor who conferred upon him the title *Chung-chieh* (Loyal Integrity). The Manchus could appreciate loyalty even when it had served the family they had overthrown.

On November 8, 1633, the Church in China suffered its most grievous loss since the death of Ricci. On that day Hsü Kuang-ch'i passed away, not many months after reaching the pinnacle of success. Already grand secretary of the *Tung-ko*, he had been named grand secretary of the *Wên-yüan-ko*. He was recognized as "the first man in China after the monarch himself."[13]

The last years of Hsü's life had been energetic ones. He had put great effort into organizing the work of the Calendrical Bureau and much of its later success was due to the orientation given by him in the beginning. The initial need was to translate specialized literature for the use of Chinese assistants. As had Terrenz before them, Schall and Rho applied themselves strenuously to the extremely demanding task set for them.

The annual publication of the calendar was one of the most important functions of government. The movement of sun, moon, stars, and conjunctions, the entry of the sun into the twenty-eighth constellation of the Chinese zodiac — all had to be exactly determined. An errorless calendar was vital to the realization of the Confucian idea that the orderly arrangement of civic life required that it be in harmony with nature.

Chinese astronomical science had a very long history and was far from being inferior in all respects to European science.[14] On the theoretical side the Chinese view of the heavenly bodies floating in infinite space was far nearer reality than the Ptolemaic-Aristotelian concept of a geocentric universe of solid spheres like plastic domes. On the other hand the European methods for calculating eclipses were far superior to the Chinese empirical methods. The Chinese had been watching the skies for hundreds of years and had accumulated an enormous mass of factual data. Errors had, however, multiplied in the course of time. As a consequence predictions of eclipses rarely proved exact. Sometimes eclipses occurred which had not been foreseen.

There had been efforts at reform. These usually were made at the beginning of a new dynasty. Thus the introduction of Arabic arithmetic at the outset of the Yuan dynasty (1280) brought about a renewal. Arabic science continued to hold a place of honor under the Ming dynasty (1368-1644). At least twenty-four Arabian astronomers were in the service of the first Ming emperors. In 1370 the Mohammedan school was recognized as part of the Bureau of Astronomy. Its directors gave lectures in spherical geometry and algebra. They translated into Chinese hundreds of Arabic manuscripts which were found in the capital when the descendants of Ghengis Khan were driven back into Mongolia by Chu Yuan-chang, founder of the Ming dynasty. In 1385 the Mohammedan astronomers presented a treatise to the court on the theory of the calendar. It underwent revision in 1470 and again in 1477. When the Jesuits began their work, the Mohammedan school still functioned as part of the Bureau of Astronomy, but, according to Schall, its calculations were scarcely less inexact than those of the Chinese, there having been no thorough reform for 381 years.[15]

The Jesuits could not simply substitute the European calendrical system. They had to preserve the Chinese time-measurement system and the basic structure of the calendar. Väth says that this was the chief reason why, although many of them were Copernicans, they did not abandon the Ptolemaic system.[16] Needham suggests that it was also due to the fact that "they could not but be sensitive to the condemnation of Galileo by the Church."[17] They hoped in time to persuade the Chinese of the advantages of the Gregorian calendar, but for the moment there was no possibility of so radical a break with tradition.

Needham notes several other items which must be marked down on the debit side of the ledger when assessing the Jesuit contribution to Chinese astronomy, but he recognizes that the value of the contributions on the credit side greatly outbalance them. In listing these latter under six headings, he remarks:

> In the history of intercourse between civilizations there seems no parallel to the arrival in China in the 17th century of a group of Europeans so inspired by religious fervour as were the

> Jesuits, and at the same time so expert in most of those sciences which had developed with the Renaissance and the rise of capitalism.[18]

Schall and Rho worked quietly in their residence in order not to provoke unnecessarily the opposition of adherents of the old schools. So rapidly did their work advance that twice in 1631 and once in 1632, Hsü was able to present to the throne translations on astronomical subjects, comprising seventy-two *chüan* and one table of the fixed stars. It was a prodigious feat on the part of the two Jesuits, but it is unlikely that they could have succeeded except for the devoted co-operation of Hsü. The great scholar, moreover, gave to the translations a classical literary flavor.

He also founded an academy for the training of specialists in mathematics and astronomy. Here, under the direction of Schall and Rho, the students, all Christians, worked at the translation of astronomical and logarithmic tables.

When Hsü fell ill on September 11, 1633, the work was well in hand. The year before he had recommended to the throne the appointment of (Peter) Li T'ien-ching as head of the Calendrical Bureau to succeed him. He no doubt hoped to groom him to carry on the mission of furthering the interests of Christian culture, a task to which he himself had devoted the best years of his life. In 1632 Li was provincial judge of Shensi. At that time he could not be spared from his post. Another scholar whom Hsü had recommended for the post, declined on account of ill health. The postion of head of the Calendrical Bureau was not a sinecure. On all sides there smoldered the sullen jealousies of adherents of the old astronomical schools and the fierce resentment of old guard reactionaries.

Now, on his deathbed, Hsü Kuang-ch'i's thoughts continued to center upon the cause of Christianity and the work of the Jesuits in the Calendrical Bureau. On October 31, from his sickbed he despatched two memorials to the throne. In one of them he reported to the emperor the progress which had been made in the Calendrical Bureau, called attention to the unsparing way in which the Jesuits had devoted themselves to the work entrusted to them, and asked that they be rewarded in a manner commensurate with their services. In the other memorial Hsü again recommended that Li T'ien-ching succeed him as head of the bureau. This was his last public act. It rang the curtain down on a life of rare unselfishness, a life utterly devoted to public service: the service of learning, the service of his country, the service of his faith. The few remaining days of his life he devoted to preparing for death. He passed these days peacefully, spending long hours in prayer, but speaking freely, often on the subject of eternal beatitude, with Longobardo, Schall, and Rho. He confessed at least three times, received viaticum and extreme unction, and on November 8, "passed to receive from God," writes Bartoli, "the reward for his great services to the Church of China, services which should preserve immortal and glorious in its history and among its posterity the memory of Kolao Paul Hsü Kuang-ch'i."[19]

The emperor, who had sent his own doctors to attend the grand secretary during his illness and who frequently sent officers to inquire into his condition, gave signs of unusual grief when informed of his passing. He sent a special coffin of precious wood to receive the body and ordered the Board of Rites to see that solemn funeral services were conducted at state expense.

His body was carried in state to Shanghai; but, due to the disturbed condition of the time, he was not buried on his estate at Zikawei until 1641. In 1933 his tomb, which lies behind the major seminary, was the scene of an elaborate program commemorating the tercentenary of his death.

The emperor posthumously conferred upon him the honorary title of Junior Guardian (changed in 1643 to Grand Guardian) of the Heir Apparent and the honorific posthumous name of *Wên-ting* (Illustrious Tranquility).

Posthumous honors could not compensate for the sense of personal loss felt by every Jesuit in China. There was not one center of Jesuit activity which could not trace its establishment directly or indirectly to the influence of Hsü Kuang-ch'i.

From the moment of his conversion to that of his death, Hsü's personal life showed forth the best of Christian virtues. The Jesuits, who knew him well, filled pages with anecdotes to illustrate his spirit of faith, his humility, modesty, tranquillity, rectitude; his spirit of prayer and of penance; his mastery over his emotions; his love for his enemies, the moderation of his heart, language, and countenance. As for his zeal, it knew only the bounds of prudence. There is no record of how many he brought to the Christian faith. In 1623 alone it is recorded that he was directly responsible for one hundred and twenty conversions, most of them scholars or students.

In Peking he lived next door to the Jesuit residence. A private passageway led from his home into the fathers' chapel. Even when as grand secretary he was burdened with the weightiest affairs of state he never failed to pass some time in prayer there each day.

There was nothing nationalistic in his Catholicism. His faith was universal. He felt intimately united to the whole body of the Church. The letters which the missionaries received from Europe aroused his keen interest. The rapid progress of the Church in Indo-China was a source of joy to him. He wrote to the new Christian centers in Tonkin encouraging them to hold firm against attack and "to esteem themselves blessed to live in the Church, more blessed to be worthy to die for her."

He never hesitated to risk his career in defense of the faith. Every published attack upon Christianity received an answer from his pen. His *Apologiae*, unlike much of polemical literature, never violated Christian charity in defending Christian truth. Even when most aroused he never lost his urbanity. So effective were his essays in defense of the faith that he robbed many pamphleteers of desire to attack it again.

Like Ricci he was a man of the long view: it was to the future that he looked. The morrow's harvest was more important to him than the tangible, but ephemeral, fruits of today. This is why, through years of disappointments and reverses, he never lost sight of the project of calendar reform. Through this he hoped to obtain a position of security and liberty for the Church. His hopes were realized.

In a land where public office is too often a road to riches Hsü Kuang-ch'i lived and died a poor man. He had no more than enough to maintain himself and his family. Special emoluments received from the emperor for outstanding service, he devoted to charity. On his birthday anniversaries he gave four large alms: to the sick, to those in prison, to the old, and to the missionaries to distribute among needy Christians. In provinces swept by famine he was known as the "Father of the Poor." As grand secretary he held the highest office of the land. Yet in his last illness the Jesuits who were with him noted that he did not have sufficient money on hand to pay for ordinary medicines.

The words of Bartoli make a fitting epitaph for this great man:

Such was the patrimony which Kolao Paul left to his family, and with which he enriched his household: great merits, a great example, and of worldly substance very little.[20]

NOTES

(1) Pasquale D'Elia, S. J., "Daniele Bartoli e Nicola Trigault," *Revista storica italiana* XVI (June 30, 1938), 77-92.

(2) *ARSI*, Jap-Sin 161 II, ff. 116-117.

(3) Athanasius Kircher, S. J., *China monumentis, qua sacris qua profanis, nec non variis naturae et artis spectaculis, aliarumque rerum memorabilium argumentis, illustrata* (Antwerpiae: J. à Meurs, 1667), p. 110.

(4) The full story is told by Pasquale D'Elia, S. J., *Galileo in China*, tr. by Rufus Suter and Matthew Sciascia (Cambridge: Harvard University Press, 1960).

(5) *Eminent Chinese*, II, 955.

(6) On his Japanese career cf. C. R. Boxer, *The Christian Century*, page references in the Index.

(7) Semedo, *op. cit.*, pp. 152 ff.

(8) *Ibid.*, pp. 359 ff. for these quotations and for other estimates of Li Chih-tsao.

(9) *Eminent Chinese*, II, 686.

(10) Joannes Gabiani, S. J., *Incrementa Sinicae ecclesiae a Tartaris oppugnatae* (Vienna, 1673), p. 594.

(11) *Eminent Chinese* II, 808.

(12) Joseph Siao, S. J., *T'ien-Chu-chiao ch'uan-hsing chung-kuo* (Hsien-hsien, 1931), p. 209.

(13) Väth, *op. cit.*, p. 103.

(14) Cf. Needham, *op. cit.*, pp. 171-497, especially 437 ff.

(15) Schall, *op. cit.*, p. 7.

(16) Väth, *op. cit.*, p. 102.

(17) Needham, *op. cit.*, p. 438.

(18) *Ibid.*, p. 437 f.

(19) Bartoli, *op. cit.*, IV, 429.

(20) *Ibid.*, p. 448.

Chapter XIV

Brother Helped by Brother

THE DEATH of Hsü Kuang-ch'i marked the end of an epoch. To win for Christianity a position in the empire safe from the danger of sudden destruction had been in Ricci's conception the primary objective of the mission. That goal had by now been attained. Serious storms had been weathered. Persecution had failed to uproot Christianity and the evil figure of Wei Chung-hsien had passed from the scene. With the association of the Jesuits, by imperial decree, in the work of the Calendrical Bureau, Christianity at last enjoyed relative security. So with the death of Hsü Kuang-ch'i, the last as he was the greatest of the intellectuals who had collaborated with Ricci in the effort to enracinate Christianity in Chinese soil, the mission closed the first chapter of its history.

It now moves into a new phase of development. The sense of insecurity is gone. Quiet confidence prevails. It is different from the false, and disastrous, optimism which colored Longobardo's view and shaped his policies twenty years earlier. It is a confidence tempered by experience and strengthened by a deeper respect for Ricci's insight.

Now for the first time the fruits of the half-century of pioneering effort begin to appear in a growing movement of conversions in the provinces. The movement is sustained by the constantly increasing prestige won for Christianity by the labors of Schall in the Calendrical Bureau.

There is, however, another side to the picture. The second phase of the mission's history is marked, not only by expanding prosperity, but also by the appearance of new adversities. The adversities demand first attention because chronologically they appear on the first page of this chapter of the story. As the death of Hsü Kuang-ch'i in 1633 rang down the curtain on the first scene, the arrival in China of Franciscan and Dominican missionaries in the same year rings up the curtain on the second scene.

The enterprise in China seemed fated to emerge triumphant from one crisis only to encounter another. That this should have been so will surprise those only who fail to understand the significance of what the Jesuits were trying to do. They were attempting to effectuate an amalgamation of Christian and Chinese culture to produce a Sino-Christian civilization. It was a work of accommodation of the utmost delicacy.

In Rome alone had Christian missionaries encountered so organized a society, so mature a culture, so proud a civilization. Yet one cannot draw a parallel between the Roman empire and China. For all of its Semitic background Christianity took its rise in what was part of the Hellenic world. It came to China from a totally different world; and so the pride, complacency, jealousy, and conservatism of a deeply entrenched culture hostile to innovation constituted a far more massive obstacle here than had been the case in Rome. The contradictions which the Jesuits had suffered during the first fifty years in the empire had arisen chiefly in this quarter. Thanks to the policies developed by Ricci, these contradictions were overcome. But the accommodation demanded by the effort to amalgamate two cultures worked both ways. If Chinese culture had to change, Christianity had also to adapt itself to the new environment. In opposition to accommodation arising within the Church lay a potential source of other contradictions.

The adaptation of Christianity to Chinese culture was not easy. It was complicated by the fact that Roman Catholic Christianity was not simply a culture; it was a revealed religion. There could be no tampering with the body of dogmatic and moral truths which constituted its deposit of faith. In addition, however, to the body of revealed truths, Christianity had developed cultural forms. It had accommodated itself and contributed to the development of European art forms, social customs, modes of dress, of language, of thought. It had also developed a body of ecclesiastical laws, Roman in character, regulating the discipline of Catholic life. A part of history as they were, these cultural and juridical forms were not divinely revealed. Nor did they possess the value of absolutes. Had Christianity in the first centuries moved east instead of west the cultural forms developed would have been quite different. It is likely that the chiselled formulas of Roman law and the logical forms of Hellenic thought provided more security for the integrity of a body of absolute doctrines than the more undulating modes of thought and nebulous concepts of law peculiar to the Orient. Accordingly the movement of Christianity to the west may be considered providential. Nevertheless, it is true that no absolute value attached to European cultural forms. Adaptation in respect to these was possible without affecting the character of Christianity as a revealed religion.

The potential source of difficulties lay, of course, in the fact that certain Christians were unable to make the necessary distinction between the universal, absolute, and immutable in Christianity and the particular, relative, and adaptable in its cultural forms. The early Church had experienced difficulties on this head. But at that time those who were confused, and who therefore opposed the policy of cultural adaptation, were a small minority. Tertullian was the only outstanding churchman of their party and his views led him out of the Church.

By the time of the seventeenth Christian century the situation had changed. Europeanism was now deeply entrenched and the principle of accommodation had been so far lost sight of that it was little understood. The identity of Christianity and European cultural forms and social customs was so much taken for granted that even slight concessions to non-European usages or attitudes ran the risk of being regarded as a betrayal of the faith. If in the early Church adaptation aroused the opposition of a small minority, in later centuries it could not avoid arousing the opposition of a strong majority.

Alessandro Valignano, in shaping the mission policy of Japan and China, was fully aware of this. He knew that the policy which he sponsored ran counter to the accepted notions of most of his contemporaries and that, not understanding it, they would inevitably attack it. He wanted to keep the seeds of conflict out of the mission field. He realized that division, strife, conflict, and controversy must prove disastrous to the missionary enterprise. The difficulties likely to be encountered from the side of the indigenous cultures were imposing enough. They would be increased fourfold if to them were added the complications of disunity among the missionaries with consequent divisions among Christians and scandal to non-Christians. Furthermore, he was convinced that Europeanism offered no hope of converting these countries, least of all China. The only hope of success lay in keeping out divisive and hostile influences until the policy of cultural adaptation had proved itself, until its nature was better understood, and until the Church was firmly established.

Chief threat to Valignano's policy lay in the Philippines where their experience gave the missionaries no reason to question the efficacy of Europeanism as a missiological method. Although some of the most forceful writing against Europeanism had been done by Spaniards and the practice of adaptation was not unknown in Mexico and South America, the missionaries in the islands were not inclined to see much force in ethical and missiological theories which found fault with methods which, in their experience, had come through the pragmatic test with flying colors. Eminently successful in their conquests they were impatient to storm the stronghold of China. Children of an age which was inclined to reduce all non-Christian people to a common denominator, they were little disposed to concede more to Chinese culture than they had to Philippine and Indian culture.

When Rosso lightly dismisses the question of missionary method as having nothing to do with the case and, with reference to Jesuit-Franciscan friction in Fukien, affirms that: ". . . not a single feature of the so-called Jesuit method was alien to [the friars]," he ignores the record and is directly contradicted by one of the leading participants and most prolific letter writers in the Franciscan enterprise.[1] The Jesuit methods Buenaventura Ibañez, O.F.M., described as "purely human means directly contrary to those used by the Apostles, recommended by Christ Our Lord, and, except for the fathers of the Society, everywhere employed by those who evangelize the Kingdom of God."[2] The intellectual apostolate carried on by the Jesuits appears to Ibañez simply as "posturing before the gentiles as men of wealth, power, authority, and nobility." If the "gentiles" should see missionaries of other orders, "apostolic, poor, humble," the Jesuits would be put to shame; hence their desire to keep other orders out of China.

The differences, finally centering around the rites controversy, between Jesuits and other orders reached their highest point much later. The conflict spread from China to Europe where the issues involved were argued with far more bitterness and passion than they ever were in China. It involved popes of Rome and emperors of China, cardinal legates and bishops, theologians, humanists, and rationalists. The debate swirled through the academic halls of European universities. It became a *cause célèbre* at the Sorbonne in Paris. Certainly at no time before, and probably at no time since, has any question affecting China been the object of such universal, feverish, even impassioned, interest in the European world.

It is upon this later period that the attention of historians has chiefly focused. The result has been to throw the general picture out of perspective, because in the later period the conflict became at once overcomplicated and oversimplified. It was complicated by the introduction of extraneous factors; the *esprit de corps* of religious orders required defense of the policies of their missionaries; the Jansenists and Gallicans seized upon the dispute as a weapon against their traditional foes, the Jesuits, and thus the controversy became a part of the complex politico-religious struggle in Europe; the long-drawn-out character of the debate inevitably raised the temperatures of the disputants. As the arsenal of arguments on both sides was exhausted, passion, personalities, the *argumentum ad hominem*, the imputation of unworthy motives, were more and more substituted for reason. On the other hand, the conflict was oversimplified in the sense that the question of the rites assumed so large an importance that the broader issue of the purpose of the Christian mission and of missiological method was forgotten. To some the affair becomes a supposed plot by the Jesuits to beguile the Chinese into accepting an *ersatz* form of Christianity. To others it is simply a matter of Dominican and Franciscan jealousy of Jesuit success.

As Goyau points out: "To reduce [the controversy] to a quarrel between missionary orders, differing among themselves in custom and temperament, is to miss its whole significance."[3] The real significance of the controversy is that it represents a direct clash between the philosophy and policy of Europeanism and cultural adaptation. This is its deeper meaning. Everything else, including the question of the rites, which later assumed overshadowing importance, is a detail against the background of this larger canvas.

In 1580 Valignano assembled the leading Jesuits in Japan to discuss the difficulties attendant upon the rapid growth of the Church in that country. Among the questions considered was whether, in view of the increasing number of Christians, it would be wise to invite other orders to enter the field. The question was fully discussed. Weighty reasons, pro and con, suggested themselves. Without reaching a decision, Valignano submitted the question, with the reasons advanced on both sides, to the pope. Gregory XIII decided that for the time being it was unwise to admit members of other orders to Japan. In his Brief *Ex Pastorali Officio* of January 28, 1585, he banned missionary activity in that country to all but the Jesuits.[4]

The missionaries in the Philippines could hardly be expected to accept this discrimination with equanimity. With some, annoyance grew into anger and even bitterness. They held the Jesuits responsible for their exclusion from fields which held so strong an appeal for them and which they thought were ripe for the harvest. Attacks upon the Jesuits became so numerous and extravagant, that Valignano felt moved to explain the Jesuit position. In January, 1598, he published his *Apologia en la cual se responde a diversas calumnias que se escribieron contra los PP. de la Compania del Japon y de la China*, a document indispensable to an understanding of this period.[5] It also affords an insight into the character of Valignano's mind. Devoid of partisanship, it sets forth clearly and objectively the history of events leading up to the decision of Gregory XIII and the reasons for that decision.

It is clear from this document that there were two basic reasons for Valignano's policy. He wanted to keep the Europeanizing missionary, Jesuit, Franciscan, or Dominican, out of Japan and China and he wanted to avoid a head-on collision between Spanish and Portuguese nationalism.[6]

He was as much disturbed by the activities of the Jesuit Sanchez as he was by the activities of the friars and he brought pressure to bear upon the general of the Society to forbid Jesuits from the Philippines to enter China. On the other hand, he was as ready to give encouragement to a member of another order who eschewed Europeanism as he was to a Jesuit. His relations in 1583-1584 with the Dominican Silvestre de Azevedo prove this. De Azevedo, a missionary in Cambodia, found himself abandoned by his fellow missionaries because of his repudiation of Europeanism. Using the same methods that Ricci was developing in China, he succeeded, through his assimilation of the indigenous culture and his scholarly and diplomatic attainments, in winning the confidence of the king of Cambodia, Préah-Berom-Intoréachéa II. De Azevedo's reward was to be excommunicated by the vicar of Malacca because, instead of devoting himself exclusively to the direct preaching of the Gospel, he had concerned himself with science, philosophy, and other profane subjects. For five years he could find no priest to hear his confession. From distant Japan, Valignano encouraged him and sent him everything he needed for the celebration of Mass.[7]

If Valignano was uninfluenced by animus against other orders as such, neither was he inspired by antipathy for Spaniards as such. Manoel Dias, Senior, in a letter to the general states that one of the reasons de Pantoia was assigned to the China mission was "to destroy the legend that we do not want to admit Spaniards to China."[8] Ironically enough, six years after Valignano's death, Pires, one of the Portuguese Jesuits in Japan, sourly complained that he had promoted Spaniards and Italians rather than Portuguese.[9] De Couros, who succeeded Carvalho as provincial of Japan when the latter was removed by the general for having badly handled the persecution there, charged Valignano and other Italians with having wrecked the province![10] Vieira, who had followed Pasio as visitor, complained to the Portuguese assistant that the general preferred Italians and Spaniards to Portuguese.[11]

It is clear that intense nationalism was a hard fact. Valignano might deplore it, as he did in a letter from Goa on November 18, 1595, but he had to take it into account.[12] Jesuits whose attitudes did not fit into his policy could be kept out by the internal discipline of the Society. In Japan Francisco Cabral, the provincial, had been unable to stomach Valignano's policies. He will be remembered as the superior whose policy of imposing an inferior status upon native priests, adopted in India, was criticized by Ricci. Because he could not rid himself of the prejudices of Europeanism Valignano removed him from office and sent him back to Macao.[13] But the Society had no control over members of other orders. And in the seventeenth century the question of the entry of other orders in China meant only one thing: missionaries from the Philippines where a Europeanism entirely sure of itself and little disposed to take lessons from others colored missiological views.

In China the Jesuits had learned from their own mistakes. The friars from the Philippines were little disposed to learn from Jesuit mistakes. A Franciscan apologist admits as much: "They gave too little heed to the missionaries who had already been working in the country and made insufficient use of their experience."[14]

Subsequent events fully verified Valignano's prediction that the encounter in Japan and China of advocates of different schools of missiological thought and of nationalistic pride would lead to contentions, discord, strife, divisions, and disaster. C. R. Boxer remarks: "The rivalry between the various Roman Catholic orders in Japan was one of the prime causes of the ruin of their missions, just as it was two centuries later in China. Irrespective of the rights and wrongs of the disputants, it was inevitable that this fratricidal strife would have disastrous repercussions on the mission as a whole, as Valignano foresaw in 1583."[15]

Neither did Valignano exaggerate when he attributed designs upon China to the Philippine Spaniards. Within two years after he had occupied the island of Cebu in 1565, Legazpi, commander of the expedition, was proposing to Philip II the construction of a fleet of ships to explore the coasts of China and neighboring islands. In 1569 the view was common to the *conquistadores* that the conquest of China would offer little difficulty.[16]

Valignano also knew that these ambitions were supported by missionaries and ecclesiastics in the Philippines. Sanchez, a Jesuit, and Martin Ignacio de Loyola, a Franciscan, saw nothing incongruous in the ideal of the missionary, "The Gospel in one hand, the sword of his King in the other."[17] The views of Sanchez prompted a fellow Jesuit in Mexico, José de Acosta, to write a tract proving that war against China for the purpose of forcing the Middle Kingdom to grant freedom of action to missionaries would be an unjust war.[18] Its very title "Opinion on War with China," and its publication in far-off Mexico is clear evidence that the tempting thought of a "holy war" against China enjoyed wide diffusion. Small wonder that Valignano was angered by Sanchez' repeated appearances at Macao and that he was deeply disturbed by the expeditions of Martin de Loyola. Nothing so clearly reveals the state of mind in the Philippines as a letter written by the bishop of Manila, Domingo de Salazar, to King Philip II, on June 18, 1583. De Salazar was a Dominican of outstanding ability. In Madrid he had signalized himself in the great debate which raged over the question of whether military force could be used to blaze a path for the Gospel. With most of the theologians of his order he defended the full freedom of the Indians against the arguments of official legalists anxious to justify to the court the brutal policies of some colonial administrators. Appointed bishop of Manila in 1579 de Salazar arrived at his See in February, 1582. Apparently de Salazar's view, which had easily resisted the dialectics of Madrid lawyers, could not long survive the supercharged atmosphere of Manila. On June 18, 1583, he wrote to Philip II:

> Granting as established the titles and rights which Your Majesty holds and possesses in all the Indies as King of Spain, and those which you have in China as King of Portugal . . . I maintain . . . that you can send an army so strong that the whole power of China will be helpless to injure it, and that this army has the right to enter and traverse the provinces of China; it can impose peace upon those who disturb order; it can oblige the king and the officials of this realm to allow the Gospel to be preached and to protect its heralds. . . .
>
> If the King of China should be so perverse as to prohibit the preaching of the Gospel, Your Majesty can even deprive him of his kingdom; although the truth of this proposition is no less certain than that of the preceding, . . . this would be more difficult to carry out.
>
> Let Your Majesty set everything else aside, even were it question of the conquest of a thousand Flanders or the recovery of the Holy Land: neither Julius Caesar nor Alexander the Great were ever confronted with the challenge of so magnificent a military venture; there has not been since apostolic times a spiritual undertaking of such high importance.[19]

Hideyoshi, intoxicated by his dreams of world conquest, could hardly strike a more exalted tone. Those who think that Valignano exaggerated either Chinese fears or the grounds for those fears are much mistaken.

Gregory XIII's exclusion of the mendicant orders from Japan did not long remain in effect. Clement VIII in the Constitution *Onerosa* of December 12, 1600, removed the restriction, giving permission to members of any order, regardless of nationality, to labor in China and Japan. Nevertheless, non-Portuguese missionaries to southern and eastern Asia were required to pass through Lisbon and Goa. This restriction of the *Padroado* was in turn soon lifted. The struggle between France and Spain made it difficult for prospective missionaries to reach Lisbon. Once arrived there, they were sometimes kept waiting for as much as two years before being allowed to sail. As a result of the war raging between Spain and the Netherlands, Portuguese vessels were often captured by the Dutch and their English allies. In Goa the Inquisition frequently interfered with, and mistreated, non-Portuguese missionaries. In consequence of these factors Pope Paul V in the Constitution *Sedis Apostolicae Providentia* of June 2, 1608, granted permission to members of the mendicant orders to follow any route they chose to the Far East.[20] Urban VIII, on February 22, 1633, in the Brief *Ex Debito Pastoralis Officii* extended this permission to members of all other orders and congregations.

Accordingly after 1608 no ecclesiastical restriction stood in the way of the Dominicans and Franciscans. Nor is there evidence that the Jesuits took any steps to prevent their advent to China. Nevertheless, they looked upon such an eventuality with deep misgiving.[21]

The Spaniards had long had their eye upon Formosa as a possible base of operations from which to protect their commerce against Dutch depredations. To missionaries in the Philippines it suggested possibilities as an advanced post for effecting an entry to China. On May 10, 1626, an expedition from Manila effected the unopposed occupation of several ports on the northeastern coast of Formosa. In the stronghold of San Salvador the Dominicans built a church and residence.

In 1631 the governor, Don Juan de Alcarazo, decided to send a mission to the viceroy of Fukien in an effort to obtain trading privileges. Angelo Cocchi, head of the Dominican group in Formosa, was deputed as his envoy. Cocchi took Thomas de la Sierra, a fellow Dominican, as his companion. De la Sierra had learned some Chinese in Formosa; Cocchi, who had worked for two years among the Chinese in Manila had a smattering of the language.[22]

Accompanied by two Spanish soldiers, seven Filipinos, a Chinese interpreter, and a Mexican, the two priests sailed from San Salvador on December 30, 1631. Tragedy sailed with them. Unwittingly they had hired a pirate crew to take them to the mainland. During the night the gang of cutthroats fell upon the passengers. In the melee that followed de la Sierra, five of the Filipinos, and the Mexican were slain; two others were wounded. Cocchi and the other survivors barricaded themselves in a cabin. During the following night the ship was boarded by a superior force of pirates who, after robbing and massacring the crew, abandoned the ship to the waves. Cocchi and his companions freed themselves from their cabin and managed to make a landing on an island off the coast of Fukien. Local fisherfolk took them to the mainland.

The foreigners were turned over to the local prefect who in turn sent them to Chüanchow. Here the authorities had them conducted to the viceroy at Foochow. At first disturbed by the uninvited appearance of foreigners on Chinese soil, the story of their hair-raising experiences at sea aroused his sympathy. He gave them lodging and provided for their needs, while he sent a report of the affair to Peking.

As a result of his violent adventure, Cocchi fell ill and almost died. At this time he wrote a letter to his superiors in which he formulated certain conclusions upon the basis of his experiences. The character of ambassador from the Spanish governor had been of no service to him. The Chinese were unimpressed. In the future, missionaries should come wearing Chinese dress. They should have a knowledge of the mandarin tongue, and should imitate the methods employed by the Jesuits. Simply to land a group of missionaries on the coast, as so many continued to advocate, would be "the greatest foolishness." They would only be subjected to vexation and unfailingly be sent back whence they had come.

Considerable significance attaches to this document. Cocchi was quick to recognize the errors inherent in the method of *Sturmangriffe*, and the wisdom of a policy of adaptation. It should be noted that he was an Italian. It cannot be too much emphasized that the difficulties which arose between Jesuits, Dominicans, and Franciscans in China had their roots more in differences of national temperament than in differences between religious orders. Nowhere in Europe was nationalism so strong in the sixteenth and early seventeenth centuries as in the Iberian peninsula. Most of the Jesuits who played leading parts in the mission in China came from countries where the spirit of nationalism had not yet developed. Perhaps had the first Dominicans and Franciscans in China been predominantly Italian much of the conflict with the Jesuits would have been avoided.

Cocchi had been in Foochow four months when orders arrived from Peking directing the viceroy to send him back to Formosa. The court was not interested in the subject of trade with the Spaniards. A boat was prepared to take him back; but Cocchi did not sail.

He managed to substitute a Japanese Christian, anxious to go to the Philippines. The scheme had been suggested by one Luke Liu, a Christian living in the village of Fuan, north of Foochow. Cocchi made his way undetected to Fuan and concealed himself in Liu's home. He donned Chinese clothes and had his hair and beard trimmed in Chinese style. Liu undertook to teach him the language.

Meanwhile he had managed to contact Aleni. A warm friendship sprang up between the two and Aleni helped the Dominican priest in many ways.[23] Nevertheless, the Jesuit was thoroughly out of sympathy with the Dominicans' idea of attempting at this time to establish themselves in China. He made every effort to convince Cocchi of the inadvisability of such a move. Cocchi made no commitments and kept his counsel to himself.

Fuan was a village of some three thousand inhabitants of whom ten were Christians. In view of the gloomy opinions expressed by certain later arrivals from the Philippines, Cocchi's impressions of the calibre of these Christians are important. Cocchi found them much superior to the new Christians in Manila. Often in Manila new converts had in view only the material advantages to be gained by accepting Christianity, whereas his limited observations in Fuan indicated to him that "in China converts . . . are persons of ability and learning."[24]

Anxious to develop the bridgehead established by Cocchi, the Dominican provincial ordered Juan Bautista de Morales to Formosa to prepare to join Cocchi. De Morales had arrived in Manila from Mexico in 1622. In 1629 he had led a group to Cambodia, but had soon returned to the Philippines.

No less anxious than their Dominican confrères to realize their long-cherished ambition to carry the Gospel to China, the Franciscans appointed Francisco de la Madre de Dios and Antonio Caballero a Santa Maria to accompany de Morales.[25] Antonio was destined to play a pre-eminent role in the development of Franciscan missionary effort in China. He was a man without narrowness, incapable of bitterness, who never allowed his general attitude towards the Jesuits to be warped by isolated conflicts with a few individuals. Although he differed radically with them on the question of the rites and did more than anyone else, with the possible exception of the Dominican de Morales, to initiate the famous controversy, he earned the respect and admiration of the Jesuits in China. Writing from

Peking, January 20, 1673, four years after Antonio's death, to the Franciscan Buenaventura Ibañez, the Jesuit de Magalhães paid him tribute as "a great religious . . . an apostolic missionary . . . an outstanding man."[26]

The three men sailed from Manila on March 9, 1633. They had been in Formosa three months when de Morales and Antonio started for China on a small ship sent by Cocchi which was manned by Cocchi's interpreter and four other Christians. The group landed in China on June 25. The interpreter got them to Fuan on July 2 without detection.

Their first encounter with a Jesuit seems to have been unfortunate. As Antonio later told it, they sent a bottle of Mass wine to the Portuguese Jesuit, Bento de Mattos, as a token of good will. Apparently de Mattos' stomach had a low tolerance point for sweet wine. In a reply to his benefactors de Mattos rudely complained that the wine was sweet and that it had nauseated him! He also pointed out that thieves, not shepherds, entered through the back door. The front door to China was through the bishop of Macao. They should obtain his authorization for their enterprise or at least present themselves to Manoel Dias, the vice-provincial, who administered this mission field. His rudeness seems somewhat tempered by his assurance that they would be graciously received by the vice-provincial. While complaining about the disagreeable tone of the letter, Antonio acknowledges that in other letters during the ensuing year de Mattos showed better manners.

De Mattos gave his version of these events several years later. It is found in a letter, written from the island of Hainan, whither he had been transferred shortly after the incidents he describes.[27] It is addressed, under date of May 1, 1636, to Alvarô Semedo who had evidently asked for information. "I will reply without departing from the truth to your Reverence's inquiries concerning the religious with whom I had dealings when in Fukien," he begins. Admitting that he does not recall all the details, he describes his relations with Angelo Cocchi as friendly and mentions many favors he extended to him. As for the three who arrived in 1633, he does not remember any untoward incident. He mentions that, informed by Cocchi that he was short of Mass wine, they sent him some and that he sent them "other things" in return. He supplied them with books, including a Portuguese-Chinese dictionary which he obtained in Macao. When

Cocchi died and de Morales sent word that he was at a loss for a place to bury him, he supplied a burial plot alongside the tomb of the young Jesuit priest Rudomina who had died the previous year in Foochow. Several times he saw to it that letters of de Morales were carried to Macao to be forwarded to the Dominican prior in Formosa who wrote to express his gratitude. Apart from a conflict of opinion, which still surprises him, about their requiring authorization from the bishop of Macao, the picture de Mattos paints is one of rather normal relations.

When Antonio arrived in China he had, as he himself wrote, only "commenced to learn a few rudiments of the mandarin language." Four months later he resolved "to set out for Nanking."[28] He started out on foot, on November 2, 1633, accompanied by a Christian to serve as guide and interpreter, and by a coolie, hired to carry his Mass equipment. In Kienchang, which he reached on December 16, he received a warm welcome from Gaspar Ferreira who invited him to stay for a few days and to celebrate Mass in his chapel. On the third day Ferreira told the Franciscan that he could not very well keep him longer without authorization from the vice-provincial.

Many years before, realizing that they would have to face the problem of what to do about extending hospitality to members of the mendicant orders whose methods might endanger the security of the mission, the Jesuits had asked the general to establish a policy. This was one of the *postulata* submitted by Trigault in 1616.[29] Vitelleschi had replied that, in view of the danger, a negative policy seemed to be required, but that the question should be decided by the superior on the spot in accordance with prudence and charity.

Antonio arrived in Nanchang a few days before Christmas. As de Mattos had predicted, the Jesuit superior received him cordially, offering him the hospitality of his home and church. Apparently Antonio expected that Dias would allow him to stay on indefinitely; but after several weeks Dias suggested he would be better advised to try to establish himself elsewhere. He supplied him with a new guide to whom he entrusted letters for certain Christians in Nanking.

It was on January 23, 1634, that Antonio arrived in the ancient capital. Here his guide moved him from house to house, explaining that it was necessary to conceal his presence in the city. Apparently there was a general reluctance to shelter the Franciscan for fear of official reprisals should his presence become known. At length the guide left him with a family where he stayed for six weeks. They and other Christians tried to persuade him to leave Nanking. They said that if he did not do so, an official persecution of all the Christians in the city might ensue.

Antonio would not be persuaded. Ignorant of the history of the Nanking persecution he was inclined to look upon all such remonstrances as strategems invented to get rid of him. What he could not understand, and his still meager knowledge of Chinese no doubt made it doubly difficult to make him understand, was that these fears were real. Shên Ch'üeh and the edict of banishment of 1617 had not been forgotten in Nanking. Some remembered only too well prison cells and floggings endured. For years after the Jesuits had returned to their other residences, the church in Nanking remained without a pastor. Official feeling was still hostile. Many office-holders had belonged to Shên's party. Visits of the missionaries had of necessity been secret.

The Christians of Nanking, among the most fervent in China, bore this situation with difficulty and looked forward impatiently to the restoration of the Church in their city. It was not until 1634, at the very moment of Antonio's untimely arrival, that their hopes seemed about to be realized. One of the last acts of Hsü Kuang-ch'i was aimed at the restoration of the Church in Nanking. Shortly before his death he appointed Francesco Sambiasi to go to Nanking on the business of the Calendrical Bureau. The fact that he was charged with an imperial mission would assure his proper reception by officialdom. The nature of his task would enable him to remain indefinitely in the city.

Sambiasi arrived in Nanking early in 1634. It was the first time since 1617 that a priest had openly entered the city. Official proclamations notified the people of his presence and enjoined respect for his residence and person.

It is against this background that the unfortunate experience of Antonio a Santa Maria must be judged. The arrival of the Franciscan in Nanking in 1634 coincided with that of Sambiasi. The advent of the latter brought the promise that the Christian community would be able to emerge into the light after seventeen years of quasi-underground existence. At the same moment that its hopes, so long disappointed, surged high, the appearance on the scene of the zealous friar threatened it with disaster. At least so it seemed to the Christians.

One false step at this moment could bring renewed oppression. Antonio could not have arrived at a more inopportune moment. This explains their anxiety to keep him out of the streets and, as soon as possible, to get him out of the city.

When Antonio refused to be moved by their urgent pleas that he leave Nanking, his hosts resorted to drastic action. A boat was made ready. Through a subterfuge Antonio was led to the point of embarkation. When he refused to go aboard, the committee of Catholic laymen seized him and, despite his valiant resistance, bound him hand and foot, carried him on board and locked him in a cabin! He was taken back to Fukien and released.

Whatever its unfortunate aspects, the incident is not without its amusing side. It is perhaps the only case on record of a priest being shanghaied by devout Catholics. It is a tribute to Antonio that, unlike some of his later companions who allowed their attitude towards the Jesuits to be permanently colored by Antonio's ordeal in Nanking, he himself harbored no grudge. At the time, however, he was inclined to view everything that happened as part of a plot masterminded from the beginning by Dias. He never saw the letters which Dias had sent to certain Christians in Nanking. (Since they were written in Chinese, he could not in any case have read them.) But he assumed that everything that happened in Nanking, the fears of persecution expressed by Chinese Christians, the transference from house to house, the close confinement, the pleas to go somewhere else, were all part of an elaborate charade for which Dias' letters had provided all the stage directions. This merely reflects Antonio's ignorance at this time of his environment. Nanking was the last place in China that Dias would have chosen for this kind of *mise-en-scène*. Again it should be noted that, through no fault of his own, Antonio did not talk with either Sambiasi or Dias in Nanking. All of his impressions were based on what he was told by two young Chinese boys in the house in which he was confined.

What part did the Jesuits really play in this episode? To date, research in their archives has failed to turn up any report on the affair. Perhaps Sambiasi and Dias felt the less said the better. From Antonio's own account, controlled by what is otherwise known, it is not difficult to piece together the probable sequence of events. When Dias suggested to Antonio that he go to Nanking he did not know that Sambiasi was there or would shortly be there. Neither did he give enough thought to the fears of Nanking Christians. These fears are reflected in the reluctance of any family to keep the friar for any length of time. Not only were they mindful of their own experience with persecution, but they were vividly aware of the terrible persecution still raging in Japan which they, like the Jesuits, blamed upon the indiscreet methods of the Franciscans. This is clear from Antonio's own record of their arguments with him. They frequently cited Japan as a frightful example of a flourishing Church laid waste. They communicated their fears to Sambiasi, who arrived in Nanking either just before or in the midst of these events. He fully shared their concern. When Dias stopped in Nanking en route to Peking, Sambiasi persuaded him that he had been unwise in sending Antonio to Nanking. If they did not themselves hatch the kidnapping plot, they certainly sanctioned it.

No doubt they should have discussed the situation with Antonio. They must have felt it useless to do so in view of his refusal over a period of weeks to listen to reason. Perhaps too, the fact that he was Portuguese and Antonio a Spaniard made Dias less sensitive to the demands of charity. In a letter some years later Dias asked pardon of Antonio for the incident of 1634.[30]

If Dias is charged with flagrant violation of charity, it should perhaps be remembered that he owed a duty of charity to the Christians of Nanking as well as to Antonio. For almost two decades they had endured persecution with a constancy which had won the admiration of every Jesuit in China. At the moment when the arrival of Sambiasi brought hope of final deliverance, were they to be abandoned to new dangers out of regard for the feelings of a strange priest who had wandered into their midst and who, unmindful of the situation, stubbornly refused to accept counsel? Dias thought not.

A few years later the Christians in Fukien had to endure a violent persecution provoked by the obstinacy, confused with principle, and the imprudence, confounded with zeal, of a group of friars who, having stirred up the tempest, went blithely on their way rejoicing that "they had been found worthy to suffer." The ones who really suffered were the Chinese Christians, left behind to bear the brunt of official anger and to weep over the ruins of their churches and chapels. One is tempted to feel that, if their sufferings could have been averted by the painless removal of a few too-ardent missionaries the draconian measure would have been well justified.

NOTES

(1) Antonio Sisto Rosso, O. F. M., *Apostolic Legations to China* (South Pasadena: P. D. and Ione Perkins, 1948), p. 109.
(2) *SinFran*, III, 90.
(3) Georges Goyau, *op. cit.*, p. 104.
(4) *Ius Pontificium de Propaganda Fide* (Roma: ex typographia polyglotta S. C. de Prop. Fide, 1888-1909), I, 143-146.
(5) The text is in Colin-Pastels, *op. cit.*, II, 682-692.
(6) There are many letters of Valignano in the Jesuit archives which give evidence of his continuing concern over the danger to the mission involved in the activities of the mendicant orders: e.g., October 28, 1583, *ARSI*, Jap-Sin 9 II, ff. 170-172; November 21, 1588, Jap-Sin 11 I, ff. 13-15; February 22, 1599, Jap-Sin 13 II, ff. 266-267; October 16, 1601, Jap-Sin 14 I, ff. 81-82 (this was a letter to Cardinal Bellarmine); October 15, 1602, Jap-Sin 14 I, ff. 102-106.
(7) Henri Bernard, S. J., *Aux portes de la Chine*, p. 117, n. 30.
(8) *Opere storiche*, I, 339, n. 1.
(9) Letter of March 10, 1612, *ARSI*, Jap-Sin 15 II, ff. 212-216.
(10) Letter of October 5, 1617, *ARSI*, Jap-Sin 17, ff. 95-96.
(11) Letter of September 30, 1618, *ARSI*, Jap-Sin 17, ff. 168-169.
(12) Letter to Aquaviva, November 18, 1595, *ARSI*, Jap-Sin 12 II, ff. 309-310.
(13) Cabral's letter of October 5, 1583, in *ARSI*, Jap-Sin 9 II, f. 167; and cf. Valignano's November 23, 1595, *ARSI*, Jap-Sin 12 II, ff. 315-319.
(14) Maas, *op. cit.*, p. 77.
(15) C. R. Boxer, *The Christian Century*, p. 247.
(16) Montalban, *op. cit.*, p. 105.
(17) Pierre D'Orleans, S. J., *La vie du père Matthieu Ricci* (Paris, 1693), p. 30.
(18) His treatise, *Paracer sobre la guerra de la China*, is in *Opere storiche*, II, 450-457.
(19) The text, quoted by Bernard, *op. cit.*, p. 186, is in P. Pastells, S. J., *Catalogo de los documentos relativos a las Indias Filipinas existentes en el Archivio de Indias de Sevilla, por D. Pedro Torres y Lanzas, precedido de una historia general de Filipinas* (Barcelona, 1925), II, CLVII.
(20) *Jus Pontificium*, I, 444 f.
(21) Cf. Semedo, *Histoire universelle*, pp. 374 f.
(22) Biermann's remark that Cocchi had "not mastered the language," is an odd understatement to make in the same note in which de Morales is quoted as saying that Cocchi had to use an interpreter because he had great difficulty with the language; Benno M. Biermann, O. P., *Die Anfänge der Neuren Dominikanermission in China* (Münster in Westfalen: Aschendorff, 1927), p. 28, n. 4.
(23) Biermann, *op. cit.*, p. 33.
(24) *Ibid.*, p. 34.
(25) For a biographical note on de Morales cf. Maas, *op. cit.*, p. 50, n. 9. On Francisco cf. *ibid.*, p. 51, n. 12, and *Archivum Franciscanum Historicum*, VIII (Ad Claras Aquas prope Florentiam [Quaracchi-Firenze], 1909 et seq.),

NOTES

581, n. 2, hereafter cited as *AFH*. On Antonio cf. Maas, *op. cit.*, p. 51, n. 13, and *SinFran,* II, 317 ff.

(26) *SinFran,* II, 331.

(27) *ARSI,* Jap-Sin 161 II, ff. 161r-162v.

(28) *AFH,* II, 551. For the encounter with de Mattos and for the events which follow, relating to his round trip to Nanking, I have relied upon Antonio's own accounts. A published account, written in 1636 as a contribution to the polemics induced by the trip to Peking described in the next chapter, is in *SinFran,* 319, n. 1. An earlier, more detailed, and as yet unpublished account is in a letter which he wrote on July 16, 1634, immediately after the events, to the provincial of the Dominican order in Manila. Two years later Antonio himself made a copy of this letter which he sent to Spain to the Franciscan superior general. This copy is in the *Biblioteca Nacional* in Madrid, 5930, 160-171.

(29) *Postulatum* no. 26, *ARSI,* Jap-Sin 100, f. 10r.

(30) So Antonio reported to his provincial, January 24, 1652; *SinFran,* II, 413.

Chapter XV

"How Good and Delightful —"

In November, 1634, Francisco Dias, a Dominican, and Francisco de la Madre de Dios, a Franciscan, arrived in Fukien. The Dominicans and the Franciscans now separated, the former remaining at Fuan, the latter establishing themselves in the village of Tingtow. Neither met with much success in his efforts to evangelize his surroundings. They encountered opposition even from those who were already Christians. The reasons are clear. They were unwilling to make concessions to Chinese susceptibilities or to local conditions. They sought to impose upon the Chinese not only acceptance of the doctrines of faith but observance of all ecclesiastical laws and customs observed in Europe and in Spanish possessions. In these spheres the Jesuits had made concessions which they refused to grant. The inevitable happened.

The attempt to impose, under pain of being refused the sacraments, new obligations and new prohibitions aroused discontent among Christians. They appealed to the authority of the Jesuits who had brought them the faith. "The missionaries of St. Dominic and St. Francis teach us things which are different from what the fathers of the Society preach. The teachings of these latter seem better, for the Jesuits are also servants of God and besides have already preached the Gospel for sixty years in China," they said.[1] Soon the Jesuits in Foochow were receiving complaints from Christians in Fuan and Tingtow of the severity of their new pastors. The complainants added that the missionaries were saying that the Jesuits from the time of Matteo Ricci on had misled the Christians and that they had been sent by the Sovereign Pontiff to deliver them from error! The Jesuits had been long enough in China to know with what caution the reports of talebearers must be received. Consequently vice-provincial Francisco Furtado, in reporting these incidents to the general of the Society, by letter of November 10, 1636, is careful to note that the remarks attributed to the mendicants were probably an invention.[2]

It was not long before the different interpretations of their obligations caused serious divisions among the Christians. "Divisions and great scandal" is the way the Dominican Francisco Dias described the situation. Valignano's fears were being justified.

Antonio a Santa Maria undertook to question one of the Jesuits upon the character of their teaching. What the situation required was a frank exchange of views. As the account by Buenaventura Ibañez reveals, Antonio was not looking for an explanation of Jesuit policy for the purpose of arriving at an understanding. He was seeking confirmation from the Jesuits themselves of the character of their teaching with a view to lodging charges against them. Ibañez writes:

> In order to confirm the reports of his neophytes, Frater Antonius went to a certain church of the fathers of the Society where one of the Jesuit fathers resided. Entering he visited with him and, with cautious dissimulation, asked him: "Will your reverence please tell us how your neophytes are instructed in this realm, what obligations are imposed upon them by your reverences and what [practices] are permitted them, in order that we may conform [our methods to those of] your reverences.[3]

The Jesuit explained briefly the policy of his order. Armed with this information Antonio reported to de Morales, and the two men, assisted by Francisco Dias and Francisco de la Madre de Dios, immediately began to prepare a report for their respective provincials in Manila. The report comprised two documents. The first was based upon an interrogation of eleven Chinese Christians which began on December 22, 1635, and ended on January 9, 1636. The second contained the observations of the four missionaries themselves.[4] Their testimony was put down in juridical form during a series of meetings held by the four men, January 21 - February 10, 1636. Before the month was out Francisco Dias and Antonio a Santa Maria had set sail for the Philippines to submit the reports to theologians in Manila.[5] The die was cast; the step which was to lead to the long-drawn-out and disastrous rites controversy had been taken.

Dias stopped on Formosa with a copy of the documents. Antonio sailed for Manila with the originals. En route his ship was seized by the Dutch and the intrepid Franciscan was taken prisoner. He spent eight months at hard labor in Java and a year in Molucca. Not until June, 1637, did he reach Manila.

In the spring of that same year Gaspar Alenda, another Franciscan, arrived in China to join de Morales and Francisco de la Madre de Dios. Within a few months, he and Francisco played the leading roles in an incident which illustrates the kind of thing Valignano had feared. It is also an illuminating case-study of the origin of legend.[6]

A scholar in the village of Fuan published an attack upon Christianity. He was a mere *hsiu-ts'ai* of no importance whatever. Yet when, shortly after publishing his piece, he set out for Peking the two friars concluded that he intended to present his pamphlet to the emperor. With characteristic crusading spirit, admirable in its elan, less admirable in its imprudence, they promptly resolved, as Alenda put it, "to follow him [to the imperial court] and to defend our immaculate doctrine with argument and with [our] lives, and to preach Jesus Christ, our crucified Lord. . ."[7] An enterprise more dangerous to the security of the Church and revealing greater ignorance of Peking realities could scarcely be conceived.

Accompanied by three young boys who served as interpreters, Francisco and Gaspar set out in June, 1637. That they reached the capital at all must be attributed to the chaotic conditions which made it easy to escape official attention. At this time the activities of the bandit revolutionary leaders Li Tzu-ch'êng and Chang Hsien-chung had plunged the north-central provinces, through which the Franciscans passed, into turmoil.[8] On August 14 they arrived in Peking. Here they were met by Adam Schall who installed them in the house which stood on Ricci's burial ground. During their fourteen days' stay they observed and found fault with everything. In reading their accounts it is difficult to escape the feeling that the two guests behaved like spies in the Jesuit house, and spies who saw everything through highly prejudiced eyes.

The thing that shocked them most was a painting of Christ and the twelve Apostles which hung in the chapel. Out of regard for

Chinese feelings on the subject of bare feet, the artist had fitted them with shoes. The friars were scandalized. "It gave me the deepest pain," Alenda wrote his friends Valencia and Nadal.[9] He and his companion saw to it that the subject was given the importance it deserved in reports to their confrères in the Philippines.

This otherwise trivial incident uncovers the root of the difficulties which divided Jesuits and mendicants in China and made rapprochement almost impossible. As Valignano had been aware, the spirit of Europeanism and that of cultural adaptation were poles apart. The mind which could cry scandal at so minor a concession to cultural prejudices could never be expected to understand a policy of accommodation.

This picture was not the only shocking discovery made by Francisco and Gaspar. To Manila they reported that the Jesuit chapel in Peking contained two "altars," one dedicated to the Saviour, the other to the emperor! Upon the former was a picture of Christ, upon the latter a picture of the Son of Heaven! This tale, carried to Europe, is the source of an odious legend the ghost of which has not yet been laid. It depicts the Jesuits as idolators who had raised the pagan emperor to the honors of the altar where he was worshipped upon an equal footing with the Son of God!

Neither Gaspar Alenda nor Francisco de la Madre de Dios made the charge of idolatry but it was implicit in their story. The accusation lacked all *prima facie* probability. The fact is that there was no idolatrous altar in the chapel and it never occurred to Schall that his guests would read sinister import into an innocent commemorative plaque. The accounts of Escalona and Alena make it possible for one with a little knowledge of Chinese customs and the Chinese language to establish beyond doubt what the supposed "altar" actually was. First of all, the alleged picture was no picture at all, but a wooden panel with a half dozen Chinese characters engraved upon it in gold letters.

It is easy to trace to its source the origin of the fable about the emperor's picture. It is in the sworn testimony of Francisco de la Madre de Dios, signed in Manila, June 16, 1639. He describes what he saw as an "altar . . . dedicated to the picture or tablet of the king of China."[10] An "imagen" is not the same as a "tablilla," as his statement would suggest. Despite the fact that even a cursory reading of the full accounts of the two friars shows unmistakably that it was a tablet and not a picture, legend fixed upon the "imagen" and overlooked the "tablilla." Dr. Otto Maas unconsciously reveals how reluctant even scholars are to abandon an old legend. Although admitting in a footnote that the object in question was a tablet, he continues in his text to call it a picture.[11]

Escalona gives Francisco's version of the text: "Our mighty Prince, may he live thousands of millions to thousands of millions of years!" This removes all doubt about the real character of the scandalous "altar." This is clearly a rendering of the common Chinese expression "Wan sui, wan wan sui!" ("Ten thousand years, ten thousand ten thousand years!"). It is the Japanese "banzai," the Latin "ad multos annos," the French "vive le roi!"

As the friars themselves were aware, the chapel was a gift of the emperor to the Jesuits in honor of Matteo Ricci. In acknowledgment of the imperial beneficence the Jesuits had placed upon a table a wooden plaque bearing the equivalent of "Long live the emperor!" It was fraught with no more idolatrous significance than the custom observed in Catholic Churches in the United States of placing an American flag in the sanctuary.

To the two visitors, poorly adjusted to the Chinese environment and inclined to put the worst interpretation upon Jesuit activities, the table became an "altar," the wooden panel became a "picture" of the emperor. By the simple metamorphosis of a few details an innocent gesture in recognition of an imperial favor is transmuted into a darksome excursion into idolatry. What would Gaspar and Francisco have thought if they had known that some three and a half centuries earlier, during the Yuan dynasty, one of their great Franciscan predecessors used to go out to meet the emperor when he rode into his capital and in public ceremony incense his person and bestow his blessing upon him!

During their stay in the Jesuit house, Schall tried to point out to his guests the dangerous character of their undertaking and to dissuade them from attempting to carry it further. He suggested they go to Korea, a virgin field for missionaries. His efforts were in vain. They expected Schall to arrange an interview with the emperor and to obtain permission for them to establish a residence in Peking. The Jesuits themselves, after almost four decades in the capital, had yet to meet the emperor. And as far as a residence was concerned almost twenty years of patient preparatory effort by Ricci had preceded their establishment in Peking and some thirty more years of effort at making friends and building up prestige had been needed to render their position more or less secure. Yet Gaspar and Francisco naively supposed that all that stood between them and establishment of a residence in the capital were the Jesuits. The attitude of his uninvited guests made it impossible for Schall to move in any direction without his action receiving the worst possible interpretation. By temperament Schall was an irascible man. It is surprising that he kept his temper; yet he seems to have done so, there being no indication that he lost his urbanity.

A fortnight had passed when two officials from the Board of Rites accompanied by a detail of gendarmes, appeared at the house to question the visitors, who appeared before their interrogators crucifixes in hand "prepared to give their lives to preach Jesus Christ." When the officials asked them what had prompted them, foreigners, to make their unauthorized visit to the imperial capital, they launched into a spirited sermon. Escalona describes the scene:

> The religious replied that they had come to oppose and confute the errors contained in a book which had attacked our holy faith, etc., and to preach and defend that there is but one God-Man, who is Jesus Christ crucified, whose image they held in their hands, etc.

When the officials, nettled by their tone, began to argue with them the missionaries "seized the occasion . . . to preach how they were deceived; because there is but one God, all powerful, upon whom depend all things in their existence and their conservation; [they preached] the mystery of the most holy Trinity and the principal [mysteries] of our holy faith, the Incarnation, death, and resurrection, etc."[12] A rather comprehensive sermon!

The officials lost patience and ordered the gendarmes to take away the crucifixes from the missionaries. They were forbidden to leave the house. Their interpreters were led away in chains. In the eyes of the friars, inflamed with holy zeal, the conduct of the officials appears due to "an infernal fury" caused by their "pride, which could not stand the spirit and truth with which the religious and their interpreters spoke." In the eyes of the officials, no doubt, these strangers were arrogant and defiant barbarians ignorant of the elementary notions of Chinese courtesy.

One of the officials stayed on the premises while the other left to make his report. Soon an order arrived from the president of the Board of Rites. It noted that the two foreigners had been living "for some days" in the Jesuit residence and for this it held Schall and Longobardo culpable. The significance of this reproach escaped Alenda who himself reported it. His obsessive belief that behind every adversity was Jesuit intrigue blinded him to the obvious. Perhaps as revealing as anything of his distorted view of the state of affairs in Peking and of the Jesuit position there is his reference to Longobardo as "a favorite of the king."[13]

Normally the two foreigners would have been haled before Peking courts and sentenced, expulsion being the mildest punishment they could hope for. Schall, anxious to keep the affair out of the courts for fear of repercussions against the Church, persuaded the officials in charge to omit judicial proceedings and to send the friars back to Fukien without punishment. The judicious distribution of seventy *taels* in silver helped him make the point.

Two days later a high police official accompanied "by a large troop of men" took the Franciscans into custody. They were led conspicuously through the streets of Peking to the terminus of the Grand Canal. Here they were put aboard an official boat, placarded with large signs announcing that on board were two foreigners who, for having dared to enter China without authorization to spread novel doctrines, were being taken to Fukien to be put to death. The voyage to Fukien lasted three months. In all the cities and villages where the boat stopped the foreigners were the object of curiosity. "Even the women peered out their windows to see what was happening."

And all this, according to Alenda, was the work of the Jesuits! Francisco de la Madre de Dios was willing to swear "on the word of a priest" that the Jesuits were responsible. Domingo de Jesus after giving a highly colored and inaccurate account of the experiences of Gaspar and Francisco, was even more specific in his sworn testimony: "It is common report in China that all this was the work of the fathers of the Society and of their Christians and mandarins . . ."[14]

The accusations hardly deserve comment. The accounts by Escalona and Alenda, if controlled by what is otherwise known of conditions in Peking and of the situation of the Jesuits at the time, supply the best refutation. The charge supposes a situation in Peking which did not exist. In 1637 Schall was far from enjoying either the authority or the influence imputed to him by those who held him responsible for the events described. More than ten years later, when his authority was much greater, he was unable to free two of his fellow Jesuits who, as a result of their indiscretions, had fallen under a cloud of official suspicion. Twenty years later his influence was possibly second to none in the realm. But in 1637, although his work on the calendar reform, just completed, had won him many friends, it had also made him many enemies. His influence was not even strong enough to move the emperor officially to adopt the reformed calendar. For that he had to await the rise of a new dynasty. The picture of Schall in 1637 as a master intrigant behind the scenes, moving high Peking dignitaries, including the president of the Board of Rites, the "chief of police," and a large detail of gendarmes, like so many marionettes, is fantasy without relation to historical reality. More fantastic, if that were possible, was the suggestion that he arranged a parade of the victims through Peking streets and had them shipped off on a boat bearing the imperial colors and blazoned with signs denouncing Christianity.

Shortly after the departure of Gaspar and Francisco from Peking, Schall, writing to his close friend and onetime fellow novice, Alexandre de Rhodes, told the story of what had happened in Peking. The sarcastic touches in this letter of November 8, 1637, are characteristic of Schall, who had a "Cologne" sense of humor: robust, hearty, but with a strong vein of sarcasm, the sting of which was felt upon occasion by more than one of his fellow Jesuits. Perhaps had he foreseen that his letter would be read by others than de Rhodes, he would have eliminated a few of his expressions:

> I want to tell your Reverence part of a history which took place here little more than two months ago. There came to this capital two Fathers of Saint Francis determined to be martyrs or to convert the emperor and all the Chinese. Neither of them knew how to speak Chinese. . . . Both of them wore their habits. . . . Each of them carried his crucifix in his hand and wanted to begin preaching. They came in sedan chair, accompanied by three young Chinese boys. . . . Our Father vice-provincial was here, but since he did not want to deal with them, he dropped the affair into my lap since I am a German.[15] I went to meet them before they entered the city gate and explained to them quietly, but earnestly, why they should act prudently and peacefully. I did not have much success. They

harangued me angrily, especially the provincial procurator, Fray Gaspar de Alenda, who had recently arrived from Manila. His companion, Fray Francisco de la Madre de Dios, who had been in Fukien for two or three years, spoke more moderately. (One of the advantages of spending considerable time in China is that it mitigates our natural pride.) I then brought them to the burial place of our Father Matteo Ricci . . . and did not fail them in anything which brotherliness requires, giving them rooms and [the means of celebrating] Mass, etc. There are thousands here who make their living by acting as informers. And so through such spies their presence here was made known to the authorities who sent to have them seized. . . . [The gendarmes] made me their whipping post. I was accused, spoken harshly to, cuffed and pushed about, and prevented from sleeping all night. [As for the friars] no thought of martyrdom came to them then. They surrendered their crucifixes with little or no protest and with clasped hands uttered more than enough 'laoyes,'which means 'Señor! Señor!' concluding with a *Dimitte nos in pace*. . . I employed all the diplomacy I had learned in Italy in an effort to free them. With the help of some bribes I persuaded officials not to hale them before the higher tribunals or the emperor. They were content to send them to Fukien, whence [they] said they would sail for Manila. They did not try to take with them their three Chinese boys, whom they had allowed to be imprisoned and enchained, knowing well that they were subject to death for bringing foreigners to the capital without permission. But I managed to obtain their release. The boys sufficiently regretted the 'fiesta' in which they had taken part. This is, in brief, the case and the story of the service which I rendered the Seraphic Father Saint Francis, delivering his sons from the death which awaited them had the Chinese known what our servants knew about how frequently they spoke of the conquest of China. Certainly they would have been cut into pieces nor would we have emerged whole. Macao would hardly have been safe. It is better to die in bed than to become a martyr in this fashion. . . . We received them into our house, our servants waited upon them, and despite this they spoke with [our servants] most unfavorably about our affairs, as if they alone had the apostolic spirit. For this we pardon them as our older brothers. The worst is that the whole comedy cost us seventy *taels* besides much unpleasantness during the fifteen days that they were here.[16]

Schall's letter itself became an "incident." When stories holding him responsible for the Peking events circulated in the Philippines, de Rhodes, who was in Macao, sent the letter to Manila where the Jesuits published a Spanish translation. This only added fuel to the fire.

Schall's account conforms to the factual situation in Peking. This is not to say that the two friars were dishonest when they attributed all their misfortunes to the Jesuits, especially to Schall. In all probability they believed him responsible. They were self-deceived, and a careful reading of their own accounts reveals the factors that entered into their self-deception: a deep-seated prejudice, not always without spite, against the Jesuits; ignorance of the Chinese language and of Chinese customs; and an erroneous appraisal of the situation in the empire in general and in the capital in particular.

That the prejudice existed is revealed, for example, in Escalona's reluctance to call the Jesuits anything but "Theatine Fathers." This is an echo of an old protest against the name given his order by St. Ignatius and an attempt, made during his lifetime, to force him to merge his group with the Theatines. But this issue had been long dead when Escalona wrote his *Relacion*. The Society of Jesus was over one hundred years old. In these circumstances Escalona's unwillingness to give it its name is symptomatic of a deep-seated antipathy. No doubt part of the prejudice was rooted in the jealousy which many members of the more venerable orders shared for this young upstart which had shown such extraordinary vitality and which had in many respects broken with monastic and mendicant tradition. Part of it was due to resentment over Jesuit opposition to their intervention in the China mission. And a large part of it was due to their abhorrence for every measure of cultural adaptation, which they regarded as a betrayal of the faith.

Of their ignorance of the language there is no room for doubt. Alenda had been in China a few months. Francisco had been in the empire nearly three years, but he had studied the language in Fukien, where a dialect substantially different from mandarin is spoken. Escalona's account makes it clear that they both had to rely upon their boy interpreters. Anyone who knows China can easily imagine that the interpreters told them what they thought they wanted to hear. As Antonio a Santa Maria learned in the course of time, the Chinese have a great penchant for spreading "chimeras and falsehoods."[17] Gaspar and Francisco were nothing if not gullible. There is no other reasonable explanation of their notion that everyone who had anything to do with their case in Peking, from the president of the Board of Rites to the lowliest gendarme, was a Christian! This, both Escalona and Alenda solemnly affirm more than once. José Gonzalez, O.P., maintains that one of the three interpreters was the future Bishop Gregorio Lopez, the first native Chinese bishop.[18] This is by no means certain, but in any event it adds nothing to his credibility in 1637. He was not a bishop then, but a young Chinese new to the faith (he was baptized by Antonio a Santa Maria) and as much a stranger in Peking as were the friars.

The friars brought with them to China an exaggerated notion of the favorable position of Christianity in the empire. Their optimism was hard to correct. Among other effects, it gave them an altogether distorted idea of the power and influence of the Jesuits in the realm. The conviction that the Jesuits could obtain whatever they wished is implicit in all of their complaints, as it is in their habit of attributing every adversity to Jesuit intervention. In 1651 in a rather bitter letter to the cardinals of the Congregation *de Propaganda Fide*, signed by Buenaventura Ibañez, Joseph de Casanova, Antonio Rodriques, Andrea Fragozo, Francisco Yorge, it finds explicit expression:

> The Jesuit Fathers are powerful in the whole world, and so they are here with the emperor of China and the grandees of the empire, and it is very certain that should they seek to do so it would be easy for them to drive other religious from the empire. . .[19]

At no time did the Jesuits in China enjoy the power ascribed to them here. The statement is without relation to fact.

When Gaspar and Francisco arrived in Foochow they managed to communicate with the Jesuit missionary stationed in that city. Still under the impression that they were to be put to death, they asked him to bring them viaticum. He sent word that he would speak to the official in whose custody they had been remanded. That night he visited them and assured them that the death penalty was not contemplated.[20]

During their absence Francisco Dias had returned from Formosa. With him came Juan Garcia and Pedro de Chaves, Dominicans, and Francisco de Escalona, Onofre Pellega, and Domingo Urquiçcio, Franciscans. They were all in Tingtow. The two prisoners must have been overjoyed when the official in charge gave them their freedom and directed them to join their confrères there. He also told them that he would solicit for them the friendly interest of officials in Fuan and Ningteh. The ever suspicious friars who looked upon charity as well as cruelty as part of a wily plot knew how to interpret this. "I saw through this knavery," says Alenda.[21] Never men to let well enough alone they had hardly rejoined their confrères when Francisco, accompanied by Onofre Pellega and Domingo Urquiçcio, returned to Foochow. Alenda was too ill to accompany them.

They do not say what they intended to do there. Judged in the light of their journey to Peking, it may be supposed they went to Foochow to protest to the higher authorities of the province. Whatever they did, the results were disastrous. Shortly after their arrival in the metropolis the military commandant issued a decree proscribing Christianity, threatening anyone who harbored a missionary with the bastinado and with confiscation of his property, and offering a reward to anyone who delivered a missionary into the hands of the authorities. The three Franciscans were put under arrest and taken to Ningteh.

To a detached observer it must appear that until now the Chinese authorities had shown considerable moderation in the face of no little provocation. Now evidently their patience had given out. It did not seem so to the friars. To Escalona the only explanation of the outburst was that the military commandant was "a sworn enemy of Christians." To Alenda the culprit is the familiar scapegoat, the Jesuit. Giulio Aleni must have plotted with this "sworn enemy of Christians" to stir up this tempest which would lay all his own work in ruins and drive him from the province! At this point credulity, already badly strained, cries for quarter.

During the next three months the three friars were haled before various tribunals in the metropolis. The younger Manoel Dias did everything he could for them. At the risk of compromising himself he took them into his home, nursed one of them through a grievous illness, and supplied them with funds and a guide when, at the end of their trial, they were ordered to Macao.[22]

Meanwhile the brunt of the persecution fell upon the Chinese Christians. Many were cruelly beaten. Scholar-officials, legally immune from corporal punishment, were deprived of offices, titles, possessions and disqualified from literary examinations.

The persecution increased in intensity. Dominicans and Franciscans, including Onofre who had secretly returned to Tingtow, hid in the woods. The commandant in Foochow issued new decrees of proscription and posted a list of missionaries with orders that they be arrested. Included in the list were Manoel Dias and Giulio Aleni.[23]

When word reached the Dominicans and Franciscans that these decrees had been placarded upon the walls of Foochow, they came together in Tingtow to confer on a course of action. Their decision was characteristically audacious and imprudent. Says Escalona:

> . . . We formed the firm resolution to go and preach against these placards where they had been posted up and to tear them down, and to go through the public streets making known Jesus Christ our crucified one, and proclaiming our holy immaculate law: that it alone is the law which converts and leads souls to heaven, and that the idols and sects of China are frauds of the devil. In this agreed all the religious, Franciscans and Dominicans, unanimously. . .[24]

Alenda confirms this:

> . . . P. Fr. Juan Bautista Morales, vice-provincial of the fathers of Saint Dominic, together with P. Fr. Pedro de Chaves, of the same order, and Fr. Francisco de Escalona and Fr. Juan de San Marcos, decided to go to Foochow and tear down the edicts, and to preach publicly Jesus Christ crucified. . .[25]

Escalona further describes how they gave effect to their decision. Entering the metropolis, they marched through the streets, holding their crucifixes high in the air and, in a loud voice ("en voz alta") proclaiming:

> . . . that this was the image of the true God and Man, Savior of the world, creator of all things, who punishes those who do not keep His law and rewards eternally those who keep it; and that the idols and sects of China are false and deceits by which the devil leads them to hell forever, and that whoever ordered these placards posted, if they did not repent of the offence they had committed against our Lord, the true God, would be condemned to hell, whether they be viceroy, judges, military commandant, mayor, or any other mandarin. . .[26]

This was a method of procedure which possibly had its points when employed in South America or in the Philippines, but which had no place in China unless its purpose was deliberately to antagonize. This was the sort of thing that Valignano had hoped to keep out of the Middle Kingdom.

As might have been expected, the apparition of the fiery crusaders in the streets of Foochow provoked a commotion. They were soon surrounded by a shouting, tumultous crowd so great, reports Escalona, "that we could not move forward." One of the charges brought against the missionaries in China by Shên Ch'üeh had been that they were disturbers of public order and fomenters of rebellion. The Japanese invasions of Korea, the incursions of the Manchus, the activities of secret societies, and, finally, the rise of rebellion in the provinces, had made Chinese officialdom during the last decades of the Ming dynasty, acutely sensitive to public gatherings and disturbances. One wonders about the reaction of the Foochow authorities when word reached them that four foreigners were haranguing a shouting crowd in the streets of the city, threatening with eternal damnation the viceroy and any other official who dared proscribe Christianity. It is surprising that the four men got off as lightly as they did. They were arrested, but the judge before whom they appeared merely ordered them to leave the city and released them from custody.

The four stormy petrels returned to Tingtow. Their attitude, as described by Escalona, is revealing. They were clearly unconcerned about the added impetus they had given to the persecution. They went their way rejoicing "because they had succeeded in preaching Christ crucified in Foochow." It seems to have been a matter of indifference to them that the Christians in Foochow were being subjected to draconian measures of repression: that Aleni and Dias were driven from the city; that the churches were closed; that the persecution was spreading through the province as a consequence of their exploit, with chapels being pulled down, Christians hunted and harried until as they said, "the time of the great persecutions of Christians in the early centuries seemed to have returned." All that mattered was that they had preached "Christ crucified in Foochow." It is plain that this sort of preaching had in no way advantaged the cause they represented. Its only positive gain, if it be one, was to give the preachers a sense of personal satisfaction in their deed of derring-do.

This attitude of satisfaction over having stirred up a tempest betrays itself on almost every page of Escalona's recital of events. Typical is his remark anent the outbreak of persecution: "It was for us a joy and delight, with the hopes which we had of making some good use of our lives given for Jesus Christ, as happened in

Japan with our holy martyrs."

The missionary with a more equilibrated conception of his vocation, while prepared to accept martyrdom as a crowning grace, will never solicit it by unnecessarily stirring up a storm, heedless of the consequences to the community. And in acting thus he will often practice greater heroism than some of his less balanced colleagues. One may be permitted to think that there was more of the heroic in Ricci's twenty-eight years of patiently persevering effort or in Longobardo's fifty-seven years of unremitting apostolic toil than in the brief, though exciting, adventure of these men from Manila, most of whom were soon back in the relatively tranquil surroundings of the islands. Schall's acid comment is in point: "It is better to die in bed than to become a martyr in this fashion."

The Foochow incident did not change their attitude. Still left surprisingly free, whenever they heard that placards had been posted anywhere derogatory to Christianity they still felt obliged "for the honor of God" to go and tear them down.

These activities led to the re-arrest in April, 1638, of the mendicants. Alenda, accompanied by Onofre, had returned to Formosa. The others were brought to Foochow and imprisoned. The Dominicans, Juan Bautista de Morales and Francisco Dias, were deported to Macao. The Franciscans were not long in duress. Upon their release they went to Lingchiang, where they were joined by Onofre who had returned from Formosa.

Onofre was a restless character. Scarcely back from Formosa, he and three others "seeing the little or no fruit which could be gathered in these circumstances, abandoned the mission." The other three were the Dominicans Pedro de Chaves and Antonio de la Torre and a Franciscan, Juan de Sancto Marco. The only ones left in China were Escalona and Juan Garcia, and of these the former soon followed his companions back to Manila. Few of these men ever returned to China. Among those who did not return were Escalona and Alenda. It is not irrelevant to point out here that these men lived less than two years in China. Yet it was chiefly their accounts, with the reports of Francisco de la Madre de Dios, another who never returned to China, which, uncritically accepted, established the Jesuit legend.

Prior to the events of 1637-1638 Fukien province had rivalled Shansi as the most promising center of missionary activity in the empire. There were Christian establishments in each of the eight districts into which it was divided. The younger Manoel Dias, assisted by Ignacio Lobo, worked from the residence in Foochow as a center. Aleni had his headquarters in Chüanchow whence he endeavored to serve the needs of Christian communities in thirteen nearby cities and towns. In the summer of 1637 Pietro Canevari was sent to assist him. Relieved of the necessity of spending most of his time in Chüanchow, Aleni was engaged in carrying the Gospel into the more remote parts of the province when the storm broke.

By 1637 the number of conversions averaged between eight and nine hundred annually. There were some ninety Christian chapels in the province, and a number of full-sized churches. The largest and most beautiful, built in large part by contributions of non-Christians who wished thus to manifest their esteem for Aleni, was in Foochow.

The merit of these achievements was that of Giulio Aleni. Twelve years earlier, when he first entered Fukien, there had been neither Christian nor missionary in a province where xenophobia ran high. By his tact he had dissolved prejudice and given to Christianity a position of prestige. Franciscans, as well as Jesuits, testify to Aleni's virtues and accomplishments. Ignacio Lobo, one of Aleni's assistants in Fukien, in a letter to Antonio a Santa Maria, has this to say:

> Father Giulio Aleni is a man of great virtue and the fear of God. Besides, he is learned and one of the most intelligent men we have in China today. In both word and deed he is circumspect. Everything he does is preceded by mature reflection.

Antonio gives his own estimate of Aleni:

> He was one of the most highly esteemed and most valuable missionaries the Society had in China. Highly regarded by both Christians and heathens as a courteous, learned, and able man and as a master of the Chinese language, he was really the oracle of the province in which he lived.[27]

The dour Alenda, in a context not innocent of spite, admits that he was "the idol of this province."[28]

Driven from the province by the storm, Aleni soon returned secretly to visit as many of the Christian communities as he could. He wrote to the governor of the province, successfully soliciting his support. Other interventions followed. The intendant whose jurisdiction embraced the four largest cities in the province sent a reprehension to the Foochow authorities for having included Aleni and Dias in the proscription aimed at the troublemakers from the Philippines. A celebrated academy of scholars petitioned the same intendant in support of the two Jesuits, pointing out that they belonged to the same organization as Matteo Ricci who had merited well of the empire. At the request of Sambiasi several leading officials in Kiangsu province sent letters to Fukien defending Christianity.

These interventions proved effective. They resulted in the suspension of new edicts of proscription which were about to be promulgated. Before long Aleni was able to return to Foochow. With characteristic prudence he did not immediately enter the city, but lodged in an inn some three miles away. During the several weeks he stayed here Christians and friendly officials came out from the city to visit him.

Aleni was well acquainted with Chinese psychology. He had mobilized influential support for his cause, but he made no effort to press his advantage at the expense of the dignity of those authorities in Foochow who had been chiefly responsible for the edicts of persecution. By not appearing in the city to demand the restoration of his church and residence and the rehabilitation of Christianity, he enabled the officials to "save face." They could then restore his church to him without appearing to yield to external pressure. They soon did so. Aleni celebrated Mass publicly in the church on July 14, 1639. The restoration amounted to a tacit quashing of the edicts of proscription and banishment. It had been accomplished with tact, courtesy, and without injury to official dignity. It was more effective than flaunting public authority by tearing down edicts from walls and one has the feeling that the "honor of God" was at least as well served.

Meanwhile Escalona and Garcia had been forced to flee into the woods from Tingtow, their church being destroyed and the materials given to a Buddhist temple. Their Christians were subjected to severe penalties. Eventually the two separated, Escalona making his way to Ningteh, whence he succeeded in reaching Foochow, hoping to take refuge with Aleni. It was about this time, that Aleni returned to Foochow and Escalona, who had escaped detection, found safety with him. Aleni received him with kindness.

It would not have been surprising had Escalona's recent experiences shaken his confidence in the infallibility of his own judgment, but evidently they had not. No sooner had Aleni received him into his home than he began to lecture his host on the wrongness of his views on the subject of the ceremonies with which the Chinese honor their dead.

It must be remembered that Escalona had been less than two years in China, while Aleni had had a quarter of a century of rich and varied experience in the empire and had won a reputation for his mastery of Chinese culture and language. Like most of his confrères in China he had devoted long study to the subject of the rites and engaged in serious discussions carried on over many years among the Jesuits on the subject. Aleni, wishing to avoid argument with his guest, graciously conceded to him that he and his associates held "the safer doctrine." Escalona's comments upon this incident are typical. He attributes the outcome to his own dialectical ability and preens himself upon having overcome Aleni in debate.[29]

When Aleni preached a sermon to his congregation in which he warned against confusing the veneration due to the saints with the respect paid to the memory of the dead, Escalona describes it as a condemnation of the rites and hails it as further proof that he had converted Aleni to his views. Yet from his own text it is clear that the sermon represented no change in Aleni's teaching.

If the disastrous experiences of the preceding year had not taught Escalona humility, neither did the kindly treatment he received at the hands of Aleni teach him charity. During his sojourn with Aleni (a "Theatine," as he insists upon calling him), a non-Christian scholar-official in another part of the province published a book inspired by recent events. It praised Christian doctrine, expressed high esteem for Aleni (which moves Escalona to some invidious comments about flattery and adulation), commended the other Jesuits in China, especially praised Ricci and the older Dias. It then attacked the missionaries who had come from Formosa, criticizing severely their conduct and suggesting an affinity between them and the notorious White Lotus Society.

"Aleni," concludes Escalona, "is the author!" Because the reports of Escalona and his companions have been taken seriously and have established a quite unflattering portrait of the Jesuits in China, it is important to understand the type of mind which originated these reports. All the clinical evidence necessary is supplied by the reports themselves. Here Escalona says that he can prove "syllogistically" that Aleni paid for the publication and dictated at least part of its contents. The "proof" that Aleni paid for the book is that "in China, generally speaking, the Chinese don't give anything to anybody ["nada a nadie"] unless they have been paid or promised payment." The "proof" that Aleni dictated the contents is that no infidel could speak of or praise Christianity in this fashion!

In the next paragraph Escalona, with a kind of incredible ingenuousness, tells how Aleni, as soon as the contents of the book were called to his attention, set out on a four days' journey to the home of the author, whom he persuaded promptly to withdraw his book from circulation until he had amended its objectionable features. Yet this is told without any advertence to its bearing upon the damaging charges he has just made and, needless to say, without any retraction.[30]

Aleni must have been relieved when Escalona decided to move into Kwangsi province. He did not stay there long, but his account of his activities does not lack interest. In the "principal city of the province" which he calls "Voe-cheu-fu," (probably Wuchow), he posted placards in the public places of the city. One poster declared the truth of the Christian faith; a second announced the passion and death of Christ; a third denounced China's false sects and idols; a fourth listed the favors granted by the emperor in behalf of the Christian religion. He failed to note that these favors represented the fruit of a type of apostolate of which he did not approve.

Then he marched through the streets in Franciscan habit and sandalled feet, holding his crucifix high above his head and proclaiming in a loud voice ("a voces grandes") that this was "the image of the true God and Man, Savior of the world; that all their idols and sects were false; that by means of them the devil led them, beguiled, to hell; that if they wished to escape and go to heaven, they must believe in one God . . . God had sent him to this empire 'to tell you that you are on the road to hell, and to put your souls on the road to heaven. If you pursue the crooked road that leads to hell and the hour of death arrives, you will not be able to escape falling into hell and there enduring bitterness and travail without end.' "[31]

Escalona seems to have so high an opinion of the favorable impression he made that one is surprised to learn that he did not stay. Instead he soon turned up in Macao, whence he embarked for Manila. He too had decided to "abandon the mission." His ship was driven from its course by storm and, near the end of 1639, Escalona landed in Cochin-China. He reached Manila early in June, 1640, and never returned to China.

Garcia was the only one of the group left. Incidentally he was the only one to indicate that he had learned anything from his experiences. On November 16, 1639, he wrote a letter to Aleni. He was still in hiding and asked the Jesuit to use his influence to make it possible for him to leave his place of concealment and show himself in public. He assured Aleni that he would conduct himself with discretion. Unlike Escalona he had been chastened by his experiences and frankly admitted that he and his companions had erred:

> I am now convinced that it will be many years before the cause of our Lord can be served by using any other method to preach the Gospel in this country than that which your fathers employ and have employed up to now. I have written in this sense to my superiors, because the experience of the unhappy results brought about by our fathers, now exiled, shows that for the present God did not approve the line of conduct they followed: although they were motivated by honest zeal in acting as they did, in an effort to see if they could thus convert the infidels. For this reason they are to be excused. . .[32]

As Valignano had foreseen, conflict was inevitable in the face of such widely divergent missiological views. The only way to avoid trouble was for the two groups to work in different parts of the empire. In his letter of November 10, 1636, to Vitelleschi, Furtado, the vice-provincial, reported that in conferences with de Morales and Francisco de la Madre de Dios the previous year he had attempted to work out an informal arrangement along these lines. "I have little confidence," he had added, "that they will abide by these arrangements."[33] When Semedo left for Rome the next year he carried with him Furtado's proposal that the mission field of China be divided between the several orders, each group to confine its apostolic efforts to the territory assigned to it.[34] *Propaganda Fide* pigeonholed the suggestion. Two centuries of friction, and not only in China, finally convinced *Propaganda* that there was merit in the idea. Today it is the basis upon which Roman Catholic missions are organized throughout the world.

As far as their personal contacts with the Jesuits are concerned, the record reveals only three actual incidents about which the mendicants had reason to complain: the unpleasantness with de

Mattos who could not stomach their wine, Antonio's rude expulsion from Nanking, and a conflict with Pietro Canevari in 1649 in Amoy in which the blame could be pretty evenly divided. The other "incidents" mentioned in the sources are without merit.

The picture, firmly fixed in history, of constant friction, strife and Jesuit intrigue is not supported by the evidence. The tales of a naive and inexperienced Francisco de la Madre de Dios and of a misanthropic Gaspar Alenda were uncritically accepted at their face value. The tireless recriminations of a Buenaventura Ibañez in letters to the cardinals of *Propaganda Fide*, to the bishops of Tonkin, and to others, were given ready credence.[35] Yet when one examines these letters it becomes clear that he is merely repeating, years after the events, the few actual incidents and indulging a tendency to report as fact every idle tale that comes to him.[36]

A clue to the way Ibañez' mind worked is found in his letter of February 20, 1651, to the cardinals of *Propaganda Fide* in which he cancels out his admission of Schall's benevolence to Antonio a Santa Maria by gratuitously asserting that Schall acted thus "against the will of his superiors."[37] Schall's superior at the time was the same Manoel Dias who, as Antonio reported in a letter to his provincial, had cared for Ibañez himself during a serious illness "with much charity, care, and tenderness."[38]

The proper perspective is restored to the picture by the correspondence of Antonio a Santa Maria which unfortunately lay unread in the archives while the legend perpetuated itself. The truth so sharply contradicts the fiction that the editor of Antonio's correspondence was himself "not a little surprised" upon reading the letters.[39]

Instead of a group of quarrelsome, arrogant men, endeavoring at every turn to frustrate missionaries of other orders, as they have so often been described, the Jesuits appear in Antonio's letters as men whose charity and kindly dispositions are so much in evidence that he never tires of writing about them. Most of these letters were written to his own Franciscan superior. Jean Valat is "an angel . . . a learned and peaceable man who has done us many good deeds." De Ferrariis is "very quiet, peaceable, and truly virtuous."

It is the charity of the much maligned Schall, however, that Antonio especially praises in letter after letter. It is plain that he would not have so readily believed his confrères' version of their experience in Peking in 1637 had he then known Schall personally. Schall's attitude "towards our people," he wrote his provincial in 1652, "is, and has always been characterized by great friendship and by good words and deeds. We are under obligation to him from whom we have received much help."[40]

Antonio had moved to Shantung province and there established the Franciscan mission which still exists. For several years he was entirely dependent upon the alms which Schall sent him. His own superiors in Manila were opposed to his Shantung venture and ordered him back to Fukien. Despite their promise of disciplinary measures if he failed to obey, Antonio chose to remain where he was. His superiors cut off all financial support.[41] "During the [four or five years] that I have been here," he wrote his provincial, "I have had no other succor than the alms which P. Johann Adam [Schall], who is located in the capital city of Peking, has sent me without my asking him, but because he knew my need . . ."[42] On another occasion he urged his provincial to write a letter of appreciation to the Peking Jesuit. Writing in 1667, the year after Schall's death and two years before his own, he recalls that it was Schall "who, after God, alone made it possible for me to establish, in the city of Tsinan in the province of Shantung, the first house and church of our order in this empire."[43]

If Schall's charity was outstanding, it was not exceptional. In 1656 Antonio reported that "the vice-provincial, and all the Fathers in other places, treat us with so much kindness and love, proved by good deeds."[44] And in 1660 he informed the archbishop of Manila, Antonio a S. Gregorio, that "a close bond of love and fraternal charity" united him with the Jesuits. "We receive in everything a thousand charities from the said reverend fathers," he testified.[45] With scarcely a year's experience in China the dour Alenda had written: "To fall into the hands of the Jesuits is the thing which, in this empire we find almost the most painful experience."[46]

Antonio painted a picture on the basis of more than a quarter of a century of experience. Alenda drew a caricature.

NOTES

(1) From the testimony of Francisco de la Madre de Dios and Juan Bautista de Morales; cf. Maas, *op. cit.*, p. 58, n. 26.

(2) *ARSI*, Jap-Sin 161 II, ff. 164-165.

(3) Buenaventura Ibañez, O.F.M., "Brevis relatio de oppositionibus quas tres missionarii Franciscani passi sunt ab ingressu in Sinam anno Domini 1649 usque ad annum 1662," *SinFran*, III, 93.

(4) These two documents are in the Franciscan archives in Pastrana, Spain. They will be cited as *Inf. 1* and *Inf. 2*.

(5) Lorenzo Perez, O.F.M., "Los Franciscanos en el Extremo Oriente," *AFH*, II, 554.

(6) Francisco de la Madre de Dios' account is given by Francisco a Jesu de Escalona in his "Relacion del Viaje al Reino de la Gran China," which is published in *AFH*, VIII, 558-591 (the pertinent passages are in pp. 582-591), and IX, 184-218; it is re-edited in *SinFran*, II, 225-314. Alenda's story is told in his letter to Fathers Joseph de Valencia and Heironymus Nadal of March 12, 1638, *ibid.*, *passim.*

(7) *AFH*, *VIII*, 582, n. 2.

(8) *Eminent Chinese*, I, 37 f., 491 f.

(9) *AFH*, VIII, 583, n. 1.

(10) *AFH*, IV, 54 f.

(11) Maas, *op. cit.*, p. 64, n. 42.

(12) *SinFran*, II, 252.

(13) *Ibid.*, n. 1.

(14) *AFH*, IV, 56.

(15) The vice-provincial, Furtado, was Portuguese and must have felt the Spaniards would be more likely to heed a German.

(16) A copy of the original Portuguese version of Schall's letter is in *ARSI*, Jap-Sin 161 II, ff. 196-197. There is a Spanish version published from a manuscript in the Pastrana archives in *AFH*, VIII, 588-589, in the note.

(17) *SinFran*, II, 541.

(18) José Gonzàlez, O.P., *Biografia del primer obispo Chino* (Manila: U.S.T. Press, 1946).

(19) *SinFran*, III, 28 f.

(20) *Ibid.*, II, 254, n. 5.

(21) *Id.*

(22) Pfister, *op. cit.*, I, 108.

(23) Maas, *op. cit.*, p. 69, n. 55, in noting this fact does not seem to see that it has any bearing upon the credence to be given Alenda's assumption that Aleni was master-minding the persecution.

(24) *SinFran*, II, 263.

(25) *Ibid.*, p. 264, n. 3.

(26) *Ibid.*, p. 264.

(27) Maas, *op. cit.*, p. 67, n. 46.

(28) *SinFran*, II, 254, n. 5.

(29) *Ibid.*, p. 281.

(30) *Ibid.*, p. 285.

(31) *Ibid.*, p. 293.

NOTES

(32) Quoted by Noel Alexandre, O. P., *Apologie des Dominicains missionaires de la Chine*, 2d. ed. (Cologne: C. d'Egmond, 1700), pp. 201 f.

(33) *ARSI*, Jap-Sin 161 II, ff. 164-165.

(34) The document is in the archives of *Propaganda;* cf. Robert Streit, O.M.I., *Bibliotheca Missionum* (Münster-Aachen: Veröffentlichungen des Internationalen Instituts für missionswissenschaftliche Forschung, 1916-39), V, 775, n. 2168.

(35) *SinFran*, III, 24 ff.

(36) For striking examples of the idle tale reported as fact, cf. *ibid.*, pp. 122, 125 f.

(37) *Ibid.*, p. 28.

(38) *SinFran*, II, 453.

(39) *Ibid.*, p. 350.

(40) *Ibid.*, pp. 417, 419.

(41) Perez, *op. cit.*, *AFH*, II, 559 f.

(42) *SinFran*, II, 433.

(43) *Ibid.*, pp. 593 ff.

(44) *Ibid.*, pp. 445 f.

(45) *Ibid.*, pp. 498 f.

(46) *AFH*, IX, 187, n. 1.

Chapter XVI

Accommodation Under Fire

THE CHARGE THAT the Jesuits, by their policy of accommodation, compromised the integrity of their Roman Catholic faith has enjoyed wide currency. To arrive at a judgment it is necessary to establish the nature of the concessions which they made in the name of accommodation. Five primary sources make it possible to do so. In addition to the two *Informaciones* carried to Manila by Antonio a Santa Maria in 1636 and Furtado's letter to the general of November 10, 1636, there is a reply by Furtado to a letter of June 3, 1639, sent by de Morales to Manoel Dias making twelve charges against Jesuit practices. Finally there is an important report written by Furtado to Pope Urban VIII, dated November 1, 1639.[1]

All that needs to be known is found in these five documents. The century of controversy which followed added nothing to the charges made and answered here. The controversy added heat, but no more light.

In his letter to the pope, Furtado expresses his grave concern that the tender young shoot planted "if not with our blood, at least with a lot of sweat, labor and trouble," was endangered by the activities of the Franciscans and Dominicans. The danger comes not from any lack of "holy zeal," but from their inexperience in dealing with the Chinese and from their ill-advised method of preaching.

In this document Furtado states briefly but clearly in fifteen subdivisions exactly what has been the Jesuit practice. He also states what it is the Jesuits object to in the methods employed by the mendicants. In conclusion, he extends to the whole mission field of the Church the suggestion he had already made about the division of China among the orders. As the pope, in order to minimize the danger of conflict, had drawn a line of demarcation between the colonial activities of Spain and Portugal in his famous Bull of May 3-4, 1493, so he should do the same with the missionary activities of the religious orders.[2] With so many mission fields available, with the immense needs of the Spanish colonial empire itself, it should be possible to satisfy everyone. Granted that many are needed in China, it is better, wrote Furtado, sometimes to use fewer sails than by breaking out all the canvas at the moment of launching to sink the ship.

The objections of the mendicants to Jesuit practice may be divided into two groups: a number of points relating to Christian practice and missionary method; questions concerning certain rites universally observed by the Chinese in paying honor to the recently deceased members of their family, to their ancestors, and to Confucius. This second group of questions will be considered in the next chapter.

The first group of questions involved mainly the following points: failure to promulgate the laws of the Church; the method of administering the sacraments; the alleged failure to preach the doctrine of the crucifixion of Christ; the problem of Christian terminology; the general procedure of the Jesuits, i.e., their adoption of Chinese dress, their intellectual apostolate, their refusal to say that Confucius was in hell, etc.

In the course of the controversy as it later developed, it was the question of the rites which monopolized attention. Actually, what scandalized the newcomers more than toleration of the rites was the failure of the Jesuits to promulgate the positive precepts of the Church.

As Dr. Maas remarks, this "so shocked and so astonished the new missionaries that they accorded this question first place in their investigations."[3] It occupies first place too in the list of questions submitted by de Morales to Dias.[4] It was also the first question raised by de Morales and Francisco in an interview with Furtado in 1635. At that time they added to the other omissions which astonished them the fact that Christians were not obliged to abstain from work on Sundays and feast days.[5]

The charge was true. The Jesuits did not oblige their Christians to observe these ecclesiastical laws under pain of mortal sin. In his tour of the mission in 1629 the Jesuit Visitor André Palmeiro, new to China, was also astonished by this. He reported his surprise to the general in a letter of December 20, 1629.[6] The fathers on the mission when he questioned them seem to have had a rather firm legal position. They said that no bishop in the Far East had promulgated the positive laws of the Church. They seemed also to have the impression that there had been a papal indult in the matter.

In 1615 when in Rome Trigault had inquired of the theologians of the Roman College what causes would justify not promulgating the positive precepts and whether the Society had been granted any privilege in the matter. The theologians replied that the popes had settled these questions for Japan, thus inferring that the same answers would apply to the China mission.

It is true that in 1595 Clement VIII had granted an indult to Jesuit missionaries in the "East Indies" to omit the usual ceremonies from the baptismal rite and to dispense from fasting. What other papal acts the theologians had in mind is not certain. In any case it seems probable that the policy in China had originated simply as an application of the policy established by Valignano in Japan.

Conditions in Japan did not make the general observance of the positive laws of the Church possible. It was plain to Valignano that it would be many years before they could be introduced. As long as the laws were not promulgated they did not obligate the Japanese Christians. The absence of any possibility of their being observed dispensed from the necessity of promulgating them. This was Valignano's reasoning. He had been a doctor in law before becoming a Jesuit and it was as a trained lawyer that he arrived at these conclusions. He insisted that the Holy See should grant to the highest superior in Japan the power to dispense from the positive laws of the Church, but until that was done he forbade the missionaries to promulgate them as binding upon conscience.[7]

It was in somewhat the same terms that Furtado defended Jesuit policy in China. In his letter to Vitelleschi and in his report to Urban VIII he appeals not to indults, but to simple considerations of charity. To impose the ecclesiastical precepts under pain of mortal sin would, in the conditions of the time, impose upon most Christians an intolerable burden of conscience. Most of them would find it impossible to comply.

"So far as fasting is concerned," he wrote, "the Chinese live so close to the margin of subsistence, that in Europe itself Christians of long standing would be exempted from fasting if they lived in like circumstances. For most Chinese live simply on rice and herbs, to which they sometimes add a few vegetables."

The obligation of hearing Mass on feast days and that of abstaining from work were related. Most of the Christians, in order to attend Mass, would have been forced to forego their work day. Furtado puts the position clearly. In general the Chinese "are so poor and earn so little each day, that to forbid them to work would be the same as to forbid them to eat."

The law could have been promulgated, it being understood that those for whom circumstances made observance impossible were excused. On the other hand, there is little wisdom in promulgating a universally binding law from the observance of which the large majority are excused by reason of circumstances. This can only lead to a general lowering of respect for the binding force of the law itself.

In China the missionaries were confronted with conditions not envisaged by Church authorities when they formulated these disciplinary laws. When the laws of fast and abstinence were promulgated in Europe, China was not thought of. There seemed no point in blindly insisting upon the literal application of the whole panoply of ecclesiastical legislation to every country newly opened to the Gospel, irrespective of local conditions. Charity was thought to take precedence over the letter of the law.

Europeanism, however, tends to look upon any divergence from the external forms observed in the homeland as a betrayal of the faith. This assumption shows through one of the questions submitted by de Morales to the Congregation *Propaganda Fide* in 1645:

> Are Chinese Christians obliged to observe the positive law, with respect to fasts, annual confession and communion, the observance of feasts, *in the same way* that the Indians are obligated *in New Spain and the Philippine Islands?* (Italics added.)

Which is to say: the way they are observed in old Spain.

The second charge made by de Morales in his letter to Dias is that: "The Fathers in baptizing women fail to apply saliva to their ears, salt to their mouths, and oil to their breast and head."[8] The

Jesuits deemed the rigid conceptions of decorum governing conduct towards women more than sufficient reason to omit these ceremonies in China, inasmuch as none of them affects the validity of the sacrament. Says Furtado:

> Among the Chinese it is [regarded] as highly irregular and indecent to expose a woman's breast, to touch her hands and her mouth. If it is necessary everywhere for ministers of the Gospel to observe circumspection in their conduct with women, it is certainly far more necessary in China.

It requires no more than an elementary notion of Chinese social attitudes governing sex in the seventeenth century to recognize the solid foundation of Furtado's argument.

From the beginning the problem of ministering to the spiritual needs of Chinese women was a thorny one. The interdiction of contact with the opposite sex, except within the bosom of the family, made it difficult even to talk with women without arousing suspicion. Both Ricci and Longobardo had been falsely accused of adultery. At a later date the far from Carthusian manner of life of the free-wheeling Adam Schall enabled hostile tongues to stir up such a swarm of calumnious gossip that for a time some of his fellow Jesuits were inclined to believe them. Such gossip was none the less injurious to the reputation of its victims because it was without foundation.

Hence the Jesuits had adopted a policy of great circumspection in their dealings with women. Bartoli describes, for example, how they overcame deep-seated prejudices and at the same time protected themselves against wagging tongues in hearing the confessions of women. At one end of the largest room in the house a large mat was suspended. The confessor sat on one side of the mat, the penitent on the other. At the other end of the room whence he could see everything, but hear nothing, stood "the grave master of the house, (Ignatius) Sun Yüan-hua, a Christian of great virtue."[9]

One might think that "a Christian of great virtue" would have greater confidence in the probity of these priests whom he knew well. The fact is that the presence of Ignatius was not an indication of mistrust on his part, but was a protection against the irresponsible gossip of others. The word of a domestic to a neighbor that the women of the house were wont to shut themselves in a room alone with these foreign men was enough to start a scandalous tale that would spread like prairie fire. The presence of "the grave master of the house" in the room prevented the possibility of such scandal-mongering at its source.

Another objection of de Morales charged "that when they are interrogated by scholars or other persons on certain important points: whether Confucius has been damned; whether it is legitimate to have several wives, as did Yao and Shun, Kings who reigned over them in antiquity and are considered holy men, and similar questions, the Fathers of the Society answer with equivocations, because they well know that the Chinese would take ill a response derogatory to their Master, their holy men, the laws of their realm, and hence the ministers of the Gospel would be expelled."[10]

Furtado denies categorically that equivocation is used but he freely admits that the Jesuits do not answer the question about Confucius' present whereabouts apodictically. When they are confronted with the explicit question, they answer it with a statement of the conditions required for salvation: "All those who know God and love Him above all things, and who pass out of this life with such knowledge and love, are saved. If Confucius knew God and loved Him above all things, and passed out of this life with such knowledge and love, without doubt he is saved."

From the point of view of Roman Catholic theology this answer is impeccable. No theologian, whatever elaboration he might give to Furtado's formula, could answer the question of the salvation of Confucius, or of anyone else, in any but this hypothetical way. No one could say whether Confucius was in hell. Possibly the Jesuits, who admired many features of his ethical system, entertained a secret hope that he was not. It is good to know that they were free to indulge in such occult charity without incurring the taint of heresy.

As far as the question of monogamy is concerned, Furtado is justified in stating that nothing could be farther from the truth than to charge the Jesuits with equivocation. "Among the truths of our holy religion, none is more familiar to the pagans than this: that the holy law of God does not allow more than one wife, even to the emperor."[11] Sufficient evidence has appeared in these pages to leave no doubt that the Catholic position had been made perfectly clear. Time and again the missionaries refer to it as one of the chief obstacles to conversion. If they had deep sympathy for the dilemma with which the exigencies of Christian monogamy confronted sensitive-minded Chinese, they nevertheless refused to compromise.

Yao and Shun were a different matter. These two heroes of China's mythical Golden Age had lived, if they ever did live, thousands of years before. The Jesuits felt no compulsion to pass judgment upon them. Their business was to enunciate the Christian doctrine of monogamous marriage and to refuse to receive into the Church anyone who was unwilling to accept that ideal. If they were asked whether Yao and Shun were to be condemned for having a plurality of wives, they avoided passing judgment.

This did not satisfy their critics, who wanted retroactive anathemas pronounced against the shades of Yao and Shun. Because the Jesuits were not interested in the marital arrangements which were said to have prevailed in the establishments of these legendary rulers, they were accused of equivocating on the doctrine itself. It must be said that the charge is based not only upon bad logic, but upon questionable theology. Many theologians hold that the primeval dispensation of polygamy was granted not only to the patriarchs and people of Israel, but to all other peoples as well.[12]

Undoubtedly the most serious charge in the first indictment was that the Jesuits suppressed the doctrine of the crucifixion of Christ. This is the accusation that has received such wide acceptance as to become an historical commonplace. Thus even a serious writer like Gerald Brenan, in making a point about marxist distortions of history, can for purposes of comparison refer casually to "the feats of those Jesuit missionaries of the seventeenth century who, the better to convert the Chinese, suppressed the story of the Crucifixion."[13]

The mendicants themselves did not explicitly make this charge. They inferred it from the fact that the Jesuits practiced a certain discipline of the *arcana;* and in their letters and reports they implied it. As might have been expected, it was not long before both in the Philippines and in Europe the implication was accepted as fact.

A simple examination of the works published by Jesuits prior to 1637 exposes the calumnious nature of this accusation. Almost every Jesuit who published anything in Chinese had written something on the passion and crucifixion of Christ.[14] The only ones who did not are men who wrote little in Chinese, like Cattaneo who left only two short essays; or men like de Ursis and Terrenz who wrote entirely on scientific subjects.

The works of Aleni are of special interest, inasmuch as they appeared in Fukien province shortly before and at the very time that the mendicants were reporting their shocking discovery to Manila. In 1635 Aleni published his *T'ien Chu chiang-shêng ch'u-hsiang ching-chieh* (Sacred Explanation of the Life of Christ Illustrated with Pictures). Among the fifty illustrations are dramatic drawings of the agony in the garden, the scourging at the pillar, the crowning with thorns, and the crucifixion.[15] Between 1635 and 1637 there appeared in Foochow the first edition of Aleni's eight *chüan T'ien Chu chiang-sheng chi-lu* (Life of God Incarnate). This is how Aleni, in unadorned synoptic style, describes the crucifixion.

> Jesus carried the cross upon his shoulder to the mountain. The Soldiers first gave him wine with gall to drink. Jesus tasted it but did not drink. Next his sweat and blood-stained clothes were taken off. He was stretched out bodily upon the cross. Above, his two hands were spread out and nailed to the cross-piece. Below, his two feet were nailed together to the upright. The cross was hoisted up and dropped into the hole. (This punishment was regarded as the cruelest and most pitiful and was therefore administered to the lowest criminals.) Two wicked robbers were nailed on Jesus' left and right. Jesus suffered the same punishment as the wicked robbers. Pilate ordered a wooden plaque fixed to the top of the cross inscribed in Hebrew, Greek, and Latin characters proclaiming: Jesus Nazarenus, King of all the people of Judaea. The people of Judaea seeing it, regarded it as a national humiliation. They asked that the words "King of the people of Judaea" be removed. Pilate stubbornly turned a deaf ear, saying: 'What I have written, I have written'. . . .[16]

If further proof were needed it would be found in the diatribes of Yang Kuang-hsien who devoted years to a relentless effort to bring about the downfall of Adam Schall and the proscription of the Christian religion. The anti-Christian books which he published show complete familiarity with the doctrine of the crucifixion. His *Pu-tê-i* (I Cannot Refrain) has remarkably graphic illustrations of Christ being nailed to the cross and hanging from the cross between the two thieves.[17]

Writing to his provincial on January 3, 1653, Antonio a Santa Maria, the most experienced of the Franciscan missionaries in China, writes:

> I spent holy week in Peking; Father John Adam Schall cele-

The Crucifixion as portrayed in Giulio Aleni's pictorial life of Christ, the *T'ien Chu chiang-sheng ch'u-hsiang ching-chieh,* published in Fukien in 1635. From a copy in the Jesuit archives.

> brated with great devotion, with a procession of palms within the cloister, with six pictures of the principal scenes of the passion set up in the church, and on the main altar a picture of the Crucified, whose passion he preached word for word on Good Friday morning with so many tears that at times he could not speak.[18]

In view of the massive weight of evidence it is not surprising that Francesco Brancato should have branded the story of the suppression of the doctrine of the crucifixion "a lie," or that Martino Martini should have protested vigorously to the Holy See about the calumnies being spread abroad in and from the Philippines by members of the mendicant orders.[19] How could the latter have invented this tall tale? Jacques Le Favre, in a letter of September 8, 1657, to the procurator of the Jesuit province of France, puts his finger on the explanation:

> I cannot end without expressing to your reverence my astonishment at the report which some people have broadcast in Europe that our Fathers in China do not dare to preach Jesus crucified. It is true that to go out into the public places with a crucifix in the hand would only expose our religion to the contempt of the gentiles; but after they have been instructed in the other mysteries, there is nothing that moves them as much as the passion of our Lord.[20]

To the men from Manila the only way to preach the Gospel was in the public places with crucifix in hand. Presumably this is the way they acted in the Philippines. This is the way they preached in Fukien. Narrowly interpreting the ringing declaration of St. Paul: "I preach Jesus Christ and Him crucified," they regarded this as the only legitimate way to preach the Gospel. They forgot that St. Paul himself did not always begin his preaching with the crucifixion. In his famous discussion with the Greek philosophers in the Areopagus he began, as the Jesuits in China began, by taking as his starting point a partial truth already obscurely recognized and attempting by a process of natural reasoning to lead the Greeks to a knowledge of the whole truth. In his famous phrase St. Paul was enunciating an axiom of theology; he was not expounding a theory of methodology.

The Jesuits did not give wide public display to visual representations of the crucifixion. (Interestingly enough, no pictorial representations of the crucifixion are to be found in the catacombs. The Church was several hundred years old before Christians began to represent the crucifixion in anything but symbolic forms.)

Furtado gave the reason for this reserve: *ne det sanctum canibus.* The hue and cry raised by the eunuch Ma-t'ang when he came upon Ricci's crucifix had not been forgotten. They did not view lightly the danger of the Christian symbol of man's redemption being assimilated to a Taoist charm. There was also the danger that a wide display of the crucifix to a world ignorant of the Christian dispensation would expose the doctrine itself to ridicule. Francisco de la Madre de Dios testified that he had never found that the pagans abominated the cross.[21] At the time, he had been in China thirteen months, living in the village of Tingtow in Fukien. The fears of the Jesuits rested upon more than half a century in China, dealing with all classes, and in all the provinces of the empire. Whether they or Francisco were right may easily be judged by examining Yang Kuang-hsien's anti-Christian tract, *Pu-tê-i.*

Ignoring the abundance of evidence — they must surely have known of Aleni's books — the friars despatched to Manila heavily melodramatized accounts which could but lead their readers to infer much more than they explicitly said. Typical is Francisco de la Madre de Dios' description of a conversation with Ignacio Lobo in Foochow on the occasion of the meeting between himself and de Morales on the one hand and Furtado and Lobo on the other. It is part of his sworn testimony in the *Informaciones* which Antonio carried to Manila. In reading it one assists again at the birth of a legend.

Lobo is advising de Morales not to display the cross on the door of his house which opens onto the street. In the accents of melodrama Francisco describes his reaction to this perfectly sound advice: "I stood there leaning against the window and listening, for his words were also meant for me, and the Lord God alone knows with what a sorrowful heart I heard such words, words entirely without foundation. . . ."[22] Thus the collective experience of the Jesuits over a half a century is brushed aside by the neophyte who has been a single year in China.

In the same style he goes on to report that the only crucifix he saw in the Jesuit house where this meeting took place was in a room on an upper floor. The ecclesiastics in Manila reading this were not likely to realize that the "upper floor" was without a doubt the second floor where, as is the case in many Catholic missions to this day, a room had been set aside to serve as the domestic chapel.

Instead they probably got the impression of the crucifix hidden away in some attic nook.

This is the whole story of the famous "Jesuit suppression of the doctrine of the crucifixion." It is not the whole story of the legend itself, for that has had a long life. Like most wraiths it is hard to kill.

NOTES

(1) Furtado's letter of November 10, 1636, in *ARSI*, Jap-Sin 161 II, ff. 164-165, is also published in *Informatio antiquissima de praxi missionariorum Sinensium Societatis Jesu, circa ritus Sinenses, data in China, jam ab annis 1636 et 1640 a P. Francisco Furtado antiquo missionario, et vice-provinciali Sinensi ejusdem Societatis* (Parisiis: N. Pepié, 1700), pp. 10 ff., cited hereafter as *Informatio antiquissima.* The reply to de Morales' letter of June 3, 1639, is published in the same book, but with its own pagination. It will be cited as *Responsio*. The report to Urban VIII is in *ARSI*, Jap-Sin 123, ff. 69-74.

(2) Writing from his Japanese prison cell, where he awaited martyrdom, Carolo Spinola in a letter of February 26, 1620, had made the same suggestion; *ARSI*, Jap-Sin 36, ff. 205-207.

(3) Maas, *op. cit.*, p. 123.

(4) *Responsio*, pp. 2 f.

(5) *Informatio antiquissima*, p. 11.

(6) *ARSI*, FG [Fondo Gesuitico] regist. 1, 2 ff., n.c.

(7) For Valignano's views on the subject cf. Josef Franz Schütte, S. J., *Valignanos Missionsgrundsätze für Japan* (Roma: Edizione di storia e letteratura, 1951-1958), I, 374, 376; II, 294, 296, 314, 319, 389, 394.

(8) *Responsio*, p. 3.

(9) Bartoli, *op. cit.*, IV, 89.

(10) *Responsio*, p. 34.

(11) *Ibid.*, p. 39.

(12) Bernard J. Otten, S. J., *Institutiones dogmaticae in usum scholarum* (Chicago: Loyola Press, 1925), VI, 397.

(13) Gerald Brenan, *The Spanish Labyrinth* (New York: Macmillan Company, 1943), p. 326.

(14) Cf. Pfister, *op. cit.*, nos. 17, 18, 19, 21, 26, 31, 39, 54.

(15) Cf. the copy in *ARSI*, Jap-Sin I, 188.

(16) Translated from the copy, bound in three volumes, in the Jesuit archives, *ARSI*, Jap-Sin, I, 73/80. The text quoted is in *chüan* 7, chapter 20, pp. 15v/16r. A copy of this work, under the title *T'ien Chu chiang-shêng yen-hsing chi-lüeh* (Record of the Words and Deeds of God Incarnate) is in the Smithsonian deposit of the Library of Congress, the text here quoted in *chüan* 7, p. 53. It is under this title, which also appears on the table of contents page in the copy in the Jesuit archives, that the work is described by Pfister, *op. cit.*, I, 131.

(17) *Pu-tê-i, chüan* 1, pp. 33, 34, in the copy in *ARSI*, Jap-Sin 89, 1-2.

(18) *SinFran*, II, 417.

NOTES

(19) Francesco Brancato, S. J., *De Sinensium ritibus politicis acta seu responsio apologetica ad R. P. Dominicum Navarrete Ordinis Praedicatorum* (Paris, N. Pepié, 1700), II, 186. Brancato wrote this tract while interned with Navarrete in Canton in 1669. The original manuscript signed on September 5, 1669, is in the Biblioteca Nazionale, Rome, *Fondo Gesuitico* 1250, fasc. 5.

(20) *Lettre du R. P. Jacques Le Faure de la Compagnie de Jésus au P. Procureur de la province de France, et des Missions d'Orient de la mesme Compagnie, sur son arrivée à la Chine, et l'estat present de ce royaume* (Paris: Edme Martine, 1662), pp. 35 f.

(21) *Inf. 2,* fol. 47, quoted by Maas, *op. cit.*, p. 130.

(22) *Ibid.*, fols. 46-47

Chapter XVII

A Question of Rites

The Jesuits had not formulated answers to the thorny problems encountered in China without themselves experiencing divisions of opinion. For more than two decades before the advent of missionaries from the Philippines they had carried on a debate concerned mainly with questions of terminology for the expression of Christian concepts. A mere outline of the history of this debate is enough to establish that they did not adopt their policies lightly or without mature consideration of the issues involved.[1]

The problem of finding Chinese words with which to express Christian ideas was one of the most difficult encountered by Ricci. It were clearly futile to look for words in the Chinese vocabulary which would immediately signify the Christian concept. How, for example, could one expect to find a Chinese word signifying "grace" in the sense in which it was understood in Roman Catholic theology when such a concept was foreign to the Chinese mind?

The problem was the same as that encountered by early Christianity when it entered the Greco-Roman world. Although not going as far as did the early Church, Ricci on the whole solved it the same way. He sought for words which had an approximation of the Christian idea and, by process of explanation and instruction, endowed them with the power to evoke the correct Christian concept.

It is difficult to understand why this solution should seem less sensible when applied in the China of the sixteenth century than when applied in the Roman empire of the first century. The only alternative was to foist upon the Chinese language a collection of barbarisms signifying nothing in themselves. Thus "ke-la-chi-a," a phonetization of the Latin word "gratia," was merely a queer concatenation of sound to the Chinese ear. No less educational effort was required to make this barbarism evocative of the Christian concept of grace than would have been needed to infuse a genuine Chinese expression such as *t'ien-ên* (heavenly favor) or *shêng-ên* (sacred favor) with the same significance.

The dispute centered upon Ricci's selection of the words *Shang-ti* and *T'ien-chu* for God, *t'ien-shên* for angel, *ling-hun* for soul. Valignano, after a conference held in Macao in 1600, had approved Ricci's suggestion of this terminology. The first misgivings about the use of these words arose among the Jesuits in Japan who communicated them to their confrères in China. St. Francis Xavier unwittingly rendered his preaching ambiguous when he selected the Japanese word *Dainichi* to signify God. The term had a fixed significance in Japanese Buddhism. St. Francis was shocked to learn that in summoning the Japanese to worship *Dainichi* he was sponsoring the cause of a Buddhist deity quite different from the Christian God. He immediately proscribed further use of the term.[2]

This initial experience made the Jesuits in Japan wary of adapting Japanese words to Christian usage. For the next fifty years they debated the problem. In the end those who argued that the integrity of the faith required that Christian concepts be expressed by introducing into the Japanese vocabulary phoneticized Portuguese and Latin words prevailed.

The danger of equivocation was much greater in Japan than in China. In Japan Buddhist thought had given to certain expressions a fixed and well defined connotation, whereas in China the classics made free use of certain terms evidently referring to the spiritual world without effort to render their meaning precise. Where the Deity was concerned, the Chinese used words of majestic but vague import. Was *Shang-ti* (Ruler on High) a personal God, or a mere force, or an anthropomorphized "ancestor"? Was *T'ien* the material sky or a deity who was Lord of heaven and earth? The Chinese had never bothered to define their terms. When the question was put to them they found it as difficult to express an opinion as the missionaries found it to interpret their minds. The reason is clear: in general the Chinese had no fixed opinions on the subject. Religious thought to them has always been anthropocentric and practical rather than theocentric and speculative.

This fact made it easier to take certain expressions and by definition give them Christian content. It was no more than a matter of supplying to Chinese terminology the precision which, as a consequence of Chinese disinterest in speculative theology, it lacked.

The Jesuits in Japan failed to recognize that the data of the problem were not the same in China as in Japan. Hence when the Chinese works of Matteo Ricci were introduced in Japan they were disturbed by his use of the terms listed above. They communicated their misgivings to Jesuits in Macao and through them to some of the men elsewhere in China.

In Nicolò Longobardo the Jesuits in Japan found an ardent advocate of their views. From the year of his arrival in China in 1597 Longobardo questioned the legitimacy of these expressions; and, as soon as he assumed the office of superior after Ricci's death, he urged the visitor, Francesco Pasio, to re-examine the entire question. The opinions of Hsü Kuang-ch'i, Yang T'ing-yün, Li Chih-tsao, and other scholars, were sought. They endorsed Ricci's views. Consequently, although Pasio, whose own missionary career had been spent in Japan, was himself inclined to agree with Longobardo, he left the question in abeyance.

Longobardo continued to press his views. Sebastiano de Ursis agreed with him. In 1615 Francisco Vieira succeeded Pasio as visitor of the Japanese and Chinese missions. Camillo di Costanzo, one of the Jesuits in Macao, entered the lists with a treatise attacking the use of the disputed terms. Vieira shared di Costanzo's opinion, but knowing that de Pantoia and Vagnoni disagreed he asked them to write an exposition of their views. They did so, defending the terminology chosen by Ricci.

In 1617 Longobardo presented Vieira with a tract on the subject. The following year de Ursis, banished to Macao by the edict of 1617, contributed both an essay and a formal treatise supporting Longobardo. In 1621 Jerónimo Rodrigues, who had succeeded Vieira, called a conference of missionaries at Macao to discuss the problem. The majority opinion supported Ricci's view and Rodrigues issued a set of directives approving this position.

Longobardo was not a man to surrender easily. He urged a review of the findings of the Macao conference and in 1623 wrote another treatise arguing his case.[3] The next year he subjected Ricci's *T'ien-Chu shih-i* to a critical analysis in another tract to which Vagnoni replied in a long letter to the visitor dated October 8, 1626. In 1627 Rodrigo de Figueredo wrote an essay in support of Ricci's terminology and van Spiere threw his thesis into the ring on the side of Longobardo.

The missionaries being as far from agreement as ever it was decided to hold another conference. In a letter to Vitelleschi dated May 14, 1628, André Palmeiro, who was visitor in 1627 and 1628, says that this decision had been made before he assumed office and, although it had "its inconveniences," he judged it better to let it stand.[4]

In the last days of December, 1627, nine Jesuits came together in Kiating. The younger Dias, as vice-provincial, presided. Longobardo, Vagnoni, Trigault were certainly there; probably there, were the older Dias, Sambiasi, Cattaneo, and Semedo. An eleven-point agenda was agreed upon. Many hours each day were devoted to a discussion which often generated considerable warmth. There was little difficulty with the problems relating to the less solemn Confucian ceremonies and the ancestral rites. Here substantial agreement was reached and the policies hitherto followed approved. The major controversy centered upon the question of terminology. With Longobardo holding out strongly for his opinion, no agreement was possible. When, towards the end of January, word arrived of the death the previous September of the T'ien-ch'i emperor, the meeting hastily broke up, it being thought dangerous in the circumstances to have so many foreigners gathered in one place.[5]

Longobardo, the irrepressible, was not through. In 1633 he wrote another manuscript attacking use of the term *Shang-ti.* Gaspar Ferreira answered him. Longobardo, determined to have the last word, riposted with a lengthy tract in which he went further than he had in his earlier arguments. He now rejects both *Shang-ti* and *T'ien-chu* and holds out for a phoneticized form of the Latin *Deus*. He failed to have the last word, for both Aleni and Semedo wrote critiques of his final salvo. It may not be amiss to point out that the term which ultimately won sole possession of the field and which has been used by Catholics in China ever since without injury to orthodoxy or to clarity of concept is *T'ien-chu.*

Even this brief survey supplies abundant evidence of the conscientious manner in which conclusions were reached and policies formulated in these difficult questions. It is also worthy of note that, despite the sharp divergence of opinion and the intensity of the debate, no echoes of the controversy reached the Christian community to spread division in its ranks. The Jesuits took leading Christian scholars into their confidence, but the discussion was not carried on in the public forum. The Christian community remained united and undisturbed. Neither did the conflict of views result in discord among the Jesuits. There was a clash of minds, but not of hearts. The visitor, André Palmeiro, bears witness to this fact. Following the Kiating conference he visited every mission in the empire. He wrote to the general:

> The truth is that I found no disunion of hearts or of affection . . . and that is the more important matter. But in matters of speculative judgment . . . they have contrary opinions. Hence it has been a cause of great admiration in me to see that this wide diversity of view and this contention, which has lasted so long a time, have nevertheless produced neither exasperation of spirit nor the slightest indication of malevolent affection which might disunite them and disturb the mission.[6]

In this passage Palmeiro refers to the dispute as a "speculative controversy." The real issue would seem to lie within the sphere of prudential judgment. The question which should have been debated was this: "Regardless of the primitive meaning of *Shang-ti*, *T'ien-chu*, *t'ien-shên*, *ling-hun*, can we confidently hope that constant explication of the Christian concept can infuse these terms with Christian meaning? Can we not say to the Chinese, 'whatever your ancestors understood or many of your contemporaries understand by *Shang-ti*, Christians by *Shang-ti* mean a being who is eternal, infinite, unique, omnipotent, creator of heaven and earth'?" This in fact was what the missionaries had done and whatever ambiguities may have arisen in Japan, there was no evidence to indicate that Chinese Christians had a faulty concept of the nature of the Christian God.

Unfortunately the debate was argued out in the speculative field where the uncertainties of terrain rendered a meeting of minds impossible. The controversy revolved around an effort to determine the original meaning of these terms in Confucian thought. Even today scholars, while agreed that the position of the pro-Ricci group was basically sound, are hesitant before some of the problems disputed at Kiating.[7]

The importance of this point lies in the fact that what happened in this debate happened again in the controversy about the Chinese rites. A problem essentially practical in character became the subject of a speculative controversy bristling with uncertainties.

To understand the rites problem it is necessary to know something about Confucian thought, which was the basis of the entire Chinese social and political system. The central concept is harmony. The Confucian world is an ordered universe in which the object of man's striving is the maintenance of harmonious relations with nature, with himself, and with his fellowman. If for nature one substitutes God, this statement would be an exact formulation of one of the fundamental theses of Catholic moral philosophy.

The chief weakness of his system stemmed from Confucius' fundamental agnosticism and his innocence of metaphysics. This is why nature took the place of God. Possibly because there, rather than in any other of its manifestations, the greatest order, symmetry, and serenity seemed to prevail, nature came to mean chiefly astral phenomena.

It was a major concern to bring human events and human decisions into accord with the stately movement of the heavenly bodies. This explains the importance given to astronomy in China and to the preparation of the calendar. High affairs of state and low affairs of family were decided with an eye upon the calendar. Faulty calculation upset the balance between heaven and earth. It disrupted the harmony between nature and man. It introduced discord and disorder into the harmonious and ordered Confucian world. It threw the smoothly operating machinery out of gear. Hamlet is a Confucianist when he attributes the disasters of his day to the fact that "the times are out of joint."

The major emphasis of Confucius' thought, however, was upon harmonious regulation of the relations between men. It is this which accounts for the predominantly social character of the Confucian ethic. It is this phase of his system which has impressed itself most deeply upon the Chinese mind.

Society is governed by five fundamental relations: sovereign and subject, parents and child, husband and wife, older brother and younger brother, friend and friend. There is harmony and order in society when the reciprocal duties which spring out of these relationships are observed. Neglect of these duties wounds the social organism, destroys the harmony of the universe, and thus does violence to the moral order.

The most important of the five relationships, and the exemplar of the others, is that of parent and child. The central virtue governing this relationship is *hsiao:* filial piety. Upon that primary virtue, and through the accompanying virtues of obedience, respect, and service which it implied the structure of Chinese society had in the main been erected. To it, more than to any other factor, were the stability and continuity of that society due.

Only with this in mind is it possible to understand the so-called Chinese rites. In view of the importance which Confucius had given to *hsiao*, it is not surprising that he should, by a logical projection of his thought, have insisted that for the dutiful child the exercise of filial piety must not cease with the death of his parents. He must continue to serve them dead as though they were still living. No less logical was it to extend the obligation to all the familial ancestors.

This did not imply metaphysical or even religious views on the part of Confucius as to survival after death. The Occidental naturally tends to infer this, inasmuch as he can see no point in rendering service to those who have died unless they still survive. But it must be recognized that in this respect Confucius was an agnostic. His only reference to life after death is his reply to a question put to him by a disciple: "Why do you ask me about life after death who know so little about life before death?"[8] He neither affirms nor denies immortality. He gives no indication of being concerned about it. His concern, and the concern of his entire teaching, was with this life. It can scarcely be doubted, therefore, that his insistence upon the discharge of the duties of filial piety towards those who had died had as its object the fostering of that virtue in this life.

In this he was not deceived. By projecting the obligations of the virtue beyond the limits of time and space Confucius succeeded in investing it with a transcendent importance among the living which it would not otherwise have enjoyed.

Towards the living, filial piety could operate in the form of actual services rendered. Towards the dead, the virtue could operate only in the form of ceremonial acts symbolizing the abiding will to render such services. This was the function and the meaning of the ancestral rites. In the place of acts of obeisance to living progenitors there were substituted similar acts directed towards ancestral tablets, wooden plaques bearing the names of the ancestors. To these tablets were directed expressions of reverence and respect; on days prescribed by ritual, offerings of food were made to the ancestors represented by the ancestral tablet. The food was then consumed in a family banquet. In essence these were the ancestral rites.

The rites observed in honor of Confucius did not differ essentially from ancestral ceremonies. Only the scholar class, however, performed the Confucian ceremonies, whereas all Chinese observed the ancestral rites. The cult of Confucius was of comparatively late development in China. It was natural that the posthumous honors accorded him should have modelled themselves after the ancestral rites.

The ceremonies in honor of Confucius were of two kinds. Rather simple ceremonies accompanied the conferring of the *hsiu-ts'ai* degree upon successful candidates. These ceremonies were held in a hall dedicated to Confucius. Upon receiving their degree from the presiding officer the candidates performed the customary obeisance to a tablet representing the Sage. Similar rites, obeisance and the burning of incense, were observed by officials and scholars at the new moon and the full moon. Solemn ceremonies were held on certain days of the year which in their external aspects had nearly all the appearances of religious sacrifice: the offering of an animal slain on the spot, of wine, silk, and so forth, followed by a solemn banquet.

To a Christian observer these ceremonies must be disturbing. On their face they seem clearly to suggest a religious cult. This is especially true of the solemn ceremonies just described. To a less extent it was true of the ancestral rites. At the least they seemed to imply certain preternatural beliefs. If one took literally certain of the expressions by which the ancestral tablets were apostrophized, one could hardly fail to conclude that the ancestral spirits were thought to dwell in the plaque itself, referred to as the "seat of the spirit."

The first impulse of Ricci had been so to interpret them; but Ricci had not been long in China before he discovered that things are not always what they seem. There were many reasons to doubt the validity of the obvious interpretation of the rites. Elaborate ceremonial played a considerable part in Chinese life, as might be expected of an ethic which stressed the concept of order and harmony. It was not certain that ritualistic acts, which to the Occidental immediately suggested superstition or religious adoration, were to the Chinese any more than the symbolic expression of the virtue *hsiao*. The fact that many of these same acts were in common use as part of the ceremonial observed towards the living suggested the wisdom of reserve in interpreting them in a religious sense when applied to the dead. This was notably so in the case of the burning of incense. This custom was in universal use in Chinese society and had no religious connotation. It was the custom for a well-bred host to receive his guest with incense, as part of the ceremonial of etiquette which gave grace and harmony to social relations. It was a simple mark of honor and respect. Was there then reason to think it any more than that when used at funerals, at ceremonies before the ancestral tablets, or in the hall of Confucius? To the Westerner incense suggested religious cult. Did it make the same suggestion to the Chinese?

Another noteworthy example was the ceremonial of obeisance, called the *k'o-t'ou* (or kotow), in which one kneels and bows profoundly until the forehead touches the floor. When the missionaries from Manila saw this act being performed before the coffins of the recently deceased and before ancestral tablets, they immediately pronounced it adoration.[9] Among Europeans such a profound obeisance is reserved for acts of adoration directed to the Divinity. Was it legitimate to infuse Chinese symbols with European interpretative values? The fact that the *k'o-t'ou* was widely used among the living without religious connotation strongly suggested the contrary. Those received in imperial audiences *k'o-t'ou*'ed nine times to the emperor's throne. Those appearing before government tribunals directed the *k'o-t'ou* to the presiding officer, children to their parents and parents-in-law. Symbols mean no more than they are meant to mean.

Other reasons to question the superstitious or idolatrous character of the rites lay in the agnosticism of Confucius himself and in the frank materialism of Sung neo-Confucianism. It seemed improbable that in the eyes of Confucius the rites had a religious significance. As for the neo-Confucianists, they denied the survival of any human soul, including that of Confucius, and at the same time were the most insistent upon the faithful observance of the ancestral rites and the rites in honor of the Sage.

These were the factors which caused Ricci to revise his original opinion. As usual his attitude was distinguished by an absence of dogmatism in matters of uncertain opinion. He was satisfied that the Confucian ceremonies were not superstitious. As for the ancestral rites, his final judgment was one of reserve. After studying the subject at length and discussing the rites with his Chinese friends he concluded that "all this has nothing to do with idolatry, and perhaps it can also be said not to involve any superstition, although it will be better to change this into giving alms to the poor where it is a question of Christians."[10]

Neither Ricci nor those who followed him ever went beyond this contention. They all conceded that the view which condemned the rites as superstitious was the "safer doctrine." They claimed no more than a probability that the rites were not in themselves superstitious and so long as that probability existed they had no right to demand as an obligation of conscience that Chinese Christians abandon these usages so central to their social and political way of life.

As Jacques Le Favre put it:

> Every people has its own customs and its own way of judging things. Neither charity nor prudence permit [us] to impose [our] own measure of judgment upon others and thus condemn the innocent as guilty before the case is thoroughly understood.[11]

Ricci submitted his opinions to Valignano who discussed the problem with his consultors in conferences held in 1603 and in 1605. These discussions terminated in an endorsement of Ricci's views and Valignano issued a set of directives for the guidance of missionaries.[12] It was this document which formally determined Jesuit policy vis-à-vis the rites, prescribed the limits within which they were to be permitted, and pointed out the measures to be taken to make sure that Christians in observing them kept themselves free from the taint of superstitious beliefs. Because the document itself has not been found in any of the archives, what it allowed and what it disallowed must be determined from an examination of the actual policy pursued by the Jesuits.

They did not allow Christian scholars to participate in the solemn ceremonies in honor of Confucius. Their testimony on this head is unanimous and categoric, and the Holy See in its final decision banning the rites acknowledged this fact. After admitting that they permitted Christian scholars to take part in the simple ceremonies accompanying the awarding of the degree of *hsiu-ts'ai*, Furtado adds that participation in the solemn ceremonies "we under no conditions permit because it strongly smacks of superstition."[13] Prosper Intorcetto, writing in 1668, is equally emphatic: "The Fathers who preceded us in the China mission did not allow Christians [to take part] in these [solemn] Confucian rites . . . nor do we ever allow [them]."[14]

As explained by Le Favre, these ceremonies had "nearly all" the external appearances of what constitutes the "essence of a sacrifice strictly understood." However empty of superstitious belief might be the a-religious minds of the scholars participating in the ceremonies, the simple citizen looking on might easily interpret them in a literal sense.

Clearly the same objection could be raised against the toleration of the other rites. But in the other rites the appearance of superstition was not so strong. Here, it was thought, the danger, which admittedly existed, could be more easily offset by education and instruction. It was a matter of balancing risks, of prudential judgment rather than of logical categories. In the one case it was thought the risk was too great to be undergone; in the other case it was the confident hope that the danger could be surmounted.

The Jesuits permitted participation in the solemn rites observed in honor of familial ancestors upon condition that the burning of paper money be eliminated; that the participants repudiate any notion that the spirits of the dead derived sustenance from the food offerings; that no prayers or petitions be directed to the dead. The first condition was based upon the erroneous idea that this particular ceremony was of Buddhist origin.

Inasmuch as the danger of contamination could not be entirely eliminated except by weaning the Christians away from these deeply rooted customs, this too was part of the policy. In the words of Furtado:

> As far as in us lies we try to bring Christians to give up these practices. When we are unable to do so, we tolerate them with St. Augustine in whose day similar exaggerations in oblations were practiced by Christians upon the tombs of the dead, when St. Augustine was the coadjutor of Hippo and the future successor of St. Valerian. In these practices the holy Doctor condemned only the belief that the souls of their dead

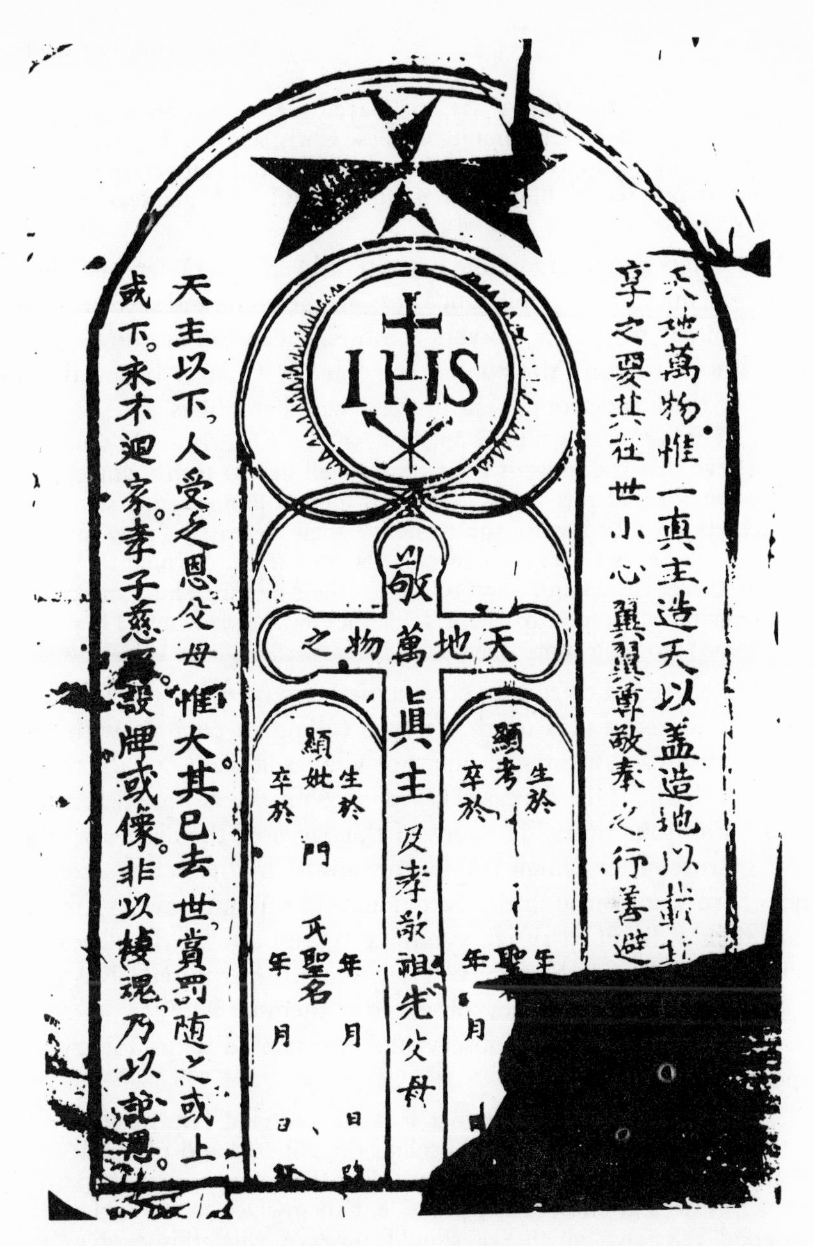

Photostat of an early Ch'ing Christian ancestral tablet, the original of which is in the *Bibliothèque National de Paris*. The text within the outline of the cross says: "Worship the true Lord, creator of heaven, earth and all things, and show filial piety to ancestors and parents." The text in the side columns explains the Christian attitude: It is through father and mother that one receives his greatest favors from God. After death, whether they receive punishment or reward, they will not return home. "Therefore," the instruction concludes, "the filial son or kind grandson sets up a tablet or a picture by no means that their spirits might dwell therein, but in order to serve as a reminder of his debt."

> came to eat and drink what was placed there. This error, as I have said, is not found among Chinese Christians. St. Augustine undertook to do away with these and similar [exaggerations] not at one severe blow, but gradually and with gentle condescension.[15]

The Jesuits also tolerated the custom of keeping a tablet, inscribed with the names of the family ancestors, in the home and surrounding it with marks of honor: flowers, candles, incense. Furtado rejects, not without sarcasm, the contention that the Chinese believed the spirits of their ancestors dwelt in these wooden tablets:

> The Chinese gentiles, much less the Christians, do not believe that the souls of their dead dwell like so many worms in the pores of this wood. . . . Their intention in erecting such tablets inscribed with the name of their deceased father or grandfather is to set up a certain place or term to which they can direct their minds; and to it as to their picture, show those accustomed honors to them as if they were present. [They intend] nothing more than this.[16]

There were other simple ceremonies observed by the Chinese upon the occasion of a death. Friends calling to condole with the family put on a mourning garment of white silk. Entering the room where the body of the deceased lay in its coffin, the visitor performed the *k'o-t'ou* four times. The sons of the deceased then repeated the same gesture, after which the visitor, advancing nearer the coffin, once more went through the ceremony. The Jesuits saw in this no more than a dignified ritual, symbolic of respect for the deceased and of sympathy for the family. They not only permitted Christians to observe this custom, they observed it themselves. Furtado categorically denies that these observances are tainted with idolatry or superstition:

> It is abundantly clear that it is a mere civil [rite] established for the purpose of consoling the afflicted and of manifesting sorrow at another's death. For this reason our fathers permit it, and on occasion practice it themselves, as far as the good relations which we should observe with this people require.[17]

Such, in its essentials, was the Jesuit practice vis-à-vis the rites. In view of the sharp differences of opinion that existed among them in the question of Christian terminology, it is interesting that there was no difference of opinion among them about the rites policy. Difficulties arose about the application of the principles laid down by Valignano to concrete cases and these were ironed out among themselves, but there was agreement on the principles. Longobardo would later be cited by Navarrete as an enemy of the rites; but Navarrete was wrong. Strongly as he disagreed with the prevailing view in the matter of terminology, Longobardo agreed with the others about the rites.

In the controversy which followed, the Jesuits took the position that the rites were originally mere civil ceremonies which had in the course of time become infected with erroneous preternatural or superstitious beliefs. This they attempted to prove by appealing with considerable scholarship to the original Confucian texts. They then argued that these beliefs were already widely abandoned and that it was therefore possible to purge the rites of the superstitious accretions and restore them to their primitive purity. In modern terminology their contention was that the rites were in process of being laicized.

In their argument they assumed that the rites had originated with Confucius and that in studying them as they appeared in his writings one saw them in their original character. There they appeared essentially as filling a functional role directed to the cultivation of *hsiao* and with little or no indication of superstition. This view, however, failed to explain satisfactorily the strongly superstitious appearance of the rites. If they had originated as mere civil ceremonies why had they been given a liturgy so strongly suggestive of religious beliefs?

Had the Jesuits possessed the data which later archeological studies would make available to the twentieth century they could have made a stronger and more satisfying argument. The truth is that the rites did not originate with Confucius, but long before in the animistic superstitions of primitive Chinese society. By the time of Confucius they had already been to a large extent laicized in the sense that the animistic beliefs in which they had originated were no longer generally held and had lost precision and importance. Yet the rites, with long tradition behind them, continued to be observed. Confucius simply incorporated them into his system.

Confucius was not an originator. He called himself "only a transmitter and not a maker, believing in and loving the ancients."[18] His object was to restore and conserve the traditions of the past, among which were the rites. Their preternatural suggestiveness concerned him not at all. Since they were admirably suited to foster the virtue of *hsiao*, he simply made them a part of his teaching.

Because of the survival of the external ritualistic forms, with their symbolism strongly suggestive of the superstitious beliefs in which they had originated, these beliefs themselves never wholly ceased to exist. Because they were largely laicized, however, the extent to which the beliefs survived varied almost without limit. There were Chinese, and this was true of the majority of the scholar class, who observed the rites as a part of good citizenship while positively repudiating belief in the survival of the soul. There were those, probably the largest number, who observed them without concerning themselves one way or the other about the questions suggested by the symbolism. There were those who, in observing them, felt a strong presentiment of the preternatural, but whose beliefs remained vague and imprecise. Finally, there were those who explicitly subscribed to the beliefs in which the rites had first originated: who believed that the spirits of the dead derive nourishment from the exhalations of the food offerings, that the burned paper money is converted into useful gold in the other world. The Jesuits by no means held that the Chinese people were relatively free from superstition. On the contrary, they fully recognized that China was rife with superstitions, most of which they attributed to Taoism; but the only question at issue was the extent to which superstitious beliefs were held respecting the rites.

The real crux of the question was whether the process of laicization had proceeded so far that the rites could be performed by Christians as merely civil ceremonies without being contaminated by the external suggestiveness of the liturgy. Because of preoccupation with the speculative question of the original meaning of the rites, the disputants did not center enough attention upon this question. However, the Jesuits, upon the basis of their fifty years' experience, were confident that the facts merited an affirmative answer. There was no evidence to indicate that Christians did in fact subscribe to superstitious beliefs.

An analogous problem had arisen in the early Church and was settled by the Council of Elvira in 303 in favor of tolerance. In permitting Christians to discharge the duties of the flaminat, an office associated with the imperial cult, the Council proceeded upon the theory, as two eminent specialists in the study of Christian antiquities put it: "That the *line which separates Christian discipline* from idolatry could change its position by reason of the *laicization of idolatry*."[19]

This was substantially the position of the Jesuits in the Chinese rites controversy. However, in the end the Holy See decided against them. Later, and long after the question had ceased to be of critical importance, the Holy See returned to the problem and in a decree of December 8, 1939, authorized Christians to participate in the ceremonies honoring Confucius, which the Chinese government had declared to be mere civil ceremonies, and also to perform the ancient "manifestations of civil respect before the deceased or before pictures of the deceased or even a tablet inscribed with only the name of the deceased. . . ."[20] Times had changed. In 1939 the Holy See was persuaded that the process of laicization had evolved to a point where the rites could be tolerated without endangering the purity of the faith.

If there is no reason to criticize their concern for the integrity of the faith, there are grounds upon which to criticize the manner in which the missionaries from the Philippines initiated the controversy. They were hasty, leaped to conclusions, and demanded immediate solutions to thorny problems to which there was no easy answer.

Thus Antonio a Santa Maria, a novice in China, is taking his first lessons in Chinese. His instructor attempts to explain the character *ch'i*. Antonio translates it as "sacrifice," and since this word is used with reference to the Confucian and ancestral ceremonies he immediately concludes that these are superstitious.[21] Yet it is clear that whether *ch'i* is rightly translated "sacrifice" in a theological sense depends upon the prior determination of the nature and meaning of the ceremonies rather than the other way around.

Then there is the matter of the two *Informaciones* which brought the question out into the public forum. The information, evidence, and conclusions represented the opinion of four missionaries, two of whom, Antonio and de Morales, had been in China two and a half years, two of whom, Francisco Dias and Francisco de la Madre de Dios, had been in China thirteen months; and of eleven Chinese living in two or three small villages in a province into which Christianity had been introduced less than ten years before. The four missionaries devoted two weeks to the compilation of the first

Información and some eighteen days to the second, a record of summary judgment which is highlighted rather cruelly when placed alongside the chronology of conference, discussion, and debate about the question of Christian terminology.

The same impatience is shown by de Morales who was unwilling to await an answer to the twelve questions he submitted in 1639 to Manoel Dias before carrying the matter to Rome. His apologists have argued that deliberate delay by the Jesuits was responsible. A simple chronology of events refutes this contention. De Morales submitted his questions to Dias in a letter of June 3, 1639; but on the previous February 15 he had sent a long memorandum to Rome to *Propaganda Fide*.

Dias replied to de Morales on June 4, informing him that he would transmit the questions to Furtado, the vice-provincial. Furtado in turn sent them to Vagnoni, ablest exponent of the Jesuit policy, to be answered. Vagnoni's answer was returned within six months. In view of the fact that he was in the distant province of Shensi it is absurd to contend that there was deliberate delay.

De Morales embarked for Manila from Macao in April, 1640. The archbishop of Manila and the bishop of Cebu, on the basis of the *Informaciones* of 1637, had written to Rome condemning the Jesuit practices. Later, upon hearing the Jesuit defense, both wrote again to Rome retracting their charges. Their religious superiors now decided to send both de Morales and Antonio to Rome. They set sail in May, 1640. Arrived in Macao, Antonio chose to remain there while de Morales continued to Rome.

De Morales submitted to *Propaganda Fide* a series of questions on the permissibility of the rites. His description of the rites assumed as established all the questions that were in fact disputed. In view of the manner in which they were described it was certain that the Congregation would condemn them. It did so in a decree of September 12, 1645.[22]

Convinced that the rites had been misrepresented, the Jesuits sent one of their most learned men, Martin Martini, to represent their views. Martini had met de Morales in Goa in 1641 when the latter was en route to Rome. The statement of *dubia* which Martini submitted to the Congregation is a terse and straightforward description of the various rites as practiced by the Chinese. Omitted was the solemn Confucian rite because this, not being permitted by the missionaries, did not enter into the case. Together with this document he also submitted a long brief. In it he appealed to the authority of Ricci, who was known in Europe through Trigault's *De Christiana Expeditione*, of de Pantoia, Furtado, Dias, and others. He argued that the description of the rites by de Morales was misleading and pointed out that the conclusions of the mendicants had been reached upon the basis of an experience limited to a few small villages and to contacts with unlettered rustics.

The result was another decree, issued on March 23, 1656, permitting Christians to practice the rites under the conditions observed by the Jesuits.[23] There is no contradiction here, as some have claimed. If the rites were what de Morales had said they were, they could not be tolerated. If Martini's description was correct, they could be permitted. That, in effect, is what each decree said.

The subsequent history of the rites controversy falls outside the purview of this work. Before it ended it had solicited the attention of Popes Urban VIII, Innocent XII, Alexander VII, Clement XI, Innocent XIII, Benedict XIII, Clement XII, and Benedict XIV. It had led to the repeated intervention of the Congregation *de Propaganda Fide* and of the Holy Office, and to two apostolic legations to China. On November 20, 1704, a decree of the Holy Office banned the rites. On March 19, 1715, Clement XI in the Bull *Ex illa die*, reaffirmed the prohibition in more solemn form. On July 11, 1742, Benedict XIV, in the Bull *Ex quo singulari*, again forbade any toleration of the rites and banned further debate under pain of severe ecclesiastical penalties.

Actually the favorable decree of 1656 may have ill served the Jesuit cause. The Jesuits in China, confident that this decree had said the final word on the subject, were lulled into a false sense of security. Far removed from the scene of battle, they were unable to realize the intensity with which the controversy raged in Europe and the seriousness of the danger to their position. Busy with their work, they ignored repeated appeals from the general for documentation to assist the Roman theologians who were trying to defend their cause. Not until the end of the century did the general succeed in arousing them to a realization of the gravity of the situation. They then hastily despatched Gaspar Castner and François Noel, able sinologist, to Rome to present their case. It was too late. By the time they reached the Eternal City at the end of 1702 minds had been made up.

The practical effect of the prohibition of the rites was twofold. By banning the Confucian ceremonies it made it impossible for a scholar-official to become a Christian or for a Christian to become a scholar, thus destroying the possibility of those sympathetic *rapports* upon which, in the Jesuit method, the peaceful penetration of Chinese society had been based. By banning the ancestral rites the Church was forced to assume a posture that seemed hostile to the Chinese environment. Instead of leaven Christianity became a foreign substance in the body of Chinese social culture. It meant the effective ending of the policy of cultural adaptation. If these consequences were fully understood by the Holy See, it must have felt that the integrity of the faith required payment of so high a price.

Where there is clear conflict between purity of doctrine and the principle of accommodation there is only one course open to the Church, no relativist in matters of religious faith. But there may arise problems where it is far from certain that the conflict exists. The matter of forming a sound prudential judgment then becomes extremely difficult.

This was the situation created by the question of the rites. The obscurity surrounding their origins, the contradiction between their seeming preternatural implications and the professed materialism of many of their most observant practitioners, the uncertainty of the extent to which the people as a whole interpreted them in a superstitious sense, were the elements which made the problem one of peculiar complexity. The Jesuits, not without much debate and exhaustive scrutiny, concluded that with proper precautions Christians could be permitted to practice at least some of the rites without compromising the integrity of their faith. Eventually and after long uncertainty the Holy See decided that the risks were too great. In doing so it exonerated the Jesuits of bad faith. The fact that when essentially the same question came up three hundred years later in Japan and again in China all the old doubts, uncertainties, and differences of opinion immediately arose is enough to indicate the complexity of the problem. In the latter case the Holy See decided that historical circumstances and the evolution of thought permit a policy of tolerance. In the earlier day the Holy See decided that, contrary to the Jesuit view, the circumstances of the time and the state of thought did not permit a policy of tolerance. That, in its simplest terms, is the story of the rites problem.

NOTES

(1) The history of this debate can be largely reconstructed from the documents listed by Robert Streit, O.M.I., *op. cit.*, V, 728-779.

(2) The problem of terminology in Japan has been dealt with by Georg Schurhammer, S. J., *Das Kirchliche Sprachproblem in der Japanischen Jesuitenmission des 16 und 17. Jahrhunderts* (Tokyo: Deutsche Gesellschaft für natür- und völkerkunde Ostasiens, 1928).

(3) This treatise, entitled *Reposta breve sobre as Controversias do Xamty, Tien Xin, Lim hoên, e outros Nomes e termos sinicos; par se determinar quaes delles podem ou não podem uzarse nesta Xrandade*, is found in the archives of *Propaganda Fide: APF*, SR Congr. I, ff. 145-168. This copy of the Portuguese original was made by Fray Antonio de Santa Maria for *Propaganda.* With it he sent his own Latin translation, *ibid.*, ff. 171-197.

(4) *ARSI*, Jap-Sin 161, f. 99r.

(5) The story of the Kiating conference is told in a document found in the archives of *Propaganda Fide: APF, Inform. Lib. 157*, f. 348. It is entitled: *Brevis ac Historica Relatio Controversiae de Ritibus aliquot Sinicis, ac Vocibus ad Appelandum Deum Optimum Maximum abhibendum.* The text is incomplete and hence unsigned. The author is very probably Gaspar Castner, S. J., who came to Rome from China in 1702 to represent the Jesuit cause with the Holy See in the rites controversy. His account of the Kiating meeting is based upon two letters of Palmeiro, one of May 8, 1628, the other of January 31, 1631, and a letter of Manoel Dias, who presided at the conference, written November 18, 1629. Domingo Navarrete, O.P., printed what he claimed were the minutes of the Kiating conference in his *Controversias antiguas y modernas de la mission de la gran China* (Madrid, 1679), pp. 109-138. This work was suppressed by the Inquisition before it was completed and there are but a few copies in existence, one in *ARSI*, FG 728. Navarrete's account of how these "minutes" (according to which Longobardo's position emerged triumphant) came into his hands years after the meeting would make a sceptic of the most credulous. Despite Rosso's airy dismissal of the charge (Rosso, *op. cit.*, p. 101, n. 21), these "minutes" are certainly a forgery as was demonstrated long ago by the author of *Monumenta sinica* (1700, s.l.), pp. 22-100.

(6) Bartoli, *op. cit.*, IV, 240 f.

(7) Cf. Y. C. Yang, *China's Religious Heritage* (New York: Abingdon-Cokesbury Press, 1943).

(8) *Analects*, ix, 11:1.

(9) *2 Inf.* fols. 29, 30, quoted by Maas, *op. cit.*, p. 90, n. 101.

(10) *FR*, I, 118.

(11) Jacques Le Favre, S. J., "Responsio ad dubitationem a R. P. Dominico Navarrete propositas seu brevis synopsis de cultu Sinico Confucii ac mortuorum," in Brancato, *op. cit.*, p. 14.

(12) Streit, *op. cit.*, V, 728.

(13) Furtado, *Responsio,* pp. 16 f.

(14) Prospero Intorcetta, S. J., *Testimonium de cultu Sinensi datum anno 1668* (Paris: N. Pepié, 1700), p. 141.

NOTES

(15) *Responsio*, p. 22.

(16) *Ibid.*, pp. 29 f.

(17) *Ibid.*, p. 24.

(18) *Analects*, vii, 1.

(19) Louis Bréhier et Pierre Batiffol, *Les survivances du culte impérial romain, à propos des rites shintoiste* (Paris: Auguste Picard, 1920), 12.

(20) *Acta Apostolicae Sedis* (Roma: Polyglot Press, 1909 et seq.), XXXII (1940), pp. 24 f. for the full text of the decree.

(21) Francisco Varo, *Historia de China*, cap. 15, quoted by Perez, *op. cit.*, *AFH*, II, 553, n. 2.

(22) *Collectanea S: Congregationis de Propaganda Fide* (Roma: ex typographia polyglotta, 1897), pp. 653-655 gives the text of the decree.

(23) *Ibid.*, p. 655 f., gives the *dubia* and the decree. Martini's autograph copies of his long Latin brief together with two shorter briefs in Italian, all addressed to the cardinals of *Propaganda Fide*, are in *ARSI*, FG 724, regis. 5, n. 1.

Chapter XVIII

Green Fields

EXCEPT FOR THE setback suffered in Fukien, the Church made notable advances during the 1630's. Outstanding was the work of Vagnoni in Shansi. Aided in his apostolate by a group of scholars, he made that province one of the main centers of Christian activity in the empire.[1] His most stalwart supporters were the brothers (Thomas) Han Lin and (Stephen) Han Yün. At their instance Vagnoni visited Chiangchow in 1625. They built a church and a residence for him and, with their friend and fellow townsman, (Peter) Tuan Kun, became his zealous assistants. Han K'uang, an uncle of the Han brothers, who had held the office of grand secretary in Peking, was hardly less devoted to Vagnoni, although not himself a Christian. Through him the faith entered the city of Puchow, important not only because of its size and prosperity, but because it was a mecca for Shansi scholars. Han K'uang urged Vagnoni to visit Puchow and prepared his way in the scholarly circles of the city. When Vagnoni arrived he received a cordial welcome. When he left at the end of four months he had laid the foundations for a Christian center which within a few years rivalled that of Chiangchow.

In 1634 Han K'uang provided Vagnoni with a residence. Three years later the number of Christians in Puchow had become so large that it was necessary to give them a permanent pastor. Ignacio da Costa was transferred from Shensi for this purpose. This freed Vagnoni to attend to the needs of other communities.

His tireless zeal won the admiration of fellow Jesuits. Three years earlier, in 1634, Francisco Furtado, after completing a visit to the twelve Jesuit residences in the empire, had written a report to the general in which he signalled out Vagnoni and Longobardo for special praise:

> I found in all twenty-three of our European priests and in the four Chinese brothers, natives of Macao, great zeal for the conversion of souls and for their own perfection. But above all, I derived the greatest consolation from Father Alfonso Vagnoni, in the province of Shansi, and Father Nicolò Longobardo, in the imperial province of Peking. Both are well advanced in age, having passed their seventieth year, and both labor in this vineyard of the Lord as if they were but thirty years old.[2]

Shansi during these years offered full opportunity for the practice of Christian charity. From 1633 to 1641 it was ravaged by famine. Preceded by eight months "without a drop of rain or the shadow of a cloud," the disaster struck in 1633. It was the worst famine in the memory of the oldest people living. Desolation and death stalked through the province. In Chiangchow the streets were covered with corpses. Outside the city walls four large ditches were filled with bodies.

The famine passed its zenith within eight months, but starvation and want continued to haunt the province for six years. On the heels of the famine a raging epidemic swept through the province. Banditry, the normal consequence of such conditions, raised its head on all sides to add to the general terror. Driven by desperation, men roamed the province, in unorganized mobs and organized armies, pillaging and slaying, looting and burning. The wild disorder spilled over from Shansi into the provinces of Shensi and Honan.

In Chiangchow Vagnoni established the first orphanage mentioned in the annals of the mission. He rented a house for his purpose in 1634, putting in charge Father Etienne Le Fèvre and (Manoel) Lu Yu-chi, a Macaist lay-brother. Soon they were caring for three hundred children. The work received the approbation and support of the governor. From this beginning the work spread throughout the province. Wherever possible Vagnoni established similar institutions under the administration of lay Christians.

In his untiring efforts in behalf of the distraught people of Shansi, Vagnoni was ably supported by his Christians. The first to contribute to famine relief in Chiangchow were Han Lin and Han Yün. Han Lin, in addition to five hundred *taels* of silver given by himself, raised a subscription of an equal amount.[3] Tuan Kun, besides distributing food to hungry crowds at his gate, converted his home into an orphanage and quasi-hospital. As many as one hundred orphans were in his home. It became a common sight in Chiangchow to see Tuan making his way towards his home with an abandoned baby in each arm. When his wife protested, he laughed at her and urged her to be a Christian in deed and not in name alone. His arguments and example won her, as well as his younger brother and sister, over to his side. His sister, the wife of a wealthy non-Christian, was among the first to give her jewels to Vagnoni to be used to support his orphanages and hospitals.

Until two months before his death, Vagnoni carried on his unremitting labor with the spirit and energy of a young man. Finally, in February, 1640, while supervising the building of a church, he collapsed. Brought back to Chiangchow he lingered on for two months. Christians came from far and near to see him. On April 9, 1640, surrounded by as many of his flock as could crowd into the room, he died at the age of seventy-four.

As soon as word of his death spread abroad, officials, scholars, shopkeepers, peasants, and the poor, flocked to pay their respects. The head of a branch of the imperial family came in state. Han K'uang sent two members of his family from Puchow to represent him at the funeral. He also wrote a eulogy of Vagnoni which he wished to have read before his coffin in the presence of the scholarly elite of Chiangchow. A large number of scholars and officials, many of them non-Christians, composed similar eulogies in praise of Vagnoni's virtues and merits.

For eight days his body lay in state while groups of Christians maintained constant vigil, chanting their prayers beside the coffin. On the eighth day, after a solemn Mass of Requiem celebrated by Father Michel Trigault, the funeral procession wended its way to the burial ground, a gift of the Han family. Two thousand Christians walked in the procession; four hundred of them carried torches; another four hundred carried alms to be distributed to the poor. After them came the more prominent Christians, each one carrying a rosary in one hand, an incense burner in the other. They were followed by all the officials of the city, the Ming prince, and finally by Father Trigault in surplice and stole. Vagnoni's body was laid to rest amid scenes of unaffected grief.[4]

When Vagnoni entered Shansi there were no more than two dozen Christians, converts of Nicolas Trigault in the province. When he died there were more than eight thousand Christians in one hundred and two Christian communities. More than two hundred of these Christians were graduates in letters; some were important officials.

The mission suffered several other losses in this same year. After two years of paralysis, Lazzaro Cattaneo, companion of Ricci and founder of the Shanghai and Hangchow missions, passed away on January 19 in Hangchow.[5] In the same residence also died Pedro Ribeiro, who had struggled with poor health throughout his forty years in China. In Peking on August 26, the invaluable lay brother (Pascal) Ch'iu Liang-hou closed out his career. The previous year had witnessed the death of another grand old man of the mission, Manoel Dias, Senior. The only contemporaries of Ricci now left were Nicolò Longobardo, Gaspar Ferreira, and the younger Manoel Dias. One is struck by the longevity of many of these pioneers: Vagnoni, seventy-four; Cattaneo and the older Dias, both eighty; Ferreira would live to be seventy-eight, the younger Dias eighty-five, and Longobardo ninety-five!

As in Shansi, so in Shensi, these were years of growth for Christianity. The apostle of the latter province was Etienne le Fèvre, who began his missionary career as assistant to Vagnoni in Shansi in 1633-1634. In 1635 he had moved into Shensi where, except for a few years as aide to Schall in Peking in the early 1640's, he remained until his death. He was assisted at various times by Michel Trigault, Ignacio da Costa, Augusto Tudeschini, Jozé d'Almeida, and others. But to Le Fèvre goes much of the credit for the multiplication of Christian communities and the ever increasing number of conversions. At his death in 1657 there were 12,000 Christians in Shensi.[6]

Legend has pullulated about the name of Le Fèvre. Tales of prodigies performed by him — of lands delivered from locust plagues, of miraculous healings, of his taming the ferocious tigers in the Ch'in-ling mountains — became a persistent Shensi tradition which was kept alive by non-Christians and Christians alike. Over two centuries after his death the stories were still told. In 1873 the vicar-apostolic of Shensi wrote that his tomb was still the mecca of frequent pilgrimages by both Christians and non-Christians.[7] Whatever the truth of the legends, there is no doubt that Le Fèvre was a man of more than ordinary sanctity who greatly furthered the cause of Christianity in Shensi — and Shensi has kept his memory green.

In 1636 the aged Longobardo carried the faith to Shantung when he went to visit a grandson of Hsü Kuang-ch'i in Tsinan. At the time he carried the burden of caring for the Christian community in Peking, Schall and Rho having little time to spare from their labors in the calendrical bureau. He still managed, despite advancing age and dangers incident to increasing political disorders, to make an annual visit to Shantung. In 1641 at the age of eighty-two he fell into the hands of bandits who released him at the intervention of a resident prince of the imperial family in Chingchow. The prince and his family later entered the Church, but were swallowed up in the deluge of Manchu invasion. After 1649 Giovanni de Ferrariis took over the burden of the Shantung mission, but Longobardo seems to have continued his annual visits until shortly before his death in 1654 at the age of ninety-five.

In 1637 Antonio de Gouvea founded the first Christian community in Hukuang.[8] In 1640 Ludovico Buglio introduced the faith into Szechwan province. Two years later he was joined by Gabriel de Magalhães. It was the beginning of an inseparable companionship which death alone terminated thirty-five years later. They worked with no little success for the next year, establishing churches in the cities of Paoning and Chungching, as well as a number of chapels in nearby towns.

Along with the establishment of new Christian centers during the last years of the Ming era, the older missions forged steadily ahead. In Nanking, Sambiasi's tact and patience went far towards restoring the fortunes of his faith. The governor of the southern capital sent an agent to Macao in 1638 to facilitate the entry of more missionaries. Unfortunately only two priests were available and neither of them lived very long. Nicholas Fiva, a Swiss, died in Hangchow in 1640; and Michael Walta, a German, was murdered in 1644 by the ravaging soldiery of Li Tzu-ch'êng in the sack of Puchow.[9]

In 1638 the governor of Nanking also wrote the provincial authorities of Fukien defending Christianity and the missionaries and urging that they put an end to persecution in that province. He gave Sambiasi permission to build a new church in Nanking and, in public edicts, promised severe penalties against any who should commit outrages against the Christian edifice.

With funds raised by Nanking Christians, Sambiasi built a church within the city walls, near the western gate — the *Han-hsi-men.* A celebrated Nanking scholar composed a eulogy of Christianity which was engraved upon stone before the church door. On a hill outside the south gate the Christians established a cemetery where they raised a large stone cross which Sambiasi blessed before a large concourse of people.

Members of the Ch'in family were still among the most loyal Christians in Nanking. In 1643, Ignatius Ch'in had Sambiasi celebrate Mass on his flagship before setting sail for Peking with the annual shipment of rice destined for the court. Upon each of the five hundred ships in his fleet he raised a standard with a red cross, symbolic of his Christian faith, imposed upon the imperial yellow background.

Scene of the greatest expansion of Christianity in these years was the mission centering in Shanghai. In 1637 Francesco Brancato was assigned to this mission and for the next twenty-eight years carried on an outstandingly successful apostolate. Writing in 1650, Bartoli reported that Shanghai "has from eighteen to twenty thousand faithful and is one of the most splendid Christian centers in the empire."[10]

Much of the credit for his success belongs to Candida Hsü, granddaughter of Hsü Kuang-ch'i. Among the many remarkable women in Chinese history Candida Hsü (1607-1680) deserves a high place. As her grandfather is the outstanding layman in the history of the Catholic Church in China, so she stands at the head of Catholic laywomen.[11] Widowed at an early age, she devoted most of her long life to furthering the cause of Christianity. She was a dynamic force behind Brancato. She it was who won for him the good will of officials in the areas he served. Most of the one hundred and thirty-five churches and chapels left by Brancato were made possible by her generosity.

No doubt many of these "churches" were chapels and many of the "chapels" oratories, but several were full-sized churches, just how many it is impossible to say. Among them was the church in Sungkiang and that in Soochow. Madame Hsü financed the construction of the former, and she and a military commander that of the latter. To the church in Soochow the Shun-chih emperor sent a golden-lettered inscription: *Ch'in-ch'ung t'ien-tao* (Revere the Celestial Doctrine). Through all the vicissitudes of later years Shanghai remained one of the two most flourishing centers of Roman Catholicism on the Asiatic continent. The other was Peking.

The fortune of Christianity in Peking shared in the general wave of expansion. Missionary work was not confined to the city but extended over a wide area outside the capital. In 1637 there were sixteen Christian communities at varying distances from Peking. Stationed in the capital were Longobardo, Schall and, until his death in 1638, Rho. Others were there for short periods of time including Walta (1640-1641) and Le Fèvre (1641-1642).

Schall and Rho were chiefly occupied with their scientific tasks. Early in 1635 the last installment of their series of translations was presented to the throne by (Peter) Li T'ien-ching. The collection, in 137 *chüan*, was printed under the title *Ch'ung-chên li-shu* (Ch'ung-chên Astronomy Books). It has since been reprinted many times under different titles. Under the title *Hsin-fa suan-shu* (New Method of Calculation) it was copied, in 100 *chüan*, into the *Sse-k'u* manuscript library.

It was one thing to reform the calendar. It was quite another to obtain official adoption of the reform. Not until the advent of a new dynasty was Schall able to realize this objective. From the outset there was strong opposition rooted in the chauvinistic pride of a clique led by one Wei Kung. He was supported by "many powerful personages at the court," wrote Schall, "resentful that the honor of so important an undertaking has been entrusted to us foreigners and [resentful of] the esteem and benevolence of the emperor, they give every aid, whether of influence or money, to our adversaries."[12]

As long as Hsü Kuang-ch'i lived, Wei Kung was able to raise no effective opposition. But Li T'ien-ching was a man of different kidney. His choice as Hsü's successor was not a happy one. He lacked the energy and firmness to override opposition. Of a peace-loving disposition he was too inclined to yield to pressure in order to avoid friction. Furthermore, he had once been Wei Kung's pupil and felt constrained to defer to his old teacher.

In the hope of appeasing Wei, Li T'ien-ching asked the emperor to allow the old man to establish his own astronomical school. The court concluded from this that Li was not sure of the way things were going in the calendrical bureau and doubts were raised concerning the value of European astronomy. Wei was permitted to open his own school and the administrative expenses were paid by the state. It became a center of intrigue against the work of the Jesuits.

In 1638 Schall lost his associate, Giacomo Rho, and the full burden of the work fell upon his own shoulders.[13] Rho fell suddenly ill on the night of April 17, apparently suffering from food poisoning. The best doctors in Peking were called in, but were unable to diagnose his illness. The various treatments prescribed seemed only to aggravate his condition. On April 26 he insisted upon celebrating Mass, but collapsed immediately afterwards. By evening he was unconscious. Some hours later he recovered consciousness and, although unable to speak, fixed his eyes upon a crucifix held before him by Brother Ch'iu Liang-hou. At two hours past midnight he breathed his last. He was forty-seven years old and had been sixteen years in China.

Funeral services were held on May 5. A long procession wound its way from the church through the principal streets of Peking to Ricci's burial ground. In front walked members of the Christian community. They were followed by the coffin, carried by sixteen men. Behind came torch-bearers and incense-bearers. In the rear walked Li T'ien-ching, the members of the calendrical bureau, several eunuchs representing the emperor, and a large number of scholar-officials. In the chapel at the cemetery Longobardo sang a solemn Mass of Requiem and preached. After Mass the mourners filed slowly past the coffin, each one stopping to *k'o-t'ou.*

Until now the original subsidy granted for the maintenance of Schall and Rho scarcely sufficed for one of them. On his deathbed Hsü had called the emperor's attention to their niggardly allowance, but no action followed. Now, with Rho's death, the emperor, in recognition of his services, gave the Jesuits 2,000 *taels* to invest in income property. He also ordered that the sum of 12 *taels* be paid to Schall each month.[14]

In this same year the emperor conferred the highest mark of imperial favor possible in China, presentation of a *pai-pien,* i.e., four characters chosen by himself, embroidered in gold upon a silken scroll. The legend selected by the Son of Heaven read: "*Ch'in-pao t'ien-hsüeh*" (Imperial praise for the celestial doctrine). The words "*t'ien-hsüeh*" were ambiguous. They could be understood either as referring to astronomy or to Christianity. They had often been used by the Jesuits in their books in the latter sense. It was in this sense that the Christians chose to interpret them in the *pai-pien*.

On January 6, 1639, a high court official brought the imperial *pai-pien* to the Jesuit residence. Four heralds rode at the head of the procession to warn all passersby, of whatever rank or position, to *k'o-t'ou* when the imperial scroll passed by. Then came the scroll itself, carried by its custodian, and followed by a troop of mounted men and a glittering cortege of high officials.

Schall, Longobardo, Li T'ien-ching, the officials of the calendrical bureau, and the students of the academy, awaited the procession at the entrance to the residence. They received the scroll with the accustomed *k'o-t'ou*. It was displayed in the principal room of the house. A banquet followed, while a huge crowd, attracted by the concourse of dignitaries, milled about in the street outside.

Shortly after this the first ranking grand secretary sent a *pai-pien* eulogizing the Jesuits and the religion they taught. The president of the Board of Rites followed suit. His scroll announced that "the services of the two astronomers Schall and Rho equal those of Hsi and Ho" (two famous savants of legendary times). Copies of the imperial *pai-pien* were sent to all Jesuit residences in the empire. They were publicly displayed and local officials came to pay their respects.[15]

The *Imperial Gazette*, which was read throughout the empire, made the work of Schall and Rho known. For ten years the subject of calendar reform had been dealt with in numerous memorials and imperial rescripts. These had been widely read. Furthermore, the *Gazette*, which recorded all the emperor's activities, had publicized every mark of imperial esteem bestowed upon the Jesuits.

During these years Christianity for the first time penetrated the precincts of the palace. In 1632 two eunuchs, brothers, were converted by Longobardo and baptized under the names of Achilleus and Nereus. The former was P'ang T'ien-shou, who at a much later date would win renown as the stalwart supporter of the last Ming pretender. In 1632 neither he nor his brother was in a position to carry on an apostolate within the palace. They did, however, establish a first contact and in 1635, the conversion of another respected eunuch, named Wang, furnished Schall with his first effective aid within the Forbidden City. Through him Schall undertook to sow the seed of the Gospel among the women of the palace.[16]

These women were not, as one might suppose, concubines. Many were ladies-in-waiting to the emperor's consorts; but others were more than that. Inasmuch as no full-blown man was allowed to live within the Forbidden City, all palace offices were filled with eunuchs and with women, many of them well educated. Some women were secretaries. Others served as ghost-writers and produced the emperor's rescripts, edicts, and other documents.

Wang's first convert took the Christian name Catherine. The annual letter of 1637 speaks of eighteen women converted. Like the mandarinal order, the ladies had their own hierarchy. In 1637 of the twelve women who belonged to the highest grade, three were Christians: Donna Agatha, esteemed by the emperor for virtue and intelligence; the very zealous Donna Helena, and Donna Isabella. One of the converts, Lucia, belonged to the second class; four, Cecilia, Cyrene, Cyria, and Thecla, were members of the third class; eight belonged to the fourth class. Two others, Donna Agnes, nurse to several emperors, and Donna Antonia, both of whom belonged to the first class, were retired from active duty.

In 1638 the number of Christian women within the Forbidden City rose to twenty-one, in 1639 to forty, and in 1642 to fifty. They formed an unusual Christian community. Their only contact with the missionaries was by correspondence. Schall wrote instructions in Christian doctrine which Wang transmitted to them. They in turn wrote to Schall for spiritual direction, listing their faults and asking for forgiveness. A chapel was prepared for them within the palace. Here they met several times a week for common prayer and to receive instructions from Wang. Here too Wang baptized new converts. In 1640 Furtado, superior of the northern missions, appointed one of the ladies as directress of the community.

Although the contrary has at times been affirmed, it is extremely improbable that Schall ever celebrated Mass in the chapel of the palace ladies. He did on occasion celebrate Mass for Christian eunuchs within the palace; but he states clearly that the missionaries were unable to conduct services for women within the Forbidden City.[17]

The emperor was aware of the Christian ferment at work. He and the empress were impressed by the piety and zeal of the converts, some of whom did not hesitate to urge the emperor to follow their example. Only one of his consorts, a devout Buddhist, was hostile. It was even reported that the emperor had urged his consorts to become Christians.

In 1640 the spinet that Ricci had presented to the Wan-li emperor forty years earlier was found in the imperial storehouse. The emperor wanted to hear European music and Schall was summoned to repair the instrument. With the aid of the Jesuit lay-brother, (Christopher) Hsü Fu-yuan, who was called to Peking for the purpose, Schall put the spinet in order. He wrote directions for playing it, translated one of the Psalms into Chinese, and composed a plainsong accompaniment.

The presentation of the repaired spinet offered a long-awaited opportunity to give the emperor two other gifts. Two decades earlier Trigault had brought from Europe a number of presents from Maximilian, Duke of Bavaria. Because the presentation would have been published in the official gazette as tribute from Bavaria, they had not been presented. Among the gifts, so long withheld, were two works of Christian art: an illustrated life of Christ on one hundred and fifty parchment pages, and a lifelike representation, on finely colored wax, of the Adoration of the Magi. The first mentioned work contained forty-five pictures showing the principal scenes in Christ's life, with the appropriate Gospel text engraved on the facing page. Schall translated these texts into Chinese which he had engraved in golden letters on the back of the pictures. In addition, he wrote a more complete description of the life and death of Christ.

The two gifts, together with the spinet, were presented to the emperor on September 8, 1640. After the fall of the Ming dynasty in 1644 when the ladies-in-waiting returned to their families, one of them, Donna Helena, told Schall about the more than ordinarily favorable impression they had made upon the emperor. Usually, after a cursory examination of gifts, he turned them over to his eunuchs to be stored away. On this occasion, he sat down before the open book and the wax sculpture. He was so absorbed in examining them that he three times ignored the signal for dinner. He called the empress and, pointing to the infant Jesus, said: "He is greater than all our revered ancients." The empress *k'o-t'ou*'ed before the sculpture. Both gifts were set up in the throne room. Here they remained on display for ten days. The emperor had his consorts and chief eunuchs pay homage to them. After they were removed to the storeroom, the emperor often had them brought to him and spent long hours reading the Gospel texts and Schall's description of the life of Christ.[18]

These were years when, everywhere in China, the fields were green with promise and rapidly ripening for the harvest. The prevision of Ricci was now becoming a vision that all could see. Although it is idle to seek in figures an exact measure of the growth of Christianity, a glimpse of reality is offered in the statistics given by Martini. These represent the number of Chinese received into the Church up to the years indicated: in 1627, 13,000; in 1636, 40,000; in 1640, 60,000-70,000. Eleven years later the number had reached 150,000.[19]

If one has in mind how few were the missionaries at all times, how strong the prejudices they had to overcome, one will be strongly inclined to agree with Dr. Jann that these "astonishing results" of well under one hundred years of effort were "without parallel in the history of the Church."[20]

What these figures reveal beyond question is that, starting in the last decade of the Ming dynasty, the growth of Christianity began to assume geometric rather than arithmetic proportions. The Christian leaven was working as Ricci had anticipated.

If, however, the sun seemed to be rising upon the Christian cause in China, darkness was closing in upon the descendants of Chu Yuan-chang who, almost three hundred years before, had driven the Mongols from the Dragon Throne and founded a dynasty which he called *Ta Ming* (The Great Effulgence). The sands of time were running rapidly out.

NOTES

(1) Two of Vagnoni's letters tell of his work in Shansi, one to the older Dias, June 25, 1634, *ARSI*, Jap-Sin 161 II, ff. 154-155; the other to G. Ferrari, April 4, 1639, *ARSI*, Jap-Sin 161 II, ff. 219-220. Cf. also Bartoli, *op. cit.*, IV *passim* and Fortunato Margiotti, O.F.M., *Il cattolicismo nello Shansi dalle origini al 1738* (Roma: Edizioni "Sinica Franciscana," 1958), pp. 89-105.

(2) Bartoli, *op. cit.*, IV, 535 f.

(3) *Eminent Chinese*, I, 274.

(4) Bartoli, *op. cit.*, IV, 758.

(5) D'Elia in *FR*, I, 334, n. 5. There is an unsigned letter to the Portuguese Assistant dated January 1, 1641, which says, probably erroneously, that Cattaneo died in February, 1640; *ARSI*, Jap-Sin 161 II, f. 227.

(6) Everyone who has written on Le Fèvre has erroneously given the year of his death as 1659. The correct date has been established as 1657 by Francis A. Rouleau, S. J., "The Death of Stephen Faber, S. J." *Archivum Historicum Societatis Iesu*, *XXIX* (Roma, 1960), pp. 130-148.

(7) Cf. Pfister, *op. cit.*, I, 206.

(8) Annual letter of 1637, *ARSI*, Jap-Sin 115 II, ff. 370-435.

(9) Cf. Margiotti, *op. cit.*, pp. 137 f.

(10) Bartoli, *op. cit.*, III, 45 f.

(11) Cf. Phillipe [Philip] Couplet, S. J., *Histoire d'une dame chrétienne de la Chine* (Paris: Estienne Michallet, 1688).

(12) Bartoli, *op. cit.*, IV, 652, quoting from a letter of Schall's.

(13) His death is reported by Monteyro in the annual letter of 1638, *ARSI*, Jap-Sin 121, ff. 114-193, on f. 147v.

(14) Furtado to Dias, December 24, 1638, *ARSI*, Jap-Sin 161 II, f. 217r.

(15) Cf. Vagnoni's report from Shansi, April 25, 1639, in *ARSI*, Jap-Sin 161 II, f. 219r.

(16) Schall himself has told the story of the apostolate within the Forbidden City: cf. *Lettres et mémoires d'Adam Schall, S. J.*, ed. par le P. Henri Bernard, S. J. (Tientsin: Hautes Etudes, 1942), pp. 46-64. Schall's memoirs of his Peking experiences were originally published as *Historica relatio de ortu et progressu fidei orthodoxae in regno Chinensi* (Ratisbonae: August Hanckwitz, 1672). The unnamed editor took it upon himself to embellish the Latin style. Schall's original manuscript is in the Jesuit archives in Rome. It is this text which Bernard edited and published together with a French translation by Paul Bornet, S. J. It will hereafter be cited as Schall, *Mémoires*.

(17) Väth, *op. cit.*, p. 123, n. 66.

(18) Schall, *Mémoires*, p. 48.

(19) Martinus Martini, S. J., *Brevis relatio de numero et qualitate christianorum apud Sinas* (Romae: Ignatius de Lazzeris, 1654), pp. IV ff.

(20) Dr. P. Adelhelm Jann, F. Min. Cap., *Die katholischen Missionen in Indien, China und Japan. Ihre Organisation und das portugiesische Patronat vom 15. bis ins 18. Jahrhundert* (Paderborn: F. Schöningh, 1915), p. 393, n. 2.

Chapter XIX

Survival of the Fit

It is doubtful if anyone then living could have saved the Ming dynasty. It is certain that the Ch'ung-chên emperor (1628-1644) could not. He inherited an empire that hovered on the brink of disaster. Since the beginning of the Wan-li period (1573) governmental power had been wielded for the most part by unprincipled, self-seeking reactionaries who debased administrative standards and political morals to an unprecedented low. Their insatiable greed imposed ever heavier burdens upon the people in the form of confiscatory taxes. The result was general impoverishment and economic chaos.[1]

Corruption in both central and local government reached new depths during the regime of the notorious Wei Chung-hsien. "He was the principal cause of the evil," wrote the Jesuit Martini, analyzing the causes of the Ming collapse. The dynasty never recovered from the effects of his rule.

When, in 1628, the Ch'ung-chên emperor mounted the throne, the country was in the grip of general economic depression. The government had forfeited the confidence of the people. The emperor's failure to sweep the reactionaries into oblivion and smash the influence of eunuchs sealed the fate of his dynasty. So long as these elements retained influence and power, efficient government was impossible.

From 1630 on the country seethed with discontent. A great famine in Shensi in 1628 and another in Shansi a few years later led to large-scale banditry. By 1631 there were thirty-six bandit leaders with more than 200,000 adherents in these two provinces. One of them was Li Tzu-ch'êng, a native of Shensi, destined to bring an end to Ming rule.

Hung Ch'êng-ch'ou, made governor-general of Shensi in 1631 and, in 1634, of the five provinces of Honan, Shansi, Shensi, Szechwan, and Hukuang, repeatedly defeated the forces of Li Tzu-ch'êng; but Li could not be destroyed as long as the sufferings of the people went unrelieved. In 1639 famine hit Honan. Li immediately capitalized upon it. Thousands of disaffected citizens flocked to his standard when he moved into the province. Two scholars, Li Yen and Niu Chin-hsing, joined his cause and became his political mentors. Following their sage counsel Li Tzu-ch'êng won increasing support from the people. A slogan devised by Li Yen: *Yin Ch'uang Wang, pu nei liang* (Welcome Ch'uang Wang, pay no taxes) had strong pulling power. Ch'uang Wang (the Dashing King) was Li Tzu-ch'êng's *nom de guerre*. Confiscation and distribution to the peasants of large estates did his cause no harm.

By 1641 he controlled most of Honan. He captured the Prince of Fu, good friend of Sambiasi, fired his palaces which burned for three days and executed the prince. This was the same Chu Ch'ang-hsün who had narrowly missed being emperor.

In the same year the stupidity of a Ming general led to terrible disaster at Kaifeng. The city was besieged by Li Tzu-ch'êng. The general commanding imperial troops sent to lift the siege thought he could drown Li's army by breaching the dikes of the Yellow River. Instead he drowned most of the 300,000 inhabitants of the city. The Jesuit Rodrigo de Figueredo perished in the flood with his Christian flock.

In July, 1642, the court turned to Adam Schall for aid in strengthening the defenses of the capital. He was asked to manufacture cannon. Schall strove mightily to be excused, insisting that the manufacture of weapons of war did not pertain to his calling and that he had only a little book knowledge of the subject, but no practical experience. His excuses were not accepted and he had to yield to imperial insistence. A large open field within the Forbidden City was set aside for the purpose. Schall was supplied with material and a large force of workmen.

In order to forestall the superstitious who proposed ceremonies paying homage to the god of fire, Schall set up a table upon which he placed a picture of Christ, donned a surplice, stole, and biretta and directed the work force to join him in prayers to the true God for assistance in their work. These are the simple facts of an incident by which many have affected to be scandalized.

Twenty cannon were cast. They were tested in a field forty *li* from the city in the presence of a staff of officers and a committee of palace eunuchs. The test was a complete success. The emperor, highly pleased, ordered five hundred cannon, to weigh no more than sixty pounds each so that soldiers could carry them upon their shoulders. The often ironic Schall thought this amusing. Chinese soldiers, he wrote, were not so stupid as to burden themselves with cannon when fleeing from the field of battle, which was what they did best!

No doubt Schall was aware that whatever lack of soldierly qualities Chinese troops displayed was due to the fact that, badly trained, poorly equipped, rarely paid, frequently driven to slaughter by incompetent officers, they had little incentive to fight courageously. What they could do under efficient or inspirational leadership the soldiers of Yüan Ch'ung-huan had demonstrated.

While Schall was occupied with the manufacture of cannon, his school of astronomy came to an unfortunate end. Schall puts the blame upon the complacent Li T'ien-ching who, as he ironically remarks, "was asleep as usual." A onetime student in science of de Pantoia and de Ursis usurped Schall's office, undermined his prestige and even spread stories that he had embezzled part of the money allotted for the construction of cannon. Schall had foreseen the possibility of such charges and had protected himself by insisting that all finances be handled directly by the Board of Public Works.

The troublemaker succeeded, however, in remobilizing the irreconcilables. Renewed attacks upon the foreigners and their science met with partial success. It was decided to put an end to the independence of the calendrical bureau, nominally presided over by Li T'ien-ching, actually directed by Schall, and make it a subordinate division of the old Bureau of Astronomy. Schall, never an appeaser, rather than entrust his science to "idiots," as he characteristically dubbed these adversaries, closed his academy.

Schall has been criticized for his activities both as manufacturer of cannon and as consultant on fortifications. It has been suggested that they cannot be reconciled with his character as priest and missionary. Contemporary relations contain no word of reproach on this score. Since he gave a large part of his time for more than a year to this work it is obvious that he had the approval of his superiors.

The Catholic Church is opposed to priests taking up arms even in a just war but she does not absolutely forbid it. The fierce resistance of the Spanish people to the armies of Napoleon, which had as much to do with the collapse of Bonaparte's European fortress as the Russian debacle, was led by priests and monks. None but a pacifist could find fault with Schall's participation in the defense of Macao in 1622, and the pacifist cannot logically distinguish in this respect between priest and layman. His objection goes against both.

China was a cultured state whose civilization, whatever its tares, was the highest to be found in the Orient. She was sorely beset by rebels and by wandering nomadic tribes, the Manchus. The government of the Ming had fallen upon evil days. Many of China's ills could be laid at the door of her own rulers. Nevertheless, the Ming dynasty was the legitimate government. Heaven might, indeed, be withdrawing its mandate, but at the moment defense of the state seemed synonymous with defense of Chinese civilization. That is why most of the leaders of the Tung-lin party, who for years had deplored the corruption of Ming government and led the fight against reactionaries, remained loyalists when the dynasty fell.

In retrospect it is easy to observe that the conquest of China by the Manchus resulted in an infusion of new strength and vigor. It is easy to note that the new dynasty, before its own decline, gave to the empire a series of remarkable rulers. But this is hindsight. In 1642 or 1643 these developments could not be foreseen.

The issue then seemed simply to be the defense of the state against an aggression by Tatar hordes which threatened the foundations of state, society, and culture. Schall's first loyalties were to the propagation of Christianity, but he was a subject of the emperor. And in the present instance he saw no conflict between the two loyalties. Service to the state, justified in itself, indirectly served the cause of Christianity.

Events proved Schall's efforts to have been in vain. Treachery within the capital was more potent than Schall's cannon. In the spring of 1644, Li Tzu-ch'êng, after declaring his own dynastic pretensions and naming Sianfu his capital, moved upon Peking. He swept rapidly through Shansi. In the fall of Chiangchow (Stephen)

Han Lin lost his life. The Catholic Church in Puchow was burned to the ground, the Jesuit priest, Michael Walta, slain.

On April 23, 1644, Li encamped before the western gate of Peking. The emperor, who had rejected the pleas of his councillors to flee the city, now made the crowning mistake of his life. He put the force of 70,000 picked troops defending the city under the command of 3,000 eunuchs. There was poetic justice in this. A dynasty which had repeatedly betrayed its own interests, as well as those of the people, by its reliance upon these emasculates, chose an appropriate way to destroy itself.

Li, with wholesome respect for Schall's cannon, had not attacked the city. He did not have to. On April 25 Ts'ao Hua-ch'un, the eunuch commanding at this point, opened the western gates and Li's troops poured into the capital.

When he heard the news, the emperor mounted horse and with a few faithful followers rode toward the gate in the south city. His traitorous enunuchs opened fire on him with Schall's cannon and forced him to turn back. Schall watched him ride by the Jesuit residence.

Returning to the palace, the emperor ordered the empress to hang herself and his three sons to hide. His fifteen-year-old daughter he attempted to slay to keep her from falling into the hands of the soldiery. In warding off the blow of his saber she lost a hand and fled. Her distraught father then climbed *Mei shan* (Coal Hill) to the north of the palace. From here he had once inspected Schall's cannon. He wrote a note in his own blood directed to Li Tzu-ch'êng, asking him not to oppress the people and not to employ his faithless ministers. Then he hanged himself from a rafter in a garden house.

Thus ended the Ming dynasty after 276 years of rule. It was not overthrown by the Manchus. Thanks to the efforts of capable generals, who had to struggle against obscurantism, apathy, and corruption within as well as against the enemy without, the Manchu threat had been held in check. When the capital fell, the Manchus were outside the Great Wall. The dynasty collapsed of its own weight, undermined by political corruption and ineptitude from within.

For several days terror reigned in Peking. Li's soldiery embarked upon a career of looting and killing. Schall, the only foreigner in the city, stood guard over his Christians. Longobardo and Furtado had left the capital before the debacle. Schall insisted upon sharing the fate of his Christians. He especially feared for the women, and spent most of his time going from house to house to make sure that they were safe.

Commanding Ming troops facing the Manchus at Shanhaikuan was Wu San-kuei. When Li was investing the capital the emperor had ordered him to come to its rescue. Wu delayed and had hardly set out from Shanhaikuan when word reached him of the fall of the city. He turned back to await developments. Li Tzu-ch'êng, who held Wu's father hostage, invited him to join him. According to the Jesuit accounts, Wu, torn between filial love and his duty as a Ming officer, refused to betray his allegiance to his dead emperor even to save his father. According to the more romantic version popular among the Chinese, Wu was about to capitulate to Li when he learned that the latter had appropriated his favorite concubine, Ch'ên Yüan. The Jesuits make no mention of Ch'ên Yüan. Perhaps they did not know of her. Perhaps, less romantic than the Chinese, they preferred to believe that fidelity to a trust rather than love for a concubine drove Wu to sacrifice his father.

Li Tzu-ch'êng, at the head of 200,000 men, marched to meet Wu San-kuei. The latter elected to form an alliance with the Manchus. On May 27, 1644, their forces joined those of Wu.

Abahai, the Manchu ruler, had died in September of the preceding year and his ninth son, Fu-lin, had been selected to succeed him. Inasmuch as Fu-lin was only six years old, two of his uncles, Dorgon and Jirgalang, had been elected regents. Dorgon, fourteenth son of Nurhaci, dominated the regency.

In the last days of May, 1644, the combined armies of Dorgon and Wu San-kuei inflicted a series of crushing defeats upon Li Tzu-ch'êng. Li fled back to Peking. He had postponed his own coronation as emperor. He now hastily ascended the throne and as hastily descended. Leaving behind a rearguard of 3,000 men with orders to plunder and burn the capital, he fled with his disorganized army towards Shansi. Dorgon bypassed the city to press home the pursuit.

The days that followed Li's flight were days of new terror in the capital. His rearguard fired the imperial palace, then the subsidiary palaces, and finally the homes of the people. From his house Schall heard the roof of the Audience Hall crash in ruins as the flames destroyed the magnificent supporting columns. Many in the neighborhood took refuge in Schall's residence. Firebrands were hurled in from the street, incendiary arrows fired into the roof. Hot ashes and burning embers poured down. But the vigilance of the refugees saved the residence while everything else in the area was being devoured. A mob, led by two Chinese who nursed a grievance because Schall had refused some months before to lend them money, tried to break into the mission compound. Schall seized a huge Japanese sword and planted himself inside the gate. The sight of this sturdy figure, made more impressive by a luxuriant beard which, wrote Schall not without a certain note of satisfaction, would have sufficed to supply the whole mob with whiskers, unnerved the would-be looters who abandoned the attack.

Meanwhile Dorgon had turned over command of the forces pursuing Li Tzu-ch'êng to his brothers Ajige and Dodo, while he returned with part of his army to Peking. The Manchus entered the city on June 7. The people, happy to be delivered from the terror (half the city had been burned), lined the streets and greeted them with shouts of "Wan-sui, wan-sui, wan-wan sui!" Some months later Fu-lin was brought to the capital and on October 30 was proclaimed emperor of China with the reign title Shun-chih. Eight years earlier Abahai had given to his succession the dynastic name Ch'ing.

Within less than a year the Ch'ing were masters of Chihli, Shantung, Shansi, and Shensi. But control of the northern provinces is not mastery of China. It was to take the Ch'ing almost twenty years of constant warfare to bring all of China under their rule. Nor was their road to ultimate victory marked by unbroken success.

That resistance was so tenacious and often so effective throws into sharp relief the full responsibility of Ming rule for the ultimate disaster. It proves that all the elements for effective resistance were present in the country. Failure of the Ming regime to mobilize the forces of the nation against collapse from within and aggression from without is a measure of its own ineptitude.

Several factors contributed to Ch'ing success. Although increasingly enmeshed in factional struggle for power, their leaders were men of more than ordinary strength and intelligence. Dorgon, Ajige, Dodo, Jirgalang, Oboi, Bolo, Nikan and others were proof that the blood of Nurhaci had lost none of its vitality. Equally important: Nurhaci's sons and grandsons won to their support a considerable number of able Chinese leaders, military and civil, who were not all traitors. Many of these had lost faith in Ming government and, embittered by its corruption and incompetence, had thrown in their lot with the Manchus long before the fall of the dynasty. Others, for much the same reason, decided that the solution of China's internal problems could be achieved only under a new dynasty. Men of this type were responsible for the military success of the Ch'ing in the long struggle in southern China. K'ung Yu-tê and Kêng Chung-ming, who as lieutenant-colonels under the command of (Ignatius) Sun Yüan-hua had led the mutiny of 1631, served brilliantly in the southern campaigns. Kêng Chi-mao, son of Kêng Chung-ming, was an able, if ruthless, commander. Shang K'o-hsi, who joined the Manchus in 1633, was in command of the Ch'ing troops which conquered Kwangtung province after a long and bitter struggle. Hung Ch'êng-ch'ou, the nemesis of Li Tzu-ch'êng, went over to the Manchus in 1642 and proved one of their most effective instruments, both as military leader and as civil administrator. In 1652, after the Ch'ing forces had suffered serious reverses, he was made governor-general of Hukuang, Kwangtung, Kwangsi, Yunnan, and Kweichow with full military and civil command. He checked the advance of Ming forces. It was he who mapped the strategy and led one of the armies which, in 1659, drove the last Ming pretender from the empire.

After their seizure of power in north China, the Ch'ing won invaluable support by the sagacious policies they pursued. They avoided the destruction which had characterized their former forays into the empire; they remitted burdensome taxes; they ordered fitting burial for the late Ming emperor, whose body had been treated with shameful disrespect by Li Tzu-ch'êng.

Behind these policies was the brain of Fan Wên-ch'êng who had thrown in his lot with the Manchus when Nurhaci took Fushun in 1618 and thenceforward served as their political adviser. It was Fan who had put into the hands of the Peking reactionaries the faked evidence which had led to the execution of Yüan Ch'ung-huan. It was Fan who, when he heard in Mukden of the fall of Peking to Li Tzu-ch'êng, had immediately urged Dorgon to invade the empire.

The transition of power in north China was accomplished with little shock to the Chinese administrative system. This gave the revolution the appearance of a simple dynastic change rather than of an alien conquest and won the support of the majority of Chinese officials. The Manchus had long before incorporated into their own state organization many features of Chinese bureaucratic administration. The Chinese, in settling Manchuria, carried their political system with them. The Manchus took over that system. Hence the substitution of their rule for that of the Ming did not involve radical change in political organization. They doubled the size of the important ministries and staffed them with an equal number of Manchus and Chinese.

The innovation which aroused the deepest resentment and provoked fiercest resistance in many parts of China was the order that the Chinese grow queues and shave their heads after the Manchu fashion. Says Martini:

> This edict gave birth to the greatest difficulties, because the Chinese were more afflicted by the loss of their hair than by the loss of their empire, and fought more courageously for this vain ornament of their heads, than in defense of their provinces. Some carried their folly to such a point that they preferred to lose their heads rather than lose their hair.

Martini is less than just. There is much to be said for the man who will fight more readily in defense of his right to cut his hair as he chooses than in defense of an empire. It is when tyranny attempts to bully its way into the sphere of personal rights that it encounters the flaming resistance of the free human spirit. So all praise to the Chinese for their "folly." They were defending human freedom, not a vain ornament of their heads.

One of the most extraordinary things about this period is the rise of Adam Schall in the favor of the Peking government while his confrères continued to enjoy the friendship of Ming loyalists and the Ming pretenders themselves. Schall got along well with the Manchus from the start. He admired their talent for organization, their military skill, and the forcefulness of their leaders. From the moment Peking fell, he was convinced that the Ming cause was doomed. He accepted the new regime and co-operated fully with it.

The Manchus on their part admired Schall. Most of their outstanding personalities cultivated his friendship. One of his most frequent visitors was Daisan, eldest son of Nurhaci, who had led in the movement to nominate Abahai as Nurhaci's successor. He related to Schall most of the legendary and real history of his people.

The new dynasty, although anxious to maintain Chinese traditions, had no intention of becoming a slave to narrow prejudice. Hence it was able to give Schall a standing which had been impossible under the old regime. Before the end of 1644, Dorgon, the regent, named him director of the Bureau of Astronomy. Schall had no desire to accept the office. Seven times he asked to be excused. Only after Furtado, superior of the northern division of the mission, had written to him six times ordering him to accept the appointment did he yield.[2] His official title was *Ch'in-t'ien-chien-chêng* (Director of the Bureau of Astronomical Observation).

Within a few years Schall's prestige was reflected upon his fellow missionaries throughout the provinces under Ch'ing control. On September 27, 1650, Brancato in a letter to the Jesuit general remarked: "All of us who are in this mission bask by divine favor in the aura of Father Adam. . . ." In the same year the vice-provincial, the younger Dias, wrote: "Would that we had a hundred Adams; for despite his distance he is so real a help to us that we need only to say that we are his companions and brothers and no one dares venture a word against us."[3]

Not all of Schall's confrères subscribed to these sentiments. Out of a misunderstanding, Gabriel de Magalhães developed an enmity for him and mounted a campaign against him that almost led to his dismissal from the Society and cast a long shadow over his brilliant career.

It had started in 1643 when at the head of his bandit hordes Chang Hsien-chung, popularly known as the Yellow Tiger and one of the most savage tyrants in the history of China, swept into Szechwan province where Buglio and de Magalhães were busily building up their Christian communities. There, on December 4, 1644, he proclaimed himself *Ta Hsi Kuo Wang* (King of the Great Western Kingdom).[4]

Chang had heard of Buglio and de Magalhães. The two Jesuits, who had fled into the mountains, were hunted out and brought back to Chengtu. Over their protests Chang made them officials and put them to work constructing terrestrial and celestial spheres. For the next two years their life was a nightmare.[5] They were prisoners of Chang Hsien-chung and involuntary eyewitnesses to his indescribable barbarities: scholar-officials were decapitated, others flayed alive, others cut to pieces upon the slightest suspicion. In a transport of sadism Chang had his soldiers slaughter 40,000 inhabitants of Chengtu in a single day.

Buglio and de Magalhães, unable to do more than save an occasional life during these holocausts, repeatedly begged to be released. They succeeded only in arousing the tyrant's fury. Condemned to die, they were saved on January 3, 1647, by the sudden arrival at Hsichung, in Szechwan, of the advance guard of a Manchu army. When the first few enemy horsemen unexpectedly appeared on the horizon, Chang, writes de Magalhães,

> in his usual maddened way, leaped on his steed and with a few followers, all unarmed, dashed out to meet them. He had not gone far when he was brought down by an arrow through the heart and died on the spot.[6]

Panic seized his army and it fled in disorder. The two Jesuits were dragged out of their hiding place and made prisoners. Both suffered arrow wounds in the course of their capture.

Upon learning that they were Schall's associates Prince Haoge, commanding the Manchu army, treated the two priests with respect. Immediately upon hearing of their capture Schall prepared a petition asking for their release. Aleni had been appointed vice-provincial, but because of the chaotic conditions he had named Francisco Furtado superior of the northern part of the mission.[7] Furtado ordered Schall not to present his petition to the authorities. The two prisoners did not want him to intervene, upon the ground that this would be an insult to their benevolent captor. They preferred to be brought to Peking and released there. What they did not know was that Haoge was hated by Dorgon, the chief regent. As eldest son of Abahai, Haoge had been the logical choice for the Manchu throne in 1643 and it was Dorgon who had prevented his accession. Now, despite Haoge's brilliant military record, he was determined to get rid of him as a threat to his own power. Upon returning to Peking in 1648 after pacifying Szechwan, Haoge was condemned to prison. Seeing the handwriting on the wall, he committed suicide after strangling two of his three wives.

His benevolence therefore availed the Jesuit prisoners nothing. They were taken under guard to the enclosure for foreigners and jailed. Schall hurried to the headquarters of the military command where he learned for the first time that Buglio and de Magalhães had held official positions in the regime of Chang Hsien-chung and were considered rebels and traitors for which the ordinary penalty was death. Schall was warned to have nothing to do with them lest he too fall under suspicion.

Schall reported these facts to Furtado and, with characteristic frankness, made it clear that in his opinion their conduct had been a choice bit of stupidity. They should have preferred death to accepting service under the tyrant. They also should have accepted their freedom when he offered to obtain it for them.[8]

De Magalhães bitterly resented Schall's strictures. He could see no difference between his serving Chang Hsien-chung under duress and Schall serving the Manchu government in Peking. Because he did not feel himself a traitor or rebel, he could not believe that the Manchus could possibly look upon him as such. Therefore, he concluded with a logical *tour de force* to make the head spin, his confinement must be due to the machinations of Schall. Nothing could persuade him otherwise. He began a campaign of vilification, bombarding superiors and fellow missionaries with an unending barrage of accusation.

Schall quietly did what he could for the two prisoners. It was out of consideration for him that they were treated more like guests than as criminals during their confinement. But Schall was warned by friends and finally by the government ministry in charge and by the regency itself not to identify himself with the two captives. He was told that so long as the country was in the throes of civil war the regency, out of regard for the attitude of the higher officer corps, could not grant them full freedom. Schall felt this was the best that could be hoped for in view of the circumstances. Perhaps he should have attempted to explain reasonably to his two confrères his point of view; but that was not in Schall's character. The situation seemed plain enough. Whether victims of their own folly or of circumstances, the two men, for the good of the mission, must quietly accept their lot until it was possible to effect their release. If they could not see this, Schall did not feel impelled to try to make them understand. Like St. Paul, Schall suffered fools; but unlike St. Paul, not gladly.

After being confined for over two years in the enclosure for foreigners, Buglio and de Magalhães were turned over to a Manchu official with the status of slaves. Again Schall's influence served them well. Their Manchu master actually gave them the equivalent of full freedom. They could go and come as they pleased. They were free to carry on their ministry. They were even given property and allowed to build a church, the second church to be established in Peking. None of this changed their attitude. De Magalhães continued his anti-Schall campaign. It is quite possible that the truly frightful experiences he and Buglio underwent during their two years with Chang Hsien-chung had unbalanced his judgment. He was ready to believe every idle rumor that came to him. Inasmuch as his receptivity to gossip was well known, an abundance of rumors reached him. Schall, blunt, outspoken, often irascible, incapable of dissembling, and impatient with charlatans, self-seekers and pettifoggers, had made more than one enemy. These found in de Magalhães a natural dupe.

The Portuguese Jesuit stirred up a storm that did not entirely subside until the death of Schall seventeen years later and that filled two large files in the Jesuit archives in Rome with letters and reports.[9] He conducted his campaign with such persistence and energy that, for a time, he succeeded in hoodwinking many of his fellow Jesuits in China and temporarily alienating them from Schall. On May 20, 1649, Furtado, Longobardo, Buglio and Ferrari joined de Magalhães in signing a petition sent to Manoel Dias, the vice-provincial, urging that Schall be dismissed from the Society of Jesus.[10] Most of the eleven reasons given show a total inability to understand either Schall's outspoken nature or his ironic sense of humor.

He was charged with refusing obedience to everyone from the pope down to his immediate superiors; this, because he was said to have remarked to someone that the only superiors he had were God and St. Ignatius! In similar vein Grueber would later tell in accents pregnant with scandal how he had with his own ears and "in great sorrow" heard Schall give expression to shocking sentiments on the subject of respect and obedience owed to superiors. Schall, who could never resist the temptation to prick the pious balloon, had interrupted a probably pompous disquisition of Grueber's on the subject with the remark: "Quivis pro se, Deus pro omnibus" (Every man for himself and God for all), a rather nice turn to the old saw, "every man for himself and the devil take the hindmost."[11] It is easy to grow quite fond of Schall from the scandalized reports of his detractors.

He was charged with holding opinions contrary to faith because to a fellow missionary who, in return for alms, promised him a moderation of "the terrible pains" awaiting him in purgatory, Schall caustically replied that talk about "the terrible pains" of purgatory was a clerical exaggeration which people from Cologne did not believe!

In other charges, that he acted as though he owned the residence and that he lived in a style proper to high mandarins but not to simple religious, it is difficult not to detect the grumbling of envy. The position held by Schall, a position which he had seven times attempted to refuse and which he had accepted only when ordered to do so by Furtado who now joined in the charges against him, obliged him to a kind of life other than monastic.

Actually Schall during his long years in Peking, often alone, had developed an unconventional life. He had succeeded in establishing extremely informal and democratic relations with his Chinese and Manchu friends. He himself remarked that he felt as much at home with them as if he were among his countrymen in Cologne.[12] He had perpetual open house. His friends came and went as they pleased. No part of the house was closed to them. The emperor himself used to drop in frequently. He was accustomed to enter Schall's bedroom, sit upon the bed, or stretch out on it with a book before him. Others did the same. All of this, of course, provided food for gossip. (Grueber reported his concern over the lack of cloister!)

It was part of Schall's democratic nature that friendship with his servant came as naturally to him as friendship with the emperor. He had allowed P'an Chin-hsiao, his majordomo, to work his way into the position of a confidant. This proved to be his vulnerable spot. He was indiscreet in freely expressing his opinion about various people, including some of his fellow Jesuits, to P'an. The latter, probably flattered by Schall's friendship, abused his confidence. His attitude towards more than one visitor about whom Schall had expressed himself critically was impudent. He even attempted to imitate Schall's natural bluntness of speech. Schall made more than one enemy because of P'an.

At the insistence of the Shun-chih emperor, Schall had adopted as his grandson the five-year-old son of P'an Chin-hsiao. The youngster's polite manners had charmed the ruler who was distressed that the celibate Schall had no one to carry on his name. The adoption was a matter of common knowledge. Early in the reign of the K'ang-hsi emperor an imperial decree of October 23, 1661, ordered the admission of the boy to the Imperial College in Peking reserved for the training of an imperial elite. Said the decree:

> In view of the fact that T'ang Jo-wang has taken a vow of chastity and lifelong celibacy and consequently like an exile must live sad, alone and without help, the [Shun-chih] emperor desired him to adopt a boy as his grandson.

After then granting to certain high mandarins the privilege of sending a son to the college, the decree continues:

> T'ang Jo-wang comes from a foreign land and has for many years served the empire. He is not married. He should not on this account be excluded from this privilege. Therefore his adopted grandson may be admitted to the College. We decree it so.[13]

These were the innocent facts from which calumny drew its sustenance. Like a doting grandfather Schall spoiled the youngster and delighted in his company. He often visited the P'an home, reported the worried Grueber. Grueber's report is a case-study on how calumny is born. He prefaces his insinuations by admitting that he has himself not witnessed any incriminating action by Schall. But he does go to his servant's home where there are young women, "even girls!" (no doubt P'an's daughters, nieces, cousins); and besides drinking rice wine, eating rice cakes and joining in family songs, who knows what more grievous things he might be doing! And then these women freely come and go in Schall's home! Who knows what that might mean! It should be pointed out that when Grueber made these observations Schall was seventy years old. It can be said for Grueber, only one year in China, that once away from Peking and de Magalhães' influence he saw things in saner perspective. During his climb of the Himalayas in search of a land route to Europe his head cleared. Arrived in Rome he warmly defended Schall.

This was the kind of gossip that was carried to de Magalhães. His chief informant was Ts'ai An-to, a young Macaist known to the Jesuits as Antonio Fernandez, who had been with him in Szechwan and had been brought with him to Peking. Ts'ai was released by the Manchus and occupied himself as chief talebearer for de Magalhães. He later entered the Society as a lay brother and died a victim of charity nursing one of the interned missionaries in Canton in 1670. But at this stage of his life he was simply a young Chinese aware of de Magalhães' feeling towards Schall and doing what he thought would please him most. Schall was here the victim, and not of charity.

Fifty years after Schall's death the fact of the adopted grandson was twisted into an ugly myth of concubinage and an illegitimate son. It originated in the same mind that gave birth to the thoroughly discredited story that the Jesuits had poisoned the papal legate, Cardinal de Tournon – the mind of his secretary, Angelita. It was given wide publicity in Europe through the writings of the ex-Capuchin Norbert Platel, who has been called by Robert Streit, O.M.I., "an undoubtedly psychopathic case,"[14] and who, by his own admission, "for more than thirty years had as my goal the destruction of [the Society of Jesus]."[15] In his obsession he enlisted his talents as a salaried writer in the service of Pombal, the powerful politico of Portugal, who shared the same hatred. Many a popular anti-Jesuit legend was born out of that union.

This myth found no credence in Schall's lifetime, because the facts were too well known. Not even Yang Kuang-hsien, who hated Christianity and who raked up every possible charge against Schall, even mentioned it, as he certainly would have had there been anyone in Peking willing to believe it. Nor is there any mention of it in the bitterly anti-Jesuit writings of Domingo Navarrete, O.P., who delighted the hearts of Jansenists in Europe with his tracts. He was in Peking with the other missionaries in China at the height of Yang Kuang-hsien's persecution, was afterwards confined with them in Canton, and was the last person to overlook so juicy a morsel as this.

To the discredit of some of his confrères, however, other tales were believed, tales of the who-knows-what-might-be-going-on-behind-closed-doors type of gossip. That Furtado allowed himself to be brought into the cabal against Schall was no doubt due to a personal grievance. He had felt the rough side of Schall's tongue. The latter had left him in no doubt about his opinion of Furtado's judgment in overruling his offer to free Buglio and de Magalhães before they were brought to Peking. Later when Furtado, ignoring official warnings, continued frequently to visit the prisoners he was haled before a tribunal and ordered out of the city. Furtado did not obey the order, but went into hiding with a Christian family in the city. On this occasion Schall did nothing to prevent this order of expulsion from issuing. De Magalhães even charged that, in a memorial to the tribunal, he suggested it. The truth seems rather to be that Schall simply failed to defend Furtado's presence in the capital. He did the same thing in the case of Martin Martini who was sent to Peking by the newly appointed vice-provincial Dias to replace him in the calendrical bureau. Schall did not feel impelled to put himself out for those who seemed to form part of a plot against him.

Furtado, who thought he was Schall's superior, naturally regarded his failure to defend him as a mortal affront. But Schall denied that Furtado was any longer superior. As it happened, Schall was in a sense right. With the death of Aleni and the appointment of Dias to succeed him, the general had abolished the office of superior of the north. Schall had evidently received word of this; Furtado had not. Actually, the general had appointed Furtado to the higher officer of visitor, but neither Schall nor Furtado was aware of this. From Schall's point of view, he was at the moment Furtado's superior and he was not inclined to help keep in Peking a subject who believed every idle tale about him.

That Furtado had quite a different opinion about Schall before this injury to his pride colored his views, is clear from his letter of February 2, 1641, to the general of the Society:

> Father John Adam [Schall] has merited greatly before God and the Society. . . . Everything that we do in this empire has been made possible by his labor and by the zeal with which he champions our cause in Peking. . .[16]

One older head who, for a short time, allowed his better judgment to be overcome by the violent persistence of de Magalhães was Longobardo. He had lived with Schall for years and knew from personal observation that the charges were untrue. Yet de Magalhães threw up so heavy a barrage of smoke that the aged Longobardo was persuaded there must be some fire. He was not long deceived, however, and in August, 1651, he wrote a letter to be read to the nearly blind Dias urging that Buglio and de Magalhães be withdrawn from Peking. They were, he said, bringing Christianity into disrepute and with the connivance of certain apostate Christians who had personal grievances against Schall were injuring the latter's good name. What brought Longobardo to his senses was the charge of faults against chastity levelled against Schall. He had been Schall's confessor and knew that there was not a shred of truth in the accusation: "I affirm to your Reverence as confessor of this Father," he wrote, "that I can swear that the good Father is altogether pure and innocent."[17]

Schall was saved by the good sense of the three consultors of the vice-province, Brancato, Smogulechi, and Gravina, and by the fact that the higher authorities in Rome kept their heads. Thorough investigation of every charge resulted time and again in Schall's complete vindication. The most that could be said against him was that long years in Peking, often alone, and not subject to the restrictions of monastic life, had accentuated his natural independence as well as certain harsher features of his character. In a penetrating report of June 3, 1652, to Piccolomini, the then general of the Society, Smogulechi, in clearing Schall, gave his reasoned judgment of all the persons involved in the dispute. Of Schall he said: "on the exterior a rather harsh man, very irascible and morose after the German fashion."[18] Smogulechi was a Pole. In a confidential reply dated December 12, 1653, the general, who had not yet received a report from either Schall or the visitor, said that Schall could not be forced or expelled from the Society and if anything of the sort were attempted it would be invalid.[19]

In 1653 Dias sent Francesco Brancato to Peking to investigate. Brancato was one of the soundest men on the mission, his judgment respected by all. During a stay of almost two months he made an exhaustive examination of the charges. His official report to Dias is a full exoneration of Schall:

> I, Francesco Brancato, professed of the Society of Jesus, was named by P. Manoel Dias of the same Society and vice-provincial of China in the year 1653 as vistor of North China. In July 1653 I visited the residence in Peking and sufficiently informed myself of the state of affairs there. I find that the accusations touching the reputation and good name of P. John Adam, professed of the same Society and superior of the house in Peking, are the lies and slanders of a few vindictive men who want to sow cockle among brothers of the Society and give free rein to their tongues because they failed to achieve certain ends of theirs which they had wanted to attain with the help of P. John Adam. By these presents I certify and affirm that in truth all the accusations arise from

> the imagination and fantasy of these evil men. Even Fathers Buglio and Gabriel de Magalhães admit to me that they have witnessed none of these things in P. John Adam, but on the contrary have only listened to this silly prattle which I most strongly affirm are lies and slanders.[20]

It is not easy to excuse de Magalhães. In a letter of May 12, 1662, to the general, the always clearheaded Ferdinand Verbiest, since 1660 assistant to Schall, remarked: "May God forgive certain of our Fathers . . . who lent such ready ears to these calumnies and lies and furthered this evil."[21]

More troublesome than the attack upon his personal character and potentially a greater threat to the security of the mission was the effort to remove him from his position as head of the Astronomical Bureau. The question of the appropriateness of his holding this office had been raised before by Aleni, as vice-provincial; but the doubts had been settled. De Magalhães raised the issue again. On September 6, 1649, he completed a closely written thirty-six page indictment, with Furtado's endorsement appended, of Schall's connection with the bureau.[22] De Magalhães had evidently found a way to keep himself occupied during his internment.

One week later Furtado signed another document purporting to be the opinion of Manoel Dias, the vice-provincial, and nine other professed Fathers of the mission, giving ten reasons why Schall should resign.[23] It will be remembered that Schall had risked the anger of the emperor by his repeated requests to be excused from accepting this appointment and had only yielded when ordered to do so by the same Furtado. Schall seldom had to look far to find occasions to indulge his temper.

There are one or two interesting things about this document. A short preamble states that it contains the judgment and the supporting reasons of Dias and the other nine, as recorded in their consultations and letters. Yet curiously enough the ten reasons given are exactly the same ten arguments developed by de Magalhães in his own tract of a week earlier. Further challenging the deductive instincts of the sleuth is the obvious fact that the handwriting of this second document is that of de Magalhães himself. While Dias and the others may indeed have agreed that Schall should leave his post, it may seriously be doubted that they had thought up these ten arguments. It may also be seriously doubted that Dias had sent to Peking the records of his consultations. These arguments are clearly de Magalhães' own. While de Magalhães may not have intended to deceive, the fact is that he did deceive at least the Jesuit archivist in Rome. In the archives this document is attributed to Manoel Dias. It is unlikely, however, that Schall was deceived.

The ten arguments employed in both tracts can be reduced to two: professed members of the Society by a special vow bind themselves to refuse to accept proferred dignities; the functions of this office were said to involve Schall in co-operation with superstitious practices and to render him subject to excommunication.

Historically it seems certain that the dignities which St. Ignatius had in mind in introducing the fourth vow were ecclesiastical. He wanted to keep members of his order out of the scramble for ecclesiastical preferment. Urban VIII, however, seems to have interpreted it as including secular dignities to which jurisdiction was attached. But, as Schall rather reasonably pointed out, the general practice in Europe made it clear that it was not intended to exclude dignities of an academic nature, to which the directorship of the Astronomical Bureau was assimilated. "Look at our colleges," he wrote, "whose *Rectores Magnifici* enjoy a dignity in many respects greater than that of this office."[24] (The heads of many European universities still bear the rather pompous title, nostalgic of the Renaissance, of *Rector Magnificus.*) Despite this eminently sensible point of view, many Jesuit consciences were agitated. Many letters, pro and con, travelled the long sea lanes to Rome. Verbiest made an interesting argument in his letter of May 12, 1662. There is an obligation of natural law to make restitution for the wrongful deprivation of one's good name, and this obligation should take precedence over any possible prohibition of the positive law against accepting dignities. Altogether apart from the fact that his many merits and the deep indebtedness of the mission make him worthy of such a reward, "for this reason alone, that he has endured such great calumny," wrote Verbiest, "do I think him most worthy of this honor . . . and I do not hesitate to desire it for him, so that in this fashion not only in the sight of the Christians in Peking, but also of others throughout the whole of China who are not unaware of this infamy, he may be restored to the honor which is his due."

The question had finally to be settled by the pope. In a letter of April 12, 1664, to Michel Trigault, the vicar-general wrote:

> We have seen here the treatise of P. Ferdinand Verbiest on the office of P. Adam Schall, and also a shorter one by P. John Adam himself; and our R.P. Revisors have approved [them]; and we order that he continue in that office as he has until now, without fear, for the better propagation of Christianity and the greater glory of God. . . . Our Holy Father lately consulted by us about the office held by P. John Adam, replied that this could be licitly allowed to our professed in favor of the propagation of the faith, and if it were necessary, he would dispense from the vow of profession and order that it be allowed.[25]

The second objection was finally settled too, but not before much ink had flowed, a great deal of it from the pen of de Magalhães; a Dominican in the faraway Philippines had joined the attack with a lengthy charge sent to Rome demanding strong measures against Schall;[26] Martin Martini had been sent on the long voyage to Rome to present the case; and learned theologians of the Roman College had considered the question.

Schall defended himself ably in a number of letters to the consultors and finally, in 1652, for the first time in a letter to the general of the Society. His replies are characteristically short and sharply pointed. If for six years he had borne in silence the injuries and calumnies inflicted upon him by de Magalhães and Buglio, he told the general in a letter of October 6, 1654, it was because he had more confidence in the providence of God than he had in companions or superiors. "Inanis hominum cura," was how he described reliance upon *them!* "No one ever hoped in the Lord and was confounded," was his conclusion; a devout sentiment, but in his context not without its barb.[27]

There was no question that the calendar served superstitious, as well as legitimate, civil purposes. Propitious days for certain public acts were determined in accordance with the calendar. The question was whether Schall's responsibilities as head of the astronomical bureau involved him in a species of illicit co-operation with superstition. Ultimately it was a problem to be resolved in terms of the well known principles of moral theology relating to formal and material co-operation.

On August 3, 1655, a commission of five theologians of the Roman College handed down an opinion unfavorable to Schall.[28] They held that there was no superstition in the part of the calendar for which he was directly responsible; but his position as head of the bureau involved him at least indirectly in the work of all his subordinates, some of which was tainted with superstitious belief. Because this opinion seemed based upon a misunderstanding of the nature of Schall's activities, the debate continued. In March, 1660, and again in May, 1662, Schall sent to the general further precisions.[29] How widely opinions differed may be judged from this: Together with the calendar, Schall issued in Chinese an explanatory booklet. On November 28, 1662, Ignacio da Costa, having just finished his three-year term as vice-provincial, wrote to the general sharply criticizing Schall's booklet.[30] Yet in his letter of May 12 of the same year Verbiest had told the general that, if Schall had done nothing else, this booklet alone should win him a memorable place in the annals of the mission.

> Not only does he in this book purge the mathematical bureau of the superstitions, which some have suspected were connected with it, but he also with outstanding authority and with reason refutes all Chinese superstitions of this nature, with the written endorsement of all the mathematicians of the tribunal, Gentiles as well as Christians, of the principal mandarins, and of the Grand Secretary Hu, who composed a prologue for the book not only approving but praising these explanations of Father Adam.

The visitor, Simão da Cunha, who himself supported Schall's position, commissioned Johann Grueber to carry with him to Rome a request for a definitive decision. Once again the question was submitted to a commission of theologians of the Roman College who, on January 1, 1664, handed down an opinion that Schall's co-operation was merely material and therefore, with so much at stake, was justified.[31] The vicar-general, later general, Oliva, in notifying da Cunha of this decision added that, as far as the fourth vow was concerned, the dignity involved in the directorship of the bureau was of an academic nature and was no greater than that enjoyed by the chancellor in certain European universities, nor was the authority exercised any greater than that wielded by teachers and prefects over their students. He thus endorsed Schall's sensible argument. In conclusion, Oliva directed da Cunha

> to stimulate Father John Adam to continue gladly in this office for the glory of God, and, if it can conveniently be done, to prepare one of our men as his successor so that, when it shall

> have pleased God to call Father John to his deserved rewards, he may fill this office.[32]

Schall had won a long and weary fight, but it is doubtful that he ever learned of his final victory. It is probable that by the time these decisions reached Peking he was already dead. De Magalhães, never one to give up, attempted still to have the last word. On October 10, 1666, less than two months after Schall's death, he wrote to Luis da Gama, the visitor, urging that in the future the appointment be refused.[33] He lost here too, however, and a Jesuit remained at the head of the Astronomical Bureau until the suppression of the Society of Jesus. After that the Lazarist fathers held the office until well into the nineteenth century, and without any noticeable damage to the integrity of the faith.

NOTES

(1) The chief sources upon which this and the following chapter are based are: Schall, *Mémoires;* Martinus Martinius [Martin Martini], *De bello Tartarico historia* (Romae: Ignatii de Lazzeris, 1654); Adrien Greslon [Grelon], *Histoire de la Chine sous la domination des Tartares* (Paris: H. Renault, 1671); Franciscus de Rougemont, *Historia Tartaro-Sinica nova* (Lovanii: Martinus Hullegaerde, 1673); and various biographical sketches in *Eminent Chinese*, cf. I, 193 ff., 195 ff., 255 ff., 231 f., 358 ff., 415, 416, 435 f., 491 f., 558; II, 635 f., 651 f., 877 ff. Schall was an eyewitness to the events in Peking. Martini was a witness to many of the events of these years. He left China in 1651, but completed his account from letters which he received from China. From 1666 to 1671 Grelon and de Rougemont were interned in Canton with the other missionaries from whom they gathered the first-hand accounts upon which they based their works. The work of Pierre Joseph d'Orleans, *Histoire des deux conquerans tartares qui ont subjugué la Chine* (Paris: C. Barbin, 1688) is based upon the accounts of Schall, Martini, Grelon and de Rougemont. Another old, but worthless, account is by Bishop Juan de Palafox, *Histoire de la conquete de l'empire de la Chine par les Tartares* (3d ed.; Amsterdam: Frederic Bernard, 1729). Said d'Orleans: "A man who wrote the history of China in Mexico upon the basis of reports which reached him from the Philippines is not a good guide to follow." This is the same Palafox whom Charles III of Spain moved heaven and earth to get canonized. Fortunately for the honor of the Church, although he succeeded in moving earth (the suppression of the Society of Jesus was related to his efforts), he was unable to move heaven.

(2) Väth, *op. cit.*, p. 159, n. 13.

(3) Quoted *ibid.*, p. 170.

(4) *Eminent Chinese*, I, 37 f.

(5) A detailed report of their experiences by de Magalhães is in *ARSI*, Jap-Sin 127, ff. 1-35. Buglio's account is published in de Magalhães' *Nouvelle relation*, pp. 371-385.

(6) *Eminent Chinese*, I, 38, 280, says that Chang was taken prisoner and executed; but de Magalhães was there.

NOTES

(7) Cf. Aleni to Vitelleschi, February 12, 1642, *ARSI*, Jap-Sin 161 II, ff. 242-243, in which he acknowledges receiving on November 3, 1641, the patents of appointment sent from Rome on January 4, 1640. The interval of almost two years was normal and added greatly to the problems of administration. More than once the appointee had died before receiving word of his appointment.

(8) Cf. Väth, *op. cit.*, pp. 253 f.

(9) *ARSI*, Jap-Sin 142 and 143.

(10) *ARSI*, Jap-Sin 142, n. 11.

(11) Grueber's complaints about Schall are in his report of July 5, 1660, in *ARSI*, Jap-Sin 143, ff. 148-159.

(12) Väth, *op. cit.*, p. 245.

(13) *Ibid.*, p. 251, quoting from Petrus Hoang, *Chêng-chiao fêng-pao* (4th ed.; Zikawei: Mission catholique, 1904), I, 43r.

(14) Streit, *op. cit.*, VI, 136.

(15) C. P. Platel Norbert, *Mémoires historiques sur les affaires des Jésuites avec le Saint Siège* (Lisbon: François-Louis Ameno, 1766), I, 8 (erroneously paginated 7).

(16) *ARSI*, Jap-Sin 161 II, ff. 228-229.

(17) Väth, *op. cit.*, p. 260, n. 39.

(18) *ARSI*, Jap-Sin 142, n. 39.

(19) *ARSI*, Lus 37 II (Assist Lusit Epist Gener Soli 1601-1674), f. 394r.

(20) Brancato left a copy of this report with Schall who, in his letter of October 6, 1654, to the general, quotes it in full in the original Portuguese; *ARSI*, Jap-Sin 142, n. 44.

(21) *ARSI*, FG 730, regis 3, 1662.

(22) *ARSI*, Jap-Sin 142, n. 14.

(23) *ARSI*, Jap-Sin 142, n. 16.

(24) Schall, *Mémoires*, p. 156.

(25) *ARSI*, Lus 37 II, ff. 394v-395v.

(26) *ARSI*, Phil II [Philippines], ff. 259-280. One wonders how this long attack upon Schall and his calendar, sent to *Propaganda Fide*, found its way into the Jesuit archives. Its author was Vittorio Riccio and he is an example of a common phenomenon of the time. Although he had never set foot in China when he wrote this tract in 1651, had been less than two years in the Philippines, had only begun to learn the rudiments of the Chinese dialect of Amoy, he did not hesitate to present his treatise to *Propaganda* as an authoritative interpretation of Schall's Chinese calendar and even of Schall's "scandalous" manner of life in far off Peking.

(27) *ARSI*, Jap-Sin 142, n. 44.

(28) *ARSI*, Jap-Sin 142, n. 46.

(29) *ARSI*, Jap-Sin 142, nn. 50, 51.

(30) *ARSI*, FG 730, regis 1662.

(31) *ARSI*, Jap-Sin 142, n. 53.

(32) *ARSI*, FG 722, regis 3, n. 5.

(33) *ARSI*, Jap-Sin 142, n. 59.

Chapter XX

Red Button and Golden Crane

HOPES OF A MING RESTORATION rested in Chinese opposition to alien rule and in the loyalty of a surprising number of capable leaders.[1] Those who had least reason to support the fallen dynasty, the members of the Tung-lin party, proved in the end its most loyal supporters. For years they had fought against corruption, incompetence, and reaction in government. When the evils they had struggled against finally brought about the fall of the dynasty, one might have expected them to find grim satisfaction in the denouement they had foreseen. Instead, for the most part, they proved the most irreconcilable opponents of the new regime and the most stalwart supporters of the Ming pretenders. And in the last and most nearly successful effort to restore the Ming, Christian leaders played the leading part.

The attempt to restore the fallen dynasty was doomed to failure. It was defeated by the factors which had brought about the initial downfall. With possibly one exception, the Prince of T'ang, the pretenders were altogether unworthy of the loyalty of the men who served them.

The first attempt at restoration occurred in Nanking. Word of the death of the Ch'ung-chên emperor, which reached the southern capital on May 17, 1644, caused the greatest confusion. "I was then in Nanking," writes Martini, "where I witnessed the strange consternation of all spirits, which prevailed until the leading mandarins, having recovered from their amazement, chose an emperor from the Ming family, giving him the title of Hungquang."

The nominee was the Prince of Fu, who had fled with his mother to Hupeh, and later to Anhwei, when his father was killed by Li Tzu-ch'êng in Honan in 1641. He was the choice of the party of reaction. Most of the reactionaries had lost no time deserting the dynasty which they themselves had scuttled. Some few thought they saw a chance to thrust themselves forward under the pretenders. Typical of these was the notorious Ma Shih-ying, commander-in-chief at Fêngyang, Anhwei. Heading the good government party in Nanking was Shih K'o-fa, a man of rare nobility of character. Supported by Tso Liang-yü, Shih advocated the candidacy of the Prince of Lu who, unlike the dissipated Prince of Fu, was regarded as having a modicum of ability. But Ma Shih-ying mustered enough political support to put over his candidate.

Other members of the Tung-lin party, besides Shih K'o-fa and Tso Liang-yü, who rallied to the support of the Nanking pretender, included Huang Tao-chou and (Thomas) Ch'ü Shih-ssu. Huang, philosopher, artist, and author, had been one of the outstanding leaders in the struggle against the reactionaries in Peking, where he held high office until 1638 when his adversaries succeeded in relegating him to a minor post in Kiangsi. He was appointed president of the Board of Rites in the government of the Nanking pretender. Ch'ü Shih-ssu was named vice-governor of Nanking.

In the autumn of 1644 the Nanking government sent a mission to Peking to propose to the Ch'ing that they withdraw from north China in return for a grant of title to all land outside the Great Wall and an annual payment of 100,000 *taels*. Dorgon rejected the offer, and, as a counterproposal, offered to leave the southern Ming court unmolested if it would abandon its claim to the northern provinces and accept the status of a dependent kingdom. The self-seeking Ma Shih-ying was strongly inclined to accept this proposal, but was forced to reject it owing to the insistence of Shih K'o-fa.[2]

The same factional struggle between corrupt politicians and good government men, which had begun in the reign of the Wan-li emperor and continued ever since, was resumed in Nanking. Ma Shih-ying, through bribery, extortion, and the unblushing sale of offices, obtained control of the Nanking court. Impeached, he bribed his way back into power. Ma got rid of Shih K'o-fa by sending him to Yangchow. Huang Tao-chou resigned and withdrew from Nanking. Ch'ü Shih-ssu was transferred to Kwangsi as governor.

Tso Liang-yü decided to oust Ma by force. He moved upon

Nanking at the head of his troops to "clarify the surroundings of the throne." Ma called in troops from the north thus weakening the defense against the Ch'ing. Tso Liang-yü died suddenly the night of April 29, 1645, before reaching Nanking.

This factional strife played into the hands of the Manchus. On May 13, 1645, a Ch'ing army, commanded by Dodo appeared before the walls of Yangchow. Shih K'o-fa rejected all demands to surrender and for seven days led a heroic defense of the city. When Yangchow fell, Dodo, angered by its resistance, put the inhabitants to the sword.[3]

Two weeks later the Ch'ing army reached Nanking. The treacherous Ma Shih-ying did not resist and Dodo entered the city unopposed. Ma fled to Chekiang where he was repudiated by the Prince of Lu. The Prince of Fu, who had fled to Wuhu in the neighboring province of Anhwei, was handed over to the Ch'ing forces by one of his own officers. Taken to Peking he died the next year.[4]

Two rival claimants to the throne now appeared. On August 18, 1645, a group of loyalists in Fukien proclaimed emperor the Prince of T'ang, eighth generation descendant of the twenty-third son of the founder of the Ming dynasty. The next day, in Chekiang, the Prince of Lu, a tenth generation descendant of the dynastic founder, assumed the title "administrator of the realm." Efforts to reconcile the two courts failed. Neither was of long duration. The forces of the Prince of Lu, commanded by Chang Kuo-wei, scored some initial success and in December, 1645, pushed the Ch'ing army back to the Ch'ien-t'ang river. But, in the following July, the treachery and incompetence of another general, Fang Kuo-an, enabled the Ch'ing forces to sweep through the province. The Prince of Lu fled to the Chusan islands. He later renounced his claims to the throne and lived until 1662, the only one of the pretenders to die a natural death.

Chief supporter of the Prince of T'ang was Huang Tao-chou, who, disgusted with the political corruption of Ma Shih-ying, had left Nanking before its fall. He now sponsored the cause of T'ang under whom he served as president of the Board of Civil Offices and grand secretary. But military power was in the hands of the freebooter Chêng Chih-lung. Huang's struggle to keep the government out of his control alienated Chêng's support. Huang, unsupported by Chêng, attempted a march into Kiangsi in 1646. He was captured on February 9 and taken to Nanking. Hung Ch'êng-ch'ou tried to persuade him to abandon the Ming cause, but like many other Tung-lin adherents, Huang steadfastly refused and was executed on April 20, 1646.

When Ch'ing armies, under Prince Bolo and General Li Ch'êng-tung swept into Fukien on September 30, 1646, they met no opposition. Chêng Chih-lung surrendered to them. On October 6, the Prince of T'ang fell into the hands of Li Ch'êng-tung and was immediately put to death. A tall, imposing man, a sincere and courageous patriot, an able writer and voracious reader, he was the most promising of the pretenders. While living at Changshu, Kiangsu, he had become a close friend of Sambiasi. Four days after being proclaimed emperor he wrote to him:

> I have been forced to accept the government of the empire. You have known me for twenty years. I swear to recover the provinces governed by my ancestors and to rule exclusively for the good of the people. You, my old friend, come and counsel me. I have already written you three times asking you to come. Now I should like to make you a military commander and then give you an ambassadorial mission. What do you think? Love me, advise me, and bring encouragement to my heart.[5]

Sambiasi had joined him in Fukien, but, declining to accept office in his government, consented only to return to Macao to seek aid for his cause.

The last pretender to the throne was the Prince of Yung-ming, or, according to the title given him in 1646 by the Prince of T'ang, the Prince of Kuei. On December 18, 1646, he was proclaimed emperor at Chaoching where sixty-four years earlier Ricci had begun his China career. His chief supporters were three Christians, (Thomas) Ch'ü Shih-ssu, (Luke) Chiao Lien, and the eunuch (Achilles) P'ang T'ien-shou. As grand secretary of the *Wên Yuan Ko* and president of the Board of Civil Offices, Ch'ü Shih-ssu was the key figure in the new regime.

The Prince of Kuei, a grandson of the Wan-li emperor, lacked courage and ability. He spent most of the time fleeing from city to city while his supporters fought valiantly against Ch'ing armies. When Canton fell to the Ch'ing on January 20, 1647, the pretender fled to Kweiling in Kwangsi. When Ch'ing forces advanced on Kweiling, he fled to Chüanchow, after adding the post of president of the Ministry of War to the other responsibilities of Ch'ü Shih-ssu.

Three times Ch'ing armies laid siege to Kweiling between April 18, 1647 and April 14, 1648. Each time they suffered defeat at the hands of Ch'ü Shih-ssu and Chiao Lien, who strengthened their defenses with the aid of cannon obtained from Macao. In recognition of his valiant efforts, the pretender conferred upon Ch'ü the title Earl of Lin-kuei and made him Grand Tutor to the Heir Apparent.

The fortunes of the Ming cause reached their peak in 1648 when all the southern provinces, except Fukien, were recovered as the result of a series of smashing victories. But in the following year two Ch'ing armies, led by K'ung Yu-tê, Shang K'o-hsi, and Kêng Chi-mao advanced successfully through Hunan and Kiangsi. After an eight months' siege, Canton fell for the second time on November 24, 1650. Three days later Kweiling was taken. Ch'ü Shih-ssu and his aide, Chang T'ung-ch'ang, were captured. K'ung Yu-tê tried in vain to persuade them to transfer their allegiance to the Ch'ing cause. Anxious to spare Ch'ü Shih-ssu, he promised him his freedom if he would but consent to shave his head and cultivate a queue as required by the Manchus. Ch'ü stoutly refused to conform to Ch'ing tonsorial standards and both he and Chang were executed.

During their forty-one days in prison, awaiting execution, the two men spent their time writing poetry. Their poems were posthumously published under the appropriate title *Hao-ch'i yin* (Odes to the Free Spirit).[6]

Before the fall of Canton, the pretender had fled from Chaoching to Wuchow. When he learned of the capture of Ch'ü Shih-ssu he moved farther west to Nanning. The advance of Ch'ing armies drove him further and further west until on March 15, 1652, he arrived at Anlung, in Kweichow province. Here he maintained his court for the next four years.

During this period the faithful P'ang T'ien-shou played an important part in the government. He was also instrumental in converting most of the imperial family to Christianity. P'ang, who gave his support to the Kuei cause after the death of the Prince of T'ang in whose government he had served, introduced the Jesuit Andreas Koffler into the court of the last pretender. P'ang himself interested the women of the household in Christianity. In 1648 Koffler baptized the pretender's wife, the empress, who took the name Anna; the pretender's mother, who took the name Maria; and the legal wife of the pretender's deceased father, who took the name

Helena.

On May 24, 1648, a few days after the baptisms, a son was born to the pretender. Koffler refused to baptize him unless his father consented to his being raised a Christian and agreed not to force him to take more than one wife. The pretender refused, but withdrew his objections when the child, stricken with illness, was at the point of death. The boy was baptized and given the name Constantine. The name did not prove prophetic of his destiny.[7]

On November 4, 1650, the empress dowager, Helena, wrote a personal letter to Pope Innocent X and another to the general of the Society of Jesus asking prayers for the Ming cause and the despatch of more missionaries to China. Two similar letters, dated November 1, were written by P'ang T'ien-shou. Michael Boym, who had assisted Koffler for a time in the court, was designated to carry the letters to Rome.[8]

Boym set out from Macao on January 1, 1651. A Chinese Christian, Andrew Chêng, accompanied him. He is probably the second Chinese to visit the Eternal City. Preceding him by several years was (Emmanuel) Chêng Wei-hsin who arrived in Rome in 1650 to enter the Jesuit novitiate the following year. Boym and his companion travelled by sea to Goa, and overland through the empire of the Great Mogul, through Persia, Armenia, Asia Minor, to Smyrna, where they took ship to Venice.[9]

The well-meaning Boym stumbled into a hornets' nest. Arrived in Venice he had, without first communicating with the Jesuit general, presented himself to the *Serenissime Doge* of the Republic to whom he carried a letter from P'ang T'ien-shou certifying the authenticity of his mission. For this he incurred the wrath of the general, Goswin Nickel, who thought it contrary to his profession that he should have presented himself as ambassador and who was not easily placated. From Loretto, Boym wrote on February 21, 1653, explaining his reasons for presenting his credentials to the Doge of Venice and concluding:

> For these and other reasons, approved by several cardinals, I desired to make this embassy public; but if this displeases your Paternity, inasmuch as I have submitted both my intelligence and will to obedience, I am ready, at the first sign, either to come to Rome or to return immediately to China, even at cost to my reputation and my health.[10]

When he got to Rome he found himself the center of a more

serious storm. The charge was freely bandied about that Boym was a charlatan, that he had never been to China, that his letters were forgeries, that the mission was a clumsy fraud invented by the Jesuits to enhance their reputation and deceive the Holy See! Boym must have longed for the relative tranquility and simplicity of life in war-torn China.

He had abundant proof of the authenticity of his mission: the notarized depositions of the ecclesiastical administrator of Macao, letters from Sebastiao de Maya, Jesuit visitor to Japan and China, from the archbishop of Meliapor and patriarch of Ethiopia. But the voice of calumny was not easily stilled. For three years Boym and his Chinese companion cooled their heels in Rome. Meantime Innocent X died. At length the skepticism and seeming indifference of the Holy See was breached and Alexander VII, in letters dated December 18, 1655, replied to the empress dowager and to P'ang T'ien-shou. The Jesuit general added his own replies, dated December 25. It is to be hoped that Boym knows, and derives consolation from the knowledge, that today the letters which he carried to Rome from the Ming court and had such trouble presenting to the Holy See are among the most prized possessions of the Vatican archives.[11]

The replies never reached their destination. Boym and Chêng sailed from Lisbon early in 1656 and arrived in Tonkin in August 1658. The empress dowager had died in Tienchow, Kwangsi, on May 30, 1651. Koffler had died the following January 4 when, fleeing with the court, he became separated from the other refugees and fell into the hands of the Manchus who slew him on the spot. The faithful P'ang T'ien-shou had died in 1657. The cause of the pretender was in the last stage of disintegration. None of these dire tidings reached Boym, and his last letter, written from Tonkin in November, 1658, is filled with optimism. He thinks the queens are still living. He has heard that P'ang has led a successful elephant charge against the Manchus. Deceived by these false reports he obtained a visa from the Tonkinese court and had penetrated Kwangsi province a distance of six days on foot before he learned of the disasters that had fallen on the Ming cause. In the face of an advancing Manchu army he turned back towards Tonkin, but was stopped at the border. He sent word to two Jesuits in Tonkin to appeal for a re-entry permit. They were unable to obtain it. Seriously ill with dysentery, worn out by his exertions, and brokenhearted over the failure of his mission, he suddenly died on August 22, 1659. The faithful Andrew Chêng buried him on the border separating Tonkin from China.

During these years, while Boym was pursuing his hopeless mission for the Ming to its tragic denouement, Adam Schall's brilliant star was in dizzying ascendancy in the Ch'ing firmament despite de Magalhães' best efforts to shoot it down. On February 1, 1651, the Shun-chih emperor, twelve years old but mature far beyond his years, dissolved the regency and assumed real direction of affairs. The relations which quickly developed between the emperor and the Jesuit have no precedent in Chinese history.

The emperor delighted in Schall's company and depended upon his advice. He never addressed the sixty-year-old Schall by any other name than "Ma-fa," a Manchu expression equivalent to "Grandpa." Their relationship was indeed more that of grandfather and grandson than that of emperor and subject.

Reports and petitions were required to be presented indirectly to the emperor through officials appointed to receive them. Schall was allowed to present his reports directly, at any hour and wherever the emperor might be found. Because they conflicted with his Mass, he was dispensed from attending the early morning audiences which, on certain days, the director of the Bureau of Astronomy was supposed to attend with other ministers of state. In October, 1651, the emperor exempted Schall from future performances of the *k'o-t'ou* in his presence, a privilege enjoyed by only two privy councillors and four ministers. On state occasions when the emperor sat upon his throne Schall sat upon a cushion placed in front of him.

Members of the Dutch mission which visited Peking in 1656-1657 witness to the position of Schall at that time. Jan Nieuhoff, steward of the Dutch party, describes their first encounter with Schall. The embassy was received by the Council of State. The presiding minister sat cross-legged on a raised bench, two Manchu members of the council sat on his right, while on his left sat "a Jesuit, with a long white beard, his head shaved and dressed in Tatar fashion. He is from Cologne on the Rhine, is named Adam Schall, and has been forty-six years in Peking (sic), enjoying great esteem with the Emperor of China." Schall spoke to the Dutch in German, congratulating them upon their safe arrival, and inquiring after several Catholic families in Amsterdam with whom he was acquainted.

Afterwards he walked with them to the gate of the palace while "the ambassadors on the way spoke to him of a great many things, to which he replied with intelligence, in which the Jesuits are not wanting."[12]

Interesting is Nieuhoff's description of the Shun-chih emperor as he saw him at the imperial audience where the Dutchmen were received together with an embassy from the great Mogul: "A young man, white of skin, of medium size; rather plain, wearing a vest which seemed woven from gold." To the disappointment and astonishment of the Dutch the audience passed in complete silence. The emperor sat upon his throne while the ambassadors knelt some thirty paces in front of him. At the end of a quarter of an hour the emperor arose, paused to look intently at the Dutchmen, and left.

The emperor often summoned Schall to his palace at night to converse with him. Whenever he kept him there until a late hour he sent several young Manchu princes to accompany him back to his residence. In utter disregard of tradition, the young ruler frequently visited Schall's home. Sometimes he kept his suite of as many as six hundred persons waiting outside while he sat in Schall's room, cross-legged on the bed, or on an old chair, or on a bench used by the Jesuit's students, questioning Schall about his religious beliefs and his manner of life. In 1656-1657 he visited Schall's home twenty-four times. Sometimes he stopped first in the church. He visited every corner of the house, picked fruit in the garden, and watched Schall's workmen making instruments for the observatory. On March 15, 1657, when Schall joined members of the imperial family, officials, and notables at the palace to congratulate him on his birthday, the emperor suddenly announced that he wished to celebrate the occasion at Schall's home. The Jesuit hurried home and prepared food. The official gazettes kept the whole empire informed of the friendship of the emperor for Schall.

There is little doubt that during these years Schall was one of the most influential men in the empire. A member of the Dutch embassy of 1656-1657 wrote: "Father Adam Schall is in such great favor with this prince that he has access to him at any hour."[13] In 1661 Verbiest reported: "Schall has more influence upon the emperor than any viceroy, or than the most respected prince, and the name of Father Adam is better known in China than the name of any famous man in Europe."[14] And de Rougemont remarked: "I do not believe that since the foundation of the Chinese empire any foreigner has received so many marks of honor and kingly favor."[15] The real proofs of "kingly favor" are in the titles conferred upon him.

The mandarinal hierarchy was divided into nine grades, with each grade containing two divisions. Through the conferring of honorary titles it was possible to raise a man in the hierarchy without the necessity of his holding particular offices. As director of the Bureau of Astronomy, Schall was *ex officio* an official of the fifth class, first division. During Dorgon's regency he received an honorary title which raised him to the fourth class, first division. On September 15, 1651, he received three titles of honor. On April 2, 1653 the honorary title "Master of Universal Mysteries," was added to the others. On March 15, 1657, the emperor ordered an inscription in praise of Schall erected in front of the church. In October of the same year he was given the title "President of the Imperial Chancery" and made an official of the third class, first division. Finally, on February 2, 1658, he reached the hierarchical summit: he was given the title "Imperial Chamberlain" and made a mandarin of the first class, first division. Only the grand secretaries and the most important princes of royal blood belonged, *ex officio*, to this class. As a sign of his rank, Schall from this time on wore the red button on his hat and, on the breast of his tunic, the gold-embroidered crane with open wings.

There was nothing obsequious in Schall's close relations with the young emperor. The primary object of his life was to further the cause of Christianity. But he had a sincere and deep affection for the emperor who had many excellent qualities: "Shun-chih is, to be sure, a youth," wrote Martini, "but singularly endowed with a sense of prudence, equity, and especially justice."[16] He also had many imperfections: a violent temper, an inclination to superstition, and a strongly-sexed nature. Only Schall had the courage to admonish him of his faults. To his official reports to the emperor he was accustomed to add personal admonitions. On one occasion, in 1655, at the emperor's request, he wrote down everything he found to reproach in the personal conduct and mode of government of his royal friend.

Schall's influence upon the ruler's thought is evident in his exhortations to officials and officers. It was the custom of Ch'ing emperors to issue written exhortations to their officials. The Shun-chih

This portrait of Johann Adam Schall formerly hung in the venerable Jesuit novitiate at San Andrea al Quirinale in Rome, where Schall had himself once been a novice. When this building was expropriated by the government it was moved and now hangs in the Jesuit house at Galloro. It is known that Johann Grueber, like many Jesuits of the time a competent artist, painted Schall's portrait during his stay in Peking in 1660. It is possible that he brought it with him to Rome and that this is it.

emperor's exhortations, collected in six *chüan*, contain a great deal that is of Christian inspiration.[17]

Schall had hopes of converting the emperor to Christianity. Many long conversations were held on such subjects as immortality, the ten commandments, the nature of God, grace, marriage, celibacy, the life of Christ. In his visits to Schall's church the emperor examined everything attentively. On one occasion he had Schall don all the Mass vestments and explain their significance. The illustrated life of Christ, presented by Schall to the last Ming emperor, fascinated him. One day he stretched out upon Schall's bed, the book open before him, while the old Jesuit, kneeling beside the bed explained the passion of Christ.

Schall was convinced that the young emperor believed in the truth of Christianity with his mind, but not with his heart. The requirements of the sixth commandment and the demands of Christian monogamy were a stumbling block to him. In the end, Schall felt, it was this which defeated him: "He could not overcome the lusts of the flesh."

Schall, a deeply humble man, thought that Le Fèvre, who had a reputation for sanctity, might succeed where he had failed. He was anxious that Le Fèvre be sent to Peking. In a letter of June 5, 1657 to Semedo he expresses himself clearly on this point.[18]

After 1658 Schall's influence upon the emperor declined. The young ruler fell more and more under the influence of eunuchs, of Buddhist monks, and, veering away from Christianity, developed a deep interest in Ch'an (Zen) Buddhism.

For several years the power of the eunuchs, who during the regency of Dorgon had practically no influence, had been growing. In 1653 the emperor established thirteen offices controlled by eunuchs in the palace. Some of them were even given a measure of control over the issuing of imperial edicts and the appointing of officials. The old sinister pattern was reappearing. Although in 1655 and again in 1658 the emperor warned them to mend their ways and scolded them for accepting bribes, their influence and power continued to grow. Using a tool they had often found effective in establishing their ascendancy over young emperors, they encouraged him freely to indulge his sexual impulses.[19]

It was usually true that Buddhist influence in the Forbidden City waxed or waned as the power of the eunuchs rose or fell. In 1657 eunuchs arranged a meeting between the emperor and Hsing-ts'ung, a Buddhist monk. Hsing-ts'ung persuaded him that in a previous incarnation he had been a monk. Other Buddhist monks who had considerable influence upon him during the last four years of his life were Tao-min, a man of charm and intelligence, and T'ung-hsiu, abbot of the monastery of Mt. T'ien-mu in Chekiang.

Not unrelated to these influences, so powerful in the last years of his life, was the *grande passion* which the emperor conceived for Hsiao-hsien, daughter of Osi of the Donggo clan. Hsiao-hsien, according to Jesuit accounts, was the wife of a young Manchu noble. According to Ch'ên Yuan, eminent historian, the young noble was, in fact, the emperor's youngest half-brother, Bombogor. [20] Determined to have her, the emperor, reports de Rougemont, so abused her young husband that he died of grief. It is more likely that, seeing which way the wind was blowing, Bombogor committed suicide. At any rate, the eighteen-year-old Hsiao-hsien entered the palace in 1656 to become the emperor's favorite consort. He was infatuated with her. She was given the title *Huang Kuei-fei* (Imperial Consort of the First Class), a rank next to that of empress. At the instigation of the eunuchs, the emperor had some time before this deposed his first empress, and would have deposed her successor in favor of Hsiao-hsien but for the determined opposition of the empress dowager and high officials. But he lavished far more favors upon her than were due her rank.

From this time on the emperor lost interest in state affairs and became more and more absorbed in Hsiao-hsien and in Ch'an Buddhism, an interest his young consort shared with him. In November, 1657, she gave birth to a son who died the following February. Two years later, in 1660, she herself died. The emperor was inconsolable. He raised her posthumously to the rank of empress and her body was borne by high officials to the Ching-shan, a small hill north of the palace, where elaborate Buddhist ceremonies were conducted by T'ung-hsiu at enormous cost.

A palatial hall was constructed for the sarcophagus. At the end of the services the abbot T'ung-hsiu applied the torch to the huge funeral pyre. Besides the costly building, a fortune in jewels, silks and other precious objects was destroyed. The distracted young emperor ordered some thirty members of the dead woman's entourage to commit suicide in order to join her in death, thus reviving a cruel Manchu custom which the Chinese thoroughly detested and the Tatars themselves had abandoned.[21]

The inevitable legends have flowered from the story of the Shun-chih emperor's love for Hsiao-hsien. Most popular is the story that his own death was a hoax to enable him to give up the throne and, in disguise, to retire to a Buddhist monastery where he lived long years with his memories. The truth is that, already suffering from tuberculosis, he was exhausted by the long and tiring ceremonies which followed her death. On February 2, 1661, four and a half months after her death, he contracted smallpox and died three days later.

During these last years Schall had been more and more shunted aside although the emperor never lost his affection for his old counsellor and friend. But his new orientation of life was in conflict with all that Schall stood for. Under the circumstances Schall's admonitions, which he continued to administer orally and in writing, were troublesome. They were unpleasant reminders which he no longer wished brought to his attention.

Nevertheless, the young emperor must at times have felt conscience-stricken for on July 28, 1660, he sent Schall a note in which one can sense an overtone of apology:

> Your law [Christianity] is already widely spread. Through your exertions the science of astronomy has become known. Thus, Jo-wang, do you labor for the empire. Should not the heart of the Emperor rejoice! You, Jo-wang, know how the empire should be governed. For this reason come to me and we will talk about it. Jo-wang, conserve my words in your heart.[22]

Schall visited him while he lay dying and made a last effort to win him to the Christian faith. The emperor appeared touched by his loyalty and read an exhortation which Schall had prepared on the subject of death and eternal life. But he put off further discussion of the subject until his recovery. Before he died Schall was able to render one last service. His successor had not been named. The emperor was inclined to name a cousin. His mother, the empress dowager, Hsiao-chuang, and the Manchu princes urged that he name one of his sons. The dying ruler asked Schall's advice. He sided with the dowager. Thereupon the emperor named the third of his eight sons, the six-year-old Hsüan-yeh, the future K'ang-hsi emperor, to succeed him. China should be grateful for Schall's part in naming one of her greatest emperors.

When the Shun-chih emperor died in Peking the flickering embers of Ming hopes were within seventeen months of final extinction in far distant south China. In its last years the regime of the Prince of Kuei found its chief military support in the armies of Li Ting-kuo and Sun K'o-wang, former lieutenants of the tyrant Chang Hsien-chung. In 1652, after several years of free-lance fighting against the Ch'ing, they joined the Ming cause. Li Ting-kuo won a number of brilliant victories, but by 1656 he and Sun, who suffered from illusions of imperial grandeur, were locked in internecine strife. Li defeated Sun, but the struggle opened the way to final Ch'ing victory. Sun K'o-wang led his troops into the Ch'ing camp, surrendering to Hung Ch'êng-ch'ou.

Three Ch'ing armies drove into Kweichow and Yunnan in 1658. In March, 1659, the pretender asked permission of the Burmese to take refuge in their country. He and his household, numbering some 646 persons, were taken down the Irrawaddy River to Sagaing where the King of Burma kept them virtual prisoners. Li Ting-kuo, after desperate fighting, occupied the northeast part of Burma, where for two years he fought off both Burmese and Ch'ing armies. Almost three hundred years later and in this same area, in what seems a re-enactment of the same historical scene, remnants of Chiang Kai-shek's nationalist troops, driven over the border into Burma by communist forces, repeated the experience.

In June, 1661, the Prince of Prome murdered his brother, the King of Burma, and seized control of the country. He put to death more than half of the Ming pretender's retinue and placed the others under heavy guard.

It was the sorry distinction of Wu San-kuei, who had played a vital if ambiguous role in the first chapter of the story of Ming collapse, to figure prominently in its final scene. At the head of a large force of Ch'ing troops he arrived at Aungbinle, Burma, on January 20, 1662, and demanded the surrender of the last Ming pretender. Two days later the Prince of Prome delivered him his prisoners. They were taken to Yunnanfu. There in June, 1662, the Prince of Kuei and his fourteen-year-old son and heir, (Constantine) Chu Tz'u-hsüan, were put to death by strangulation with a bowstring. The pretender's widow and mother were taken to the capital.

Thus, with a bowstring in Yunnanfu, ended the Ming saga which had begun more than three centuries before when an orphan boy had left a Buddhist monastery to lead the revolt which toppled the descendants of Ghengis Khan from their throne and restored Chinese rule to the empire.

NOTES

(1) For the chief sources relied upon in this chapter cf. chapter XIX, note 1.

(2) Martini gives a different version according to which the Nanking government offered to recognize the Manchu conquest of the northern provinces. On many details the sources conflict. I have not bothered to call attention to all such conflicts, but have followed the version which seemed to me more probably correct.

(3) Shih K'o-fa's correspondence with Dorgon reveals the nobility of his character; cf. Wilhelm Hellmut, "Ein Briefwecksel zwischen Dorgon und Shi Ko-fa," *Sinica* VIII (1935), pp. 239 ff.

(4) *Eminent Chinese*, I, 196. Martini, *op. cit.*, p. 57, says he was executed in Peking. Joseph de Mailla, *Histoire générale de la Chine* (Paris: P. D. Pierres, 1777-1785), X, 529 f., says he drowned in the Yangtse river while fleeing from his pursuers.

(5) In the Jesuit archives is a Portuguese translation of this letter, which is dated the 4th day of the 10th month of the first year of the reign of Lung-wu, the reign title assumed by the Prince of T'ang; *ARSI*, Jap-Sin 123, f. 174r.

(6) *Eminent Chinese*, I, 201.

(7) When visiting Macao at the end of 1648 Koffler told the story of the conversions. An Italian version of his account, taken down at the time, is in *ARSI*, Jap-Sin 125, ff. 139-153r.

(8) Boym was a Polish Jesuit whose father had been personal physician to King Sigismund of Poland. He inherited his father's interest in medicine as is suggested by his work on the Chinese method of diagnosis from observation of the pulse, the first discussion of the subject by a European. Philip Couplet sent it to Batavia in 1658 to be transmitted to Europe. The Dutch kept it for over twenty years and finally in 1682 published a plagiarized edition at Francfort Zubrodt, attributing it to one Andreas Claye. Boym also wrote another scientific work, which he illustrated himself, on various fruits and flowers of China, likewise the first *ex professo* treatment of the subject by a European. Cf. the excellent study by Boleslaw Szczesniak, "The Writings of Michael Boym," *Monumenta serica* XIV (1949-1955), 481-538; cf. also Robert Chabrié, *Michel Boym, jésuite polonais et la fin des Ming en Chine (1646-1662)* (Paris: Pierre Bossuet, 1933), and the review of this book by Paul Pelliot in *T'oung Pao*, XXXI (1935), 95 ff., and comments by Henri Bernard in *Monumenta serica* I, 215.

(9) In Smyrna Boym delivered a lecture on the royal conversions. It is published in Thevenot, *op. cit.*, I, under the title "Briefve relation de la Chine et de la notable conversion des personnes royales. . ."

(10) *ARSI*, Jap-Sin 77, f. 130.

(11) Translations of the letters together with Alexander VII's replies are in Athanasius Kircher, *op. cit.*, pp. 100 ff. Cf. also E. H. Parker (ed.) "Letters from a Chinese empress and a Chinese eunuch to the Pope in the year 1650," *Contemporary Review*, CI (London, 1912), 79 ff.

NOTES

(12) Jan Nieuhoff, "Le voyage des ambassadeurs de la compagnie hollandoise des Indes Orientales vers le Grand Chan de Tartarie, à Peking," in Thevenot, *op. cit.*, II, no. 1, 51 ff.

(13) In *ibid.*, I, no. 8, 29.

(14) *ARSI,* Jap-Sin 143, Regis. 8, f. 11v.

(15) Quoted by Väth, *op. cit.*, p. 207, n. 69.

(16) *Ibid.*, p. 171, n. 1.

(17) Cf. Philosensis, "Ta Tsing hwang ti shing Heun (Sacred Instructions of the Ta Tsing dynasty)," *Chinese Repository*, X (Canton, 1841), 593 ff.

(18) Väth, *op. cit.*, p. 199.

(19) Cf. *Eminent Chinese*, I, 257.

(20) *Ibid.*

(21) De Rougemont, *op. cit.*, pp. 142 ff.

(22) Brancato to Espinelli, October 9, 1661, *ARSI,* Jap-Sin 124, ff. 19-20.

Chapter XXI

Sturdy Oaks Brought Down

THESE YEARS OF trouble had been years of both loss and gain for the mission. The losses were chiefly in personnel and in property. Seven Jesuits lost their lives in the upheaval. Besides Walta, de Figueredo, and Koffler, three others died violent deaths when the city of Nanchang fell to the Ch'ing forces in 1644. These were Tranquillo Grassetti, Joze d'Almeida, and Brother (Manoel) Lu Yu-chi. In 1643 Augusto Tudeschini drowned en route to Macao from Foochow when his ship was boarded and set afire. Still others died natural deaths, among them the last of the great pioneers.

In 1649 Aleni, Ferreira and Sambiasi passed away. Aleni died quietly at Yenping and was buried outside the north gate of Foochow on *Shih-tze-chia shan* (Mountain of the Cross). He left at least twenty-six works in Chinese.[1] More than two centuries after his death reprints of some of his writings were still appearing.

After the regime of the Prince of T'ang collapsed, Sambiasi settled in Canton. There he built a church and a residence and there he was severely wounded in a scuffle with a band of looting Ch'ing soldiers during the sack of Canton in 1647. He owed his life to a former Jesuit brother, now a soldier in the Ch'ing army, who, passing by, saw his one-time confrère sorely beset and came to his rescue. Sambiasi never entirely recovered from his wounds and died two years later at the age of sixty-seven.

Gaspar Ferreira, like Sambiasi, barely escaped death in Canton in 1647. His death, shortly after that of Sambiasi, at the age of seventy-eight, left Longobardo as Ricci's only contemporary.

Francisco Furtado died in 1653. In the course of the next year the venerable Longobardo, within five years of the century mark, followed him. The Shun-chih emperor, fond of the old man, had commissioned an artist to paint his portrait shortly before his death. With the death of Semedo in Canton in 1658, of Manoel Dias, Junior, in Hangchow in 1659, the old familiar names are gone from the mission.

These men had all played outstanding parts in carrying forward the work begun by Ricci. With Cattaneo, the older Dias, Vagnoni, de Ursis, Trigault, Rho, and Terrenz, they formed a body of gallant men of whom Valignano and Ricci would have been proud. Christian culture has never had better representatives in China nor has Chinese culture ever had more sincere and sympathetic admirers. Scarcely more than a dozen men, they brought together two worlds and established a contact that, however weakened by later developments, has never been broken. Within the span of a man's lifetime they overcame the deep hostility of the protagonists of a proud and self-contained culture and won wide recognition for Christianity. Before the last of them had died there were Christian communities in all the provinces of the empire save two — Yunnan and Kweichow. Even these, through Christian influences in the court of the last pretender, had been touched by Christianity. The gap which these missionaries had to bridge was far wider than the one which had separated the culture of Rome from the culture of nascent Christianity. It is only by comparing the status of Christianity in China eight decades after Ricci had entered the empire with its position in Rome eighty years after the death of St. Peter that the magnitude of their achievement can be appreciated.

The mission lost a not inconsiderable number of churches, destroyed by fire in the struggles of these years. It is impossible to determine the exact number, because the reports make only passing references to churches destroyed. In Shansi, the churches in Chiangchow, Puchow and Taiyüan; in Hukuang, the church at Wuchang; in Kiangsi, the church at Nanchang; in Fukien, the church at Foochow, were destroyed in whole or in part. That there were many others is suggested by the fact that T'ung Kuo-ch'i, governor of Fukien (1653-1658), not only rebuilt the church in Foochow, but restored at his own expense church buildings at Kanchow and elsewhere in Kiangsi. A stone tablet, dated June 18, 1655, giving his account of the dedication of the new church still stands at Foochow.

He also built a large church in Hangchow, on the site of the edifice erected by Yang T'ing-yün in 1627.[2] T'ung Kuo-ch'i's wife, known in Jesuit accounts of the time as Madame Agatha, was a devout Catholic. T'ung himself did not become a Catholic until 1674 when he was baptized in Nanking by Felix Pacheco.

The Christian communities hardest hit were in Fukien. They shared in the general devastation brought about in that province during the long and fierce struggle between Chêng Ch'êng-kung and the Ch'ing. Many a flourishing Christian center was broken up by the "scorched earth" policy of the Ch'ing which, in 1662, depopulated a wide coastal area of the province.

Chêng Ch'êng-kung was the son of the famous freebooter, Chêng Chih-lung, who, after making himself master of the coastal sea lanes, had entered the service of the Ming court in 1628. Upon his defection to the Ch'ing in 1648 his son assumed command of his army and fleet and for years was a thorn in the side of the Manchus, inflicting repeated defeats upon them in Fukien over which, by 1655, he had established complete military and civil control. The Prince of Kuei made him Marquis Wei-yuan, Duke Chang-kuo, and Prince of Yên-p'ing.

He finally suffered defeat in a great battle before Nanking on September 9, 1659, and had to fall back to Amoy. Turning again to the sea he wrested Formosa from the Dutch in 1661-1662. From here he repeatedly raided the mainland. In desperation the Ch'ing authorities ordered all coastal inhabitants of Shantung, Kiangnan, Chekiang, Fukien and Kwangtung provinces removed inland a distance of 30 to 50 *li*. All cities, towns, and villages in the evacuated area were razed. The blow fell heaviest upon Fukien. De Gouvea and Canevari saw their churches and residences destroyed, their Christians widely scattered. Macao, isolated by the coastal evacuation, was almost ruined.[3]

The gains of these years, however, far outweighed the losses. The rate of growth continued at a pace that is astonishing when it is remembered that at no time were there more than two dozen missionaries in China and that they had to work amid the confusion and turmoil of a nation at war. Verbiest estimated the number of conversions each year at 10,000. According to Gabiani there were 104,980 converts between 1651 and 1664. In 1663 the visitor, da Gama, reported that there were then 114,000 Christians living in China. In the following year Le Favre, the vice-provincial, wrote to Rome that "the

Manchus allow the Gospel to be preached with the same freedom which prevails in Europe."[4]

The ink was scarcely dry on Le Favre's optimistic letter when a devastating blow struck down the freedom of the Church everywhere in the empire. Storm center was Peking. Immediate target was Adam Schall. Ultimate goal was the destruction of Christianity in China.

The death of the Shun-chih emperor had not immediately affected Schall's position or prestige. On his seventy-first birthday, April 29, 1661, he received congratulatory essays from many high officials. Later in that same year when, by a special edict signed by the K'ang-hsi emperor, his adopted grandson, T'ang Shih-hung, was granted the privileges of a student of the Imperial Academy, Schall received more congratulatory messages, among them one by the grand secretary, Hu Shih-an. For three more years he remained secure; but meanwhile the storm was gathering.[5]

Arch-conspirator in the movement against Schall was one Yang Kuang-hsien, a notorious and self-seeking charlatan, but not without courage or, as the Jesuits admitted, intelligence. A sensationalist and publicity seeker, Yang's melodramatic interventions in politics had brought him a flogging and banishment to Liaotung during the reign of the last Ming emperor. Freed in 1644, he lived for some years in Nanking. In 1659 he suddenly thrust himself again into the limelight, this time as a crusader against Christianity. In that year he began to publish treatises bitterly attacking the Christian religion and, at the same time, criticizing Schall's calendar.

His arguments reveal a bitter, bigoted, but sharp mind. He was familiar with the story of Christian origins and with the life of Christ. His philosophic argument, built around the notion of *yin* and *yang*, shows that he was under the influence of Taoist thought. His Taoist orientation is further suggested by his claims to possess the power of divination, a claim which for a time made him popular with the ladies in Peking.

His feud was not a personal one with Schall.[6] It is clear from his writings that the object of his hatred was Christianity. If he centered his attack upon Schall it was because of the latter's prominence and because, in the minds of reactionaries, the cause of European science was closely allied to the cause of Christianity.

Yang Kuang-hsien found valuable allies in certain disgruntled

Moslem functionaries in the Bureau of Astronomy. In 1657 Wu Ming-hsüan was punished with several months' imprisonment when his charges that Schall had made several faulty predictions proved unfounded. First sentenced to death he had been spared through Schall's personal intervention. This magnanimous act seemed only to intensify Wu's hatred. After his release he and Yang joined forces, Wu supplying Yang with a smattering of astronomical knowledge.

From 1660 on Yang periodically filed charges against Schall with the Board of Rites. For several years his accusations were ignored, but by 1664, political developments in Peking conspired to create a situation favorable to his intrigues. During the minority of the K'ang-hsi emperor the direction of government was entrusted to a regency composed of the four Manchu princes, Oboi, Ebilun, Soni, and Susaha. Oboi, a shrewd and unscrupulous political adventurer, succeeded with the support of Ebilun in concentrating power in his own hands. Already well-supplied with money by his sympathizers, Yang Kuang-hsien found in Oboi the political support he needed. On September 15, 1664, he submitted a document to the Board of Rites in which he charged Schall with errors in astronomical calculations and the missionaries throughout the empire of plotting against the state and indoctrinating the people with false ideals. There was nothing new in these accusations, but to them Yang added the charge that Schall had selected an inauspicious day for the burial of the infant son of Hsiao-hsien in 1658 and thus, by casting a spell, caused the early death of both the mother and the Shun-chih emperor. It was a stratagem calculated to have its effect upon the Manchu rulers, strongly influenced by Shaministic superstitions. The charge was, of course, false. Schall had nothing to do with the selection of the burial day. That belonged to the office of the Minister of Rites. But when Oboi gave his support to Yang Kuang-hsien the victory of Schall's enemies was assured. Everything played into Yang's hands. At the moment when he stood most in need of his faculties, a stroke of paralysis deprived the aged Schall of the power of speech.

On November 12, 1664, Regent Oboi committed the four Jesuits in Peking, Schall, his assistant Verbiest, Buglio and de Magalhães, to prison. Schall was stripped of his titles. For six months the prisoners were chained to wooden posts. Scarcely a day passed without their appearance before one or another tribunal. They were months of intense suffering, but also of high dramatic interest. Verbiest acting as lawyer for the defense, conducted his case with dignity and courage. Nothing better revealed the weakness of Yang's case than the manner in which it was shunted from tribunal to tribunal.

Early in January, Schall was sentenced to death by strangulation. The other three Jesuits were to be flogged and banished from the empire. Seven Christian officials of the Bureau of Astronomy received the same sentence.

Execution of the sentence was suspended while the solidity of the foreigner's astronomical teaching was subjected to a comparative test. A solar eclipse was anticipated. In his prison cell, Verbiest, with the assistance of Schall, worked out his calculations. The Mohammedan and Chinese astronomers were ordered to make their predictions. When the hour of the eclipse approached, the Bureau of Astronomy was crowded with members of the privy council, ministers of state, observatory officials, and other mandarins. In an atmosphere of tense expectation the critical moment drew near. The Chinese astronomers had predicted that the eclipse would begin at a quarter past two o'clock; the Mohammedans at half past two; Verbiest at three o'clock. At exactly the stroke of three the first shadow of darkness began to appear upon the face of the sun. The test resulted in a triumph for the Europeans.

The forces mobilized by Yang Kuang-hsien were, however, too strongly entrenched to surrender. The series of interminable hearings began again before various tribunals. By this time the case was receiving nationwide publicity. Popular sympathy was on the side of the accused. This is indicated by the apologetic title of a two-volume tract published at this time by Yang Kuang-hsien giving the reasons for his campaign against Christianity and European astronomy. He called it *Pu-tê-i* (I Could Not Do Otherwise). Buglio answered him in a four-volume work entitled *Pu-tê-i pien* (I Could Not Do Otherwise Refuted).[7]

In the earlier judicial hearings the accused had so easily and effectively answered the charges directed against their religious teaching that this part of the indictment was dropped. The only question left in issue was that of their astronomical teaching. What was really on trial was science itself. The grand council held a series of dramatic hearings lasting from March to May. While the partially paralyzed Schall looked on in forced silence, Verbiest with charts and instruments demonstrated the truth of European astronomy and answered all objections raised against it.

Verbiest's demonstrations were in vain. The Jesuits were not on trial: they were caught in a conspiracy and prejudged. In mid-April, under pressure from Oboi, the grand council condemned Schall and his seven Chinese colleagues to decapitation. Oboi himself changed the sentence to the most terrible penalty of the judicial code — the *ling-ch'ih*, dismemberment of the living body.

At this point nature intervened. An earthquake struck Peking with devastating force. Fire broke out in the imperial palace. More than one member of the grand council, ashamed of his part in the whole affair, pointed to these phenomena as signs of heaven's displeasure. At the same time the empress dowager, Hsiao-chuang, mother of the Shun-chih emperor, angrily denounced Oboi's persecution of her son's great and good friend. The regent, apparently frightened by the extent of the popular support which had rallied to Schall, beat a retreat. Although five of Schall's Christian scholar-colleagues were executed, the four Jesuits were released on May 18 and permitted to remain in Peking.

Meanwhile all the other missionaries in China, except three Dominicans who escaped detection and remained in hiding in Fukien, had been brought to Peking. Twenty-five Jesuits, four Dominicans, and one Franciscan assembled in the capital. In September, 1665, they were banished to Canton where they were kept in detention until 1671. All churches were closed.

In his years of prosperity the faults of Schall's richly human character had blinded some of his colleagues to his genuine nobility. It took adversity to reveal the stature of the man. He endured the disasters with a calm heroism that aroused Verbiest's deepest admiration. On July 2, 1665, a moving scene was enacted in his room in Peking. To his fellow Jesuits, gathered around the old man's bed, Verbiest read Schall's acknowledgment of his faults. Written by Verbiest at Schall's dictation and signed by Schall it is a truly touching human document. The pathetic evidence of Schall's paralysis is plain to be seen in the almost illegible scrawl of his signature, contrasting sharply with his customarily neat script.[8] Devoid of the affectation which easily insinuates itself into such confessions, its every sentence bears the impress of a sincere and genuinely humble nature.

Schall accuses himself of having been a source of vexation to others, especially to his superiors "whose advice and opinion I did not always follow and whose authority I called in question both in word and writing." He had been too condescending towards his servant for whose impudence and insolence he accepts the responsibility. He had offended against a strict observance of poverty by using things without necessity. His adoption of a grandson had been an imprudence. In word and writing he had offended the "brotherly love" due his fellow Jesuits. This catalogue of his own faults represents the worst that can be said of Schall. They were the faults of a strong-willed but magnanimous man whose essential goodness they but serve to accentuate.

For these faults Schall asked forgiveness and spiritual aid from his colleagues:

> . . . The compassionate God . . . in the place, at the time and in the manner which His providence and grace ordain gently touches and strongly moves the hearts [of men]. In this place and at this time the hand of God, a fatherly hand, a loving hand, a compassionate hand, has not only stricken me in body but has also touched my soul. As the compassion of God has until now patiently suffered me to live in the Society of His Son, so I trust that out of regard for your prayers and your services He will allow me to persevere unto the end and with His grace protect me. Amen.

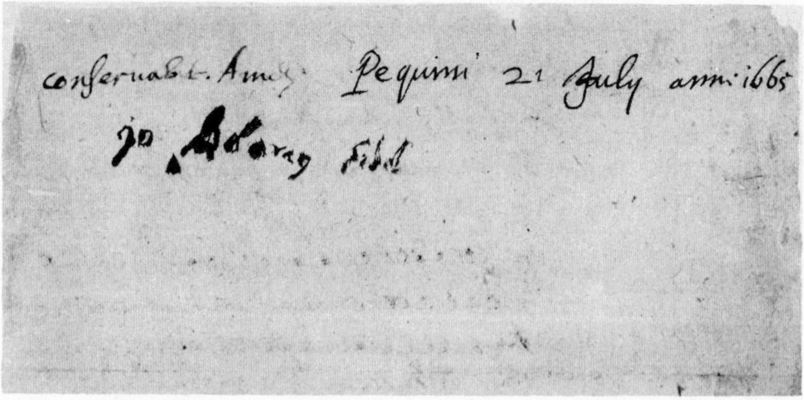

The signs of his paralysis are clearly evident in this almost illegible scrawl with which Adam Schall signed his confession of faults, read by Verbiest to all the Jesuits in Peking gathered at Schall's bedside. (From the original in the Jesuit archives in Rome.)

A little more than a year later, on August 15, 1666, Schall in his seventy-sixth year died peacefully in Peking, closing a career as exciting and colorful as his own personality. Although lacking their tact and evenness of disposition, he ranks with Ricci, who preceded him, and Verbiest, who succeeded him, as one of the three outstanding figures in the history of the Jesuit mission in China.

He was a man of exceptional attainments and of universal knowledge. Like Ricci, he had an extraordinary memory that elicited the admiration of his colleagues. Although his forte was in the positive sciences, where he kept abreast of all the latest European developments, he had a good speculative mind as well. He was proficient in dogmatic theology, in civil and ecclesiastical law, in scriptural, ecclesiastical and profane history. In his writings he quotes, often in Greek and Latin, Hesiod, Aristotle, the astronomer Hipparch, Cicero, Ovid, Vergil, Flavius Josephus, Appian, Ptolemaeus, Galenus, the Justinian Code, Tertullian, Ephraim, Philastrius, Ambrose, Jerome, Augustine, the Council of Toledo, Orosius, Gregory the Great, Venerable Bede, Bernard, Thomas Aquinas, Baronius, Cajetan, Soto, Sylvester, all the leading astronomers of the sixteenth and seventeenth centuries – and Don Quixote!

According to Verbiest and Gabiani he had such a mastery of both literary and vernacular Chinese that he could pass for a native Chinese scholar. In his old age he still wrote beautiful Latin prose. He had a perfect mastery of Portuguese, the ordinary medium of communication among the missionaries of the China mission. He was quite at home in Italian, had a fair knowledge of Spanish, easily understood Dutch. German, of course, was his native tongue.

Indicative of his practical and technical skill: he built cannons, drew plans for fortifications, constructed machines to lift heavy weights, planned and built a baroque church that Rome would not have been ashamed of, constructed astronomical instruments, refurbished a clavier, built a sailing boat for the emperor, even wrote a treatise on mining.[9] Paul Pelliot, distinguished authority on things Chinese, summed him up well: "Man of the Church, man of science, man of action, man capable of irony and of anger, a many faceted figure, attractive and intriguing, Schall would have made an impact anywhere."[10]

NOTES

(1) Cf. Pfister, *op. cit.*, I, 131-136 for a list of his writings.

(2) *Eminent Chinese*, II, 793.

(3) Jesuit accounts supply abundant details on the careers of both Chêng Chih-lung, usually referred to as "Icoan," from his childhood name, and Chêng Ch'êng-kung, referred to variously as "Cozinga," "Quesing," and "Kueising," all evidently renderings of Kuo-hsing Yeh (Lord of the Imperial Surname). The best account is that of de Rougemont, *op. cit.*, pp. 8-116. There is a Dutch eye-witness account of the siege and capture of Formosa by Chêng Ch'êng-kung in Thevenot, *op. cit.*, I, n. 9, 28-40. Chêng sent a Dominican priest who was in Formosa to Manila in an effort to enlist Spanish military support. A letter from Manila, dated April, 1622, tells of this incident; *ARSI*, Jap-Sin 124, 20-22.

(4) Väth, *op. cit.*, p. 223 f.

(5) For the events which follow the best sources are: de Rougemont, *op. cit.*, and Grelon, *op. cit.* What de Rougemont did not witness himself he had straight from Verbiest who commissioned him to write the story. There is also an account by Antonio a Santa Maria in *SinFran*, II, 502-606. *Eminent Chinese*, II, 889-892, gives the essential facts.

(6) Rowbotham, *op. cit.*, p. 83, is mistaken when he says that Schall had displaced Yang Kuang-hsien in the Bureau of Astronomy, thus suggesting that Yang's feud was a personal one. Yang, no astronomer, was not appointed to the bureau until he had accomplished Schall's downfall, and then against his wishes.

(7) There is a copy of Yang's *Pu-tê-i* and of Buglio's *Pu-tê-i-pien* in *ARSI*, Jap-Sin I, nn. 89, 90, 91, 92.

(8) The original of this moving document is in *ARSI*, Jap-Sin 142, n. 57.

(9) Väth, *op. cit.*, pp. 241 ff.

(10) *T'oung Pao*, XXXI (1934-1935), 180.

Epilogue

WHEN SCHALL DIED the work of the Jesuits seemed to lie in ruins. Appearances were deceptive. As a result of the policies inaugurated by Ricci, Christianity had too many roots in the empire to be thus easily destroyed.

In 1665 Oboi appointed Yang Kuang-hsien head of the Bureau of Astronomy. The charlatan, aware of his incapacity, made every effort to escape the responsibility. "From 1665 to 1668 he blundered along as director of the Astronomical Board with Wu Ming-hsüan assisting him in preparing the calendar."[1] In 1668 the young K'ang-hsi emperor dissolved the regency and assumed direction of the government. On December 29, 1668, he sent a copy of Yang's calendar for the following year to Verbiest for examination. The Jesuit pointed out a number of important mistakes, whereupon the emperor appointed a commission to investigate. Its report, substantiating Verbiest's critique, led to a more thorough and detailed investigation. On March 8, 1669, the emperor decreed that, inasmuch as the European method of calculation had been proved accurate, all future calendars were to be based upon that method alone, and Yang Kuang-hsien was discharged from his office. On April 17, Verbiest was named associate director of the Astronomical Board. Four months later Wu Ming-hsüan was cashiered and Verbiest was made director.

At the same time the emperor ordered the arrest of Oboi. Charged with thirty crimes, among them tyranny and treason, the ex-regent was thrown into prison where he soon died. The emperor ordered the case against Schall and his colleagues reviewed. The result was complete vindication. Yang Kuang-hsien was sentenced to exile for having lodged false charges. The emperor, out of regard for his age, commuted the sentence and allowed him to return to his home as a commoner. He died en route.

All of Schall's titles and ranks were posthumously restored and his confiscated properties were given back to the missionaries. His body was honored with an official funeral. The five Christian astronomers executed in 1665 were posthumously restored to their former ranks. Two years later the exiled missionaries returned to the provinces. Churches and residences were given back to them.

Restoration was complete and marked the beginning of an era of constantly increasing prosperity for the Christian cause in China. The next forty years saw the fortunes of the mission rise to their highest point. The foundations of that success were laid by the men who, from Ricci to Schall, labored patiently to achieve a synthesis of Chinese and Christian culture, with respect for and understanding of the former and without injury to the latter. That is their merit. For the decline which followed, when the lengthening shadow of the rites controversy darkened the face of the future and forced the Church into a position of seeming hostility to Chinese culture, thereby destroying the possibility of a rapprochement with the Chinese world of letters, they bear no responsibility.

There is a form of tolerance to which the Jesuits could not, and did not subscribe. It holds that all religions are more or less equally good, that all have a portion of the truth, but none the whole truth. It advocates a kind of religious syncretism in which Christianity, Buddhism, Taoism, Hinduism, sacrifice some of their centrally held beliefs in order to reach a common denominator of universalism. Such a view is destructive of religion itself. The Christian, who is convinced that God has spoken through the prophets and definitively through the Word made flesh, cannot sacrifice revealed truth to reach a meeting of minds.

At the other extreme is the intolerance of the Christian who thinks that outside the pale of Christianity is nothing but error and unrelieved vice. For those who have not seen the light he has neither sympathy nor understanding. His arrogance contradicts one of the articles of his own belief which insists that grace is everywhere operative — even at Teachers' College!

Between relativism and fanaticism there is a middle road. From the persuasion that Christian revelation is unique, it does not follow either that no glimmer of truth is to be found outside Christianity or that everyone who fails to believe is a scoundrel. Often enough the narrow intolerance of the believer, marring the beauty and obscuring the truth of Christianity, is responsible for unbelief in others. The will plays a vital role in the act of faith. No one will believe what he does not want to believe; and few will want to believe a doctrine which, by the bigotry of its spokesmen, is made to appear harshly repellent rather than warmly attractive.

Most religions represent, in greater or less degree, sincere strivings of the human mind to establish contact with the divine. This is certainly true of Siniticism, as the Jesuits never tired of pointing out. It is true of Buddhism, although the Jesuits here showed less perception of the fact. It is less true of Taoism. And if Confucianism showed little concern to reach the divine, it was at least a noble and not wholly unsuccessful effort to build a human society upon the foundation of sound natural virtues.

Because they are efforts to discover truth, whether human or divine, they deserve to be treated with respect. If they fall short of the full truth it is because by definition the supernatural is unattainable by human power alone. If they wander into bypaths of error, it is because human reason is a fallible instrument. To disdain the effort because of the limitations imposed by nature is to disdain human nature itself. That, despite its limitations, reason has achieved a measure of the truth should rather be a cause of admiration. If it is the part of the Christian to rejoice in good rather than evil, he will greet with joy every glimpse of the truth, however obscure, and every manifestation of virtue, however imperfect.

Such was the attitude which determined the policy of the Jesuits in China. Neither the relativists nor the fanatics can claim them for their party. Despite the legend to the contrary, they were not disposed to compromise the articles of faith for any purpose whatever. On the other hand, as the Church had done before with Greek philosophy, they sought every possible point of contact in the partial truths of Confucianism which they endeavored to enrich and complete with the supernatural revelation of Christianity. It was a work which could be accomplished only in an atmosphere warmed with human sympathy and understanding. Whatever else one may think of their efforts one must recognize that they brought to their task a warm and sympathetic understanding almost unique in the history of the cultural relations of East and West.

Measured in terms of the first century of Christianity their accomplishment ranks as one of the great achievements in the history of the Christian mission. The few dozen men chiefly responsible for that achievement revived the true concept of Christianity's world mission and restored to its proper place the tradition of earlier centuries. They opposed universalism to provincialism. What they did is of significance not only to the history of Christianity, but to the history of international cultural relations as well.

These few men, by the contacts which they established between Chinese and European thought, almost changed the course of history in China, and hence in the world. Not even the reverses of the future can obscure the fact that they contributed brilliantly, as a modern author remarks, to "that cosmopolitanism which is at the heart of modern civilization . . . and by helping to bridge the gulf between Orient and Occident, made an outstanding contribution to the ideal of universal brotherhood."[2] By their readiness to put aside European prejudices, by their adaptability, their innocence of snobbery and smugness, their alertness to discover the good and reluctance to note the bad, by the sympathy and understanding they brought to their contact with China, they pointed the way, and their example still points the way, to cultural rapprochement between the peoples of the world. They deserve to be held in honor not only by the Roman Catholic Church and by China, which has never had better friends, but by everyone who agrees with the Chinese proverb that "within the four seas all men are brothers."

NOTES

(1) *Eminent Chinese*, II, 89.

(2) Rowbotham, *op. cit.*, p. 301.

Bibliography

Chief Sources:

I. Up to the death of Matteo Ricci in 1610:

1) Ricci, Matteo, S.J., *Fonti Ricciane*, ed. Pasquale M. D'Elia, S.J., 3 vols. (Roma: Libreria dello Stato, 1942-1949).
   These are Ricci's memoirs, edited in masterly fashion by D'Elia.
2) Ricci, Matteo, S.J., *Opere storiche*, ed. Pietro Tacchi-Venturi, S.J., 2 vols. (Macerata: Giorgetti, 1911-1913). The first volume has been superseded by D'Elia's incomparably more learned edition of the memoirs. The second volume, containing Ricci's letters, will retain its importance until the hoped for appearance of D'Elia's promised edition.

II. Following the death of Ricci:

1) Unpublished material from the Jesuit archives in Rome, consisting chiefly of letters and reports written by the missionaries involved in the story. Cited under the rubric *ARSI* (Archivum Societatis Iesu).
2) Published material from the Franciscan archives in *Archivum Franciscanum historicum* (Ad Claras Aquas [Quaracchi-Firenze] prope Florentiam, 1908—); and in *Sinica Franciscana, Relationes et Epistolas Fratrum Minorum*, ed. A. Van den Wyngaert (Ad Claras Aquas [Quaracchi-Firenze] apud Collegium S. Bonaventurae, 1929-1936).
3) *Eminent Chinese of the Ch'ing Period (1644-1912)*, ed. Arthur W. Hummel. 2 vols. (Washington: U. S. Government Printing Office, 1943-44). Biographical sketches based chiefly upon Chinese sources.

Other Sources:

Acta Apostolicae Sedis (Roma: Polyglot Press, 1909 et seq.)

Alexandre, Noel, O.P. *Apologie des Dominicains missionaires de la Chine*, 2d ed. (Cologne: C. d'Egmond, 1700).

Archivum Franciscanum historicum, cf. *supra* under Chief Sources, II, 2.

Archivum historicum Societatis Iesu (Roma: Institutum Historicum S. I., 1932–).

Bartoli, Daniello, S.J., *Dell'istoria della Compagnia di Gésù. La Cina. Terza parte dell'Asia.* 4 vols. (Ancona ed.: Giuseppe Aureli, 1843). Written in mid-seventeenth century from the letters of the missionaries. In the style of his time he does not cite his sources, but checking his narrative against letters found in the archives almost invariably bears him out. "The terrible and stupendous Bartoli," as one of his editors called him, was as accurate as he was prolific.

Bernard, Henri, S.J., *Aux portes de la Chine* (Tientsin: Hautes Etudes, 1933).

——— *Le père Matthieu Ricci et la société chinoise de son temps (1552-1610)*. 2 vols. (Tientsin: Hautes Etudes, 1937).

——— "Un portrait de Nicolas Trigault dessiné par Rubens?" *Archivum historicum Societatis Iesu*, XXII (Roma, 1953).

Biermann, Benno M., O.P. *Die Anfänge der Neuren Dominikanermission in China* (Münster in Westfalen: Aschendorff, 1927).

Boehmer, H., *Les Jésuites*, tr. by G. Monod, 2 ed. (Paris: Armand Colin, 1910). Glutted with errors.

Bontekoe, William Ysbrantsa, *Memorable Description of the East Indian Voyage, 1618-1625* (New York: Robert McBride and Company, 1929).

Boxer, C. R., *The Christian Century in Japan 1549-1650* (Berkeley: University of California Press; London: Cambridge University Press, 1951).

——— *Fidalgos in the Far East 1550-1770. Fact and Fancy in the History of Macao* (The Hague: Martinus Nijhoff, 1948).

Brancato, Francesco, *De Sinensium ritibus politicis acta seu responsio apologetica ad R.P. Dominicum Navarette Ordinis Praedicatorum* (Paris: N. Pepié, 1700).

Bréhier, Louis, and Batiffol, Pierre, *Les survivances du culte impérial romain, à propos des rites shintoistes* (Paris: Auguste Picard, 1920).

Brenan, Gerald, *The Spanish Labyrinth* (New York: Macmillan Company, 1943).

Bridgman, E. C., "Paul Su's Apology addressed to the emperor Wan-lih of the Ming dynasty, in behalf of the Jesuit missionaries, Pantoya and others, who had been impeached by the Board of Rites in a report dated the 44th year, 7th month of his reign, (A.D. 1617)," *The Chinese Repository*, XIX (Canton, 1850).

Chabrié, Robert, *Michel Boym, Jésuite polonais et la fin des Ming en Chine (1646-1662)* (Paris: Pierre Bossuet, 1933).

Cibot, Martial, *Mémoires concernant l'histoire, les sciences, les arts, les moeurs, les usages, des Chinois: par les missionaires de Pekin* (Paris: Lyon, 1776-1791).

Colin-Pastells, *Labor evangelica de los obreros de la Compania de Jesus en las islas Filipinas por el P. Francisco Colin de la misma Compania.* Nueva edicion illustrada con copia de notas y documentos para la critica de la historia general de la soberania de Espana en Filipinas por el Padre Pablo Pastells, S.J., 3 vols. (Barcelona: Henrich, 1900-1902). Colin's first edition was in 1663.

Collectanea S. Congregationis de Propaganda Fide (Roma: ex typographia polyglotta, 1897).

Colombel, Auguste M., S.J., *Histoire de la mission de Kiangnan.* 5 vols. (Shanghai: Mission catholique, 1895-1905).

Considine, John J., M.M., *Across a World* (Toronto and New York: Longmans, Green and Company, 1942).

Couplet, Phillipe [Philip], S.J., *Histoire d'une dame chrétienne de la Chine* (Paris: Estienne Michallet, 1688).

Cronin, Vincent, *The Wise Man from the West* (London: Rupert Hart-Davis, 1955).

D'Elia, Pasquale, S.J., "Daniele Bartoli e Nicola Trigault," *Revista storica italiana*, XVI (June, 1938), 77-92.

________ "Due amici del P. Matteo Ricci, S.J., ridotti all'unita," *Archivum historicum Societatis Iesu*, VI (1937), 302-310.

________ *Galileo in China*, tr. by Rufus Suter and Matthew Sciascia (Cambridge: Harvard University Press, 1960).

________ "Il domma cattolica integralmente presentade da Matteo Ricci ai letterati della Cina. Secondo un documento cinese inedito di 350 anni fa," *Civiltà Cattolica* anno 86, II (1935), 35-53.

________ ed. *Fonti Ricciane*, cf. *supra* under Chief Sources, I, 1.

Delplace, L., *Le catholicisme au Japon.* 2 vols. (Bruxelles: A. Dewit, 1909-10).

Deshaisnes, C., *Vie du père Nicholas Trigault de la Compagnie de*

Jésus (Tournai: Casterman, 1865).

Du Jarric, Pierre, S.J., *Histoire des choses plus memorables advenues tant es Indes orientales, que autres pais de la descouverte des Portugais, en l'establissement et progrez de la foy chrestienne et catholique: et principalement de ce que les religieux de la Compagnie y ont faict, et enduré pour la mesme fin* (Bourdeaux: S. Millanges, 1608-1614).

Eminent Chinese of the Ch'ing Period, cf. *supra* under Chief Sources, II, 3.

Faria e Sousa, Manuel de, *Asia Portuguesa.* 3 vols. (Lisboa: H. Valente de Oliveira, 1666-1675).

Fülop-Miller, René, *The Power and Secret of the Jesuits.* Trans. by R. S. Flint and D. F. Tait. (New York: The Viking Press, 1930).

Furtado, Francisco, *Informatio antiquissima de praxi missionariorum Sinensium Societatis Jesu, circa ritus Sinenses, data in China, jam ab annis 1636 et 1640* (Paris: N. Pepié, 1700).

Gabiani, Joannes, S.J., *Incrementa Sinicae ecclesiae a Tartaris oppugnatae* (Vienna: s.l., 1673).

Gaillard, Louis, S.J., *Nankin d'alors et d'aujourd'hui; aperçu historique et géographique* (Shanghai: Mission catholique, 1903).

Gallagher, Louis J., S.J., *China in the 16th Century, The Journals of Matthew Ricci 1583-1610* (New York: Random House, 1953). This is a translation of Trigault's *De Christiana expeditione.*

Gonzalez, José, O.P., *Biografia del primer obispo China* (Manila: U.S.T. Press, 1946).

Goodrich, L. C., *A Short History of the Chinese People* (New York: Harper and Brothers, 1943).

——— *The Literary Inquisition of Ch'ien-Lung* (Baltimore: Waverly Press, 1935).

Goyau, Georges, *Missions et missionaires* (Paris: Librairie Bloud et Gay, 1931).

Greslon [Grelon], Adrien, *Histoire de la Chine sous la domination des Tartares* (Paris: J. Renault, 1671).

Havret, Henri, S.J., *La stèle chrétienne de Si-ngan-fou.* 3 vols. (Shanghai: Mission catholique, 1897).

Hay, P. J., S.J., *De rebus Japonicis et Indicis epistolae recentiores* (Antverpiae: Martini, 1605).

Hellmut, Wilhelm, "Ein Briefwecksel zwischen Dorgon und Schi Ko-fa," *Sinica*, VIII (1935), 239-245.

Histoire de ce qui s'est passée es royaumes d'Ethiopie, en l'année 1626, jusqu'au mois de Mars 1627. Et de la Chine, de l'année 1625 jusques en Fevrier de 1626. Avec une briefve narration du voyage qui s'est fait au royaume de Tumquim nouvellement descouvert. Tirées des lettres addressées au R. Père Générale de la Compagnie de Iesus. Traduites de l'italien en français par un Père de la mesme Compagnie (Paris: Sebastien Cramoisy, 1679).

Histoire de ce qui s'est passé es royaumes du Japon et de la Chine tirée des lettres escrites es années 1621 et 1622. Addressée au R. P. Mutio Vitelleschi, Général de la Compagnie de Jésus. Traduite de l'italien en français par un père de la mesme Compagnie (Paris: Sebastien Cramoisy, 1677).

Hoang, Pierre, S.J., *Concordances des chronologies néoméniques chinoise et européene* (Shanghai: Mission catholique, 1910).

Intorcetta, Prosper, S.J., *Testimonium de cultu Sinensi datum anno 1668* (Paris: N. Pepié, 1700).

Ius Pontificium de Propaganda Fide. 8 vols. (Roma: Ex typographia polyglotta S. C. de Prop. Fide, 1888-1909).

Jann, Dr. F. Adelhelm, F.Min.Cap., *Die katholischen Missionen in Indien, China und Japan. Ihre Organisation und das Portugiesische Patronat vom 15. bis ins 18. Jahrhundert.* (Paderborn: F. Schöningh, 1915).

Jäger, Fr., "Die Letzten Tage des Ku-shih-si," *Sinica*, VIII (1933), 197-207.

Jennes, Dr. Joseph, C.I.C.M., "A propos de la liturgie chinoise," *Neue Zeitschrift für Missionwissenschaft* (1946), 241-254.

Jordão, Levy Maria, *Bullarium patronatus Portugalliae regum in ecclesiis Africae, Asiae atque Oceaniae bullas, brevia, epistolas, decreta actaque S. Sedis ab Alexandro III ad hoc usque tempus amplectens*. 5 vols. (Olisipone: ex typographia nationali, 1868-1879).

Kircher, Athanasius, S.J., *China monumentis, qua sacris qua profanis, nec non variis naturae et artis spectaculis, aliarumque rerum memorabilium argumentis illustrata, auspiciis Leopoldi Primi roman. imper.* (Antverpiae: J. à Meurs, 1667).

Kuno, Yoshi S., *Japanese Expansion on the Asiatic Continent* (Berkeley: University of California Press, 1937).

Lamalle, Edmond, S.J., "La propagande du P. Nicholas Trigault en faveur des missions de Chine (1616)," *Archivum historicum Soci-*

etatis Jesu, IX (Roma, 1940), 49-120.

Laures, Johannes, S.J., *The Catholic Church in Japan* (Tokyo: Charles E. Tuttle Company, 1954).

Latourette, K. S., *A History of Christian Missions in China* (New York: Macmillan Company, 1929).

——— *The Chinese, Their History and Culture* 2 ed. (New York: The Macmillan Company, 1934).

Le Comte, Louis, S.J., *Nouveaux mémoires sur l'état présent de la Chine* (Paris: J. Anisson, 1696).

Lettere annue del Tibet del MDCXXVI e della Cina del MDCXXIV; scritte al M. R. P. Mutio Vitelleschi Generale della Compagnia di Gésù (Roma: F. Corbelleti, 1628).

Litterae Societatis Jesu e regno Sinarum annorum MDCX et XI ad R. P. Claudium Aquavivum eiusdem societatis praepositum generalem. Auctore P. Nicalao Trigautio, eiusdem societatis (Augustae Vindelicorum: Christophorus Mangium, 1615).

Ljungstedt, Aders, *An Historical Sketch of the Portuguese Settlements in China; and of the Roman Catholic Church and Mission in China* (Boston: J. Munroe and Company, 1836).

Longobardo, Nicholas, S.J., *Traité sur quelques points de la religion des Chinois* (Paris: J. Josse, 1701).

Magaillans [Magalhães], R. P. Gabriel de, S.J., *Nouvelle relation de la Chine, contenant la description des particularites les plus considerables de ce grand empire* (Paris: Claude Barbin, 1688).

Maas, Dr. Otto, O.F.M., *Die Wiedereröffnung der Franziskanermission in China in der Neuzeit* (Münster in Westfalen: Aschendorff, 1926).

Mailla, Joseph de Moyriac de, S.J., *Histoire générale de la Chine, ou annales de cet empire; trad. du Tong-kien-kang-mou.* 13 vols. (Paris: P. D.Pierres, 1777-85).

Manoel, Jeronymo P. A. Da Camara, *Missoes dos Jesuitas no Oriente nos seculos XVI e XVII. Trabalho destinado a X sessao de Congresso Internacional dos orientalistas* (Lisboa, s.l., 1894).

Margiotti, Fortunato, O.F.M., *Il cattolicismo nello Shansi dalle origini al 1738* (Roma: Edizioni "Sinica Franciscana," 1958).

Martini, Martinus, S.J., *Brevis relatio de numero et qualitate Christianorum apud Sinas* (Romae: Ignatius de Lazzeris, 1654).

——— *De bello Tartarico historia* (Romae: Ignatius de Lazzeris, 1654).

Mayers, William F., *The Chinese Government, A Manual of Chinese Titles.* 3 ed. (Shanghai: Kelly and Walsh, 1897).

Montalban, Francisco Javier, S.J., *El patronato espanõl y la conquista de Filipinas, con documentos del archivo general de Indias* (Burgos: El siglo de la misiones, 1930).

Monumenta Xaveriana (Matriti: typis Augustini Avrial, 1899-1900).

Navarrete, Domingo, O.P., *Controversias antiguas y modernas de la mission de la gran China* (Madrid, s.l., 1679).

Needham, Joseph, F.R.S., *Science and Civilization in China.* 3 vols. (Cambridge: University Press, 1959).

Nieuhoff, Jan, *Le voyage des ambassadeurs de la Compagnie Hollandoise des Indes Orientales vers le Grand Chan de Tartarie, à Peking.* Cf. Thevenot.

d'Orleans, Pierre Joseph, S.J., *Histoire des deux conquerans tartares qui ont subjugué la Chine* (Paris: C. Barbin, 1688).

——— *La vie du père Matthieu Ricci* (Paris, s.l., 1693).

Otten, Bernard, S.J., *Institutiones dogmaticae in usum scholarum* (Chicago: Loyola Press, 1925).

Pantoia, Diego de, S.J., *Relaçion de la entrada de algunos padres de la Compania de Jesus en la China, y particulares sucessos que tuvieron, y de cosas muy notables que vieron en el mismo reyno* (Valencia, s.l., 1606).

Parker, E. J. (ed.), "Letters from a Chinese empress and a Chinese eunuch to the Pope in the year 1650," *Contemporary Review*, CI (London, 1912), 79 ff.

Pastells, P., S.J., *Catalogo de los documentos relativos a las Indias Filipinas existentes en el Archivio de Indias de Sevilla, por D. Pedro Torres y Lanzas, precedido de una historia general de Filipinas* (Barcelona, s.l., 1925).

Pfister, Louis, S.J., *Notices biographiques et bibliographiques sur les Jésuites de l'ancienne mission de Chine 1552-1773.* (Shanghai: Mission catholique, 1932).

Philosensis, "Ta Tsing hwang ti shing Heun (Sacred Instructions of the Ta Tsing dynasty)" *Chinese Repository*, X (Canton, 1841), 593 ff.

Platel, C. P. [Norbert], *Mémoires historiques sur les affaires des Jésuites avec le Saint Siège* (Lisbon: François-Louis Ameno, 1766).

Playfair, G. M. H., *The Cities and Towns of China*, 2 ed. (Shanghai: Kelly and Walsh, 1910).

Relatione delle cose più notabili scritte ne gli anni 1619, 1620, 1621 dalla Cina (Roma: Zannetti, 1624).

Renan, Ernest, *Histoire générale et système comparé des langues sémitiques*. 3d ed. (Paris: Imp. impériale, 1863).

Reville, A., *La religion chinoise* (Paris: Librairie Fischbacher, 1889).

Ricci, Matteo, S.J., Cf. *supra*, Chief Sources, I, 1 and 2.

Rosso, Antonio Sisto, O.F.M., *Apostolic Legations to China* (South Pasadena: P.D. and Ione Perkins, 1948).

Rougemont, Franciscus de, *Historia Tartaro-Sinica nova* (Lovanii: Martinus Hullegaerde, 1673).

Rouleau, Francis A., S.J., "The death of Stephen Faber, S.J.," *Archivum historicum Societatis Iesu*, XXIX (1960), 130-148.

———— "The First Chinese Priest of the Society of Jesus," *Archivum historicum Societatis Iesu*, XXVIII (1959), 3-50.

Rowbotham, Arnold H., *Missionary and Mandarin, The Jesuits at the Court of China* (Berkeley: University of California Press, 1942).

Saeki, P. Y., *The Nestorian Monument and Relics in China* (Tokyo: Toho Bunkwa Gakuin, 1937).

Schall, Adam, S.J., *Historica relatio de ortu et progressu fidei orthodoxae in regno Chinensi* (Ratisbonae: August Hanckwitz, 1672).

———— *Lettres et mémoires d'Adam Schall, S.J.*, ed. par le P. Henri Bernard, S.J. (Tientsin: Hautes Etudes, 1942).

Schurhammer, Georg, S.J., *Das Kirchliche Sprachproblem in der Japanischen Jesuitenmission des 16. und 17. Jahhunderts; ein Stück Ritenfrage in Japan* (Tokyo: Deutsche Gesellschaft für natur-und völkerkunde Ostasiens, 1928).

Schütte, Josef Franz, S.J., *Valignanos Missionsgrundsätse für Japan*. 2 vols. (Roma: Edizione di storia e letteratura, 1951-58).

Semedo, Alvarez [Alvarô], S.J., *Histoire universelle de la Chine, avec l'histoire de la guerre des tartares, contenant les revolutions arrivées en ce grand royaume, depuis quarante ans: par le P. Martin Martini. Traduites nouvellement en François* (Lyon: Hierosme Prost, 1667).

Sinica Franciscana, cf. *supra*, Chief Sources, II, 2.

Streit, Robert, O.M.I.,–Dindinger, Johann, O.M.I., *Bibliotheca Missionum*. 10 vols. (Münster-Aachen: Veröffentlichungen des Internationalen Instituts für missionswissenschaftliche Forschung, 1916-39).

Szczesniak, Boleslaw, "The Writings of Michael Boym," *Monumenta serica*, XIV (1949-55), 481-538.

Thevenot, Melchisédech, *Relations de divers voyages curieux qui n'ont point este publiées, et qu'on a traduit ou tiré des originaux des voyageurs françois, espagnols, allemands, portugais, anglois, hollandois, persans, arabes et autres orientaux.* Nouv. ed. (Paris: T. Moette, 1696).

Thomas, Elbert Duncan, *Chinese Political Thought* (New York: Prentice-Hall, 1927).

Tobar, Jerome, S.J., *Inscriptions juives de K'ai-fêng* (Shanghai: Mission catholique, 1912).

Trigault, Nicolas, S.J., *De Christiana expeditione apud Sinas suscepta ab Societate Jesu ex P. Matthaei Ricci ejusdem Societatis Commentariis. . . .* (Augustae Vindelicorum: C. Mangium, 1615).

Väth, Alfons, S.J., *Johann Adam Schall von Bell, S.J.* (Köln: J. P. Boehm, 1933).

Voyages et missions du père Alexandre de Rhodes de la Compagnie de Jésus en la Chine et autres royaumes de l'Orient; nouv. ed., par un père de la même Compagnie (Paris: Julian, Lanier, etc., 1854).

Williams, S. Wells, *The Middle Kingdom.* Rev. ed. 2 vols. (New York: Charles Scribner's Sons, 1883).

Wylie, A., *Chinese Researches* (London: K. Paul, Trench, Trübner and Company, 1937).

Yang, Y. C., *China's Religious Heritage* (New York: Abingdon-Cokesbury Press, 1943).

Index

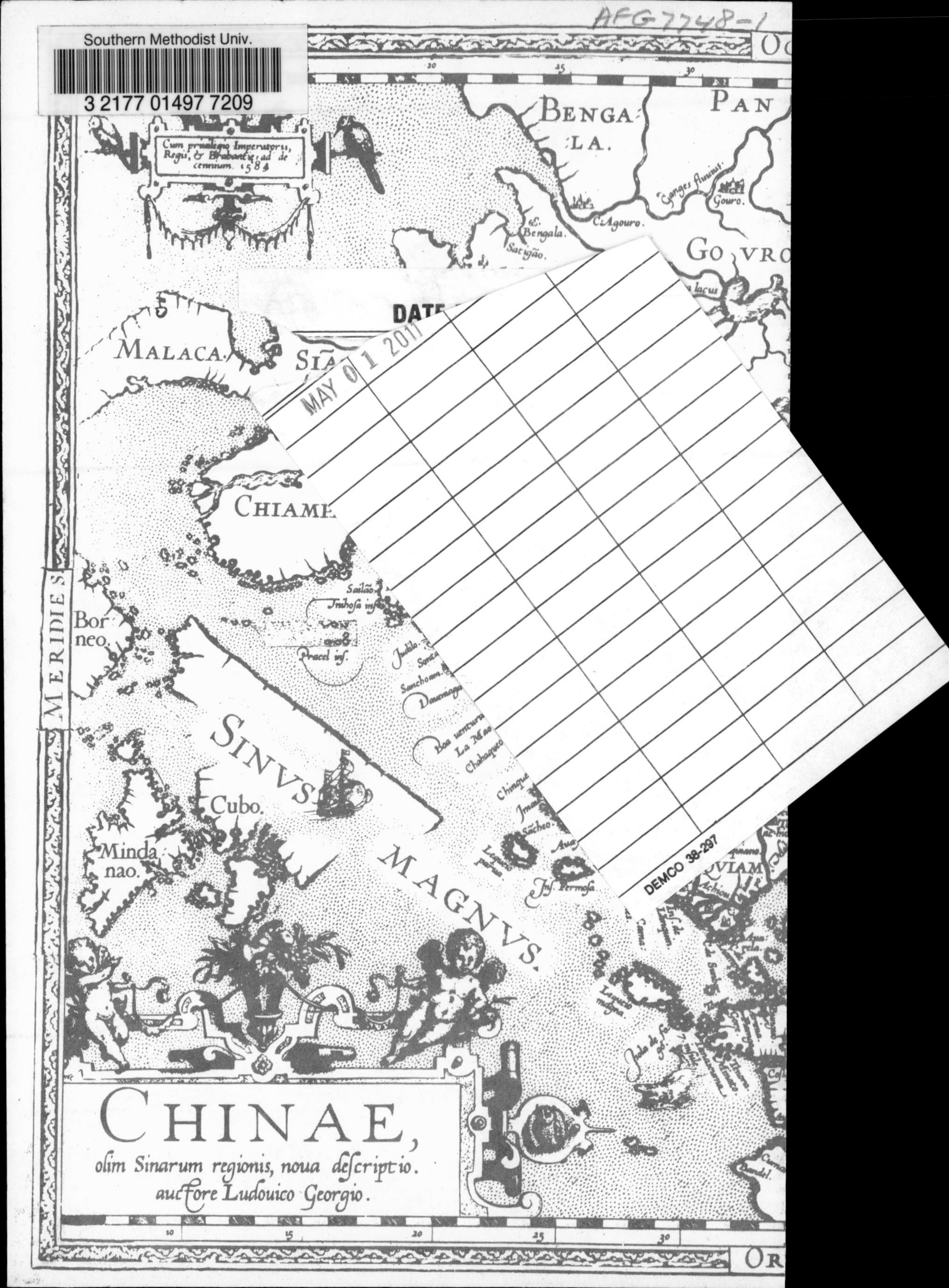
Cum privilegio Imperatoris, Regis, & Brabantiæ, ad decennium. 1584
BENGALA.
PAN
Ganges fluuius
Gouro.
C. Agouro.
C. Bengala.
Satigão.
GOVRO
MALACA.
CHIAME
Sailão
Pracel ins.
Borneo.
MERIDIES
SINVS MAGNVS.
Cubo.
Mindanao.
Ins. Fermosa
CHINAE,
olim Sinarum regionis, noua descriptio.
auctore Ludouico Georgio.
DATE
MAY 01 2011
DEMCO 38-297